AI Computing Systems

An Application-Driven Perspective

AI Computing Systems
An Application-Driven Perspective

Yunji Chen
Ling Li
Wei Li
Qi Guo
Zidong Du
Zichen Xu

MK
MORGAN KAUFMANN PUBLISHERS

ELSEVIER   AN IMPRINT OF ELSEVIER

Morgan Kaufmann is an imprint of Elsevier
50 Hampshire Street, 5th Floor, Cambridge, MA 02139, United States

Notices

ISBN: 978-0-323-95399-3

For information on all Morgan Kaufmann publications
visit our website at https://www.elsevier.com/books-and-journals

Publisher: Katey Birtcher
Acquisitions Editor: Stephen Merken
Editorial Project Manager: Ali Afzal-Khan
Publishing Services Manager: Shereen Jameel
Production Project Manager: Haritha Dharmarajan
Cover Designer: Miles Hitchen

Typeset by VTeX

Printed in India

Last digit is the print number:
9 8 7 6 5 4 3 2 1

  Working together to grow libraries in developing countries

www.elsevier.com • www.bookaid.org

Contents

Biographies

Yunji Chen is a full professor and Deputy Director at the Institute of Computing Technology, Chinese Academy of Sciences, Beijing. He led the development of the world's first deep learning dedicated processor chip. He has published more than 100 papers in academic conferences and journals and held more than 100 patents. He received the Best Paper Awards at the top international conferences on computer architecture ASPLOS'14 and MICRO'14 (the only two so far in Asia). He was reported as a "pioneer" and "leader" in the field of deep learning processors by *Science Magazine* and was named by the *MIT Technology Review* as one of the world's top 35 innovators under the age of 35 (2015).

Ling Li is a full Professor at the Institute of Software, Chinese Academy of Sciences. Her research interests include intelligent computing and video processing. She has coauthored two books and over 50 papers on journals and conferences (including TC, TPDS, TIP, ISCA, and MICRO). She has received the Best Paper Award of MICRO'14.

Wei Li is an associate professor at the Institute of Computing Technology, Chinese Academy of Sciences. Her research covers high-performance AI computing systems. She has participated in several National Key R&D Projects. As a core member, she has participated in the R&D of several deep learning processors. She has published around 30 academic papers and applied for nearly 20 patents.

Qi Guo is a full professor at the Institute of Computing Technology, Chinese Academy of Sciences. His research interests mainly include computer architecture and AI computing systems. He has published many papers in top-tier venues such as ISCA, MICRO, HPCA, IJCAI, and ACM/IEEE Transactions.

Zidong Du is an associate professor at the Intelligent Processor Research Center, Institute of Computing Technology, Chinese Academy of Sciences. His research interests mainly include novel architecture for artificial intelligence, including deep learning processors, inexact/approximate computing, neural network architecture, and neuromorphic architecture. He has published over 20 top-tier computer architecture research papers in ASPLOS, MICRO, ISCA, TC, TOCS, and TCAD, among others. For his innovative work on deep learning processors, he won the Best Paper Award of ASPLOS'14, the Distinguished Doctoral Dissertation Award of CAS (40/10000), and the Distinguished Doctoral Dissertation Award of the China Computer Federation (10 per year).

Zichen Xu received his PhD degree from Ohio State University. He is a full professor and the vice dean at the School of Mathematics and Computer Science, Nanchang

University, China. His research spans the field of data-conscious complex systems and architecture, including performance analysis, system optimization, energy-aware architecture, and database system design/implementation. He is an IEEE senior member and ACM member.

Preface for the English version

This book was mainly inspired by a letter written by Dr. Kozyrakis, a professor at Stanford University, in September 2015. He asked me to give a distinguished lecture about artificial intelligence computing systems in the Electronic Engineering Department at Stanford University. I agreed and made preparations for the lecture. Unfortunately, I was not able to give the lecture in the end due to a time conflict. However, the preparation of the lecture had somehow changed my professional career.

When I was preparing for the lecture, I found that there had been no up-to-date courses all over the world that comprehensively covered the entire technology stack across both software and hardware of modern artificial intelligence (machine learning) computing systems, not to mention a textbook that could holistically introduce such complex technical systems. To solve this problem, I started a course about artificial intelligence computing systems at the University of Chinese Academy of Sciences in 2019. Based on the lecture notes for the course, I wrote the Chinese version of this book, *AI Computing Systems*. Up to now, this textbook has been widely used in about 100 universities to train thousands of students every year in systematic thinking about artificial intelligence.

While the Chinese version of this book has attracted the interest of Chinese readers, we believe that the English version of this book will be even more important, so that more researchers and students in the world could read, discuss, and comment on it. Our research in AI computing systems started by standing on the shoulders of countless pioneers in the international academic communities of computer architecture and artificial intelligence. In these communities, I learned about quantitative research methods, and I proposed the concept of deep learning accelerator in return (along with our international collaborator Prof. Olivier Temam from INRIA[1] at that time). Our work has been cited by researchers from more than 30 countries; 40% of these citations come from the United States. Even this book was also inspired by the invitation from Stanford University.

Therefore, I would like to emphasize that science has no borders. We should always encourage scientific knowledge to flow across different nationalities, races, colors, and religions. The flow that created our highly developed human civilization will also bring that civilization to a brighter future.

We would like to thank Prof. Zichen Xu from Nanchang University for his great help in translating the book into English.

I would like to thank my colleagues and students for their great effort in translating and polishing the English version of this book together with me: Ling Li, Wei Li, Qi Guo, Zidong Du, Xin Zhang, Xing Hu, Yifan Hao, Xinkai Song, Rui Zhang,

---

[1] National Institute for Research in Digital Science and Technology, France.

Xiaqing Li, Di Huang, Zhenxing Zhang, Jiaming Guo, Yuanbo Wen, Zhe Fan, and Chang Liu.

We also thank Miao Yu and Xiaojie Hu from our AICS course team, Lifang Wen from China Machine Press, and Elsevier for the publication.

Additional resources, including a solutions manual and image bank, are available for instructors using this book in a course. Please visit https://educate.elsevier.com/book/details/9780323953993 for more information.

Yunji Chen
Institute of Computing Technology
Chinese Academy of Sciences

Preface

Motivation for this book

With the massive surge in artificial intelligence (AI)-based innovation, AI techniques have become catalysts to revolutionize nearly every scientific and industrial domain. It is not only a fundamental tool, but also an important way of thinking that everyone should learn. Hence, it is important to cultivate AI talents in modern higher education. There is one key question: What kinds of AI abilities should be mastered in higher education?

There is a popular view in China that the curriculum of AI majors only needs to teach students the development of AI applications and algorithms, while the AI computing system stack running those apps or algorithms is not the focus of this education. This view is analogous to the belief that the curriculum of an automobile major teaches assembling vehicles without explaining the mechanism of engines, or that the curriculum of a computer science major teaches how to program apps without introducing the principles of CPUs and operating systems. The ethos of emphasizing applications over systems may cause an imbalance between AI basic research and industrial development.

In stark contrast, our international counterparts place far more emphasis on AI computing systems than ordinary people can imagine. Using Google as an example, it has the world's largest AI application and algorithm research teams with the top expertise and has released the most comprehensive products. In the 2019 International Conference on Machine Learning (ICML), Google published nearly 20% of all papers. However, when we take a closer look at Google, we can find that it is more than an algorithm company; it is a system company. John L. Hennessy, Google's chairman, is a Turing Award winner, one of the most famous researchers on computer architecture. Jeffrey Dean, the general leader of Google's AI research and the designer of the MapReduce distributed computing system, is also a computer system researcher. Google's three most notable contributions to the field of AI are also related to systems, not pure algorithms: the machine learning programming framework TensorFlow, AlphaGo, which defeated the human Go world champion Lee Sedol, and Google's own AI chip, TPU.

Therefore, higher education in AI should produce researchers, designers, and manufacturers of AI systems or subsystems. Only when this goal is achieved can the talents cultivated by colleges and universities fully and consistently support the industrial application and research of AI. To achieve this goal, the curriculum of AI majors should include not only courses on machine learning algorithms and audiovisual applications, but also hardware and system courses.

In fact, many senior professors and experts are already aware of this problem. Many colleges and universities wanted to offer system courses of AI, but they met some objective difficulties in initiating such kind of courses. First of all, AI computing systems are an emerging intersection of state-of-the-art software and hardware techniques, and there is no mature course for professors to refer to. To be honest, even top international universities had little prior experience in teaching the AI field. Furthermore, the background knowledge required to teach a course on AI computing systems is very extensive, covering diverse areas across algorithms, architectures, chips, programming, and so on. There are few professors who can fully cover this knowledge.

The most crucial difficulty is the absence of a systematic textbook to provide the basis for the course. It is impossible to provide a good course without an appropriate textbook. To the best of our knowledge, there was no textbook that comprehensively covers all aspects of AI computing systems in depth (especially modern machine learning computing systems). Because the research directions of our lab cover various aspects of AI computing systems and we have experience in teaching courses on AI computing systems at the University of Chinese Academy of Sciences, Peking University, and BeiHang University, many professors asked us if we could write a textbook with comprehensive content. Therefore, we wrote this textbook, *AI Computing Systems*, based on the audio and video recordings of our past lectures. We hope that this textbook can get the ball rolling, provide a small boost to the development of system courses of AI in colleges and universities, and playing a role in promoting the cultivation of AI talents.

Value of an AI computing systems course

Personally, I believe that the AI computing systems course is of great value to students, professors, and universities.

For students, AI computing systems courses can help them develop system skills and systematic thinking. System skills can help students gain stronger competitiveness in the job market. In the near future, tens of thousands of students who have learned AI algorithms will graduate every year. If a student is only able to tune parameters but has no idea about the latency and power consumption of the entire system and cannot efficiently deploy algorithms on a real system, it will be hard to find a good job. The AI computing systems course aids students to understand how AI works (including how an AI algorithm calls the programming framework, how the programming framework interacts with the operating system, and how the algorithms in the programming framework run on the chip), which enables students to build complex systems or subsystems with their own hands. Naturally, these students are more likely to stand out in the job competition.

Also, systematic thinking is beneficial to improve students' scientific research ability. Students who lack systematic thinking are prone to be too obsessed with the scores of accuracy. They may regard scientific research as a sports competition (if others achieve an accuracy of 97%, I'll have to achieve 98%; if others achieve an accuracy of 98%, I'll have to reach 99%), which eventually leads to a narrower and narrower research path. In fact, from the system's point of view, the criteria for evaluating AI are well beyond one dimension of accuracy; speed, energy efficiency, cost, etc., are all important dimensions. Regardless of in which dimension a breakthrough is made, it will be very valuable research. Therefore, some influential works in the deep learning society in recent years, such as sparsity and low-bit-width methods, are all about improving the speed and energy efficiency of the whole AI computing system, rather than just focusing on accuracy. Thus, an AI computing systems course can help students build a broader scope of scientific research.

For professors, teaching a course about AI computing systems may also be of great help to improve their own research skills. When I was a young educator, I found that professors who taught their courses well gained much more from the course than their students. This is what the *Book of Rites and Learning* reveals: "Teaching and learning grow with each other." Writing a paper can only make one familiar with certain specific knowledge points in a certain aspect, while teaching in a sense forces the professor to have a comprehensive understanding of all aspects, which in turn can broaden their research scope. The AI computing systems course covers a wide range of topics, and teaching this course is particularly beneficial, as it can make the professor grasp comprehensive knowledge from software to hardware.

For university administrators, systems research has become a hot topic in the development of AI and should be given full attention in research planning. In 2019, dozens of renowned researchers (including M. Jordan, US National Academy of Sciences member, B. Dally, US National Academy of Engineering member, J. Dean, US National Academy of Engineering member, etc.) from top international universities and enterprises (e.g., Stanford University, Carnegie Mellon University, UC Berkeley, MIT, Google, Facebook, Intel, Microsoft, etc.) have jointly released a white paper, "SysML: The New Frontier of Machine Learning Systems," which discusses the future development of software and hardware technologies for machine learning computing systems. It shows that both academia and industry in the world are highly interested in AI computing systems. Deploying and cultivating a group of professors in such emerging and popular directions as soon as possible will undoubtedly enhance the influence of universities in the international academic society.

Content of the AI computing systems course

Experienced professors may wonder: "The course on AI computing systems covers many techniques, areas, and topics; is it difficult to include them in one course?" Yes, the AI computing systems course includes algorithms, chips, programming, and other aspects, and each can be developed into a self-contained course. It is impossible to teach all the aspects in a single course or semester. Therefore, we have adopted two principles in designing this course of AI computing systems: *application-driven* and *full-stack understanding*. The course is driven by an interesting AI application and focuses on the knowledge required to complete that application at all levels of the software and hardware technology stack. This not only makes it possible for a professor to teach the AI computing systems course in a single semester, but also provides the following two benefits.

First, a good course of engineering discipline motivates students to apply what they have learned. Especially in a course of AI computing systems, the teaching goals are not achieved if students only learn the theoretical knowledge. Application-driven learning motivates students to apply the course knowledge in practice. Second, it assists students in developing a systematic understanding. In the past, computer science courses set a clear division between different parts, which may hinder students from putting all the pieces together. For example, the operating system and computer architecture were separated. There is not a single course that combined requirements from the operating system for the computer architecture and from the support computer architecture for the operating system to enable students to master this knowledge. *AI Computing Systems*, as an upper-level undergraduate (or graduate) course, can assist students in connecting all of their previous knowledge of AI hardware and software to develop a holistic understanding.

AI Computing Systems, in particular, employs the application of image style transfer (e.g., transforming a live-action snapshot into a Van Gogh-style painting) as a vehicle to introduce the entire AI computing system software and hardware technology stack. To this end, Chapter 1 of the book presents AI, AI computing systems, and style transfer as a driving paradigm throughout the book.

The course then goes over the background of neural networks and deep learning algorithms, which are the prerequisites to understanding image style transfer. The course does not go into extensive details about irrelevant algorithms beyond style transfer. In this way, the algorithmic part can be completed within a maximum of 6 credit hours. The above content is introduced in Chapters 2 and 3 of this book.

AI algorithms require the assistance of the programming framework and system software in order to run on an AI chip. On one hand, the programming framework makes it easier for programmers to write various AI applications. On the other hand, the programming framework decomposes the AI algorithms into basic operators and schedules operators onto the AI chip (or CPU/GPU). Programming frameworks are extremely complex pieces of system software. However, the programming framework background required to implement style transfer is relatively limited. For example, there are thousands of operators in the TensorFlow programming framework, but style transfer engages less than one-tenth of them. In this way, the lecturer can teach students how to use mainstream programming frameworks and the functional mechanics behind them in about 6 credit hours. The aforementioned topics will be introduced in Chapters 4 and 5 of this book.

The AI chip hardware is located below the programming framework in the system stack. Since traditional CPUs are far from meeting the increasing performance and energy efficiency requirements of AI computing, specialized deep learning processors come into play because of their astonishing efficiency. Developing an industrial-grade deep learning processor that can handle various video recognition, speech recognition, advertisement recommendation, and natural language processing tasks takes dozens of months of work by hundreds of experienced engineers. However, in this course, we only need to consider the limited goal of how to design a deep learning processor for the specific application of style transfer, including design concepts, design methodologies, and hardware architecture implementation. To show students the cutting-edge industry trends, this book also introduces the structure of a industrial-grade deep learning processor. In this way, educators can give students a more systematic grasp of the basics of deep learning processors in about 6 hours. The aforementioned content is introduced in Chapters 6 and 7 of this book.

The instruction set and architecture of deep learning processors are quite different from those of traditional general-purpose CPUs. Hence, a new, advanced, high-level AI programming language is needed to facilitate programmers to fully utilize the computing efficiency of deep learning processors. Chapter 8 introduces an AI programming language (BCL). This programming language aims to improve the productivity of programmers when writing AI algorithms and also takes advantage of the architecture features of deep learning processors. In this chapter, the book not only introduces how to design the basic operators required for image style transfer using BCL, but also provides system-level development and optimization practices. This chapter takes about 6 credit hours.

The ultimate goal of the AI computing systems course is to enable students to fully understand the entire hardware and software technology stack of AI computing systems. If students simply finish reading the above chapters, they may only grasp some fragmented techniques, but experiments are necessary to apply all this knowledge to practical use. Therefore, Chapter 9 introduces an experiment on how to develop a simple AI computing system that can perform image style transfer tasks. Theoretically, students who do this experiment well will have good understanding of the entire techniques in this course. The number of hours required to complete experiments depends on the students' expertise and can be determined according to the real situation in each university. In addition, we suggest that a special laboratory course on AI computing systems should be offered. We also write the *Experimental Course of AI Computing Systems* textbook to provide more comprehensive experiments.

In the above design of the course, we mainly considered the student profile of the University of Chinese Academy of Sciences. When we taught this course at other universities, we found that the precourse foundations of students from different universities were not quite the same, so a professor should make flexible adjustments to the credit hours of each section. For example, if students have previously taken a basic course in AI or machine learning, the number of credit hours in the algorithms sections of Chapters 2 and 3 can be shortened. If students have not yet learned computer architecture or computer composition principles, more credit hours can be invested to teach the deep learning processor sections in Chapters 6 and 7.

The chapters or exercises marked with * in the book are optional for readers who are interested in AI computing systems research.

Writing of this book

Many educators and students have contributed their efforts to the publication of this book. They are from the Research Center for Intelligent Processors, Institute of Computing Technology (ICT), Chinese Academy of Sciences (CAS), and the Research Center for Intelligent Software, Institute of Software, CAS. Specifically, I completed Chapter 1, Prof. Ling Li finished Chapters 2 and 3, Assoc. Prof. Wei Li wrote Chapters 4 and 9, Prof. Qi Guo organized Chapters 5 and 8, Assoc. Prof. Zidong Du took care of Chapter 6, and Dr. Xuda Zhou wrote Chapter 7. Prof. Ling Li and I were responsible for the overall draft of the book. Assoc. Prof. Zidong Du designed the exercise parts of the book. In addition, Dr. Zhen Li, Dr. Dong Han, Jie Wei, Chaofeng Pan, Xi Zeng, Yong Yu, Bingrui Wang, Lei Zhang, Yifan Hao, Enhe Liu, Haoyuan He, Yufeng Gao, Xinkai Song, and Weijian Du also participated in the writing and preparation of this book. Weijian Du, Zhenxing Zhang, and Xinkai Song contributed to the exercises in this book. Zhou Fang, Xi Zeng, Zhenxing Zhang, Puzhe Li, and Binchang Chen were responsible for the drawing of many of the figures in this book. Assoc. Prof. Xishan Zhang, Assoc. Prof. Rui Zhang, Xiaoyu Wu, Shuyao Cheng, Yu Wang, and Yijun Tan participated in proofreading this book. We would like to express sincere gratitude to them.

We are also particularly thankful to Prof. Xingshe Zhou from Northwestern Polytechnical University and Prof. Tao Li from Nankai University for their valuable suggestions on curriculum design and textbook writing. In addition, Lifang Wen and Liqing Liu from China Machine Press have also provided us with a lot of help.

Due to our limited knowledge, there may exist errors and omissions in this book. We would like to invite readers to highlight and correct them. If you have any comments and/or suggestions, please feel free to send an email to aics@ict.ac.cn.

Yunji Chen
Institute of Computing Technology
Chinese Academy of Sciences

Introduction

Artificial intelligence (AI), particularly deep learning, is evolving at an incredibly fast pace and has already achieved (or even surpassed) human performance in a number of applications, including image recognition, speech recognition, natural language processing, and video games. It is not exaggerated to say that human beings are stepping into the gate of a great revolution, the AI Revolution. As the physical foundation of all revolutions that happened in human history, like the internal combustion engine to the Industrial Revolution, or the general processor to the Information Revolution, the AI Revolution shall have its own physical foundation. This physical foundation is the AI computing system (AICS).

At the beginning of this chapter, we first introduce the history of AI, which can be boiled down to three main paradigms. Next, we briefly discuss the development of AICS from the very beginning to the near future. Last, we introduce the procedure of adopting AI algorithms for software and hardware implementation on chips, using image style transfer as a driving example.

1.1 Artificial intelligence

1.1.1 What is artificial intelligence?

Generally speaking, any intelligence demonstrated by machines is AI. AI can be categorized into two classes, known as weak AI and strong AI. Weak AI is a nontrivial application of computer science and usually achieves some specific tasks based on domain-specific knowledge. Strong AI, or general AI, exhibits all intelligent behaviors of human beings with equivalent or higher intellectual capability. Some weak AI can easily outperform human beings in some tasks, such as the calculation of addition and multiplication, and is thus widely adopted. However, strong AI does not only target some specific problems, but solves all problems that can or cannot be solved by a human. This book mainly focuses on computing systems for weak AI. Yet readers should not ignore the importance of computing systems for strong AI, from the perspective of long-term development of science.

1.1.2 The history of AI

The birth of AI can be traced back to the early 1940s. Warren McCulloch and Walter Pitts proposed the first model of the artificial neuron in 1943 [1]. Six years later,

AI Computing Systems. https://doi.org/10.1016/B978-0-32-395399-3.00007-X

based on this model, Donald O. Hebb advanced the Hebbian learning rule to update the connection weights between neurons in 1949 [2]. However, the concept of AI was first introduced at the renowned Dartmouth Conference [3] in 1956. After this founding event, the development of AI faced several ups and downs, as shown in Fig. 1.1. We will take a tour of these ups and downs in the history of AI.

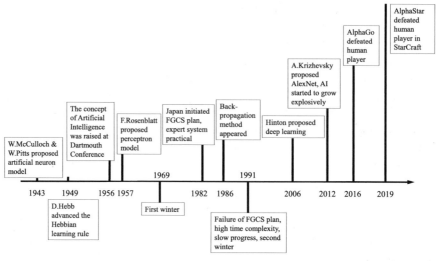

FIGURE 1.1

A brief history of AI.

1.1.2.1 1956–1960s, the First Wave

In the summer of 1956, John McCarthy, Marvin L. Minsky, Nathaniel Rochester, and Claude E. Shannon initiated a 2-month, 10-man AI study (known as the Dartmouth Conference) at Dartmouth College in Hanover, New Hampshire, from their earlier proposal for the Dartmouth Summer Research Project on Artificial Intelligence in August 1955. Their proposal was "to proceed on the basis of the conjecture that every aspect of learning or any other feature of intelligence can in principle be so precisely described that a machine can be made to simulate it. An attempt will be made to find how to make machines use language, form abstractions and concepts, solve kinds of problems now reserved for humans, and improve themselves" [4]. Many attendees of this conference have won the Turing Award afterward, including Marvin L. Minsky (1969), John McCarthy (1971), and Allen Newell and Herbert Simon (1975). Note that Herbert Simon also won the Nobel Prize in Economics three years later, in 1978.

With attendees' research background in logic, the Dartmouth Conference drove the First Wave of AI on the basis of symbolic logic (later known as symbolism). In theory, if all prior knowledge and problems to be solved can be represented as some symbols, various intelligent tasks can be solved by using a logic problem solver. Following this idea, Allen Newell and Herbert Simon demonstrated the logic theory machine Logic Theorist [5], which has been widely used for many mathematics proofs. Besides this logic theory machine, big achievements were made in geometry, such as the proving machine, the chess program, the checkers program, Q/A systems, and planning systems in the First Wave. One important and notable achievement in this period is the perceptron model from Frank Rosenblatt [6,7], attracting research attention until the present.

In the early stage of the First Wave, AI researchers were optimistic about the future of AI. In 1958, Herbert Simon claimed "there are now in the world machines that think, that learn and that create. Moreover, their ability to do these things is going to increase rapidly until in a visible future... the range of problems they can handle will be coextensive with the range to which the human mind has been applied" [8]. He visioned "within ten years a digital computer will be the world's chess champion" [8]. Yet it took computer scientists 40 years to finally develop the IBM Deep Blue to beat Garry Kasparov and become the chess champion [9]. The difficulty of the AI development was beyond the imagination of these early pioneers, and thus the First Wave was quickly over and AI had entered its first winter, lasting over one decade.

1.1.2.2 1975–1991, the Second Wave

The remarkable event of the Second Wave of AI is the 10-year Fifth Generation Computer Systems (FGCS) plan, initiated by Japan's Ministry of International Trade and Industry (MITI), which began in 1982. The plan was to build an "epoch-making computer" with a supercomputer-like performance on Prolog. In the meantime, successful expert systems appeared in multiple interdisciplinary areas, such as MYCIN [10] and CADUCEUS [11] in the medical information area. Some expert systems played practical roles in real-world business. For example, the R1 expert system [12] from DEC can automatically configure on-demand hardware components in the VAX computer system. In the mid-1980s, there was another evolutionary progress in the neural network. The *back-propagation* approach [13] brought back the research attention on neural networks, keeping the pace of connectionism up with symbolism. In the late 1980s, AI started to combine mathematical theories to build realistic applications. In this trend, the *hidden Markov model* was first used as the mathematics framework for real applications in speech recognition; *information theory* was used in machine translation; and the *Bayesian network* was used for effective representation and knowledge formulation in nondeterministic reasoning and expert systems.

As a matter of fact, symbolism is still the flagship in the Second Wave. Both the Prolog from the FGCS plan and the LISP from the MYCIN expert system mainly relied on reasoning with symbolic logic. However, researchers had encountered many limitations in the symbolism methods. For example, there lacks sufficiently representative yet effective logic, and the related logic solver has a unsolvable high time complexity. On the other hand, the connectionism approach, such as neural networks, struggled with applicability. With the failure of the FGCS plan in 1991, the Second Wave was over, and AI fell in its second winter for nearly two decades.

1.1.2.3 2006–present, the Third Wave

In 2006, Geoffrey Hinton[1] and Ruslan Salakhutdinov wrote an article in *Science* and introduced gradient descent in data dimensionality reduction. The article revealed that the multihidden layer neural network can profile key features of data, and the unsupervised layer-by-layer initialization can mitigate the difficulty in deep neural network training [14]. Many researchers today believe that this paper has blown the horn of prosperity in deep learning, i.e., the multilayer massive neural network, and started the Third Wave of AI.[2] In 2012, Alexander Krizhevsky, Ilya Sutskever, and Geoffrey Hinton proposed a novel deep learning neural network, AlexNet [15], and won the 2012 ImageNet Large Scale Visual Recognition Competition (ILSVRC) [16], attracting much attention from both the research community and industry. As the data and model size grow, the deep learning neural network has achieved better performance and wider applicability in areas of speech recognition, facial recognition, machine translation, etc. In 2016, the DeepMind team from Google developed AlphaGo [17], a Go program using deep learning techniques. AlphaGo beat Lee Sedol, the world champion in Go. This event further pushed the development of the Third Wave and drew public attention to AI, machine learning, deep learning, and neural networks.

AI in the Third Wave shows a remarkable difference from AI at the Dartmouth Conference. As shown in Fig. 1.2, hot topics in today's AI research are mainly focused on machine learning, neural network, and computer vision. These three domains are closely related with each other in some sense. The neural network is a subset of machine learning, while computer vision is an important application of machine learning and neural networks. On the contrary, symbolism, a hot topic at the Dartmouth Conference 60 years ago, is rarely picked up by researchers nowadays.

1.1.3 Mainstreams in AI

In the history of AI, three primary AI paradigms have been established, including behaviorism, symbolism, and connectionism. As mentioned, connectionism is a hot research topic in both the research community and industry today. Next, we discuss the three AI paradigms.

1.1.3.1 Behaviorism

Behaviorism is a control theory-based perception-action control system. In 1943, Arturo Rosenblueth, Norbert Wiener, and Julian Bigelow coauthored the paper "Behavior, Purpose and Teleology" and proposed that "All purposeful behavior may be

---

[1] When we wrote this book, we inadvertently discovered that G. Hinton, the winner of the Turing Prize and the pioneer of deep learning, and P. Higgs, the winner of the Nobel Prize in Physics and the prophet of the Higgs boson, are fellow apprentices under the same supervisor, C. Longuet-Higgins. What's more interesting is that C. Longuet-Higgins, the codoctoral supervisor of the two computer science and physics masters, did not study computer science nor physics. He is an expert in chemistry and cognitive science.

[2] Of course, some work from Y. LeCun and Y. Bengio at the same time also played a key role in promoting the development of deep learning. Therefore, Y. LeCun, Y. Bengio, and G. Hinton were called the three pioneers of deep learning and jointly won the 2018 Turing Award.

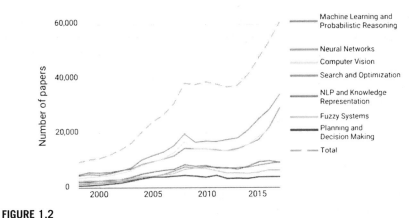

FIGURE 1.2

The number of AI papers by topic category from 1998 to 2017.[3]

considered to require negative feed-back" [19]. A few years later, Norbert Wiener defined in his book *Cybernetics* [20] cybernetics (later known as control theory) as the science of "control and communications in the animal and machine" and discussed making learning machines capable of playing chess. At the same time, William Ashby also explored AI machines, and in his book *Design for a Brain* [21], proposed that homeostatic devices with feedback loops for adaptive behaviors could train AI. The possibility of realizing AI machines via control theory attracted attention from AI research communities in the 1950s. The journal *Automata Studies* [22], edited by John McCarthy and Claude Shannon, published many research works on control theory, including finite automata, the Turing machine, and synthesis of automata, hoping to create some perception-action and reactive control systems based on control theories. Intuitively, behaviorism can simulate some kinds of AI like the cerebellum, realizing robot behaviors such as walking, grabbing, and balancing via feedback, and thus has great practical value. However, behaviorism seems not to be the ultimate path for strong AI.

1.1.3.2 Symbolism

Symbolism is built on symbolic logic and uses logic to represent knowledge and solve problems. The basic idea of symbolism is using logic to represent all knowledge, converting the problem to be solved into a logical expression, and then solving the problem by reasoning on the logical expressions of prior knowledge.

Among all symbolic logics, the most common and probably the simplest one is propositional logic. In natural deduction calculus, propositional logic only needs to consider three operations, AND, OR, and NOT, and two values of variables, 0 and 1.

However, propositional logic is weak in representation. For example, propositional logic cannot represent even a simple sentence like "not all birds can fly." Thus, logicians introduced *predicates* and *quantifiers* and designed *predicate logic* to express more subtle declarative sentences [23]. In predicate logic, quantifiers include ∃ (which stands for *there exists* or *for some*) and ∀ (which stands for *for all*), while predicates represent relations and output 0 or 1. For example, ∀x can represent "any bird," $B(x)$ can represent "x is a bird," and $P(x)$ can represent "x can fly." As such, the sentence "not all birds can fly" can be expressed as $\neg(\forall x(B(x) \rightarrow P(x)))$ [23]. Predicate logic can be further divided into first-order logic and higher-order logic. The main difference between first-order logic and higher-order logic is the presence of predicate variables. First-order logic cannot quantify predicates, while higher-order logic can.

Symbolism was the most discussed topic at the Dartmouth Conference. At that time, many believed that symbolism is the ultimate path to strong AI. However, after over 60 years of research, symbolism exposes some fundamental problems.

(1) Logic problem: From the perspective of logic, it is hard to find a concise symbolic logic framework to represent all knowledge in the world. For example, the ordinary predicate logic cannot efficiently represent time, space, probability, etc. Amir Pnueli proposed temporal logic (TL) [24], which introduced the concept of time into first-order logic, thus winning the Turing Award in 1996. However, TL is insufficient to present indeterminate future. Thus, Edmund Clarke et al. further proposed computation tree logic [25], which models time as a tree like structure, and each path in this tree represents a future possibility. Based on this contribution, Clarke et al. won the Turing Award in 2007. It is clear that only presenting time information is not an easy task. Until now, researchers have proposed hundreds of thousands of forms of logics to present knowledge. However, today, there is still not a universally accepted logic to present all knowledge.

(2) Common sense problem: People usually make decisions based on their common sense. For example, when someone says he is enjoying the beautiful sunset on his balcony, we can deduce that his balcony must be on the west side based on common sense. There exists infinite common sense in this world. The widely studied expert systems in the 1970s to the 1980s were designed to record all common sense in specific domains with logical expressions. However, even for a single domain, there could exist tons of "common senses." Even today, researchers still fail to write down all possible common senses with logical expressions in one practical domain.

(3) Solver problem: In symbolism, the key to solving problems is the logic solver. The solver decides whether a new problem holds based on prior knowledge. However, the time complexity of a logic solver is too high. Even for the simplest propositional logic, its solution is known as NP-complete. In fact, the propositional satisfiability problem (SAT) is the first proved NP-complete problem. In general, predicate logic is undecidable. That is, theoretically there exists no program which can decide whether any predicate logical expressions hold in a limited time.

Based on these aforementioned issues, symbolism usually fails in practice. Based on accepted papers from the International Joint Conferences on Artificial Intelligence (IJCAI), the number of researchers on symbolism is less than 10% in the entire research community of AI.[4]

We believe that the fundamental problem of symbolism is that it only considers rational cognitive intelligence. Human intelligence includes perceptual cognition and rational cognition. Even human beings start with low-level perceptual intelligence and recognize various objects, smells, and sounds, which cause instinctive reaction. On this basis, human beings created unique complex language in the biological world, proceeded to create characters and then mathematics and logic, and eventually formed cognitive intelligence. Symbolism skips all previous steps and starts from logic, thus inevitably encountering big obstacles. Yet, we still believe combining symbolism with other approaches shall play an important role on the path to strong AI.

1.1.3.3 Connectionism

As far as we know, the human brain is still the most intelligent object in the world. The brain is a complex network of hundreds of billions of neurons and endows human beings with the ability of thinking. Connectionism is inspired by the computational model of biological neural networks and approximates intelligent behaviors with artificial neural networks.

In fact, connectionism is not an exact copy of the human brain. It is because our brain is so complicated that even a single neuron is hard to mimic. As shown in Fig. 1.3, one neuron contains a cell body (or soma) and cell processes. A cell body consists of a cell membrane, a nucleus, and cytoplasm. Cell processes include a single axon and various dendrites. The axon is a single long fiber arising from the cell body, while dendrites are short and highly branched fibers extending from the cell body. The connection between an axon of one neuron and a dendrite of another neuron is called a synapse.[5]

The artificial neural network simplifies the biological neuron network in a high-level abstraction. That is, it models every output of the cell body and the strength of each synapse into a number. Specifically, an artificial neuron in Fig. 1.3 can receive input from outside as $\{x_1, \cdots, x_n\}$, and each input has a corresponding synapse weight as $\{w_1, \cdots, w_n\}$. The output of this neuron is the weighted sum of the input followed by a nonlinear function.

Connectionism started in 1943. At that time, the psychologist Warren McCulloch and logician Walter Pitts built up the McCulloch–Pitts neuron model to emulate biological neurons [1] as the first artificial neuron network. In the following 60 years or so, based on the relentless efforts of people like Frank Rosenblatt (perceptron

---

[4] In 2017, IJCAI accepted 710 papers with only 44 papers related to symbolism (Knowledge Representation and Reasoning Session). In fact, IJCAI is already the best venue in accepting papers in symbolism, as compared to other top AI conferences.

[5] In some rare cases, a synapse can connect two axons.

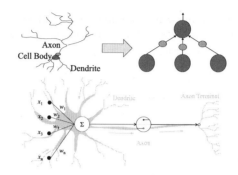

FIGURE 1.3

Biological neuron (top) and artificial neuron (bottom).

model), David Rumelhart (back-propagation model), Yann LeCun (convolutional neural network), Yoshua Bengio (deep learning), and Geoffrey Hinton (deep learning, back-propagation training, etc.), connectionism has become the mainstream in the entire AI research community.

Today, deep learning and related methods are widely applied in domains like image recognition, speech recognition, natural language processing, etc., have many interesting applications such as deep fake and image style transfer, and even win against top human players in games like Go and StarCraft. Techniques from deep learning create a nearly $100 billion-worth intelligence industry market, including intelligent security, intelligent education, intelligent phones, intelligent homes, intelligent medical services, intelligent cities, and intelligent factories. In this book, we mainly focus on intelligent computing systems based on deep learning.

However, we have to understand that deep learning may not be the ultimate path to strong AI. This method is more like a ladder, helping us reach the second or the third floor faster. Yet, this ladder cannot reach the moon. So far, the limitations of deep learning include:

(1) Limited generalization. Deep learning training requires a large number of samples, which is different from the human learning mechanism. Humans learn from a large amount of external data only in their early childhood. Afterward, adults acquire the ability to transfer learning and generalization more efficiently than the current deep learning.

(2) Lack of reasoning. The lack of reasoning prevents deep learning from solving cognitive problems efficiently. In this case, it is promising to combine symbolic logic with deep learning in the future to overcome this limitation.

(3) Lack of explainability. In some areas placing strong emphasis on security, the lack of explainability can cause some problems. For example, how is one certain decision made, and why does the deep learning model make an incorrect prediction?

(4) Less robustness. For example, by changing a few pixels invisible to human eyes on an image, deep learning can be fooled and make incorrect predictions, such as identifying pigs as cats and cows as dogs.

1.2 AI computing systems

1.2.1 What are AI computing systems?

A complete intelligent agent requires input from the wild and can solve some specific problems in reality (i.e., weak AI) or various kinds of problems (i.e., strong AI). However, the AI algorithm or code itself cannot create a full intelligent agent, but relies on a physical foundation. Hence, AI computing systems (AICSs) are the physical foundation for AI.

The current AICS is a heterogeneous system with generic CPUs and AI chips from the hardware perspective and a developer-oriented intelligent programming environment, including the programming framework and programming language from the software perspective.

The reason behind adopting a heterogeneous system is that the growth of the computing capacity of a generic CPU has almost stagnated in the past decade while the demand for intelligent computing is growing exponentially. This scissors gap calls for a solution that integrates AI chips (like the deep learning processor) to obtain the demanding computational capacity. Deep learning processors such as the Dian-Nao Family can achieve at least $100\times$ better performance in AI-related processing with one magnitude of order lower power consumption as compared to the general-purpose CPU.

While achieving better performance, the heterogeneous system does bring difficulties in programming. Programmers need to write instructions and schedule tasks for these two chips in this system. Without system-level software support, it may bring undesired overhead in the development. Thus, the AICS usually integrates a programming environment, in order to help programmers to develop energy-efficient AI applications in an agile way. This environment contains the programming framework and programming language. Common deep learning programming frameworks include TensorFlow [26] and PyTorch [27]. Deep learning programming languages include CUDA [28] and BCL.

1.2.2 The necessity of AICSs

Traditional generic CPU-centered computing systems fail to meet the performance and energy efficiency demand of today's AI applications. For example, in 2012, the Google Brain used 160,000 CPU cores to train a deep learning model to recognize cats for three days [29]. Traditional computing systems fail to meet the demand. In 2016, when AlphaGo played chess with the Go master Lee Sedol, it adopted 1202 CPUs and 176 GPUs [30] for each game, at an expense of thousands of dollars in electricity bills. In comparison, the equivalent power consumption of Lee Sedol is only

20 W. Thus, the energy efficiency of traditional computing systems is low. Therefore, AI may not rely on the traditional computing systems but shall have its own physical foundation—AICSs.

1.2.3 Trends in AICSs

Based on the history, today's AICSs can be divided into two generations: the first generation of AICS, which appeared around the 1980s, targeting specific computing for symbolism, and the second generation of AICS, which appeared in the 2010s, targeting specific computing for connectionism. At the same time, we predict there will be a new generation of computing systems, as the physical foundation for strong AI or general AI. This new generation of computing systems could be the third generation of AICSs.

1.2.3.1 The first generation of AICS

As mentioned, the 1980s saw the Second Wave of AI. The first generation of AICS is the computing systems developed in this wave, targeting symbolic logic processing. Their main function is to run programs written in popular programming languages at that time like Prolog or LISP.

In 1975, Richard Greenblatt from the MIT AI lab built the first LISP machine, CONS [31], to efficiently run LISP programs, which is also one of the earliest AICSs. In 1978, the same MIT lab published CADR, the successor of CONS. In 1982, Japan announced the "Fifth Generation Computer System" plan. The plan claimed the former four generations of computers were made of a vacuum tube, transistor, integrated circuit, and very large-scale integration, respectively, while the Fifth Generation Computer System is the AICS. With this AICS, all a human needs to do is to provide problems as the input, and the system could solve it automatically. In fact, Japan's Fifth Generation Computer System is a Prolog machine. Almost at the same time, in 1982, the US founded Microelectronics and Computer Technology Corporation to make AICSs. During this wave, in the entire decade of the 1980s, universities, research institutes, and companies in the US and Japan made various kinds of Prolog and LISP machines.

By the end of the 1980s and the early 1990s, the heat of AI cooled down, entering the winter of this wave. The first generation of AICSs failed to succeed in real-world scenarios, leading to the collapse of the market and the cessation of funding from the government. All these startups were closed down one after another. Fig. 1.4 shows a LISP machine made at MIT, now exhibited in the MIT museum.

Technically, the first generation of AICSs had a high-level programming language-oriented computing architecture. In this architecture, the programming language and the hardware are highly correlated, such as LISP and Prolog. The reasons behind the failure of this computing system are twofold. On the one hand, unlike the large application demand, such as speech recognition, image recognition, machine translation, etc., in today's AI market, there was little demand for symbolic programming languages like Prolog and LISP at that time. On the other hand, at that time, the development speed of the specific computing system failed in catching up with the fast development of the general-purpose CPU. In the golden era of Moore's law of the 20th century, the performance of CPUs doubled every 1.5 year. With this being said, the performance of CPUs can grow up to 100× in one decade. Besides, a specific AICS is less adaptive than the general-purpose CPU, and often takes a few years to develop with sufficient funds. In comparison, the specific AICS may not be better than a generic CPU-based system after several years of development. Thus, the first generation of AICSs gradually withdrew from the stage of history.

FIGURE 1.4

The existing first generation of AICS (LISP machine).[6]

1.2.3.2 The second generation of AICSs (2010–present)

The second generation of AICSs is computers or processors targeting connectionism-oriented processing, or deep learning. The Institute of Computing Technology (ICT), Chinese Academy of Sciences, started the interdisciplinary research on AI and chip design in 2008. In 2013, they codesigned the world's first deep learning processor architecture, DianNao, with Inria. After that, ICT developed the world's first deep learning processor chip, "Cambricon-1." Subsequently, over 200 institutes from 30 countries/regions worldwide, including Harvard, Stanford, MIT, Google, and Nvidia, and two Turing Award laureates, over 10 academicians from China and the US, and over 100 ACM/IEEE fellows conducted their follow up research citing the ICT paper. Thus, the magazine *Science* reported that the ICT team is "pioneering in terms of specialized chip architecture," "by all accounts among the leaders" with a comment that the team has achieved "groundbreaking advances" [32]. Table 1.1 lists a few representative works on the second generation of AICSs.

---

[6] Source: https://en.wikipedia.org/wiki/Lisp_machine, under a CC BY-SA 3.0 license, see https://creativecommons.org/licenses/by-sa/3.0/.

Table 1.1 Representative deep learning processors/computers.

Year	Deep learning processor/computer	Development organization	Features
2013	DianNao [33]	ICT, CAS	The world's first deep learning processor architecture
2014	DaDianNaostartup [34]	ICT, CAS	The world's first multicore deep learning processor architecture
	cuDNN (DL library)	Nvidia	Upgrade GPU for deep learning
2015	PuDianNao [35]	ICT, CAS	The world's first general-purpose machine learning processor
	ShiDianNao [36]	ICT, CAS	Shifting vision processing closer to the sensor
2016	Cambricon [37]	ICT, CAS	The world's first deep learning instruction set
	Cambricon-X [38]	ICT, CAS	The world's first sparse neural network processor
2017	TPU [39]	Google	Systolic array architecture
	FlexFlow [40]	ICT, CAS	Dynamic data flow architecture
2018	TPUv3 cloud	Google	Cloud computing based on TPUv3 chip
	DGX-2 server	Nvidia	Integrating 16 Nvidia V100 graphics cards
	Summit supercomputer	IBM	Integrating 27,684 Nvidia V100 graphics cards
	MLU100	Cambricon	Cambricon's cloud intelligent computing chip
2019	E-RNN [41]	Syracuse University	Recurrent neural network accelerator
	Cambricon-F [42]	ICT, CAS	Fractal von Neumann architecture
	Float-PIM [43]	UCSD	Supporting training with in-memory computing architecture

Compared with the first generation of AICSs, there are two advantages of the second generation of AICSs: (1) There are a lot of industrial applications for deep learning, which already form an ecosystem. Thus, related AI and system research can receive continuous funds from both government and industry. (2) The slowdown of Moore's law in the 21st century results in halted performance improvement of general-purpose CPUs. Thus, the performance advantage of specific AICSs continues to increase. As such, in the foreseeable future, the second generation of AICSs will continue to thrill and maintain its fast development in iteration and performance optimization.

In fact, today's supercomputers, computers in data centers, smartphones, vehicle electronics, and edge devices are processing a large number of deep learning applications, evolving towards AI computing systems. For example, the fastest supercomputer in 2018, SUMMIT, made by IBM, is called an intelligent supercomputer [44]. The weather analysis project using deep learning techniques in SUMMIT won the Gordon Bell Prize, the highest supercomputing application award, in 2018. Smartphones are commonly considered typical small AI computing systems, since smartphones use deep learning techniques to process many tasks like image processing, speed recognition, and machine translation. There are hundreds of millions of smartphones integrated with Cambricon chips. One day, our society will enter the era of AI, in which most computers are AICSs. Therefore, our book mainly focuses on the second generation of AICSs.

1.2.3.3 The future of the third generation of AICSs

To achieve better performance and higher energy efficiency, the first and second generations of AICSs are both designed towards specific AI algorithms. The only difference between them is that the first and second generations of AICSs are based on the intelligence defined by symbolism (i.e., Prolog and LISP) and connectionism (deep learning), respectively. One important and interesting question arises: What would the third generation of AICSs look like?

In our humble opinion, the third generation of AICSs will no longer naïvely chase after performance acceleration, instead providing almighty AI to human beings with nearly unlimited computation capability. The key problem now is, how could we improve the intelligence from higher computation capability? By building a bigger and more complex deep learning model, one can improve the accuracy of specific pattern recognition problems by a few percent; however, this approach never touches the essence of intelligence.

At our wild guess, the third generation of AICSs will be a virtual sandbox world to nurture generic/strong AI. This sandbox emulates the real world, in which it can nurture, grow, and reproduce countless intelligent agents (or artificial lives) with nearly infinite power of computation. Intelligent agents grow in the sandbox world, interact with the environment, and gradually form their power of perception, cognition, and logic. Eventually, they can understand and change the virtual world, in which the agents can possess strong/general AI. It may take three to five decades or even 500 years to achieve the goal. Still, we believe, for the progress of mankind, it is worthwhile to pursue this ultimate goal.

1.3 A driving example

As mentioned in the Preface, the theme of this book is application-driven and full-stack understanding. Thus, we introduce how an AICS works, from algorithms to programming until chip architecture, using a driving example of a deep learning task of image style transfer. Fig. 1.5(a) is a picture of outer space. Fig. 1.5(b) highlights the picture of outer space in Van Gogh's "Starry Night" style using deep learning techniques. The transfer procedure between Fig. 1.5(a) and Fig. 1.5(b) consists of the following steps.

(a) Outer space image

(b) Outer space image in Van Gogh style

FIGURE 1.5

Image style transfer example.[7]

The first step is building up the deep learning model for image style transfer. This step mainly involves algorithms in neural networks and deep learning, including extracting features from the content and style images, training models, etc. More details on neural network and deep learning algorithms are introduced in Chapters 2 and 3.

The second step is implementing the neural network algorithm in an AICS. First, we will use some deep learning programming frameworks, such as Caffe [46], TensorFlow [26], or MXNet [47]. Such programming frameworks package common operations in deep learning as operators or components, helping users to reproduce algorithms or design new ones. Taking TensorFlow as an example, the matrix multiply process can be described as in Fig. 1.6. Chapters 4–5 provide details of principles behind programming frameworks. Second, we need specific deep learning processors to run these programming frameworks, in order to effectively support deep learning algorithms and applications. Chapter 6 describes how to design a deep learning processor. Chapter 7 introduces architecture of industrial single-core/multicore deep learning processors. Chapter 8 discusses hardware abstraction, programming models, programming language, APIs, functions debugging, and performance tuning. The chapter ends with an example of using an AI programming language (i.e., BCL) to

---

[7] Fig. 1.5(a): reprinted with permission from [45].

develop AICS applications. An example of this AICS application is illustrated in Fig. 1.7.

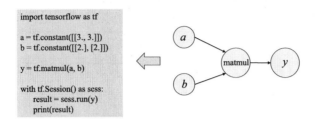

FIGURE 1.6

A TensorFlow example.

The last step is setting up the environment, debugging the program in real chips, and running it. In practice, one may face problems like low functionality, low accuracy, and bad performance. Related content on training and deployment will be introduced in Chapter 9.

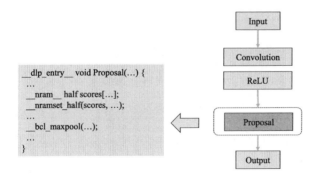

FIGURE 1.7

An example of AI programming language.

1.4 Summary

AICSs are the physical foundation of AI. In this chapter, we introduce the history of AI and AICSs. This book is mainly focused on AICSs for deep learning, i.e., the second generation of AICSs. To help understand the basic principles behind the entire computing system, the book chooses a case study on image style transfer as a driving example to systematically introduce the software/hardware stack in an AICS from the perspectives of algorithm design, programming, and chip design. We hope this book can help readers develop the ability to build a simple AICS.

Exercises

1.1 Briefly describe the difference between strong AI and weak AI.

1.2 Briefly describe the three types of AI research.

1.3 What task can a perceptron composed of a single neuron with two inputs accomplish?

1.4 What are the limitations of deep learning?

1.5 What is an AICS?

1.6 Why do we need AICSs?

1.7 What are the characteristics of the first generation of AICSs?

1.8 What are the characteristics of the second generation of AICSs?

1.9 What are the characteristics of the third generation of AICSs?

*1.10 If you are asked to design an AICS, how do you plan to design it? In your design, how will users use the AICS?

Fundamentals of neural networks

2

Neural networks are a subset of machine learning. Today, neural networks have become the mainstream of artificial intelligence (AI). For example, the aforementioned driving example of this book, i.e., image style transfer, is implemented based on neural networks. This chapter begins with linear regression and then details the basic principles of machine learning, focusing on neural networks. Next, the training process of neural network is described, as well as some optimization techniques to improve training accuracy. The chapter is closed with cross-validation in neural networks.

2.1 From machine learning to neural networks

This section distinguishes some confusing concepts, including AI, machine learning, neural network, and deep learning. Then, the basic principles of machine learning are detailed using linear regression. With a basic understanding of these principles, the basic ideas in neural networks are described, including the artificial neuron model (perceptron) [6,7], the two-layer perceptron [48], and deep learning (i.e., deep neural networks).

2.1.1 Basic concepts

We often see hot words like AI, machine learning, neural networks, and deep learning being misused by nonprofessionals in media, papers, and novels. Hence, it is necessary to clarify their concepts and relationships. Fig. 2.1 lists the containment relationships among AI, machine learning, neural networks, and deep learning. Among them, AI is the largest set that includes branches like machine learning, computer vision, symbolic logic, etc. Machine learning can be divided into several branches as well, for instance, artificial neural networks, Bayesian networks, decision trees, linear regression, etc. At present, neural networks are the mainstream machine learning algorithm, and the most advanced technique in neural networks is deep learning.

    Machine learning has been defined by many researchers. Tom Mitchell defined machine learning as the study of computer algorithms that improve automatically through experience [49]. Ethem Alpaydin believed "machine learning is programming computers to optimize a performance criterion using example data or past experience" [50]. Zhi-Hua Zhou considers machine learning as a technique that improves

AI Computing Systems. https://doi.org/10.1016/B978-0-32-395399-3.00008-1

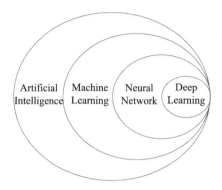

FIGURE 2.1

Relationships among artificial intelligence, machine learning, neural networks, and deep learning.

system performance by learning from experience via computational methods [51]. The common theme behind these definitions is that computers progressively improve their intelligent ability by continuously learning from experience or data.

Machine learning can be roughly divided into two categories, supervised and unsupervised learning, based on whether the training data is labeled [52]. Supervised learning learns a model function from labeled training data to predict labels for new data. Unsupervised learning reveals underlying features and patterns from unlabeled training data.

Fig. 2.2 presents a standard process of supervised learning. In the training/learning process, first, training data x and their labels y need to be prepared. Then, for the training data, a machine learning algorithm should be selected, such as a Bayesian network, neural network, etc. Finally, a model $H(x)$ is learned from the training data. In the inference process, the model $H(x)$ accepts new data as input and then outputs a predicted value $\hat{y}$. During training, the difference between the predicted value $\hat{y}$ and the actual label y is measured with loss function $L(x)$. The smaller the loss value, the more accurate the prediction.

For a better understanding, Table 2.1 provides all symbols and notations used in this book.

2.1.2 Linear regression

Linear regression is the most straightforward machine learning algorithm. It is used as an example in this subsection to help readers understand the principle behind machine learning.[1] Linear regression aims to find some patterns behind a set of points. For example, if a set of points can be fitted with a straight line, the parametric char-

---

[1] Note that linear regression does not belong to the neural networks.

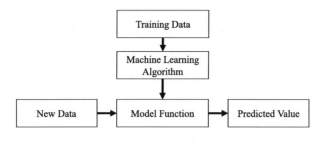

FIGURE 2.2

Typical machine learning process.

Table 2.1 Description of common symbols.

Definition	Symbol	Description
Input data	x	
True value	y	The desired value, ground-truth label, or actual label
Predicted value (model output)	$\hat{y}$	The predicted value of machine learning aims to be consistent with the true value
Model function	$H(x)$	The input and output of the model function H are x and $\hat{y}$, respectively
Activation function	$G(x)$	
Loss function	$L(x)$	Used to measure the difference between the output value $\hat{y}$ and the true value of the model y
Scalar	a, b, c	Represented with italic lowercase letters
Vector	$\boldsymbol{a}, \boldsymbol{b}, \boldsymbol{c}$	Represented with black italic lowercase letters
Matrix	$\boldsymbol{A}, \boldsymbol{B}, \boldsymbol{C}$	Represented with black italic capital letters

acteristics of this fitted line are the patterns behind the set of points found by linear regression.

The example in Table 2.2 is used to introduce how to use linear regression for solving the house pricing problem. Assume a real estate company has a sales center, determining house price y based on house size x_1 in square meters (m^2). Based on existing data, a 50-m^2 house sells for USD 250,000, a 47-m^2 house sells for USD 210,000, a 60-m^2 house sells for USD 400,000, and a 55-m^2 house sells for USD 260,000. In this case, what is the price of a 65 m^2 house? These data could be plotted into a coordinate system with house size x_1 and house price y on the x and y axes, respectively, as shown in Fig. 2.3. Based on the relationship between x_1 and y, a fitted line could be found such that the sum of the distances between all points to this line is minimal. This fitted line reveals the pattern between x_1 and y, which is the linear regression model. In this example, the house price y only depends on one variable (i.e., feature) x_1. Thus, this is a univariate linear regression model.

The univariate linear regression model can be represented as

$$H_w(x_1) = w_0 + w_1 x_1, \tag{2.1}$$

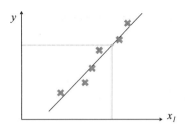

FIGURE 2.3

Linear regression.

Table 2.2 An example of linear regression. y is the price of the house ($\times 10,000$ USD), x_1 is the house size (in m^2).

x_1	50	47	60	55	...	65
y	25	21	40	26	...	?

where $H_w(x_1)$ is a linear function fitted to known data. This function is a straight line with one variable. The parameters w_0 and w_1 can be calculated from known data points, where w_1 represents the slope and w_0 is the intercept, which is the intersection of the fitted line and the y axis. With w_0 and w_1, the price of a new house could be predicted.

However, the price of a house is not only correlated to its size but also closely related to factors like the floor number x_2, orientation x_3, location x_4, etc. Assume there exist some price data in Table 2.3. A 50-m^2 (x_1) house on the second floor (x_2) sells for USD 250,000; a 47-m^2 (x_1) house on the first floor (x_2) sells for USD 210,000; and a 60-m^2 (x_1) house on the fourth floor (x_2) sells for USD 400,000. Then, how much is a 65-m^2 house on the 10th floor?

Table 2.3 An example of linear regression. y is the price of the house ($\times 10,000$ USD), x_1 is the property size (in m^2), and x_2 is the floor of the house.

x_1	50	47	60	55	...	65
x_2	2	1	4	3	...	10
...					...	
y	25	21	40	26	...	?

The aforementioned problem has two variables/features, and thus it can be presented with a binary linear regression model $H_w(x)$ as

$$h_w(x_1, x_2) = w_0 + w_1 x_1 + w_2 x_2. \tag{2.2}$$

If the problem has n variables/features (an n-dimensional vector x), it can be represented in a multivariate linear regression model $H_w(x)$ as

$$H_w(x) = \sum_{i=0}^{n} w_i x_i = \hat{w}^\top x, \qquad x_0 = 1, \tag{2.3}$$

where the parameter vector $\hat{w} = [w_0; w_1; ...; w_n]$, input vector $x = [x_0; x_1; ...; x_n]$, and $\hat{w}^\top$ is the transpose of $\hat{w}$.

How to evaluate the prediction accuracy of a linear regression model? The error ε between the predicted value $\hat{y}$ and the true value y is

$$\varepsilon = y - \hat{y} = y - \hat{w}^\top x. \tag{2.4}$$

If the sample size is sufficiently large, the error ε follows a Gaussian distribution with mean $\mu = 0$ and variance σ^2:

$$p(\varepsilon) = \frac{1}{\sqrt{2\pi}\sigma} e^{-\frac{\varepsilon^2}{2\sigma^2}}. \tag{2.5}$$

Then, we have the likelihood

$$p(y|x; \hat{w}) = \frac{1}{\sqrt{2\pi}\sigma} e^{-\frac{(y-\hat{w}^\top x)^2}{2\sigma^2}}. \tag{2.6}$$

Finally, by calculating the maximum likelihood, the objective function (i.e., loss function) is obtained. Minimizing the loss function can narrow the gap between the predicted value and the true value. We have

$$L(\hat{w}) = \frac{1}{2} \sum_{j=1}^{m} \left(y_j - H_w(x_j)\right)^2. \tag{2.7}$$

The loss function is the sum of the squares of the difference between the predicted and true values in m times. Linear regression aims to find the optimal parameters $w_0, w_1, \cdots, w_n$ such that the value of the loss function $L(\hat{w})$ is minimized. One common method to find these optimal parameters is gradient descent. The process of gradient descent is as follows. First, the parameter vector $\hat{w}$ is initialized, e.g., a random vector, and the partial derivative of the loss function with respect to $\hat{w}$ (i.e., gradient) is calculated. Second, the values of parameters are tuned with a step size η (also known as the learning rate) by following the direction of the negative gradient as in Eq. (2.8). Such computations are repeated to minimize $L(\hat{w})$ until the minimum $L(\hat{w})$ is reached, and finally, appropriate parameters are obtained for the regression model. We have

$$\hat{w} \leftarrow \hat{w} - \eta \frac{\partial L(\hat{w})}{\partial \hat{w}}. \tag{2.8}$$

The training and inference process of the neural network is similar to linear regression. Take, for example, training a neural network for animal classification. First, a number of animal samples should be collected and labeled. Then, the parameters of the neural network model are tuned to minimize the difference between the predicted outputs and true values (i.e., loss function). In the inference process, the trained neural network receives an unlabeled animal image and predicts its class.

2.1.3 Perceptron

After the warm-up on linear regression, let us introduce a simplest neural network: a single-layer neural network with one neuron, which is known as the perceptron [6,7]. It can perform simple linear classification tasks. Fig. 2.4 shows a two-input perceptron. The input and output of the neuron are $x = [x_1; x_2]$ and $y = \pm 1$, respectively, w_1 and w_2 are synapse weights, and b is the bias. This perceptron can classify input samples into two categories. This perceptron is formalized as

$$H(x) = sign(w_1 x_1 + w_2 x_2 + b) = sign(\mathbf{w}^\top \mathbf{x} + b),$$
$$sign(x) = \begin{cases} +1 & x \geq 0, \\ -1 & x < 0, \end{cases} \tag{2.9}$$

where $(\mathbf{w}, b)$ are model parameters.

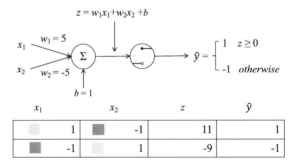

x_1		x_2		z	$\hat{y}$
	1		-1	11	1
	-1		1	-9	-1

FIGURE 2.4

A single-layer perceptron.

The goal of perceptron training is to find a hyperplane $S(\mathbf{w}^\top \mathbf{x} + b = 0)$ which can separate all samples in the linearly separable dataset T into two categories. A hyperplane is a subspace whose dimension is one less than that of its ambient space. That is, a hyperplane of an N-dimensional space is a subspace of dimension $N - 1$. For example, the hyperplanes of a 2D space are 1D lines, while the hyperplanes of a 3D are 2D planes.

For the two classes of points in Fig. 2.5, the perceptron training needs to find a hyperspace (a line) in the 2D space to separate these points. To find the hyperspace, the model parameters $\mathbf{w}$ and b should be found. Compared to linear regression, the

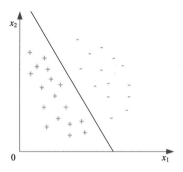

FIGURE 2.5

Two classes of points.

perceptron model adds the $sign(x)$ computation, which is denoted as the activation function. This increases the complexity in finding parameters.

The training of a perceptron requires finding a proper loss function first. Then, through minimizing the loss function, a optimal hyperplane is found. That is, the optimal parameters of the hyperplane are found. Consider a training set $D = \{(x_1, y_1), (x_2, y_2), ..., (x_m, y_m)\}$, where samples $x_j \in \mathbf{R}^n$ and labels of these samples $y_j \in \{+1, -1\}$. The hyperplane $\mathbf{S}$ should separate the two classes of points. If the points are inseparable, the hyperplane shall be close to the misclassified points. Thus, the loss function is defined as the sum of distances between misclassified points to the hyperplane $\mathbf{S}$ ($w^\top x + b = 0$).

The distance from any point x_j to the hyperplane $\mathbf{S}$ is

$$d_j = \frac{1}{\|w\|_2}|w^\top x_j + b|, \tag{2.10}$$

where $\|w\|_2$ is the L^2 norm of w, denoted as $\|w\|$ and calculated as $\|w\| = \sqrt{\sum_{i=1}^n w_i^2}$.

Assume the hyperplane $\mathbf{S}$ can correctly classify samples in training set D. Then, when $y_j = +1$, $w^\top x_j + b \geq 0$; when $y_j = -1$, $w^\top x_j + b < 0$. For all misclassified points, the predicted values may appear above the hyperplane but actually will be below it. Thus, the product of y_j and the predicted value will be negative. That is, the misclassified points in the training set will satisfy the condition $-y_j(w^\top x_j + b) > 0$.

By removing the absolute value symbol in the distance equation (2.10) between point x_j and hyperplane $\mathbf{S}$, the distance becomes

$$d_j = -\frac{1}{\|w\|}y_j(w^\top x_j + b). \tag{2.11}$$

Suppose the set of all misclassified points is M. The sum of distances between all misclassified points to the hyperplane is

$$d = -\frac{1}{\|\boldsymbol{w}\|} \sum_{\boldsymbol{x}_j \in M} y_j(\boldsymbol{w}^\top \boldsymbol{x}_j + b). \tag{2.12}$$

As the value of $\|\boldsymbol{w}\|$ approaches a constant, the loss function can be defined as

$$L(\boldsymbol{w}, b) = -\sum_{\boldsymbol{x}_j \in M} y_j(\boldsymbol{w}^\top \boldsymbol{x}_j + b). \tag{2.13}$$

The goal of training a perceptron is to minimize the loss function. When the loss function is small enough, all misclassified points are either none or sufficiently close to the hyperplane. The variables in the loss function are $\boldsymbol{w}$ and b, similar to the variables w_1 and w_2 in linear regression. Gradient descent can be used to minimize the loss function. The partial derivatives of the loss function $L(\boldsymbol{w}, b)$ with respect to $\boldsymbol{w}$ and b, respectively, are

$$\nabla_{\boldsymbol{w}} L(\boldsymbol{w}, b) = -\sum_{\boldsymbol{x}_j \in M} y_j \boldsymbol{x}_j, \tag{2.14}$$

$$\nabla_b L(\boldsymbol{w}, b) = -\sum_{\boldsymbol{x}_j \in M} y_j. \tag{2.15}$$

If random gradient descent is used, a misclassified sample $(\boldsymbol{x}_j, y_j)$ is randomly selected and $\boldsymbol{w}$ and b are updated at a step size of η:

$$\begin{aligned} \boldsymbol{w} &\leftarrow \boldsymbol{w} + \eta y_j \boldsymbol{x}_j, \\ b &\leftarrow b + \eta y_j. \end{aligned} \tag{2.16}$$

By repeating the above computations, the value of loss function $L(\boldsymbol{w}, b)$ can be reduced to a very small value close to 0, if not equal to 0. From the aforementioned process, the perceptron model with parameters $(\boldsymbol{w}, b)$ could be trained.

2.1.4 Two-layer neural network: multilayer perceptron

Between the 1980s and 1990s, the most commonly used network was the two-layer neural network, also called *multilayer perceptron* (MLP) [48]. The MLP, shown in Fig. 2.6, consists of an array of input, one hidden layer, and one output layer.[2] Since the MLP contains two layers, the number of parameters increases significantly, as compared to the aforementioned perceptron.

The principle of MLP is illustrated with the example in Fig. 2.6. This MLP receives three neurons as inputs, represented in vector form as $\boldsymbol{x} = [x_1; x_2; x_3]$. The hidden layer has two neurons, represented in vector form as $\boldsymbol{h} = [h_1; h_2]$. The output layer has two neurons, represented in vector form as $\hat{\boldsymbol{y}} = [\hat{y}_1; \hat{y}_2]$. The connection

---

[2] In this book, the input is not considered as an individual layer when counting the number of layers in a neural network.

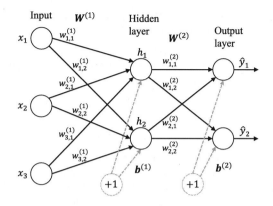

FIGURE 2.6

Two-layer neural network: multilayer perceptron.

between each input neuron and each hidden-layer neuron is represented with an individual weight. Thus the input vector corresponds to six weights, represented in matrix $\boldsymbol{W}^{(1)}$ as

$$\boldsymbol{W}^{(1)} = \begin{bmatrix} w_{1,1}^{(1)} & w_{1,2}^{(1)} \\ w_{2,1}^{(1)} & w_{2,2}^{(1)} \\ w_{3,1}^{(1)} & w_{3,2}^{(1)} \end{bmatrix}. \tag{2.17}$$

The neurons in the hidden layer are computed from inputs as follows. First, the multiplication between the transpose of weight matrix $\boldsymbol{W}^{(1)}$ and the input vector $\boldsymbol{x}$ is calculated to get the values of the hidden neurons before nonlinear activation. Then, the bias vector $\boldsymbol{b}^{(1)}$ is added to the hidden neurons. Finally, a nonlinear activation function is applied to the hidden neurons to get the output of hidden layer $\boldsymbol{h} = G(\boldsymbol{W}^{(1)^\top}\boldsymbol{x} + \boldsymbol{b}^{(1)})$.

In a similar way, the output layer could be computed using the output of the hidden layer and the weight matrix $\boldsymbol{W}^{(2)}$:

$$\boldsymbol{W}^{(2)} = \begin{bmatrix} w_{1,1}^{(2)} & w_{1,2}^{(2)} \\ w_{2,1}^{(2)} & w_{2,2}^{(2)} \end{bmatrix}. \tag{2.18}$$

The multiplication between the transpose of the weight matrix $\boldsymbol{W}^{(2)}$ and the output vector of the hidden layer $\boldsymbol{h}$ is calculated, the bias vector $\boldsymbol{b}^{(2)}$ is added, and then the nonlinear activation function is applied to get the output $\hat{\boldsymbol{y}} = G(\boldsymbol{W}^{(2)^\top}\boldsymbol{h} + \boldsymbol{b}^{(2)})$.

The MLP in Fig. 2.6 has two weight matrices and two bias vectors. The weight matrix $\boldsymbol{W}^{(1)}$ has six variables and the bias vector $\boldsymbol{b}^{(1)}$ has two variables; hence, eight variables are present in total in the first layer. The weight matrix $\boldsymbol{W}^{(2)}$ has four variables and the bias vector $\boldsymbol{b}^{(2)}$ has two variables; hence, six variables are present in total in the second layer. In all, this MLP has 14 variables to train, which does not require a large number of samples, so it could be trained quickly.

The MLP with only one hidden layer is the most classic shallow neural network. The problem with the shallow neural network is that the architecture is too simple, thus limiting the representation for complex functions. For example, it is unrealistic to recognize thousands of objects using a shallow neural network. However, researchers in the 1980s and 1990s were all working on shallow neural networks, not deep neural networks. The reason is twofold. On the one hand, Kurt Hornik proved that theoretically, a shallow neural network with one single hidden layer is capable of approximating any function [53]. It is a very strong conclusion, yet it can be misleading in practice because the one-hidden-layer neural network may have huge errors in approximating any random function, and it may require a very large number of neurons in each layer. On the other hand, at the time no sufficient computation resources or data to train a proper deep neural network existed. Today's deep learning models commonly contain tens or hundreds of layers with billions of parameters. Training such models requires a large number of samples and powerful computers. This was not affordable in the 1980s or 1990s. The performance of a single server at that time could be far lower than that of a smartphone today.[3] Constrained by the computation capability, researchers in the 1980s and 1990s could not make solid progress on deep neural networks.

2.1.5 Deep neural networks (deep learning)

Compared to shallow neural networks, deep neural networks (also known as deep learning) have more than one hidden layer. As a simple example, a multilayer neural network with two hidden layers is shown in Fig. 2.7. The forward computation of this neural network consists of three parts: computing the first hidden layer from the inputs, computing the second hidden layer from the first hidden layer, and computing the output layer from the second hidden layer. With increasing numbers of layers, the number of parameters in the neural network increases significantly. This three-layer neural network has 29 parameters in total, including 6 weights and 2 biases in the first hidden layer, 6 weights and 3 biases in the second hidden layer, and 9 weights and 3 biases in the output layer.

The early deep learning models learn from the six-layer architecture in the cerebral cortex of primates. To improve the accuracy of applications like image recognition and speech recognition, deep learning is no longer constrained by biological neural network architectures. Instead, today's deep neural networks have hundreds or even thousands of layers, which are significantly different from biological neural networks. As the number of layers increases, the number of parameters scales tremendously. AlexNet [15] from 2012 has 60 million parameters, whereas some modern neural networks have tens or hundreds of billions of parameters [54,55].

---

[3] In 1995, the frequency of Intel server CPU Pentium Pro was 200 MHz; in 2017, the frequency of the smartphone processor designed by Huawei, KIRIN 970, reached 2.36 GHz.

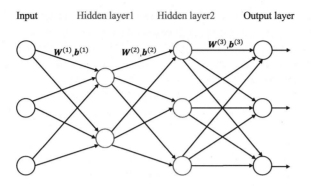

FIGURE 2.7

Multilayer neural network.

The principle of deep learning is to extract and process information through multiple layers to enable complex functionalities. Fig. 2.8 shows the extracted features from different layers of deep neural networks. At the first layer, deep neural networks use convolution to extract simple and local features, such as diagonal structures. At the second layer, deep neural networks can obtain more complex features in a larger scope, like striped structures. At the third layer, deep neural networks achieve better feature extraction, like the honeycomb grid structure. At last, by per-layer extraction and processing, deep neural networks can complete complex functionalities. Technical details about deep learning will be further elaborated in Chapter 3.

It should be mentioned that the development from shallow neural networks to deeper ones is not hard to imagine. However, the bloom of deep learning (deep neural networks) did not start until 2006. Besides the devoted promotion by researchers as Yann LeCun, Yoshua Bengio, and Geoffrey Hinton, the main reasons behind the maturity of deep learning are ABC: A (algorithm), B (Big Data), and C (computing). In the algorithm aspect, the training algorithm behind the deep neural network is maturing with higher accuracy. In the Big Data aspect, internet companies have sufficiently large numbers of data to train deep neural networks. In the computing aspect, the computation capacity of a deep learning processor chip is more powerful than 100 CPUs were at that time.

2.1.6 The history of neural networks

The history of neural networks can be divided into three periods, similar to the three waves in the whole history of AI.

In 1943, psychologist Warren McCulloch and mathematical logician Walter Pitts proposed the famous McCulloch–Pitts (M-P) neuron model to emulate the functions of biological neurons [1], known as the first mathematical model of an artificial neural network. In 1957, psychologist Frank Rosenblatt proposed the perceptron model [6, 7]. A perceptron is a single-layer neural network based on the M-P neuron model and

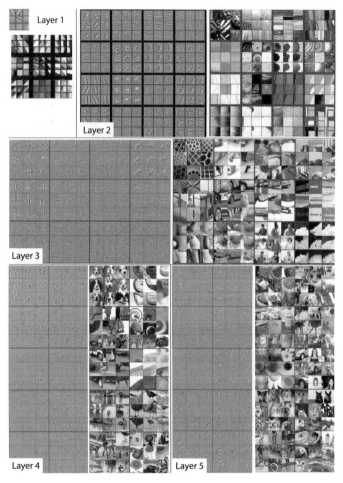

FIGURE 2.8

Working principle of deep learning.[4]

can solve linearly separable problems on input datasets. Since the perceptron, neural networks became a research hotspot until the end of the 1960s, when the research on neural networks began to stagnate. In 1969, Marvin Minsky and Seymour Papert proved that the perceptron proposed in 1957 could not solve linearly inseparable problems [57], discouraging the research of neural networks.

---

[4] Reprinted with permission from Springer Nature: Springer Nature, Visualizing and understanding convolutional networks, by Matthew D. Zeiler, Rob Fergus, [56] ©2014, https://doi.org/10.1007/978-3-319-10590-1_53.

In 1986, David E. Rumelhart, Geoffrey E. Hinton, and Ronald J. Williams proposed the back-propagation algorithm for neural network training [13] in *Nature*. The back-propagation algorithm minimizes the difference between the predicted output vector and the desired output vector by continuously adjusting the weights of the neural network. This improvement breaks through the limitation that the hidden unit cannot represent the features of the task domain during the convergence of the perceptron and improves the representation and training performance of the neural network. Today, back-propagation is still a classic algorithm in training neural networks. In 1998, Yoshua LeCun [58] proposed LeNet, a convolutional neural network for handwritten character recognition. LeNet defines the basic framework and components of the convolutional neural network (convolution, activation, pooling, full connection), which are still used today. This is the prelude to deep learning.

In 2006, Geoffrey E. Hinton built deep belief networks based on a restricted Boltzmann machine, using a greedy layer-by-layer training approach that improved the efficiency of training deep neural networks [59]. In the same year, Hinton and Salakhutdinov published the paper entitled "Reducing the dimensionality of data with neural networks" [14] in *Science*, which promoted the popularization of deep learning. With the improvement of computing performance and dataset size, the deep learning network AlexNet [15] proposed by A. Krizhevsky et al. won the ImageNet Large Scale Visual Recognition Challenge (ILSVRC) competition in 2012. AlexNet achieved a top five error rate that was 10.9% lower than that of the second place model, causing a sensational bloom in the AI industry. Since then, the academic community has further proposed a series of more advanced and accurate deep learning algorithms, including VGG [60], LSTM [61], and ResNet [62]. These models have reached notable advances in image recognition, speech recognition, machine translation, etc. In some specific areas, such as Go, these models beat humans.

2.2 Neural network training

Neural network are trained to minimize the difference between the predicted value $\hat{y}$ and the true value y by tuning parameters in the hidden and output layers. The training includes two procedures, forward propagation and backward propagation. Forward propagation starts from a trained neural network model, computes the first hidden layer output by input vectors, weights, and the activation function, and then calculates the next hidden layer from the previous one. After such layer-by-layer iterative computing, input feature vectors are extracted from low-level features to abstract features. The final output is the classification result. Backward propagation (known as back-propagation) operates conversely, first computing the loss function $L(\boldsymbol{W})$ based on the forward propagated result and the true value and then using a gradient descent method to calculate partial derivatives of the loss function with respect to each weight and bias based on the chain rule. These derivatives reflect the impact of each weight and bias on the loss function. At last, the back-propagation method updates the weight and bias. This section introduces the process of forward and backward propagation based on the example in Fig. 2.9.

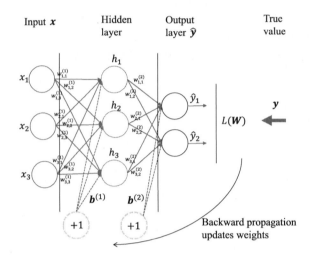

FIGURE 2.9

Neural network.

2.2.1 Forward propagation

The forward propagation of each neural network layer consists of two steps: first, the transpose of the weight matrix is multiplied by the input vector. Then, the products pass through the nonlinear activation function to get the output vector.

The input of the neural network in Fig. 2.9 has three neurons, denoted as $x = [x_1; x_2; x_3]$. The hidden layer contains three neurons, denoted as $h = [h_1; h_2; h_3]$. The output layer contains two neurons, denoted as $\hat{y} = [\hat{y}_1; \hat{y}_2]$. The corresponding bias vector of the connections between the input and the hidden layer is $b^{(1)}$, and the weight matrix is

$$W^{(1)} = \begin{bmatrix} w_{1,1}^{(1)} & w_{1,2}^{(1)} & w_{1,3}^{(1)} \\ w_{2,1}^{(1)} & w_{2,2}^{(1)} & w_{2,3}^{(1)} \\ w_{3,1}^{(1)} & w_{3,2}^{(1)} & w_{3,3}^{(1)} \end{bmatrix}. \tag{2.19}$$

The corresponding bias vector of the connections between the hidden layer and the output layer is $b^{(2)}$, and the weight matrix is

$$W^{(2)} = \begin{bmatrix} w_{1,1}^{(2)} & w_{1,2}^{(2)} \\ w_{2,1}^{(2)} & w_{2,2}^{(2)} \\ w_{3,1}^{(2)} & w_{3,2}^{(2)} \end{bmatrix}. \tag{2.20}$$

In this neural network, the sigmoid function is used as the activation function,

$$\sigma(x) = \frac{1}{1 + e^{-x}}. \tag{2.21}$$

In the forward propagation process of computing the hidden layer given the input, the transpose of the weight matrix $W^{(1)}$ is multiplied by the input vector x, and then the bias vector $b^{(1)}$ is added:

$$v = W^{(1)\top} x + b_1 = \begin{bmatrix} w_{1,1}^{(1)} & w_{2,1}^{(1)} & w_{3,1}^{(1)} \\ w_{1,2}^{(1)} & w_{2,2}^{(1)} & w_{3,2}^{(1)} \\ w_{1,3}^{(1)} & w_{2,3}^{(1)} & w_{3,3}^{(1)} \end{bmatrix} \begin{bmatrix} x_1 \\ x_2 \\ x_3 \end{bmatrix} + b^{(1)}. \tag{2.22}$$

With the sigmoid activation function, the output of the hidden layer is

$$h = \frac{1}{1 + e^{-v}}. \tag{2.23}$$

The forward propagation process of computing the output layer given the hidden layer is similar.

Example. Suppose the input data of the neural network is $x = [x_1; x_2; x_3] = [0.02; 0.04; 0.01]$, the bias vector is $b^{(1)} = [0.4; 0.4; 0.4]$, $b^{(2)} = [0.7; 0.7]$, and the desired output is $y = [y_1; y_2] = [0.9; 0.5]$. Before training, two weight matrices are randomly initialized as

$$W^{(1)} = \begin{bmatrix} w_{1,1}^{(1)} & w_{1,2}^{(1)} & w_{1,3}^{(1)} \\ w_{2,1}^{(1)} & w_{2,2}^{(1)} & w_{2,3}^{(1)} \\ w_{3,1}^{(1)} & w_{3,2}^{(1)} & w_{3,3}^{(1)} \end{bmatrix} = \begin{bmatrix} 0.25 & 0.15 & 0.30 \\ 0.25 & 0.20 & 0.35 \\ 0.10 & 0.25 & 0.15 \end{bmatrix}, \tag{2.24}$$

$$W^{(2)} = \begin{bmatrix} w_{1,1}^{(2)} & w_{1,2}^{(2)} \\ w_{2,1}^{(2)} & w_{2,2}^{(2)} \\ w_{3,1}^{(2)} & w_{3,2}^{(2)} \end{bmatrix} = \begin{bmatrix} 0.40 & 0.25 \\ 0.35 & 0.30 \\ 0.01 & 0.35 \end{bmatrix}. \tag{2.25}$$

Then, the output of the hidden layer before the activation is calculated as

$$v = \begin{bmatrix} v_1 \\ v_2 \\ v_3 \end{bmatrix} = W^{(1)\top} x + b^{(1)} = \begin{bmatrix} 0.25 & 0.25 & 0.10 \\ 0.15 & 0.20 & 0.25 \\ 0.30 & 0.35 & 0.15 \end{bmatrix} \begin{bmatrix} 0.02 \\ 0.04 \\ 0.01 \end{bmatrix} + \begin{bmatrix} 0.4 \\ 0.4 \\ 0.4 \end{bmatrix}$$

$$= \begin{bmatrix} 0.4160 \\ 0.4135 \\ 0.4215 \end{bmatrix}. \tag{2.26}$$

By applying the sigmoid function to the above three numbers, the output of the hidden layer is

$$
\boldsymbol{h} = \begin{bmatrix} h_1 \\ h_2 \\ h_3 \end{bmatrix} = \frac{1}{1 + e^{-\boldsymbol{v}}} = \begin{bmatrix} \frac{1}{1+e^{-0.4160}} \\ \frac{1}{1+e^{-0.4135}} \\ \frac{1}{1+e^{-0.4215}} \end{bmatrix} = \begin{bmatrix} 0.6025 \\ 0.6019 \\ 0.6038 \end{bmatrix}. \tag{2.27}
$$

The output of the output layer before the activation function is computed as

$$
\boldsymbol{z} = \begin{bmatrix} z_1 \\ z_2 \end{bmatrix} = \boldsymbol{W}^{(2)\top} \boldsymbol{h} + \boldsymbol{b}^{(2)} = \begin{bmatrix} 0.40 & 0.35 & 0.01 \\ 0.25 & 0.30 & 0.35 \end{bmatrix} \begin{bmatrix} 0.6025 \\ 0.6019 \\ 0.6038 \end{bmatrix} + \begin{bmatrix} 0.7 \\ 0.7 \end{bmatrix}
$$

$$
= \begin{bmatrix} 1.1577 \\ 1.2425 \end{bmatrix}.
$$

$$\tag{2.28}$$

After applying sigmoid to the above two numbers, the final output is

$$
\hat{\boldsymbol{y}} = \begin{bmatrix} \hat{y}_1 \\ \hat{y}_2 \end{bmatrix} = \frac{1}{1 + e^{-\boldsymbol{z}}} = \begin{bmatrix} \frac{1}{1+e^{-1.1577}} \\ \frac{1}{1+e^{-1.2425}} \end{bmatrix} = \begin{bmatrix} 0.7609 \\ 0.7760 \end{bmatrix}. \tag{2.29}
$$

2.2.2 Backward propagation

For backward propagation, first, the loss function is calculated with the difference between the neural network output and the true value. Then, partial derivatives of the loss function with respect to every weight and bias are computed. Finally, the weights and biases are updated.

The mean squared error (MSE) is used as the loss function in the example of the previous subsection. The value of the loss function on the sample $(\boldsymbol{x}, \boldsymbol{y})$ is

$$
L(\boldsymbol{W}) = L_1 + L_2 = \frac{1}{2}(y_1 - \hat{y}_1)^2 + \frac{1}{2}(y_2 - \hat{y}_2)^2
$$

$$
= \frac{1}{2}(0.9 - 0.7609)^2 + \frac{1}{2}(0.5 - 0.7760)^2 = 0.0478. \tag{2.30}
$$

As the weights $\boldsymbol{W}$ are randomly initialized, the value of the loss function is large.

To measure the impact of $\boldsymbol{W}$ on the loss function, we take the weight between the second node of the hidden layer and the first node of the output layer $w_{2,1}^{(2)}$ (denoted as ω) as an example, and we compute the partial derivative of the loss function $L(\boldsymbol{W})$ with respect to ω using the chain rule. First, the partial derivative of the loss function $L(\boldsymbol{W})$ with respect to $\hat{y}_1$ is computed, then the partial derivative of $\hat{y}_1$ with respect to z_1 is computed, as well as the partial derivative of z_1 on ω, and finally the three derivatives are multiplied together as

$$\frac{\partial L(W)}{\partial \omega} = \frac{\partial L(W)}{\partial \hat{y}_1} \frac{\partial \hat{y}_1}{\partial z_1} \frac{\partial z_1}{\partial \omega}. \tag{2.31}$$

Combined with the example in the previous subsection, the partial derivative of the loss function with respect to ω is calculated. The overall loss function is computed as

$$L(W) = \frac{1}{2}(y_1 - \hat{y}_1)^2 + \frac{1}{2}(y_2 - \hat{y}_2)^2. \tag{2.32}$$

The partial derivative of $L(W)$ with respect to $\hat{y}_1$ is

$$\frac{\partial L(W)}{\partial \hat{y}_1} = -(y_1 - \hat{y}_1) = -(0.9 - 0.7609) = -0.1391. \tag{2.33}$$

The neural network output $\hat{y}_1$ is obtained by z_1 through the sigmoid activation function, that is, $\hat{y}_1 = \frac{1}{1+e^{-z_1}}$. The partial derivative of $\hat{y}_1$ with respect to z_1 is

$$\frac{\partial \hat{y}_1}{\partial z_1} = \hat{y}_1(1 - \hat{y}_1) = 0.7609 \times (1 - 0.7609) = 0.1819, \tag{2.34}$$

where z_1 is calculated by multiplying the outputs of the hidden layers h_1, h_2, and h_3 by $w_{1,1}^{(2)}$, ω, and $w_{3,1}^{(2)}$ respectively, and then summing the product with the bias $b_1^{(2)}$:

$$z_1 = w_{1,1}^{(2)} \times h_1 + \omega \times h_2 + w_{3,1}^{(2)} \times h_3 + b_1^{(2)}. \tag{2.35}$$

Thus, the partial derivative of z_1 with respect to ω is

$$\frac{\partial z_1}{\partial \omega} = h_2 = 0.6019. \tag{2.36}$$

Finally, the partial derivative of the loss function with respect to ω can be obtained as

$$\frac{\partial L(W)}{\partial \omega} = -(y_1 - \hat{y}_1) \times \hat{y}_1(1 - \hat{y}_1) \times h_2 = -0.1391 \times 0.1819 \times 0.6019 = -0.0152. \tag{2.37}$$

The next step is to update the value of ω. Suppose the step size η is 1 and the initial value of ω is 0.35 in the weight matrix (2.25). The updated ω is

$$\omega \leftarrow \omega - \eta \times \frac{\partial L(W)}{\partial \omega} = 0.35 - (-0.0152) = 0.3652. \tag{2.38}$$

Similarly, we can update other weights in $W^{(2)}$.

The above process is the first step of back-propagation. The remaining weights from the input to the hidden layer and from the hidden layer to the output layer can be calculated and updated using the same chain rule.

Back-propagation is used to propagate the output error back to the neural network, layer by layer. In this process, the impact of each ω on the final loss should be calculated, which is the partial derivative of the loss with respect to each ω. Based on the impact of ω on the model error, the derivative is multiplied by the step size, and then the weight matrix of the entire neural network can be updated. When a pass of back-propagation is completed, the whole parameter model is updated. After one update iteration, another sample is fed as the input, the model error is computed, and the whole model is updated. Repeating this procedure iteratively, the error between the predicted value and the true value could be minimized. At last, the training is completed when the error is smaller than a predefined threshold.

2.3 Neural network design: the principle

It is theoretically feasible to reduce the training error of the neural network by iteratively updating the model parameters so that the model output is consistent with the desired output. However, in practice, it is inevitable that the designed neural network has been trained for a long time, but the accuracy is still very low or even cannot converge. To improve the training accuracy, common techniques include adjusting the network topology, choosing the right activation function, and selecting the appropriate loss function.

2.3.1 Network topology

The architecture of a neural network includes input, hidden, and output layers. When training samples are given, the number of neurons in the input and output layers of the neural network is fixed, but the number of hidden layers and the number of neurons in these layers (also known as hyperparameters) are tunable. For example, in the simplest MLP with only one hidden layer, the number of neurons in the hidden layer can be adjusted as needed.

The hidden layer is used to extract the underlying rules from the input features. Thus, the number of neurons in the hidden layer is a key factor for the model design. On the one hand, if the number of neurons is too small, the ability to extract information from input features could be poor. On the other hand, if the number of neurons is too large, the model could be overfitting, and the noise data would undermine the model generalization. Model generalization means that machine learning not only requires the model to have a small error on the training set, but also to perform well on the test set. This is because the model is eventually deployed in a real-world scenario where no training data are available.

Theoretically, the number of hidden layers and neurons should be equal to the number of underlying rules. However, these underlying rules are often indescribable. In practice, engineers often find the number of hidden layers and neurons through repeated attempts. To avoid manually setting the number of hidden layers and neurons, many researchers are now devoted to automated machine learning (AutoML) [63].

AutoML can automate the process of adjusting optimal hyperparameters. Examples include using evolutionary algorithms or other machine learning techniques to model and predict hyperparameters.

2.3.2 Activation function

The activation function enables the neural network to represent nonlinear functions and enriches model applicability. In the 1970s, the main reason behind the decline of neural network research was that Marvin Minsky proved that the neural network could not solve linearly inseparable problems (such as the XOR problem) [57] without an activation function like sigmoid. Therefore, in a sense, the nonlinear activation function saves the neural network.

In practice, the chosen activation functions generally have the properties of differentiability and bounded output. The activation function shall be differentiable, because back-propagation-based neural network training algorithms use gradient descent. The output of the activation function decides the input of the next layer. If the activation function is bounded, feature representations are only significantly impacted by limited weights, and thus gradient descent-based optimization would be stable. If the activation function is unbounded (e.g., an output range of $[0, +\infty)$), the training speed may be very high, but an appropriate learning rate must be selected.

If a designed neural network does not meet the expected performance, different activation functions can be chosen. Common activation functions include the sigmoid function, tanh function, ReLU function [64], PReLU/Leaky ReLU function [65,66], and ELU function [67].

2.3.2.1 Sigmoid function

The sigmoid function is one of the most commonly used activation functions. Its mathematical representation is

$$\sigma(x) = \frac{1}{1 + e^{-x}}. \tag{2.39}$$

The graph of the sigmoid function is shown in Fig. 2.10. When x is small, the value of the sigmoid function is close to 0. When x is large, the value of sigmoid is close to 1. The sigmoid function transforms the continuous real number into a range of $(0, 1)$, so that the input value of the next layer is within a fixed range and the weight is more stable.

The sigmoid function has some disadvantages:

(1) **Nonzero-centered outputs.** The outputs of the sigmoid function are not zero-centered, which may shift the mean value of the next layer input, thus affecting the network convergence.
(2) **High computational complexity.** The sigmoid function contains the exponential operation e^{-x}, which requires hundreds of addition, subtraction, multiplication, and division instructions on a general-purpose CPU. Thus, the computation is inefficient.

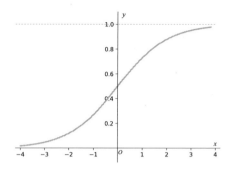

FIGURE 2.10

Sigmoid function.

(3) **Saturation problem.** The left and right sides of the sigmoid function curve are nearly flat. When the input value x is a large positive number or a small negative number, the gradient of the sigmoid function is close to 0, thus slowing down the parameter update. This phenomenon is called the sigmoid saturation problem. Moreover, the derivative of the sigmoid function is in the range of $(0, 0.25]$. If the neural network has many layers, the partial derivative calculated with the chain rule is equal to the multiplication of many numbers less than 0.25. Since the absolute values of the initialized weights are generally less than 1, the gradient would approach 0, thus causing the vanishing gradient problem.

2.3.2.2 Tanh function

To avoid the disadvantages of the sigmoid function, researchers have designed many other kinds of activation functions, including the tanh function. Tanh function is defined as

$$\tanh(x) = \frac{\sinh(x)}{\cosh(x)} = \frac{e^x - e^{-x}}{e^x + e^{-x}} = 2\sigma(2x) - 1. \qquad (2.40)$$

The graph of the tanh function is shown in Fig. 2.11. Compared to the sigmoid function, the tanh function is zero-centered, as it transforms the input into the symmetric range of $(-1, 1)$. Therefore, the tanh function solves the nonzero-centered problem of the sigmoid function. However, when the input is too large or small, the output of the tanh function is always smooth with a small gradient. This is not conducive to the weight update. Thus, the tanh function does not solve the vanishing gradient problem either.

2.3.2.3 ReLU function

The Rectified Linear Unit (ReLU) was first applied to the restricted Boltzmann machine [64], which is a universally used activation function currently. When the input is negative, the output of the ReLU function is 0; otherwise, the output is equal to the

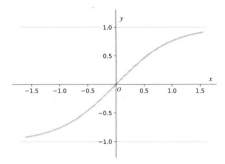

FIGURE 2.11

Tanh function.

input. Its formal definition is

$$f(x) = \max(0, x). \tag{2.41}$$

The computation of the ReLU function is particularly simple, since ReLU does not have an exponential operation in contrast to the tanh and sigmoid functions. The ReLU function only needs to return the maximum value between 0 and x, which can be implemented with one computer instruction. Moreover, when $x > 0$, the gradient of ReLU does not decay, as shown in Fig. 2.12, thus alleviating the vanishing gradient problem. Therefore, in deep learning, especially neural networks with over hundreds of layers (e.g., ResNet), activation functions like ReLU are commonly used.

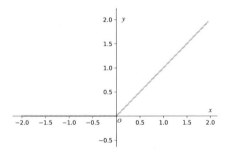

FIGURE 2.12

The ReLU function.

ReLU suffers from some disadvantages as well.

(1) The outputs of the ReLU function are not zero-centered.
(2) The dying ReLU problem may occur. In back-propagation, if the learning rate is relatively large, a large gradient passing through the ReLU neuron may cause the updated bias and weight of the ReLU neuron to be negative. As such, the input of the ReLU neuron in the next round of forward propagation is negative

and the output is 0. In the follow-up back-propagation, the gradient is 0 and the related parameters no longer change, so that the input of the ReLU neuron is always negative and the output is always 0. Thus, this ReLU neuron is dead.

(3) The output of the ReLU function is unbounded. This may cause the output amplitude to increase as the number of network layers increases.

2.3.2.4 PReLU/Leaky ReLU function

Since the ReLU function may die when $x < 0$, many improved versions of ReLU have appeared, including Leaky ReLU [66] and Parametric ReLU (PReLU) [65].

The Leaky ReLU function is defined as

$$f(x) = \max(\alpha x, x), \tag{2.42}$$

where the parameter α is a small constant in the range of (0, 1) [68]. When $x < 0$, the Leaky ReLU function has a very small slope α, as shown in Fig. 2.13, which prevents ReLU from dying.

The definition of the PReLU function is similar to that of the Leaky ReLU, the only difference being that α is a tunable parameter. Each channel has one parameter α, which is obtained through back-propagation training.

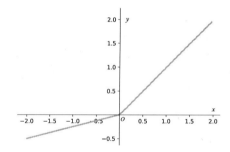

FIGURE 2.13

Leaky ReLU function.

2.3.2.5 ELU function

The Exponential Linear Unit (ELU) function [67] combines the sigmoid and ReLU functions. It is defined as

$$f(x) = \begin{cases} x & x > 0, \\ \alpha(e^x - 1) & x \leq 0, \end{cases} \tag{2.43}$$

where α is a tunable coefficient that can control the saturation position of the ELU in the negative domain.

The mean value of the ELU output shifts towards zero, which speeds up model convergence. When $x > 0$, the ELU function outputs $y = x$, which avoids the vanishing gradient problem. When $x \leq 0$, ELU is left soft saturated, as shown in Fig. 2.14, which prevents neurons from dying. The disadvantage of ELU is that it involves exponential computation. Thus the computation complexity is relatively high.

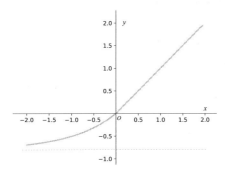

FIGURE 2.14

The ELU function.

Researchers also proposed many other different activation functions that are not included in this section. We encourage readers to follow the recent works in the top-tier conferences for more information.

2.3.3 Loss function

The gradient descent-based back-propagation process requires a clear definition of the loss function. By calculating the partial derivative of the loss function, the weight and bias can be updated along the descending direction. Therefore, finding a qualified loss function is critical in gradient calculation.

The loss function $L = f(\hat{y}, y)$ is used to measure the difference between the model-predicted value $\hat{y}$ and the expected value y. The predicted value is a function of weight matrix $\boldsymbol{w}$, as $\hat{y} = h_w(x)$. Note that $\hat{y}$ and y are not always the same, as shown in Fig. 2.15. The difference between them can be expressed as a loss function: $L(\boldsymbol{w}) = f(h_w(x), y)$.

Commonly used loss functions include the MSE and cross-entropy loss.

2.3.3.1 Mean squared error loss function

The MSE loss function is most commonly used. Taking one output neuron as an example, the model output is $\hat{y}$, the true value is y, and then the MSE loss function is

$$L = \frac{1}{2}(y - \hat{y})^2. \tag{2.44}$$

If the sigmoid function is used as an activation function, $\hat{y} = \sigma(z)$, where $z = wx + b$. The gradients of the MSE loss function to w and b are

$$\frac{\partial L}{\partial w} = (\hat{y} - y)\sigma'(z)x, \qquad \sigma'(z) = (1 - \sigma(z))\sigma(z), \tag{2.45}$$

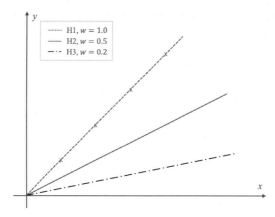

FIGURE 2.15

Fitting results under different values of w. Training sample (x, y): $(1, 1), (2, 2), (3, 3), (4, 4)$.
Points on $y = x$ are the true values.

$$\frac{\partial L}{\partial b} = (\hat{y} - y)\sigma'(z). \tag{2.46}$$

From the above, the two gradients share one characteristic: when the output of
the neuron is close to 1 or 0, the two gradients approach 0 because they both contain
$\sigma'(z)$. This implies that when the output of a neuron is close to 1 or 0, the gradient
vanishes, thus slowing down parameter updating during the back-propagation.

The MSE loss function on the training set D is

$$L = \frac{1}{m} \sum_{x \in D} \sum_{i} \frac{1}{2}(y_i - \hat{y}_i)^2, \tag{2.47}$$

where m is the number of total training samples and i is the class.

2.3.3.2 Cross-entropy loss function

Since the combination of the MSE loss function and the sigmoid function causes
the vanishing gradient problem, other loss functions can be used, such as the cross-
entropy loss function. If the sigmoid function is used, the cross-entropy loss function
can be used to avoid the vanishing gradient problem. The cross-entropy loss function
can be defined as

$$L = -\frac{1}{m} \sum_{x \in D} \sum_{i} y_i \ln(\hat{y}_i), \tag{2.48}$$

where m is the total number of samples in the training set D and i is the class. The
definition of cross-entropy is similar to the definition of entropy in information theory. For the single-label multiclass classification problem, i.e., each image sample can
only belong to one class, the cross-entropy is simplified to $L = -\frac{1}{m} \sum_{x \in D} y \ln(\hat{y})$. As

for the multilabel multiclass classification problem, i.e., each image sample belongs to multiple classes, the problem is generally converted into the binary classification problem.

For the binary classification problem, when using sigmoid as the activation function, the cross-entropy loss function is

$$L = -\frac{1}{m}\sum_{x\in D}(y\ln(\hat{y}) + (1-y)ln(1-\hat{y})). \tag{2.49}$$

The output of neural network $\hat{y}$ is

$$\hat{y} = \sigma(z) = \frac{1}{1+e^{-z}} = \frac{1}{1+e^{-(w^\top x+b)}}. \tag{2.50}$$

The gradient of the cross-entropy loss function with respect to weight w is

$$\begin{aligned}\frac{\partial L}{\partial w} &= -\frac{1}{m}\sum_{x\in D}[\frac{y}{\sigma(z)} - \frac{1-y}{1-\sigma(z)}]\frac{\partial\sigma(z)}{\partial w} \\ &= -\frac{1}{m}\sum_{x\in D}[\frac{y}{\sigma(z)} - \frac{1-y}{1-\sigma(z)}]\sigma'(z)x \\ &= \frac{1}{m}\sum_{x\in D}\frac{\sigma'(z)x}{\sigma(z)(1-\sigma(z))}(\sigma(z)-y).\end{aligned} \tag{2.51}$$

By substituting the derivative of the sigmoid function $\sigma'(z) = (1-\sigma(z))\sigma(z)$ into the above formula, $\frac{\partial L}{\partial w}$ becomes

$$\frac{\partial L}{\partial w} = \frac{1}{m}\sum_{x\in D}(\sigma(z)-y)x. \tag{2.52}$$

Similarly, the partial derivative of the cross-entropy loss function with respect to bias b is

$$\frac{\partial L}{\partial b} = \frac{1}{m}\sum_{x\in D}(\sigma(z)-y). \tag{2.53}$$

From Eqs. (2.52) and (2.53), if cross-entropy loss is used, the gradients $\frac{\partial L}{\partial b}$ and $\frac{\partial L}{\partial w}$ do not have the derivative of the sigmoid function $\sigma'(z)$, thus alleviating the vanishing gradient problem.

To sum up, the loss function is a scalar function of the weight parameter w and the bias parameter b to evaluate the network model. The smaller the loss function, the more accurately the model maps to the training sample (x, y). For one algorithm, the loss function is not fixed or unique. Besides the cross-entropy loss function, there are many other loss functions. Note that it is necessary to choose a loss function that is differentiable to the parameters $(\boldsymbol{w}, b)$; otherwise, the chain rule cannot be applied.

2.4 Overfitting and regularization

In a neural network, it is possible that the model accuracy is still low after trying all kinds of network topology, activation functions, and loss functions. This is a common problem in neural network training. At this point, you need to check whether the neural network is overfitting. On the concept of overfitting, von Neumann has a vivid metaphor: "With four parameters I can fit an elephant, and with five I can make him wiggle his trunk." If a neural network has many layers, it may learn some unimportant or even wrong features. For example, images of a person holding a blackboard eraser are used as training samples. If the trained model is overfitting, it may learn that one must have a blackboard eraser to be a person. However, this is not a real feature of humans.

If a neural network model is overfitting, its generalization becomes poor. Deep neural networks have strong representation capability but often encounter overfitting. To improve generalization, the neural networks can use different regularization techniques, including parameter norm penalty, sparsification, bagging [69], dropout [70], early stopping, etc.

2.4.1 Overfitting

Overfitting means that the model is too close to the training data, which undermines the generalization. That is, the training error is low, but the test error is high. If a neural network has too many layers and parameters, it is especially prone to overfitting. Besides overfitting, underfitting is also challenging. Underfitting is mainly caused by the lack of training features, and the fitting function cannot effectively approximate the training set, thus resulting in a large training error.

Underfitting can generally be solved by increasing the number of training samples or using a better model. Fig. 2.16(a)–(c) shows examples of appropriate fitting, underfitting, and overfitting. For such complicated classification problems, appropriate fitting may result in an arc with a small error; underfitting results in a simple straight line and the training error is relatively large; overfitting results in a strange curve. If a deep learning model has many feature dimensions, such as hundreds of millions of parameters, the overfitted function can be very close to the training set, but the resulting curve is strange and the trained model has poor generalization, thus being insufficient in prediction on new data.

The examples in Fig. 2.17 show that if there are only three variables, the samples can be fitted with a quadratic curve $y = w_0 + w_1 x + w_2 x^2$. If the model is fitted with a quartic curve, the fitting shape is twisted. Although its training error may be lower than that of the quadratic curve, it fails on new samples in real scenes. To reduce the

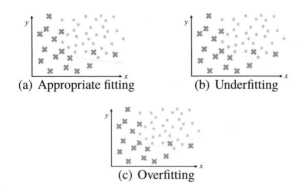

FIGURE 2.16

Types of fitting.

effect of the third- and fourth-order terms on models, regularization techniques can be applied.

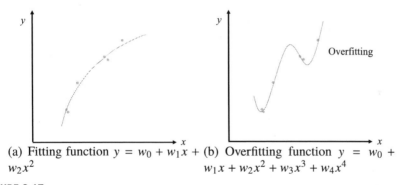

FIGURE 2.17

Different fitting functions.

2.4.2 **Regularization**

2.4.2.1 *Parameter norm penalty*

Parameter norm penalty is a key proposal in regularization. Take Fig. 2.17, for example. Overfitting can be avoided by adding a penalty on the higher-order terms in the loss function. Specifically, for a training set D with m samples, with the addition of the penalty term $C_1 w_3^2 + C_2 w_4^2$ to the original loss function $L(\boldsymbol{w}; \boldsymbol{x}, \boldsymbol{y})$, the model has the following regularized loss function:

$$\tilde{L}(\boldsymbol{w}; \boldsymbol{x}, \boldsymbol{y}) = L(\boldsymbol{w}; \boldsymbol{x}, \boldsymbol{y}) + C_1 w_3^2 + C_2 w_4^2, \tag{2.54}$$

where C_1 and C_2 are constants.

After the penalties on the higher-order terms in the loss function, not only the errors but also the parameters w_3 and w_4 are minimized. For example, if C_1 and C_2 are set to 1000, the training with the regularized loss function returns that both w_3 and w_4 approximately equal 0, and the fitted function is the dashed curve in Fig. 2.18. Without the penalty terms, the training may be overfitted, and the fitted function would be the solid curve in Fig. 2.18.

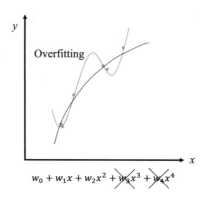

FIGURE 2.18

Solving overfitting problem by regularization.

Regularization adds penalties on the unwanted part in the loss function as follows:

$$\tilde{L}(\boldsymbol{w}; \boldsymbol{x}, \boldsymbol{y}) = L(\boldsymbol{w}; \boldsymbol{x}, \boldsymbol{y}) + \theta \sum_{j=1}^{k} w_j^2, \qquad (2.55)$$

where θ is the regularization parameter. For the neural network, the model parameters include the weight $\boldsymbol{w}$ and the bias b. The regularization generally penalizes the weight $\boldsymbol{w}$ only, such that the regularization term is denoted as $\Omega(\boldsymbol{w})$. The regularized objective function is

$$\tilde{L}(\boldsymbol{w}; \boldsymbol{x}, \boldsymbol{y}) = L(\boldsymbol{w}; \boldsymbol{x}, \boldsymbol{y}) + \theta \Omega(\boldsymbol{w}). \qquad (2.56)$$

In practice, for different purposes, different regularization terms can be chosen, such as L^2 regularization, L^1 regularization, etc.

L^2 Regularization

L^2 Regularization is defined as $\Omega(\boldsymbol{w}) = \frac{1}{2}\|\boldsymbol{w}\|_2^2 = \frac{1}{2}\sum_i w_i^2$.

L^2 Regularization can help avoid the case that the derivative values in some regions are too large, causing the curve to be particularly choppy when overfitting, as shown in Fig. 2.19. Now we analyze how L^2 regularization avoids overfitting.

The objective function after L^2 regularization is

$$\tilde{L}(\boldsymbol{w}; \boldsymbol{x}, \boldsymbol{y}) = L(\boldsymbol{w}; \boldsymbol{x}, \boldsymbol{y}) + \frac{\theta}{2}\|\boldsymbol{w}\|^2. \qquad (2.57)$$

The partial derivative of an objective function with respect to $\boldsymbol{w}$ is

$$\nabla_{\boldsymbol{w}}\tilde{L}(\boldsymbol{w};\boldsymbol{x},\boldsymbol{y})=\nabla_{\boldsymbol{w}}L(\boldsymbol{w};\boldsymbol{x},\boldsymbol{y})+\theta\boldsymbol{w}. \tag{2.58}$$

Taking η as the learning rate, the weight is updated as

$$\boldsymbol{w}\leftarrow\boldsymbol{w}-\eta(\nabla_{\boldsymbol{w}}L(\boldsymbol{w};\boldsymbol{x},\boldsymbol{y})+\theta\boldsymbol{w})=(1-\eta\theta)\boldsymbol{w}-\eta\nabla_{\boldsymbol{w}}L(\boldsymbol{w};\boldsymbol{x},\boldsymbol{y}). \tag{2.59}$$

From the above equations, a weight decay term θ is added in the gradient. That is, L^2 regularization causes weight $\boldsymbol{w}$ to become a part of the gradient. In this way, the absolute value of the weight $\boldsymbol{w}$ will be smaller, the fitted curve will be smoother, and the data is fitted better.

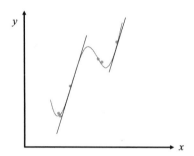

FIGURE 2.19

When overfitting, the derivative value in some intervals is very large.

L^1 Regularization

Besides L^2 regularization, there is also L^1 regularization. The L^2 regularization term is the sum of squares of all weights w_i, while the L^1 regularization term is the sum of absolute values of all weights w_i as $\Omega(\boldsymbol{w})=\|\boldsymbol{w}\|_1=\sum_i|w_i|$.

The objective function after L^1 regularization is

$$\tilde{L}(\boldsymbol{w};\boldsymbol{x},\boldsymbol{y})=L(\boldsymbol{w};\boldsymbol{x},\boldsymbol{y})+\theta\|\boldsymbol{w}\|_1. \tag{2.60}$$

The partial derivative of $\boldsymbol{w}$ with respect to objective function is

$$\nabla_{\boldsymbol{w}}\tilde{L}(\boldsymbol{w};\boldsymbol{x},\boldsymbol{y})=\nabla_{\boldsymbol{w}}L(\boldsymbol{w};\boldsymbol{x},\boldsymbol{y})+\theta sign(\boldsymbol{w}). \tag{2.61}$$

Taking η as the learning rate, the weight is updated as

$$\boldsymbol{w}\leftarrow\boldsymbol{w}-\eta(\nabla_{\boldsymbol{w}}L(\boldsymbol{w};\boldsymbol{x},\boldsymbol{y})+\theta sign(\boldsymbol{w}))=\boldsymbol{w}-\eta\theta sign(\boldsymbol{w})-\eta\nabla_{\boldsymbol{w}}L(\boldsymbol{w};\boldsymbol{x},\boldsymbol{y}). \tag{2.62}$$

L^1 Regularization adds a sign function to the gradient. In each update, when w is positive, the parameter w decreases; when w is negative, the parameter w increases. Thus, L^1 regularization makes the weight $\boldsymbol{w}$ in the neural network close to 0, thereby mitigating the overfitting problem.

2.4.2.2 Sparsification

Sparsification is making many weights or neurons in the neural network become 0 during training. Some sparsification techniques can make 90% of the weights or neurons in the network 0. The advantage of sparsification is that when using such neural networks, the calculation on the zero weights or neurons can be skipped, thereby reducing 90% of the calculation in the forward propagation. Sparsification is usually achieved by adding some penalty terms.

2.4.2.3 Bagging

The basic principle behind bagging (bootstrap aggregating) [69] is that two heads are better than one; different models are jointly trained to vote on the output for test samples. Thus, bagging has to construct k different datasets. Each dataset is obtained by sampling from the original dataset, while the set size is kept consistent. Bagging allows repeatedly using the same kind of model, training algorithm, and objective function for training, or use different kinds of models for training.

For example, in Fig. 2.20, if one pretrained neural network model does not work well on cat recognition, two other neural network models can be built. These three models may be trained with different parameters and different network topologies. Besides, the three models in Fig. 2.20 can also be built with different kinds of machine learning methods, such as one neural network, one support vector machine, and one decision tree. Given a test sample, the final recognition result can be obtained by averaging the outputs of the three models. The final result can also be obtained by training an additional classifier to choose one output from the three models. As such, bagging can reduce the recognition error.

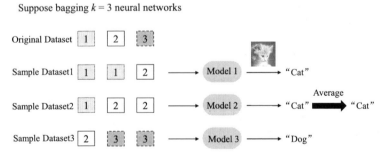

FIGURE 2.20

Bagging.

2.4.2.4 Dropout

Compared with L^1 and L^2 regularization, which penalize high-order terms in the objective function, dropout [70] randomly deletes some nodes in hidden layers during training. Since overcomplex models are prone to overfitting, dropout can avoid overfitting by dropping some hidden nodes. As shown in Fig. 2.21, different subnetworks are formed by removing a subset of hidden nodes from the basic neural network. For example, nodes h_2 and x_2 can be removed, while some other edges and nodes can also be removed [52].

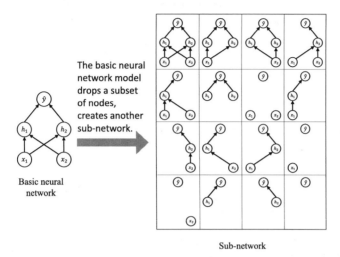

The basic neural network model drops a subset of nodes, creates another sub-network.

Basic neural network

Sub-network

FIGURE 2.21

An example of dropout.[5]

Specifically, first a mask vector μ is set. Each element of μ corresponds to an input or a node in hidden layers. Then the mask vector μ is randomly sampled, as shown in Fig. 2.22. Each node is multiplied by the corresponding mask, and the forward propagation continues along the rest of the neural network [52]. Generally, the sampling probabilities of input nodes and hidden nodes are 0.8 and 0.5, respectively. That is, half of the hidden nodes are dropped. In this way, training performance can be improved. After training with dropout, at test time, all nodes are used, and each node weight is multiplied by its sampling probability.

2.4.2.5 Summary

In addition to the methodologies introduced in this section, there are many renowned regularization methods. Each year, many papers on topics of regularization, such as early stopping, multitask learning, dataset augmentation, parameter sharing, etc., are presented in the top-tier international AI conferences. Early stopping is designed based on the observation that when training a large model, the training error decreases over time, but the validation error rises again. Therefore, once the validation error no longer decreases after a predetermined number of epochs, the training process can stop early. Multitask learning reduces the generalization error of neural networks by learning multiple related tasks at the same time. Dataset augmentation trains the

[5] Ian Goodfellow, Yoshua Bengio, and Aaron Courville, Deep Learning, p. 252, ©2016 Massachusetts Institute of Technology, with permission of The MIT Press.

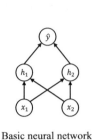
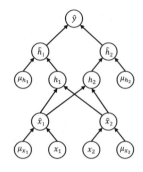

Basic neural network

FIGURE 2.22

A mask example of dropout.[6]

model with more data. The new data is created by transforming the original data and is added to the training set. Parameter sharing forces the parameters between models or model components to be equal. For example, the training models in the supervised and unsupervised modes can share one unique set of parameters.

In all, if a trained model performs poorly, many regularization techniques can be used to improve model performance. The real question is how to use these regularization techniques correctly. We need to dive deeper into these techniques in practice.

2.5 Cross-validation

As a professional machine learning researcher or researcher-to-be, one shall understand the concept of cross-validation. Cross-validation requires dividing the dataset into two parts, a training set and a test set. With this division, cross-validation can avoid overfitting and measure the practical performance of the trained model. For example, if an instructor has taught students both the exam questions and homework questions, the final exam cannot reveal the true understanding level of students. Instructors shall only teach students the homework questions and use different questions for the final exam to test the real level of comprehension of students. In this case, the training set is the homework, providing correct answers, while the test set is the final exam, determining the performance of the model.

In cross-validation, random split is the most straightforward way to obtain training and test sets. In Fig. 2.23, the light gray part is the training set, and the dark gray part is the test set. The disadvantage of this division method is that the final model and parameters are heavily dependent on the specific division of the training set and the test set, and different division may lead to large fluctuations in model accuracy.

[6] Ian Goodfellow, Yoshua Bengio, and Aaron Courville, Deep Learning, p. 254, ©2016 Massachusetts Institute of Technology, with permission of The MIT Press.

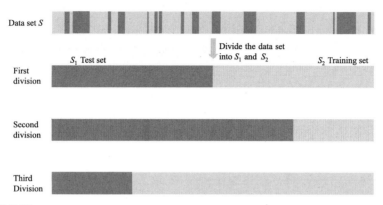

FIGURE 2.23

The simplest validation.

To reduce the fluctuations in accuracy, the leave-one-out cross-validation can be used. As shown in Fig. 2.24, for a dataset S containing n samples, each time one sample is used as the test set, the remaining $n-1$ samples are used as the training set. At last, n models are trained, and each model is tested on the test set to return MSE_i. The average of these n MSE_i values is the final test result. The main disadvantage of this leave-one-out method is the high computational overhead.

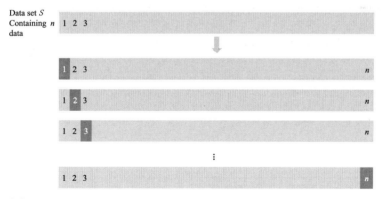

FIGURE 2.24

Leave-one-out cross-validation.

In practice, K-fold cross-validation is commonly used. For example, the entire dataset can be split into $K = 10$ subsets, as shown in Fig. 2.25. The first subset is used as the test set, and the remaining nine subsets are used as training sets; the test result of the trained model is MSE_1. Then, the second subset is used as the test set, and the remaining nine subsets are used as training sets; the test result of the trained model is MSE_2. Repeating this processes, 10 MSE values are obtained and averaged to calculate the final test result. The K-fold cross-validation method can evaluate the generalization of a neural network algorithm or model to estimate whether this model/algorithm can work well on different applications or datasets. Compared to leave-one-out cross-validation, K-fold cross-validation only needs to train K models, thus having a substantially lower computational overhead.

In summary, when evaluating machine learning methods such as neural networks with small datasets, cross-validation is needed. It is not correct to train the models with all data and take one part of the training set for testing. This may lead to some pitfalls or misleading conclusions.

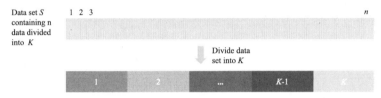

FIGURE 2.25

K-fold cross-validation.

2.6 Summary

Section 2.1 first introduces the confusing concepts of AI, machine learning, neural network, and deep learning, and then introduces the basic machine learning method—linear regression and its training process. On this basis, the principle of the simplest neural network—perceptron—is illustrated; then it is expanded to two-layer and multilayer deep neural networks. At the end of this section, the history of neural networks is introduced. Section 2.2 introduces the calculation process of forward propagation and back-propagation in neural network training. After understanding these technologies, readers can do some neural network experiments. In the process of experiment, the first experiment is often not effective. At this time, you can try different network topologies, activation functions, and loss functions. If the trained neural network model does not perform well, this may be due to overfitting. Overfitting can be solved by regularization. Finally, how to use cross-validation to determine whether overfitting occurs is introduced.

This chapter only outlines the basic content related to neural networks. Interested readers can access papers in related fields to understand more specific related knowledge, including regularization, loss functions, etc.

Exercises

2.1 What is the difference between an MLP and a single-layer perceptron? Why is there such a difference?

2.2 Suppose an MLP has only one hidden layer and the numbers of neurons in the input, hidden, and output layers are 33, 512, and 10, respectively. Then how many parameters in this MLP can be trained?

2.3 In back-propagation, how is the gradient of the neuron calculated? How are the weights updated?

2.4 Draw the graphs of five different activation functions on the same axis and compare their value ranges.

2.5 Briefly describe three ways to avoid overfitting.

2.6 The limits of the sigmoid activation function are 0 and 1. Derive its derivative expression and calculate its derivative value at the origin.

2.7 Suppose the expression of the activation function is

$$\phi(v) = \frac{v}{\sqrt{(1+v^2)}}.$$

Give its derivative expression and find its value at the origin.

2.8 Assuming that the symbols in Table 2.1 are used, how does a trained MLP with two hidden layers determine the label of each output neuron? At test time, how is the label of the current input sample determined?

2.9 One way to update the weight is to introduce a momentum term, namely

$$\Delta\omega(n) = \alpha\Delta\omega(n-1) + \alpha^2\Delta\omega(n-2) + ...$$

The value range of the momentum term α is usually [0, 1]. What effect does this value have on the weight update? What if the value range is $[-1, 0]$?

*2.10 In back-propagation, what is the difference in the calculation of the gradient using different activation functions? Design a new activation function and give the neuron gradient calculation formula.

*2.11 Design an MLP to achieve the function of a 4-bit full adder, that is, two 4-bit inputs get a 4-bit output and a 1-bit carry. Construct the training set and test set by yourself to complete the training and testing.

*2.12 Reimplement the code to solve Exercise 2.11 without using any programming framework.

Deep learning

3

The purpose of developing AI computing systems is to enable machines to understand and serve humans better. People understand the world mainly by using the senses of sight, hearing, touch, smell, and taste. Among these senses, sight and hearing are particularly important. As for machines, the completion of audiovisual understanding mainly relies on deep learning technology. The driving example of this book—image style transfer—also uses deep learning techniques.

In this chapter, we begin with discussing the basic convolutional neural networks (CNNs) for image processing. Then, we detail how to use CNNs to classify images, such as whether the animal in a picture is a cow, sheep, pig, or dog. Image classification is an important benchmark to promote the development of machine learning. However, in practice, there would be more than one animal/person/object in a picture. Thus, the principles of typical CNNs for object detection are described, including how these algorithms are developed, which may help readers design new algorithms in this path. Image processing mainly uses CNNs, while sequential information (such as speech, text, and video) processing mainly uses recurrent neural networks (RNNs), or their extension, long short-term memory (LSTM). These models will be detailed in Section 3.4. Last but not least, a relatively novel deep learning technology, generative adversarial networks (GANs), will be discussed. GANs not only relieve the demand for massive training data by previous deep learning techniques, but also has many interesting applications. For example, Deepfake, a kind of GAN, can not only transfer the style of images and videos, but also swap human heads/faces in them. Some video websites already support face swapping, which replaces the face of an actor in a movie with that of another movie star. Finally, this chapter ends with an implementation of image style transfer.

3.1 Convolutional neural networks for image processing

In computer vision, to recognize a picture, a lot of input information is needed. For example, to recognize the dog in Fig. 3.1, which is an RGB image with 32×32 pixels, the input data size is $32 \times 32 \times 3$ bytes. If using the traditional shallow neural network introduced in Chapter 2 for this recognition task, the network architecture, shown in Fig. 3.1, includes the inputs, a hidden layer, and an output layer. Given that the hidden layer has 100 neurons, the number of synaptic weights between the input and hidden layers can be as high as 307,200 ($32 \times 32 \times 3 \times 100$).

AI Computing Systems. https://doi.org/10.1016/B978-0-32-395399-3.00009-3

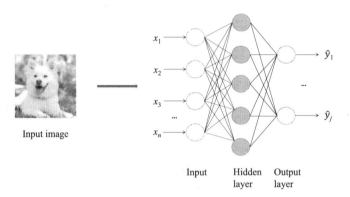

Input image
Input   Hidden   Output
         layer   layer

FIGURE 3.1

Example of image recognition using a shallow neural network.

Training such a neural network layer with 300,000 weights is prone to overfitting. As introduced in Section 2.4, overfitting could treat noise information as important hints of features in image processing, leading to failure of grasping the essence of the problem and poor model generalization. In practice, the number of weights in neural networks can be far more than 300,000. In deep neural networks, there are usually many hidden layers, and the number of neurons in each layer may exceed 100. Thus, if the simplistic fully connected layers are used in the network, given that a model input is an RGB image with 224×224 pixels and the first hidden layer has 1000 neurons, there are 150 million weight parameters between the input and the hidden layer. It is very difficult to train a neural network with such numerous parameters. Even if the network is trained, it is prone to overfitting.

CNNs can solve the aforementioned problems based on the following two features.

(1) **Local connection.** Vision has strong locality. Several adjacent pixels in an image may constitute a complete object. The longer the distance between two pixels, the weaker the connection in between. Therefore, when using neural networks for image processing, we should fully consider neighboring information to establish local dense connections instead of full connections.

(2) **Weight sharing.** CNNs use convolution kernels, known as filters/convolution templates, for convolutional processing. Different positions in an image could share the same convolution coefficients (i.e., synaptic weights). For example, the synaptic weights can be the same for the upper left corner and lower right corner of an image. The principle of this technique is that one set of weights extracts one type of features in the image. For example, to extract the feature of shape, a specific set of weights is used in different positions of an image.

Based on local connection and weight sharing, CNNs can significantly reduce the number of weights for image processing, thereby avoiding overfitting.

3.1.1 **CNN components**

In this section, the widely used CNN VGG16 [72] is used as an example to introduce the CNN components. As illustrated in Fig. 3.2, the most important layer in a CNN is the convolutional layer. Each convolutional layer has a set of convolution kernels to extract specific features. The sizes of the input and output feature maps in a convolutional layer are similar. To reduce the feature map size, a pooling layer is commonly added after a convolutional layer. For example, as illustrated in Fig. 3.2, the input is an RGB image with a size of 224×224; after the first set of convolutional layers, the output contains 64 feature maps of size 224×224. These 64 feature maps represent 64 different image features extracted by 64 different convolution kernels and have the same size as the input feature maps. This set of convolutional layers is followed by a pooling layer, which reduces the size of the feature map from 224×224 to 112×112. Convolutional layers and pooling layers appear alternately in this way. The feature map size keeps shrinking from 112×112 to 56×56, until reaching the minimum 7×7. At the same time, the number of extracted features is increasing. As shown in Fig. 3.2, 64, 128, and 512 features are extracted by the first, second, and last sets of convolutional layers, respectively. Then, three fully connected layers are used to connect every input neuron to every output neuron. In each convolutional layer and each fully connected layer, besides the vector inner product, an activation function is needed. Finally, the softmax function is applied to highlight, suppress, and normalize classification probabilities.

Next, how each layer in the CNN works is introduced in detail.

3.1.2 **Convolutional layer**

The convolutional layer can extract relatively complex features in an image through convolution, a specialized kind of linear operation. Due to the local connection and weight sharing features, nonadjacent regions in an image are calculated individually in a convolutional layer, as shown in Fig. 3.3.

Shallow neural networks use full connection, in which one single output is calculated with all inputs. However, CNNs are different, which compute each output of a convolutional layer with $K_r \times K_c$ inputs, where $K_r \times K_c$ is the size of the convolution kernel and K_r and K_c can be 1, 3, 5, 7, 9, 11, etc. In addition, the connections between all neurons in shallow neural networks use different weights. Thus, the number of weights in a fully connected layer with N_i inputs and N_o outputs is $N_i \times N_o$. In a CNN, each pair of input and output feature maps shares the same set of weights, which greatly reduces the number of weights to only $K_r \times K_c$.

3.1.2.1 *Convolution operation*

The convolution operation in CNNs is to perform the inner product between the input matrix and the convolution kernel.

Take the convolution in Fig. 3.4 as an example to illustrate the convolution process. Assume the input image or input feature matrix in Fig. 3.4 is X. The matrix size is 6×6, the convolution kernel K is a 3×3 matrix, and the convolution stride is 1.

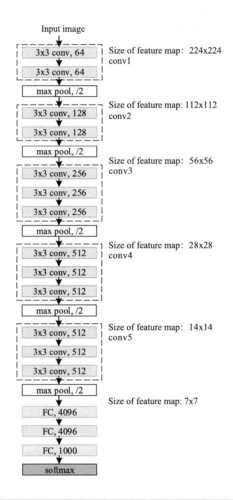

FIGURE 3.2

Architecture of VGG16.

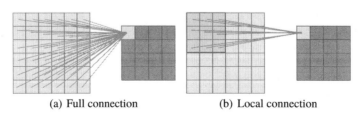

(a) Full connection   (b) Local connection

FIGURE 3.3

Full connection and local connection.

To calculate $Y_{0,0}$ in the output matrix Y, the center of the convolution kernel should be placed at the position $(1, 1)$ of the matrix X, and the inner product between the convolution kernel and the elements of X in the kernel windows is calculated as

$$Y_{0,0} = X_{0,0} \times K_{0,0} + X_{0,1} \times K_{0,1} + X_{0,2} \times K_{0,2} + X_{1,0} \times K_{1,0} + X_{1,1} \times K_{1,1}$$
$$+ X_{1,2} \times K_{1,2} + X_{2,0} \times K_{2,0} + X_{2,1} \times K_{2,1} + X_{2,2} \times K_{2,2}$$
$$= 2 \times 1 + 3 \times 0 + 1 \times 1 + 7 \times 4 + 4 \times (-3) + 5 \times 2 + 3 \times 3 + 9 \times 0 +$$
$$6 \times (-1)$$
$$= 32.$$

(3.1)

Then, the convolution kernel is slid one pixel to the right on matrix X, and the inner product between the convolution kernel and the elements of X in the kernel windows is calculated to get $Y_{0,1} = 40$. By repeatedly sliding the convolution kernel to the right on matrix X and performing the inner product, all the values of the first row of X are obtained. In the next step, the center of the convolution kernel is placed on the $(2, 1)$ position of the matrix X, and the inner product between kernel and corresponding elements of X is calculated to get $Y_{1,0} = 5$. Iteratively sliding kernels over matrix X, all the values of output Y can be calculated.

The above convolution process only uses one kernel, and thus only one kind of feature is extracted.

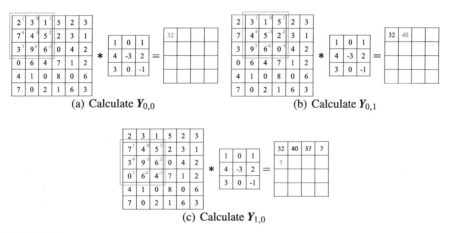

FIGURE 3.4

Convolution computation.

3.1.2.2 Convolution on multiple input-output feature maps

An image may contain edge features of different shapes, including linear, triangular, circular and twisted features. To.extract different features, CNNs need different convolution kernels. After extracting features, each neural network layer outputs multiple feature maps (also called multiple output channels). Each feature map represents one kind of feature. If the input to a network layer contains multiple feature maps (also called multiple input channels), how shall a convolution compute?

Take the convolutional computation in Fig. 3.5 as an example. Assume the input of this neural network layer contains three feature maps of size 6×6 (namely a $6 \times 6 \times 3$ tensor), and each feature map corresponds to the linear, circular and triangular feature, respectively. The convolution kernel is a $3 \times 3 \times 3$ tensor, corresponding to the input feature maps. The convolution of the above two outputs a 4×4 feature map. In the convolution operation, the number of channels between the input and convolution kernel must be the same, i.e., three channels in this case.

The value of the position $(0, 0)$ in the output feature map is the sum of three values from the convolution between the 3×3 submatrix at the upper left corner of each input feature map and the corresponding channel of the convolution kernel. For example, the submatrix extracted from the first input feature map is $[0, 0, 0; 0, 2, 2; 0, 1, 2]$, and the corresponding channel of the convolution kernel is $[-1, 1, 1; -1, 1, -1; 1, -1, 1]$. The 2D convolution outputs 1. As such, the submatrix extracted from the second input feature map is $[0, 0, 0; 0, 0, 2; 0, 1, 2]$, and the corresponding channel of the convolution kernel is $[1, -1, -1; -1, 0, -1; -1, 0, 1]$. The convolution result between the two is 0. The submatrix extracted from the third input feature map is $[0, 0, 0; 0, 1, 1; 0, 0, 2]$, and the corresponding channel of the convolution kernel is $[1, -1, -1; -1, -1, 0; -1, 1, 1]$. The convolution result between the two is 1. The above three values add up to 2, which is the value of the $(0, 0)$ position in the output feature map. Similarly, to get the output of other positions, the convolution kernel is slid on the input. For example, the value of the position $(0, 1)$ or $(1, 0)$ in the output feature map can be obtained by moving the kernel one step to the right or down, respectively, and performing convolution.

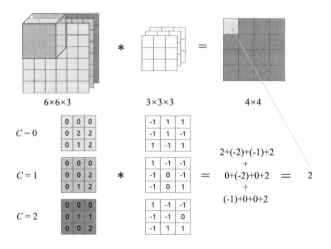

FIGURE 3.5

A convolution example of three input feature maps and one output feature map.

The above example shows the convolution process from three input feature maps to one output feature map. If the inputs stay three feature maps but the outputs are doubled as two feature maps, the number of convolution kernels needs to be doubled as well, as shown in Fig. 3.6. Similarly, the input is convolved with the first convolution kernel to get the first output feature map. Recall that both input and convolution kernel are 3D tensors. Then, the same input is convolved with the next convolution kernel until all output feature maps are obtained. In this example, there are two $3 \times 3 \times 3$ convolution kernels, i.e., 54 convolution parameters.

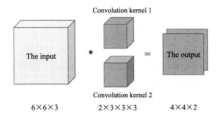

Convolution kernel 1

The input   *   =   The output

Convolution kernel 2

$6 \times 6 \times 3$ $2 \times 3 \times 3 \times 3$ $4 \times 4 \times 2$

FIGURE 3.6

A convolution example of three input feature maps and two output feature maps.

3.1.2.3 Feature detection in the convolutional layer

Fig. 3.7(a) introduces how a convolutional layer detects features. The input feature map is a 6×6 matrix, where 10 and 0 represent white and black, respectively. A line in the image separates black and white regions and is called the edge feature. What kind of convolution kernel should be designed to extract such edge features? Taking a 3×3 convolution kernel as an example, we use $[1, 0, -1; 1, 0, -1; 1, 0, -1]$ as the kernel to convolve with the input and obtain the output shown in Fig. 3.7(a). In this output, the value 0 is on both sides and the value 30 is in the middle. Observing the input and output, we can find that the smooth regions of the input correspond to low output values, while the abrupt regions of it correspond to high output values. The latter is the edge feature to be detected. In this way, the vertical edge feature in the middle of the input is detected successfully.

To detect the diagonal feature in an image, as shown in Fig. 3.7(b), one can use the convolution kernel $[1, 1, 0; 1, 0, -1; 0, -1, -1]$. The coefficients on the diagonal, right bottom, and left top of the kernel are 0, -1, and 1, respectively. Convolving this kernel with the input, we have the output shown in Fig. 3.7(b). In this output, the value on the diagonal is 30. The values on the bottom right and upper left corners are 0, since there are no changes in these regions.

Based on this process, the vertical and diagonal edge features can be detected by using specific convolution kernels.

3.1.2.4 Padding

In convolution, if there is no padding, the output size will shrink slightly. Given the input of size $N_r \times N_c$ and the convolution kernel of size $K_r \times K_c$, the size of the output feature map is $(N_r - K_r + 1) \times (N_c - K_c + 1)$. This comes from the fact

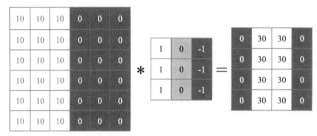

(a) Detect vertical edges

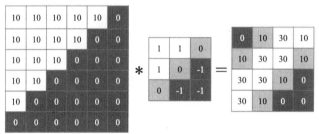

(b) Detect diagonal edges

FIGURE 3.7

Feature detection.

that the convolution kernel needs to be constrained inside the input feature map. For example, without padding, convolving a 32×32 input image with a 4×4 convolution kernel, the output feature map size is 29×29. After another convolutional layer, the output feature map size is reduced to 26×26. After yet another convolution, the feature map shrinks to 23×23. After several convolution layers, there would be no output. For a neural network with hundreds of layers, without padding, there would be no output feature map. Thus, padding is necessary in deep neural networks.

The main purpose of padding is to ensure that the sizes of the input feature map and the output feature map are the same. This is achieved by adding pixels of zeros around the outside of the image. As illustrated in Fig. 3.8(b), the size of input image or feature map is 4×4, and the kernel size is 3×3. To keep the output feature map size at 4×4, pixels of zeros should be added around the outside of the input feature map to expand the input feature map to 6×6, and then the kernel should be convolved over the padded input feature map. Through padding, the output size stays. In addition, padding can highlight the edge feature of the image. Padding with zeros leads to a strong impact on the feature extraction during convolution. Sometimes, important features may be contained at the edge of the image.

3.1.2.5 Stride

Stride is the number of pixels that a neural network filter moves over an image or video, thus changing the size of the output feature map. In previous examples, the

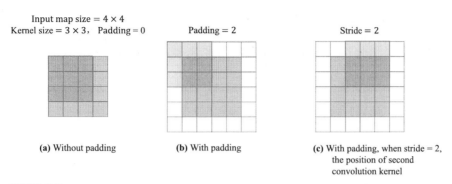

Input map size = 4×4
Kernel size = 3×3, Padding = 0   Padding = 2   Stride = 2

(a) Without padding   **(b)** With padding   **(c)** With padding, when stride = 2,
                                                                the position of second
                                                                convolution kernel

FIGURE 3.8

Example of convolution with an image size of 4×4 and a convolution kernel size of 3×3.

convolution stride is 1. That is, the convolution kernel moves one pixel on the input image at a time. Additionally, convolution with padding makes the output size equal input size. Some CNN algorithms use a stride larger than 1, thus moving two pixels or more at a time, as shown in Fig. 3.8(c). Using a larger stride can speed up the computation and shrink the output size.

The design choice of stride is on demand. If one wants to keep the feature map size unchanged, padding is the technique. Otherwise, if one wants to halve the height and width of the output feature map, padding and a stride of 2 can do the job.

3.1.2.6 Summary

In summary, the process of the convolution operation is a layered mechanism. In a convolutional layer, there is a set of input feature maps or images, represented with an $N_{ir} \times N_{ic} \times N_{if}$ tensor, where N_{ic}, N_{ir}, and N_{if} are the width, the height, and the number of the input feature map, respectively. The number of the input feature maps is also called input channels.

The convolutional layer has $N_{if} \times N_{of}$ convolution kernels of size $K_r \times K_c$, where N_{of} is the number of output feature maps (or the number of output channels) and K_c and K_r are the width and height of the convolution kernel, respectively. The convolution kernel is generally square, that is, $K_r = K_c$, such as 3×3 or 5×5. There also exist rectangular convolution kernels, which can be used as an alternative way of tuning during network training. The rectangular convolution kernel can reduce the number of parameters. For example, Inception-v3 (detailed in Section 3.2.3.3) uses a $1 \times n$ and a $n \times 1$ convolutional layer to replace the $n \times n$ convolution. Therefore, the number of parameters is reduced by $n \times n - 1 \times n - n \times 1$. After the convolution, a bias is required for the output.

The size of the output feature map is $N_{or} \times N_{oc}$, where N_{oc} and N_{or} are the width and height of the output feature map, respectively. The output size is correlated with the input size, the stride s, and padding. If the stride is larger than 1, the output feature map becomes $1/(s_r \times s_c)$ the size of the input feature map, where s_c and s_r

are the stride in the horizontal and vertical directions, respectively. Without loss of generality, assume the input feature map is padded with p_{up}, p_{bottom} rows of zeros and p_{left}, p_{right} columns of zeros on top, bottom, left, and right, respectively. The width and height of the output feature map are

$$N_{oc} = \left\lfloor \frac{N_{ic} - K_c + p_{left} + p_{right}}{s_c} + 1 \right\rfloor,$$

$$N_{or} = \left\lfloor \frac{N_{ir} - K_r + p_{up} + p_{bottom}}{s_r} + 1 \right\rfloor. \tag{3.2}$$

The convolutional layer is an important part in the deep neural network for image applications and has a relatively high computational complexity.

3.1.3 Pooling layer

Pooling layers provide an approach to downsample feature maps by summarizing the presence of features in patches of the feature map, thereby reducing the number of parameters, decreasing the computation cost, and avoiding overfitting. For example, an input image or feature map with a size of 100×100 can be pooled to 50×50. The pooling layer generally has no parameters and is easy to train. There are many pooling techniques, such as max pooling, average pooling, L^2 pooling, etc.

Max pooling is a commonly used pooling technique, which outputs the maximum value in the pooling window $K_r \times K_c$. Taking Fig. 3.9 as an example, assume that the pooling window is 2×2 and the stride is 2, without padding. We first find the maximum value 7 in the 2×2 submatrix at the upper left corner of the input feature map as the first output. The pooling window slides right two steps on the matrix, and the maximum value 5 is obtained as the second output. Continuously, we find the maximum value 3 as the third output and then keep moving the window until all max outputs are found. Max pooling only preserves the maximum values of the features in the pooling window and thus improves feature robustness.

Average pooling is another commonly used pooling technique. This technique takes the average value of all features in the pooling window, thus averaging features in the image (i.e., ambiguity).

L^2 pooling calculates the square root of the sum of squares of all elements in the pooling window.

In hardware design, the max pooling technique finds the maximum value, which is easy to implement. L^2 pooling needs to calculate the square root, thus leading to high hardware complexity. In the past, the geometric mean was used for pooling, which introduced much higher computational complexity. If the pooling window is 2×2 or 3×3, the geometric mean needs to find the fourth or ninth root, respectively, thus having a heavy computation footprint with only a slightly improved accuracy. In practice, max pooling is the most commonly used method.

2	3	1	5	2	3
7	4	5	2	3	1
3	9	6	0	4	2
0	6	4	7	1	2
4	1	0	8	0	6
7	0	2	1	6	3

max pooling

pooling window $= 2\times2$
padding $= 0$, stride $= 2$

7	5	3
9	7	4
7	8	6

FIGURE 3.9

An example of max pooling.

3.1.4 Fully connected layer

The convolutional layer and the pooling layer constitute the feature extractor, while the fully connected layer is the classifier. The fully connected layer maps the high-dimensional feature map obtained from feature extraction into a 1D feature vector. This vector contains all feature information and can be transformed into the probability of each category. For example, a 224×224 input image can be converted into 4096 1×1 feature maps after multiple convolution and pooling layers. Based on these 4096 features, a fully connected layer can be used to determine which ones are pigs, dogs, cats, cows, or sheep.

3.1.5 Softmax layer

Some CNNs end with the fully connected layer, while others end with the softmax layer.

The softmax layer normalizes the output and outputs the classification probability. The computation process is as follows:

$$f(z_j) = \frac{e^{z_j}}{\sum_{i=0}^{n} e^{z_i}},$$

(3.3)

where z_j is the jth input of the softmax layer. Therefore, the input and output have the same size. Through normalization, larger values are highlighted while smaller values are suppressed. Thus, those secondary features are ignored, without noise impact on the classification probability.

3.1.6 CNN architecture

Different CNNs are built by various combinations of convolutional layers, fully connected layers, and pooling layers. The VGG16 network in Fig. 3.2 uses convolutional layers and pooling layers for feature extraction and reduces the size of the feature map from 224×224 to 112×112, to 56×56, until 7×7. In its classification, the 512 7×7 convolutional feature maps go through the first fully connected layer to output 4096 features, the output features pass through the second fully connected layer without changing feature size, and then the resulting features are fed into the third fully connected layer to get 1000 features. Finally, these 1000 features pass through the softmax layer to produce the final output of neural network, i.e., which class out of 1000 the input object belongs to.

Fig. 3.10 presents some common layer combinations in CNNs. The convolution and pooling layers usually appear alternately, with a convolutional layer followed by a pooling layer. Sometimes, one convolutional layer can be connected to two or three more convolutional layers, followed by a pooling layer, i.e., N convolutional layers followed by a pooling layer. After repeating such pattern M times, all features are extracted, and then these features are mapped to O output features by K fully connected layers. At last, a fully connected layer, a softmax, or sometimes both are used to determine the output. For example, in Fig. 3.10, the output turns out to be a dog.

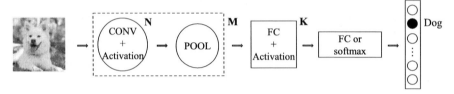

FIGURE 3.10

Common convolutional neural network architecture.

When $N = 3$, $M = 1$, $K = 2$ in Fig. 3.10, the network architecture is: input $\rightarrow$ convolutional layer (ReLU) $\rightarrow$ convolutional layer (ReLU) $\rightarrow$ convolutional layer (ReLU) $\rightarrow$ pooling layer $\rightarrow$ fully connected layer (ReLU) $\rightarrow$ fully connected layer (ReLU) $\rightarrow$ fully connected layer $\rightarrow$ output.

In some networks, such as GoogLeNet [60], there exist many more combinations, e.g., pooling layers and convolutional layers can contain branches. For example, one convolution kernel outputs a set of $76 \times 76 \times 37$ features, and another convolution kernel outputs a set of $38 \times 38 \times 99$ features. After branching, the output features of different branches are concatenated for classification. Details on branching are described in Section 3.2.3.

Why do CNNs choose a deep but not wide neural network architecture? As discussed in Section 2.1.4, in theory, a two-layer neural network with one hidden layer is sufficient to fit any function [53], provided the number of hidden neurons is sufficiently large. However, in practice, a complex feature is often composed of several simple ones. A deep network architecture can understand the image from local to global. For example, in facial recognition, the network can first find a local simple feature, e.g., a black circle. When zooming out at a larger scale, the circle could be an eye. On an even larger scale, there could be eyebrows above the eye. Scaling out again, we could find one eye and eyebrow on the left and one eye and eyebrow on the right. Scaling out again, it could be a face to identify a person. This hierarchical architecture is ideal for understanding the image from local to global.

In addition, the deep neural network can reduce the number of weights. With only one hidden layer, the number of layers is very small, but with a full connection, the number of weights in a hidden layer can be very large. For example, if the input is 1000 and the hidden layer has 10,000 neurons, the network has 10 million parameters. In a deep neural network, the number of parameters is relatively small, without any dependence on the input image size. It is because the convolution kernel used in any position of the image is the same. If the size of the convolution kernel is 3×3, the input is three feature maps, and the output is two feature maps, the number of all parameters is only $3 \times 3 \times 3 \times 2 = 54$ in all. Due to the low number of weights, the deep neural network is not prone to overfitting, and the speed of its training on massive data can be acceptable in the industry.

To further understand the neural network intuitively, Fig. 2.8 shows the visualization of a trained CNN [73]. The network is trained on the ILSVRC-2012 ImageNet dataset [16]. After several layers of convolution, a feature of black dot in a white circle in the first row can be extracted. More complex features can be well extracted after this layer-by-layer extraction.

3.2 **CNN-based classification algorithms**

CNN-based image classification algorithms go a long way back. One of the earliest can be traced back to the Neocognitron, a neural cognitive machine [74] proposed by the Japanese researcher Kunihiko Fukushima in 1980. The model borrows from the visual nervous system of the vertebrates. However, this model was not popular in practice, until 2012, when AlexNet won the ImageNet Large Scale Visual Recognition Challenge (ILSVRC), the potential of CNNs was widely recognized, and CNNs became the focus of the industry.

ILSVRC is one of the most influential academic competitions in the field of image classification. The competition provides a series of pictures and requires contestants to decide to which of 1000 categories each picture belongs. Fig. 3.11 shows the top five error rates of ImageNet classification.[1] The 2010 and 2011 champions of ILSVRC adopted traditional visual algorithms, with top five error rates of 28.2% and 25.8%, respectively. AlexNet, proposed in 2012, is an eight-layer CNN that reduced the top five error rate from 25.8% to 16.4%. Since then, deep learning became the trend, and network depth has increased rapidly, from AlexNet (8 layers) to VGG

---

[1] Classification tasks usually use the error rate as the performance metric. The top one error rate is the fraction of test images for which the correct label is not the predicted result of the highest probability by the model. The top five error rate is the fraction of test images for which the correct label is not among the five predicted results considered most probable by the model [15]. For example, given an input image the network predicts the five most probable outcomes in descending order: a water cup, chalk, eraser, pen, and mouse. If the correct label of the input image is not one of these five objects, it is considered a top five error. If the correct label of the input image is not a water cup, it is considered a top one error. According to the above definition, the top five error rate will be lower than the top one error rate.

(19 layers), GoogLeNet (22 layers), ResNet (152 layers), and even SeNet (252 layers) [75]. For the classification of 1000 objects on ImageNet, ResNet's top five error rate is only 3.57%, which is a very exciting progress.

Among these algorithms, AlexNet, which reduced the top five error rate of ILSVRC from 25.8% to 16.4%, owns the largest performance span. The next is ResNet, which reduced the top five error rate from 6.7% to 3.57%. However, the drop of the top five error rate from 6.7% to 3.57% meant that the number of incorrectly predicted images decreased by nearly half, which is very difficult to achieve.

Next, we are going to introduce several landmark algorithms in the history of CNN, including AlexNet, VGG, Inception,[2] and ResNet.

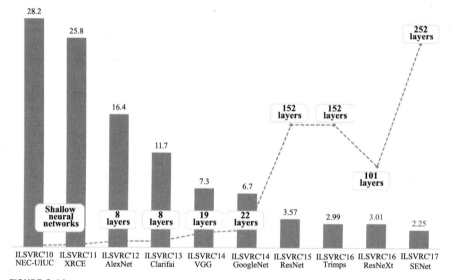

FIGURE 3.11

Top five error rate of ILSVRC from 2010 to 2017.[3]

3.2.1 AlexNet

AlexNet is one of the most important works in deep learning, known as one of the representative works from Geoffrey Hinton. The network architecture of AlexNet [15] is shown in Fig. 3.12. To deal with such a large neural network, AlexNet is trained across two GPUs.

The input of AlexNet is a 224×224 RGB image. In the first convolutional layer, AlexNet uses 48 $11 \times 11 \times 3$ convolution kernels to compute 48 55×55 feature maps.

---

[2] Note that GoogLeNet is a member of the Inception family.
[3] Data source: Russakovsky, Olga, et al., ImageNet Large Scale Visual Recognition Challenge. International Journal of Computer Vision, 2015, 115(3): 211–252.

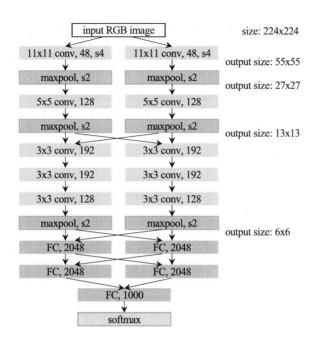

FIGURE 3.12

Network architecture of AlexNet.

On the other half of the network, another 48 55 × 55 feature maps are computed with the other set of 48 11 × 11 × 3 convolution kernels. The stride size of these two branches is 4. In this layer, the size of the image is reduced from 224 × 224 to 55 × 55. After the first layer, the network adds Local Response Normalization (LRN) and max pooling with a stride of 2 and a pooling window of 3 × 3. The resulting feature map size is 27 × 27. The second convolutional layer convolves the output of the first layer with two sets of 128 5 × 5 × 48 convolution kernels and outputs two sets of 128 27 × 27 feature maps. At the end of the second layer, the convolutional features go through LRN and max pooling with a 3 × 3 pooling window and a stride of 2, which outputs feature maps of size 13 × 13. Continuously, the third convolutional layer combines the two groups of input feature maps into one, using two sets of 192 3 × 3 × 256 convolution kernels to compute both paths in convolution. The output contains two sets of 192 13 × 13 feature maps. In the fourth convolutional layer, the input feature maps are convolved with 192 3 × 3 × 192 convolution kernels on each path. Accordingly, the fifth convolutional layer uses 128 kernels of size 3 × 3 × 192. After the fifth layer, max pooling is applied with a stride of 2 and a pooling window of 3 × 3, and outputs feature maps of size 6 × 6. With the sixth and seventh fully connected layers, the classified neurons increase to 4096, with 2048 neurons in each group. The eighth fully connected layer outputs 1000 features to the softmax, and the softmax delivers the final output of the classification probabilities.

The network configuration of AlexNet is shown in Table 3.1.

Table 3.1 AlexNet network configuration [15].

Layer number	Layer name	Input size	Convolution or pooling window size	Input channels	Output channels	Stride
1	Conv	224 × 224	11 × 11	3	96	4
	ReLU	55 × 55	–	96	96	1
	LRN	55 × 55	–	96	96	1
	MaxPool	55 × 55	3 × 3	96	96	2
2	Conv	27 × 27	5 × 5	96	256	1
	ReLU	27 × 27	–	256	256	1
	LRN	27 × 27	–	256	256	1
	MaxPool	27 × 27	3 × 3	256	256	2
3	Conv	13 × 13	3 × 3	256	384	1
	ReLU	13 × 13	–	384	384	1
4	Conv	13 × 13	3 × 3	384	384	1
	ReLU	13 × 13	–	384	384	1
5	Conv	13 × 13	3 × 3	384	256	1
	ReLU	13 × 13	–	256	256	1
	MaxPool	13 × 13	3 × 3	256	256	2
6	FC	–	–	9216	4096	1
	ReLU dropout	–	–	4096	4096	1
7	FC	–	–	4096	4096	1
	ReLU dropout	–	–	4096	4096	1
8	FC	–	–	4096	1000	1
	softmax	–	–	1000	1000	1

Compared to the conventional artificial neural network, AlexNet has four technical advantages:

(1) Dropout. In training, some hidden neurons can be discarded randomly to avoid overfitting.
(2) LRN. LRN can enhance the higher-level response and suppress the lower level one. In recent years, the industry has found that the LRN layer is less effective, and since then LRN has not been widely studied.
(3) Max pooling. Max pooling can be used to avoid ambiguity from the average pooling and improve the model robustness. Prior to AlexNet, many studies used average pooling. Since AlexNet, many agree that max pooling works better.
(4) ReLU activation function. Before AlexNet, the most commonly used activation functions were sigmoid and tanh. ReLU is simple; it outputs 0 when the input is less than 0 and outputs the input when the input is greater than 0. In the past, it was a common belief that ReLU was too simple to be effective. However,

in practice, this simple ReLU has shown impressive performance. AlexNet uses ReLU at the output of both the convolutional layer and the fully connected layer, which can effectively speed up the training convergence.

AlexNet remarkably combines these seemingly unspectacular technologies and achieves impressive performance. The architecture serves as a milestone in pushing deep learning into the mainstream. Next, we introduce LRN and dropout.

3.2.1.1 LRN

LRN performs local normalization at each position in multiple input feature maps at the same network layer to enhance higher-frequency features and suppress lower-frequency ones. The input of LRN is the output of ReLU in AlexNet. Assuming that the inputs of LRN are N feature maps, LRN shall normalize pixels at the same position from the n adjacent input feature maps to get values at position (r, c) in the output feature map $b_{r,c}^i$ [15]:

$$b_{r,c}^i = a_{r,c}^i / \left(k + \alpha \sum_{j=\max(0,i-n/2)}^{\min(N-1,i+n/2)} (a_{r,c}^j)^2 \right)^{\beta}, \qquad (3.4)$$

where $a_{r,c}^j$ is the pixel at the position (r, c) in the input feature map j. Constants $k, n,$ α, and β are manually set based on the input system. For example, AlexNet [15] sets $k = 2, n = 5, \alpha = 10^{-4}$, and $\beta = 0.75$.

Intuitively, the input of LRN is N different feature maps, including features like triangles, points, lines, rectangles, squares, etc. At the same position, if rectangles, squares, triangles, and rhombuses exist at the same time, it is necessary to normalize points at this position to find the most significant feature. However, in practice, this point may belong to triangles, squares, rectangles, and/or diamonds, such that it is not reasonable to suppress the low-frequency feature of any participation from a given point. As a result, LRN does not work well in practice and is now rarely used.

3.2.1.2 Dropout

Dropout was proposed by Geoffrey Hinton et al. [70] in 2012. This technique alleviates the overfitting problem by randomly dropping some hidden neurons, which is now becoming one of the most commonly used techniques in deep learning training.

The training process with dropout is as follows:

(1) Given a certain probability (e.g., $p = 0.5$), some hidden neurons are randomly discarded, as the outputs of these neurons are set to 0.
(2) After the forward propagation for a minibatch of training samples, weights associated with the dropped neurons are not updated in the back-propagation.
(3) The dropped neurons are recovered, and another minibatch of training samples is fed into the neural network.
(4) Steps 1, 2, and 3 are repeated until all samples have been processed.

In dropout training, none of the hidden layer neurons are deleted, but temporarily suspended in weight update. For one minibatch of samples, some hidden neurons may not be used, yet for the other minibatch of samples, these hidden neurons may be activated again, i.e., the associated weights will be updated. In inference, all neurons in AlexNet are used. The first two fully connected layers in AlexNet use dropout.

Dropout can prevent the complex coadaptation in training data. That is, a feature detector is only helpful in the context of several other specific feature detectors [70]. Thus, using dropout mitigates overfitting.

3.2.1.3 Summary

The greatest contribution of AlexNet is to demonstrate that deep neural networks can outperform other machine learning approaches on specific problems. This success can be attributed to the following.

(1) Using multiple convolutional layers. In the past, people mainly used shallow neural networks to solve problems. AlexNet applied deep learning to complex problems as ImageNet. By using multiple convolutional layers, key features are extracted effectively, and the accuracy of image recognition is significantly improved.
(2) Using ReLU to improve the training performance.
(3) Using dropout and data augmentation to mitigate overfitting.

3.2.2 VGG

The eight-layer AlexNet has significantly improved the accuracy of image classification. Can neural networks of more layers further improve the classification accuracy? In 2014, Karen Simonyan and Andrew Zisserman [72] proposed a novel neural network deeper than AlexNet, called VGG, which further improves the classification accuracy. There are many different versions of VGG. VGG16 is one of the most classic versions, which is the main focus in this section.

3.2.2.1 Network architecture

As the number of network layers increases, more problems appear, such as gradient explosion and gradient vanishing. When trained by calculating the loss function and corresponding derivatives, if the target layer is only one or two layers away from the output layer, it could be trained effectively. However, if this layer is 10 or 100 layers away, the derivative of the loss function might be decreased to a very small number, such that the neural network parameters would stop updating. Therefore, Karen Simonyan and Andrew Zisserman designed a series of VGG network architectures with different configurations, shown in Table 3.2 [72]. To train deeper neural networks, they proposed a pretraining strategy—using weights of a trained shallower neural network to initialize some layers in the deeper neural network.

Specifically, an 11-layer neural network (denoted as VGG11) is trained first. When training a deeper neural network, such as the 13-layer network (denoted as VGG13), its first four convolutional layers and the last three fully connected layers are initialized with the corresponding layers of trained VGG11, and other intermediate layers are initialized randomly. Then, VGG13 is trained.

Table 3.2 VGG [72] configuration. conv3 and conv1 denote 3×3 convolution and 1×1 convolution, respectively.

Output channels	VGG11	VGG11-LRN	VGG13	VGG16-1	VGG16	VGG19
	Input (224 x 224 RGB image)					
64	1×conv3	1×conv3 LRN	2×conv3	2×conv3	2×conv3	2×conv3
64	Max pooling					
128	1×conv3	1×conv3	2×conv3	2×conv3	2×conv3	2×conv3
128	Max pooling					
256	2×conv3	2×conv3	2×conv3	2×conv3 1×conv1	3×conv3	4×conv3
256	Max pooling					
512	2×conv3	2×conv3	2×conv3	2×conv3 1×conv1	3×conv3	4×conv3
512	Max pooling					
512	2×conv3	2×conv3	2×conv3	2×conv3 1×conv1	3×conv3	4×conv3
512	Max pooling					
4096	2×FC					
1000	1×FC					
1000	softmax					

The architecture of VGG11 is as follows: the input of VGG11 is a 224×224 RGB image. The first convolutional layer outputs 64 feature maps, followed by max pooling. The second convolutional layer outputs 128 feature maps, followed by max pooling. After two other consecutive convolutional layers, 128 feature maps are output, followed by max pooling. Then another two consecutive convolutional layers output 512 feature maps, followed by max pooling. Continuously, the last three fully connected layers are connected, which output 4096, 4096, and 1000 features, respectively. VGG11 uses softmax for the final output.

Based on VGG11, the network with LRN (denoted as VGG11-LRN) is obtained by adding an LRN layer after the first convolutional layer of VGG11. However, from experiments in [72], LRN does not improve the classification accuracy, so the LRN layer is not used in the rest of other VGG architectures.

To migrate VGG11 to VGG13, a convolutional layer should be added after the first and second convolutional layers in VGG11, respectively. Based on VGG13, two 16-layer networks (VGG16-1 and the well-known VGG16 in Fig. 3.2) are built by adding one convolutional layer after the 6th, 8th, and 10th convolutional layers, respectively. The difference between VGG16-1 and VGG16 is that the newly added convolutional layers of VGG16-1 and VGG16 adopt kernels of size 1×1 and 3×3, respectively. Based on VGG16, the 19-layer network (known as VGG19) is formed by adding one extra convolutional layer after the 7th, 10th, and 13th convolutional layers, respectively. In different VGG networks, all hidden layers use ReLU as the nonlinear activation function.

VGG creates different versions of neural networks by gradually increasing the number of layers. First, the LRN layer is added in VGG11-LRN, and is found less effective. Besides, as the number of layers increases, the model performance (i.e., the top five error rate) is improved. However, when it reaches VGG16 and VGG19, the top five error rates are both around 8% without any significant improvement.

3.2.2.2 Convolution-pooling architecture

The image size in VGG is adjusted by convolution and pooling. To avoid weakening some low-level edge features due to the large number of network layers in VGG, VGG performs padding in the convolutional layer to ensure the input and output image size is the same. The pooling window size is 2×2 at a stride of 2, such that the height and width of the image after pooling are both halved. For example, assume the input is an RGB image with a size of 224×224. After the first pooling, 64 112×112 feature maps are output. After the second pooling, 128 56×56 feature maps are output. After the third pooling, 256 28×28 feature maps are output. After the fourth pooling, 512 14×14 feature maps are output. And after the fifth pooling, 512 7×7 feature maps are output. The output shrinks every single pooling.

Except for the three convolutional layers in VGG16-1 that use a 1×1 convolution kernel, all other VGGs adopt 3×3 convolution kernels with stride 1. AlexNet uses three kinds of convolution kernels, like 11×11, 5×5, and 3×3. The larger convolution kernels are used in the earlier layers. Intuitively, a large convolution kernel has a vast field of view, or receptive field, which seems to be a better choice. However, it is not true because VGG uses continuous multilayer convolution, with all kernels of size 3×3. Therefore, a commonly used 5×5 convolution in AlexNet is equivalent to two consecutive 3×3 convolutional layers. Their receptive fields are the same, as shown in Fig. 3.13. Following the same intuition, a 7×7 convolution has the same receptive field as three consecutive 3×3 convolutions, and a 11×11 convolution has the same receptive field as five consecutive 3×3 convolutions. At the same time, the 11×11 convolution has 121 parameters, and five consecutive 3×3 convolutions have only 45 parameters. Therefore, by using a stack of small convolution kernels, VGG can perform the same task as AlexNet, with fewer parameters and less training difficulty.

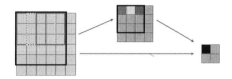

FIGURE 3.13

One 5×5 convolution and two 3×3 convolutions have the same receptive field size.

Furthermore, VGG adopts the nonlinear activation function ReLU to each convolutional layer, such that a multilayer convolution design makes the decision function more discriminative, therefore improving the classification accuracy. For example, replacing two consecutive 3×3 convolutional layers with a convolutional 5×5 layer in VGG13 could increase the top one error rate by 7% compared to that of the original VGG13 [72].

3.2.2.3 Summary

The success of VGG benefits from the following features:

(1) Adopting a regular multilayer convolution of small kernels instead of large ones. For the same receptive fields, the number of weights is effectively reduced, and thus the training speed is improved.
(2) Building a deeper CNN. Using more convolutional layers and nonlinear activation functions in the neural network improves the accuracy of image classification.
(3) Pretraining and partial initialization. The initialization approach improves the rate of convergence.

3.2.3 Inception

After VGG, Inception was developed to investigate whether a design with a smaller convolution kernel and more neural network layers could reduce the error rate. The most famous member of the Inception series, Inception-v1 (GoogLeNet) [60], won the 2014 ImageNet competition. After GoogLeNet, BN-Inception [76], Inception-v3 [77], Inception-v4 [78], etc., were proposed (see Table 3.3). Next, we introduce their featured characteristics individually.

Table 3.3 Inception series CNNs.

Network	Main innovation	Top five error	Number of layers
GoogLeNet [60]	Inception architecture	6.67%	22
BN-Inception [76]	Batch normalization (BN), replacing 5×5 conv with 3×3 conv	4.82%	-
Inception-v3 [77]	A 2D convolution is divided into two 1D convolutions. BN on fully connected layers of auxiliary classifier	3.5%	22
Inception-v4 [78]	Inception modularization, combined with the residual connections	3.08%	-

3.2.3.1 Inception-v1

The network architectures of AlexNet and VGG are relatively regular. Inception-v1 (GoogLeNet) [60] contains many complex modules, namely the Inception module, which is the core innovation of GoogLeNet.

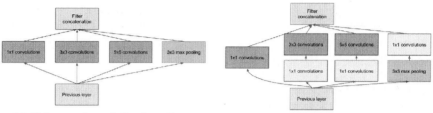

(a) Naïve version of the Inception module

(b) Inception module that supports dimensionality reductions

FIGURE 3.14

Inception module.[4]

Inception module

Fig. 3.14(a) shows the naïve version of Inception. The module provides four kinds of processing on the output of the previous layer, including a 1×1 convolution, a 3×3 convolution, a 5×5 convolution, and a 3×3 max pooling. Previous neural networks often use a set of convolution kernels with the same size (for example, 3×3 or 5×5) for feature extraction. Compared with these previous works, Inception adopts convolution kernels and pooling with different sizes, which can simultaneously extract a small or large range of features from the input. Thus, each layer in Inception can be adaptive to any scale of image features. On this basis, by adding 1×1 convolution kernels, the Inception module could reduce the dimension of features, as shown in Fig. 3.14(b). The 1×1 convolution involves convolving the pixels at the same position in multiple feature maps, which is mathematically equivalent to a fully connected layer. The advantage of 1×1 convolution is that it can normalize different features at the same position. Although it has been proved that LRN has failed in complex normalization, it could be effective on the simple 1×1 convolution in Inception.

The 1×1 convolution

Actually, 1×1 convolution is a cross-channel aggregation. The points at the same position on multiple input feature maps are fully connected, and a point at the corresponding position on the output feature map is calculated, so it is equivalent to the full connection between input and output. At the same time, each 1×1 convolutional layer uses the ReLU activation function to extract nonlinear features.

If the number of output feature maps from the 1×1 convolutional layer is less than the input, feature dimensions are reduced, and the number of parameters in the network can be reduced, and thus less computation is required. Fig. 3.15 presents such an example, where the input is a set of 256 feature maps at size 28×28 and the output only contains 96 feature maps with the same size. The left subfigure shows a one-layer convolution with 5×5 kernels. The right subfigure shows a two-layer convolution with an extra 1×1 convolutional layer, which outputs 32 28×28 feature maps. When there is only one 5×5 convolutional layer, the number of network

---

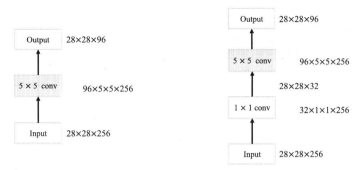

FIGURE 3.15

1 × 1 convolution parameter comparison. In each subfigure, the data in the left column is the number of features and the data in the right column is the number of convolution parameters.

parameters is $96 \times 5 \times 5 \times 256 = 614,400$, and the number of multiplication and addition operations is $28 \times 28 \times 96 \times 5 \times 5 \times 256 = 481,689,600$.

After adding the extra 1×1 convolutional layer, the number of network parameters is $32 \times 256 + 96 \times 5 \times 5 \times 32 = 84,992$ and the number of multiplication and addition operations is $28 \times 28 \times 32 \times 256 + 28 \times 28 \times 96 \times 5 \times 5 \times 32 = 66,633,728$, which is significantly less.

By adding the 1×1 convolutional layer, the input dimension of the 5×5 convolutional layer is reduced from 256 to 32, the number of parameters is reduced to $1/7.2$ of the original, thus the amount of computation is also reduced to $1/7.2$ of the original. Therefore, this 1×1 convolutional layer has been widely used in a variety of neural network architectures, including ResNet.

GoogLeNet network architecture

The network architecture of the famous GoogLeNet is shown in Fig. 3.16. It is a combination of multiple Inception modules. GoogLeNet has a total of 27 layers, 22 of which are layers with parameters and the rest pooling layers. The input of this neural network example is an RGB image at size 224×224. The first convolutional layer uses 7×7 convolution kernels with stride 2 and will output 64 112×112 feature maps. Following a max pooling layer with a 3×3 window and stride 2, an LRN process, and one 1×1 convolutional layer, 64 feature maps are output. These 64 maps go through a single 3×3 convolutional layer and are transformed to 192 feature maps, which are fed into LRN and max pooling. After nine consecutive Inception modules, two max pooling steps, one average pooling, and one fully connected layer, the output is obtained after softmax. Note that all activation functions in GoogLeNet are ReLU.

GoogLeNet is much deeper than VGG in the aspect of layers. With all layers trained together, GoogLeNet is prone to vanishing gradients. To address this problem, GoogLeNet bypasses two softmax auxiliary classification networks from the intermediate layers of the network to observe the intermediate results during train-

FIGURE 3.16

GoogLeNet network architecture (top) and configuration (bottom).[4]

type	patch size/stride	output size	depth	#1×1	#3×3 reduce	#3×3	#5×5 reduce	#5×5	pool proj	params	ops
convolution	7×7/2	112×112×64	1							2.7K	34M
max pool	3×3/2	56×56×64	0								
convolution	3×3/1	56×56×192	2		64	192				112K	360M
max pool	3×3/2	28×28×192	0								
inception (3a)		28×28×256	2	64	96	128	16	32	32	159K	128M
inception (3b)		28×28×480	2	128	128	192	32	96	64	380K	304M
max pool	3×3/2	14×14×480	0								
inception (4a)		14×14×512	2	192	96	208	16	48	64	364K	73M
inception (4b)		14×14×512	2	160	112	224	24	64	64	437K	88M
inception (4c)		14×14×512	2	128	128	256	24	64	64	463K	100M
inception (4d)		14×14×528	2	112	144	288	32	64	64	580K	119M
inception (4e)		14×14×832	2	256	160	320	32	128	128	840K	170M
max pool	3×3/2	7×7×832	0								
inception (5a)		7×7×832	2	256	160	320	32	128	128	1072K	54M
inception (5b)		7×7×1024	2	384	192	384	48	128	128	1388K	71M
avg pool	7×7/1	1×1×1024	0								
dropout (40%)		1×1×1024	0								
linear		1×1×1000	1							1000K	1M
softmax		1×1×1000	0								

FIGURE 3.16

(*continued*)

ing. Each softmax auxiliary classification network includes an average pooling layer that reduces the size of the feature map (i.e., pooling window is 5 × 5, stride is 3) and a 1 × 1 convolutional layer that reduces the feature map dimension to 128, a fully connected layer with 1024 outputs, a fully connected layer with a 70% dropout rate, and a softmax layer.[5] The auxiliary classification network processes the output of the nth layer in the middle of GoogLeNet to obtain the classification result and then adds its loss to the final classification layer with a smaller weight (e.g., 0.3). Using this auxiliary classification network, the training results of the nth layers can be observed during the training process. If the training result is not satisfied, one can back-propagate from the nth layer in advance, adjusting the weights. This approach helps train a deeper neural network to prevent the gradient from vanishing. The traditional training method back-propagates from the final output of the network. If anything goes wrong in the middle stage, it has to be back-propagated from the final output. The gradient descent approach is used to find the smallest error. In this process, the gradient is likely to vanish or explode. It is worth noting that the softmax auxiliary classification network is only used in the training phase, not in the inference phase.

Compared to VGG, GoogLeNet has deeper layers, fewer parameters, and higher classification accuracy. This is mainly due to the three pros: First, the softmax auxiliary classification network is added to observe the intermediate results of training, allowing back-propagation in advance; second, GoogLeNet adds a lot of 1 × 1 convolutional layers, which can reduce the dimension of the feature maps, the number of

---

[5] During training, the cross-entropy of the softmax output is the loss, known as the softmax loss.

parameters, and the amount of computation; third, GoogLeNet introduces a flexible Inception module, which allows adaptation to different scales of image features.

3.2.3.2 BN-Inception

On the basis of GoogLeNet, Ioffe et al. [76] introduced batch normalization (BN) in BN-Inception and achieved promising results. Specifically, BN-Inception considers a batch of samples during training. BN-Inception inserts a special cross-sample BN layer between each convolutional layer and the activation function. The BN layer applies normalization on multiple samples and normalizes the input to a standard normal distribution. This can effectively prevent the gradient from explosion or vanishing and enables the training of deep neural networks.

The principle behind BN is as follows. As the number of neural network layers increases, the parameters of each layer are changing during training. As such, the input distribution of each layer is changing and gradually shifts internally, that is, the internal covariate shift. The input distribution usually shifts towards the saturation region of the nonlinear activation function, which would cause the gradient vanishing during back-propagation. In addition, to continuously adapt to the new distribution, the training may adopt a lower learning rate and proper initialization parameters, thus leading to a slow training speed. During training minibatches, when normalizing multiple samples to a standard normal distribution (i.e., $\mu = 0, \sigma = 1$), the return value of the activation function would be close to the middle area. Some small input changes can be signified in the loss function, and thus the gradient is less likely to vanish.

If all inputs of an activation function are simplistically normalized to a standard normal distribution, the input may fall into the linear region of the activation function. In this case, the activation function cannot provide any nonlinear representation, and thus the representation ability of the network decreases. Therefore, BN needs to scale and shift the normalized value. The scaling parameter γ and the shift parameter β are trained together with the model parameters, which widens (or narrows) and shifts the normal distribution. This is equivalent to shifting the nonlinear function from the linear region to the nonlinear region, so that the model ability can be maintained.

The process of BN transformation is as follows. Suppose the input of a network layer is x_i, $i = 1, ..., M$, where M is the size of the training set and $x_i = [x_{i1}; x_{i2}; ...; x_{id}]$ is a d-dimensional vector. In theory, the model first uses all training data to normalize each dimension k of x_i as follows [76]:

$$\hat{x}_{ik} = \frac{x_{ik} - \mathrm{E}[x_{ik}]}{\sqrt{\mathrm{Var}[x_{ik}]}}. \tag{3.5}$$

Then, the normalized values are scaled and shifted to get the BN-transformed data y_{ik} [76]:

$$y_{ik} = \gamma_k \hat{x}_{ik} + \beta_k, \tag{3.6}$$

where γ_k and β_k are the scaling and shift parameters of each dimension, respectively. It is difficult to implement such BN transformation on the entire training set. Meanwhile, stochastic gradient training generally uses a minibatch of data instead of a single sample or the full training set. Therefore, in practice, the minibatch data in stochastic gradient training is used to estimate the mean and variance and perform the BN transformation.

BN-Inception draws on the idea from VGG and uses two consecutive 3×3 convolution layers in the Inception module to replace a 5×5 convolution layer [76], as shown in Fig. 3.17.

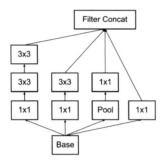

FIGURE 3.17

BN-Inception module.[6]

BN is often better than LRN, dropout, or L^2 normalization and can greatly increase the model training speed. By adding BN to Inception, the learning rate can be tuned up, which accelerates the training. By increasing the learning rate fivefold, the BN-Inception training can be 14 times faster than the original Inception [76]. More surprisingly, the accuracy can also be slightly improved by 0.8%, so BN-Inception has been described as "high-quantity, high-speed, high-quality, and cost-saving." Today, BN has not only been used in the Inception series, but it has also become one of the necessary training techniques for various contemporary deep learning neural networks.

3.2.3.3 Inception-v3

Inception-v1 (GoogLeNet) splits some 7×7 and 5×5 convolutional layers into multiple consecutive 3×3 convolutional layers. Following a similar idea, Inception-v3 [77] further reduces the convolution kernel size and splits the symmetric $n \times n$ convolutional layers into two asymmetric layers, i.e., $1 \times n$ and $n \times 1$ convolutional layers, for example, splitting the 3×3 convolutional layer into 1×3 and 3×1 convolutional layers, thereby reducing the number of parameters from nine to six. This asymmetrical splitting approach can improve the diversity of features. Therefore, three new Inception modules are formed (Fig. 3.18).

Inception-v3 is created by combining the three Inception modules in Fig. 3.18, factorizing the first 7×7 convolutional layer in GoogLeNet into three 3×3 convo-

---

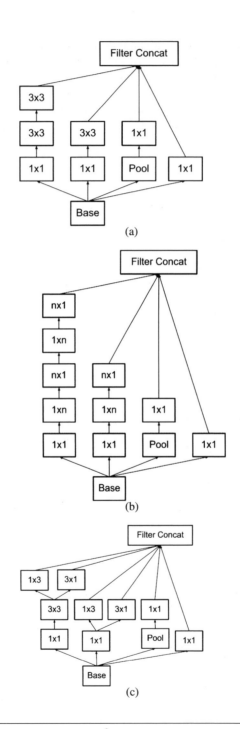

FIGURE 3.18

Three inception modules in Inception-v3.[6]

lutional layers and performing BN on all convolutional layers and fully connected layers of the auxiliary classification network, as shown in Table 3.4. The network further improves the accuracy of classification.

Table 3.4 Inception-v3 network architecture.[6]

Type	Patch size/stride or remarks	Input size
conv	$3 \times 3/2$	$299 \times 299 \times 3$
conv	$3 \times 3/1$	$149 \times 149 \times 32$
conv padded	$3 \times 3/1$	$147 \times 147 \times 32$
pool	$3 \times 3/2$	$147 \times 147 \times 64$
conv	$3 \times 3/1$	$73 \times 73 \times 64$
conv	$3 \times 3/2$	$71 \times 71 \times 80$
conv	$3 \times 3/1$	$35 \times 35 \times 192$
$3 \times$ Inception	As shown in Fig. 3.18(a)	$35 \times 35 \times 288$
$5 \times$ Inception	As shown in Fig. 3.18(b)	$17 \times 17 \times 768$
$2 \times$ Inception	As shown in Fig. 3.18(c)	$8 \times 8 \times 1280$
pool	$8 \times 8/1$	$8 \times 8 \times 2048$
linear	logits	$1 \times 1 \times 2048$
softmax	classifier	$1 \times 1 \times 1000$

3.2.3.4 Summary

The main innovations of the Inception series include:

(1) Adopting BN to mitigate gradient vanishing or explosion and accelerate the deep neural network training.
(2) Further reducing the size of the convolution kernel. This process starts from AlexNet's 11×11 convolution kernel and proceeds to VGG's 3×3 convolution kernel and to Inception-v3's 1×3 and 3×1 convolution kernels.
(3) Adding the auxiliary classification network to tune the parameters ahead by back-propagation, thus alleviating the vanishing gradient problem and solving the problem of multilayer neural network training.

3.2.4 **ResNet**

Following the path of AlexNet, VGG, and GoogLeNet, we can find a promising trend that researchers continue to try various techniques to dig deeper into the number of layers of neural networks. From the 8-layer AlexNet to the 19-layer VGG and the 22-layer GoogLeNet, deep learning technology keeps improving. However, most paradigm-shifting technology in deep neural network development is contributed by Residual Network (ResNet). Not only has ResNet achieved a much higher classification accuracy than any other algorithms in ILSVRC 2015, since it was proposed, the number of neural network layers has no upper bound. Today, although there exist many newer, deeper, and more accurate network models, most of them are generally based on the idea of ResNet.

The problem to be solved by ResNet is simple: "Is learning better networks as easy as stacking more layers?" [62]. To answer this question, the inventors of ResNet, Kaiming He et al., used conventional 20-layer and 56-layer CNNs to train and test on the CIFAR-10 dataset, respectively. As shown in Fig. 3.19, empirical results show that the training and testing errors of the 56-layer CNN are higher than those of the 20-layer CNN [62].

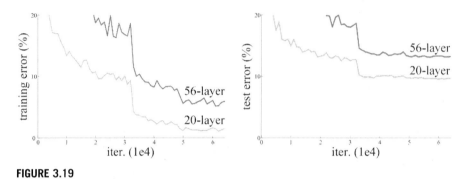

FIGURE 3.19

Training and testing error of 20-layer and 56-layer CNNs on the CIFAR-10 dataset.[7]

Why does the error increase as the number of layers increases? Some may believe that it is because of gradient vanishing. However, Kaiming He et al. have already deployed BN in the experiments, which can alleviate the syndrome of gradient vanishing, such that the gradient would not disappear completely. Therefore, these researchers believe that the decrease in accuracy of deep neural networks is due to the degradation problem caused by the increase in the number of layers [62]. In other words, the more the number of layers increases, the easier it is to converge to some local optimal points, rather than the global optimal point, resulting in larger errors.

To avoid neural network degradation, ResNet uses a different basic block. A conventional CNN adopts convolution operations similarly as using polynomial output to fit the result of image recognition. In contrast to this design, the basic block of ResNet, shown in Fig. 3.20(b), adds a shortcut connection between the input and output, and its convolution fits the difference between the input and output, i.e., the residual. Since both the input and output are normalized by BN and conform to the normal distribution, the output can be subtracted from the input as the function $F(x) := H(x) - x$ (Fig. 3.20(b)). Moreover, from the standard deviations of convolutional layer responses, the response of the residual network is smaller than that of conventional networks [62]. The advantage of the residual network is that it is more sensitive to data fluctuations and thus it is easier to find the optimal solution, such that it can improve the training performance of a very deep network.

---

[7] ©2016 IEEE. Reprinted with permission from [62].

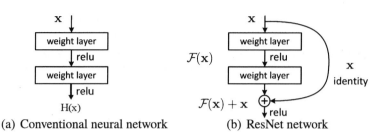

FIGURE 3.20

Network architecture comparison.[8]

The basic block of ResNet is processed as follows: The input x goes through a convolutional layer, passes the ReLU, and then goes through another convolutional layer to get $F(x)$. Adding x, the output is $H(x) = F(x) + x$. The output goes through ReLU, and the final output of the basic block y is obtained. When the dimension of the input x is different from the dimension of the convolution output $F(x)$, it is necessary to perform identity mapping on x to make them consistent, and then feed into the following procedure.

As illustrated in Fig. 3.21, the ResNet architecture is developed based on VGG19. First, the 3×3 convolutional layer in VGG is disassembled and turned into a residual block. These residual blocks are composed of two 3×3 convolutional layers. Second, the reduction of the feature map is done with a convolutional layer at a stride of 2. If the feature map size is halved, the number of feature maps doubles; if the size stays the same, the number of feature maps also stays the same. Moreover, shortcut connections have been added. For shortcut connections, the solid line indicates that the size and the number of the feature maps remain unchanged, and the dashed line indicates that the size of the feature map is halved and the number is doubled.

When the number of feature maps doubles, there are two ways to deal with the shortcut connection. One is direct mapping, i.e., the feature of the increased dimension is padded with 0; the other is to use 1×1 convolutional layers to double the number of feature maps, which introduces additional convolutional parameters. Both approaches process at a stride of 2, to halve the size of the feature map.

Besides, BN is performed after each layer of convolution and before the activation function. On the one hand, this design serves the input and output of the residual block in the same range, and on the other hand, it mitigates the gradient vanishing problem.

Using the aforementioned techniques, ResNet achieved the lowest top five error rate (3.57%) in ILSVRC 2015, which is far better than GoogLeNet's top five error rate (6.7%). Since the development of ResNet, many researchers have further improved the accuracy of image classification by increasing the number of neural network layers, but these works are all based on ResNet's unique residual network.

---

[8] Figure (b): ©2016 IEEE. Reprinted with permission from [62].

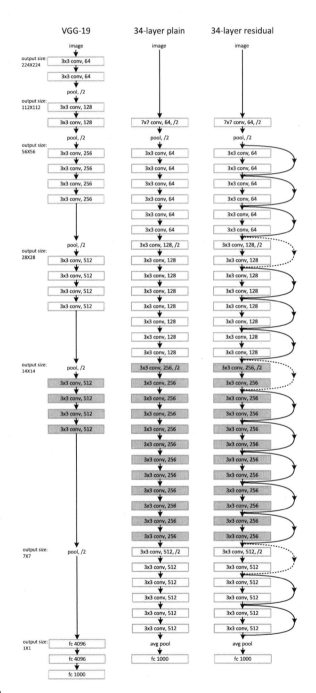

FIGURE 3.21

ResNet architecture.[7]

3.3 **CNN-based object detection algorithms**

In image classification, networks such as ResNet, VGG, GoogLeNet, and AlexNet are used to identify the category of objects in a given picture. Classification is a basic research problem, but it is difficult to play a useful role in practice. A picture in real scenarios often has a very complex scene, which may contain dozens or even hundreds of object categories. Yet, there is only one object in the picture that needs to be processed by the image classification algorithm. Furthermore, in real-world applications, objects not only need to be detected, but they also need to be located, until all objects in the picture are detected and located. This is the mission of image object detection.

At present, CNN-based image object detection algorithms are mainly divided into two categories: two-stage and one-stage algorithms. Two-stage algorithms are based on the region proposal technique. First, region proposals (bounding boxes) are generated to locate all objects. Then, each region proposal is classified using a CNN-based image classification algorithm. The R-CNN [79] series algorithms are representative two-stage algorithms. One-stage algorithms directly process the input image and output the object location and category at the same time; they are mainly represented by the YOLO [80] series and the SSD [81] algorithm.

This section first introduces the evaluation metrics of image object detection algorithms and then details three image object detection algorithms, including the R-CNN series, the YOLO series, and the SSD algorithm.

3.3.1 **Evaluation metrics**

3.3.1.1 *IoU*

Assuming that there is only one object in the input image, when we locate this object, the output result should be the bounding box of this object. The ground-truth position of the dog in Fig. 3.22 is the square box B. If the localization is inaccurate, the position may be the square box A. To measure the accuracy of image localization with only one object, Intersection over Union (IoU) is usually used as an evaluation metric. IoU is computed as the area of intersection between boxes A and B divided by the area of union between boxes A and B:

$$IoU = \frac{A \cap B}{A \cup B}.$$

(3.7)

If the localization is accurate and the square boxes A and B are completely overlapped, $IoU = 1$. If the object cannot be located at all and the square boxes A and B do not overlap at all, $IoU = 0$. If one locates only a part, the square boxes A and B overlap, and $IoU \in (0, 1)$. Usually, if $IoU \geq 0.5$, the localization is considered to be accurate. This standard can also be readjusted according to specific scenarios.

3.3.1.2 *mAP*

During object detection, if there are many objects in the input image, there may exist many boxes. In this case, some boxes may accurately locate an object, while some

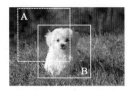

FIGURE 3.22

IoU.

other do not, or some boxes may even locate the wrong object. If a box catches the object, e.g., $IoU \geq 0.5$, and the classification is correct, the object detection is considered accurate. The accuracy of detecting all objects in the image test set is usually measured by mean Average Precision (mAP).

Taking the object detection of a picture as an example, the detection algorithm may generate $N = 1000$ boxes, among which there are $k = 50$ boxes containing object A (that is, the IoU is greater than a certain threshold). However, there exist $M = 100$ objects A in the picture. According to the notations in Table 3.5, in this example, the number of true positive cases is $TP = k = 50$, the total number of positive cases is $TP + FN = M = 100$, and the total number of all predicted results is $TP + FP = N = 1000$. The error of this detection can be measured by the following two metrics:

Recall: Among the selected N samples, recall is the proportion of the k true positive samples to the total M positive samples:

$$Recall = k/M = TP/(TP + FN). \qquad (3.8)$$

Precision: Among the selected N samples, precision is the proportion of k true positive samples:

$$Precision = k/N = TP/(TP + FP). \qquad (3.9)$$

Table 3.5 Classification results.

Predicted class	Ground-truth class	
	Positive	Negative
Positive	True positive (TP)	False positive (FP)
Negative	False negative (FN)	True negative (TN)

In the example above, the recall of object A is $Recall_A = 50/100 = 0.5$ and the precision is $Precision_A = 50/1000 = 0.05$. Obviously, by adding boxes, such as adding 1 million boxes, the recall can be improved, but the precision might be reduced.

To find a metric to measure the classification errors of different categories in the test set and to reflect both the recall and the precision of the model, the average precision (AP) will be used. Given an object detection task, the test set contains 100 images and spans 5 object categories, and 25 boxes are labeled as category A in advance. Assuming that the algorithm detects a total of 20 bounding boxes classified as A in 100 test images, the confidence values of each box and its label are shown in the left table of Table 3.6. The confidence is measured by IoU. If the label of the box is 0, there is no object in the box, and if the label is 1, this means that there is an object in the box.

The computation process of the AP is as follows:

First, sort all values according to the confidence, and get the left three columns in the right table of Table 3.6.

Second, in a descending order of confidence, we compute the precision and recall when there are only N ($N = 1, ...20$) positive examples. For example, when $N = 4$, it is considered that only four boxes (the 3rd, 7th, 11th, and 20th boxes) have object A. In this example, only the 3rd, 7th, and 20th boxes really have object A, so $Precision = 3/4$. Since there are 25 objects A in the test set, $Recall = 3/25$. Similarly, 20 precision and recall data can be calculated, as shown in the fourth and fifth columns in the right table of Table 3.6. The precision–recall curve is plotted in Fig. 3.23.

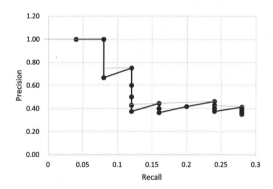

FIGURE 3.23

Precision-recall curve.

Third, according to the algorithm of AP in the PASCAL Visual Object Classes Challenge 2012 (VOC2012) [82], for each recall r, we calculate the maximum precision based on any recall $\tilde{r} \geq r$ to map the recall r, as shown in the rightmost column in Table 3.6.

Then, the area of the updated precision–recall curve is calculated as the AP. In this example, the AP of category A is

$$AP_A = (1 + 1 + (3/4) + (6/13) + (6/13) + (6/13) + (7/17)) \times (1/25) = 0.1819.$$
(3.10)

Finally, by averaging the AP for C categories in the image test set, mAP is calculated as $mAP = (\sum_{c=1}^{C} AP_c)/C$.

Table 3.6 Classification example: classification result (left) and the sorted result (right).

Number	Confidence	Label
1	0.35	0
2	0.15	0
3	0.92	1
4	0.03	0
5	0.24	1
6	0.10	0
7	0.78	1
8	0.01	0
9	0.47	0
10	0.09	1
11	0.69	0
12	0.43	0
13	0.26	0
14	0.35	1
15	0.11	0
16	0.07	0
17	0.45	0
18	0.16	1
19	0.32	0
20	0.52	1

Number	Confidence	Label	Recall (r)	Precision (p)	$\max p(\tilde{r}),$ $\forall \tilde{r} \geq r$
3	0.92	1	1/25	1	1
7	0.78	1	2/25	1	1
11	0.69	0		2/3	
20	0.52	1	3/25	3/4	3/4
9	0.47	0		3/5	
17	0.45	0		3/6	
12	0.43	0		3/7	
1	0.35	0		3/8	
14	0.35	1	4/25	4/9	6/13
19	0.32	0		4/10	
13	0.26	0		4/11	
5	0.24	1	5/25	5/12	
18	0.16	1	6/25	6/13	
2	0.15	0		6/14	
15	0.11	0		6/15	
6	0.10	0		6/16	
10	0.09	1	7/25	7/17	7/17
16	0.07	0		7/18	
4	0.03	0		7/19	
8	0.01	0		7/20	

3.3.2 R-CNN series

Regions with CNN features (R-CNN) series algorithms are two-stage algorithms and have brought great improvement over previous object detection algorithms. The main idea of the R-CNN series is to replace the traditional image processing technology with neural networks and reuse as many as possible to reduce the computation. The first algorithm in this series is R-CNN, which evolved into Fast R-CNN and later Faster R-CNN. Currently, Faster R-CNN is one of the most accurate image object detection algorithms.

Table 3.7 summarizes the main features and performance of the three algorithms. The R-CNN algorithm [79] combines Region Proposal extraction and CNN feature extraction and uses support vector machine (SVM) classification and bounding box regression (bbox regression). On the VOC2012 dataset, R-CNN achieves a mAP of 53.3%. The Fast R-CNN algorithm [83] proposes region of interest (ROI) pooling and softmax classification, which increases the mAP to 65.7% and speeds up the detection 25-fold compared with R-CNN. The Faster R-CNN algorithm [84] uses a region proposal network (RPN) to generate region proposals, further improving the mAP to 67.0% and speeding up the detection 10-fold compared to Fast R-CNN.

3.3.2.1 R-CNN

The R-CNN algorithm is the basis of the R-CNN series, with a complicated processing flow. As shown in Fig. 3.24, R-CNN includes four steps:

Table 3.7 R-CNN series.[9]

Network	Main features	mAP (VOC2012)	Single frame detection time (s)
R-CNN [79]	Combining region proposals with CNN feature extraction, SVM classification, bbox regression	53.3%	50
Fast R-CNN [83]	ROI pooling, softmax classification	65.7%	2
Faster R-CNN [84]	Using RPN to generate region proposals	67.0%	0.2

(1) Region proposals: Extract about 2000 region proposals from the original picture through selective search.

(2) Feature extraction: Warp all region proposals to a fixed size and use AlexNet (five convolutional layers and two fully connected layers) to extract a 4096-dimensional feature for each region proposal. Other CNNs can also be used, such as ResNet or VGG.

(3) Linear classification: Use category-specific SVMs to classify each region proposal.

(4) Bbox regression: Linear regression is used to correct the position and size of the bounding box. Class-specific bbox regressors (bbox regressors) are trained for each object category.

Based on the procedure above, the objects in Fig. 3.24 can be extracted with bounding boxes, including a person, a horse, a wall, etc.

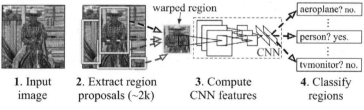

| 1. Input image | 2. Extract region proposals (~2k) | 3. Compute CNN features | 4. Classify regions |

FIGURE 3.24

R-CNN algorithm flow.[10]

Only the second step in the R-CNN algorithm is related to the neural network. The first step uses the selective search method to extract about 2000 region proposals. The third and fourth steps use SVM for classification and linear regression for fine-tuning boxes, respectively, and these methods are traditional machine learning and computer vision algorithms.

---

[9] The data in the table comes from the experimental results on the VOC dataset [79–84].

[10] ©2014 IEEE. Reprinted with permission from [79].

Region proposal extraction

Region proposal extraction usually uses a classic object detection algorithm, using a sliding window to determine all possible regions in turn. R-CNN uses selective search [85] to extract region proposals that are more likely to be objects in advance and then only extracts features on these region proposals, which can greatly reduce the computational overhead.

The region proposal algorithm based on selective search [85] uses a hierarchical grouping algorithm to generate object locations under different image conditions. The hierarchical grouping algorithm first uses an image segmentation approach to create initial regions, adds them to the region list, and calculates the similarity between all adjacent regions. Then, the algorithm groups the two neighbors with the highest similarity, calculates the similarities between the resulting region and adjacent regions, and adds the resulting region to the region list. This process is repeated until all regions are grouped into the whole image. At last, the algorithm extracts the location boxes from all regions in the region list and ranks them hierarchically. Note that the level of the region covering the entire image is 1.

To find region proposals under different conditions, the hierarchical grouping algorithm is performed under different segmentation thresholds, different color spaces, and different similarity measures. Then, regions are generated in each individual grouping strategy. The obtained boxes are sorted by priority, and then lower-ranked duplicates are removed. To avoid sorting by region size, the priority is calculated as the hierarchy multiplied by a random number. Finally, R-CNN takes about 2000 region proposals as the input of the subsequent CNN.

Classification and regression

The process of classification and regression is shown in Fig. 3.25. Region proposals are classified with class-specific linear SVM classifiers. The objects in these 2000 region proposals, including background, are categorized by 21 classifiers to determine the most likely category of each region, such as people, cars, horses, etc. Based on these results, nonmaximum suppression (NMS) is used to remove redundant boxes. For example, the same object may belong to different boxes, and thus redundant boxes need to be removed, leaving one box for this object. Finally, bbox regression is conducted to fine-tune the box localization. The to-be-calibrated box goes through a linear regression to precisely locate the object and finally improves the mAP of object detection.

One of the most important steps in the above process is NMS. In the object detection process, about 2000 region proposals are formed. For the same object position, such as the car in Fig. 3.25, there may be multiple bounding boxes, and these boxes overlap. It is necessary to use NMS to find a better bounding box and remove redundant ones. Each category needs to be processed with NMS once, in order to get the output list of the final boxes.[11]

For each category, the process of NMS includes:

---

[11] In the NMS processing process, there may exist many complicated scenarios. For example, for two people standing back and forth, the overlap of these two different objects is high. The traditional NMS used

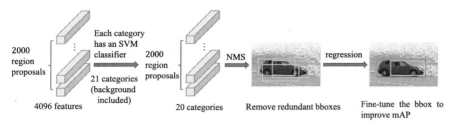

FIGURE 3.25

Classification and regression in R-CNN [79].

(1) sorting the bboxes according to the detection score as a candidate list;
(2) adding the bbox b_m with the highest score to the final output list and delete it from the candidate list;
(3) calculating the IoU between b_m and other candidate boxes b_i, and if IoU is greater than the threshold, delete b_i from the candidate list;
(4) repeating the above steps until the candidate list is empty.

R-CNN has several limitations:

(1) Repeated computation. The 2000 region proposals all need to be processed by CNN, which is computationally intensive, and there would exist redundant computation. For example, the car in Fig. 3.25 has three boxes. All three boxes need to be processed by CNN for feature extraction. However, over 80% of the three boxes is overlapping, which leads to redundant computational overhead.
(2) SVM classification. When there is sufficient labeled data, CNN is better than SVM for image classification.
(3) Multistep training. In one training, region proposal extraction, feature extraction, classification, and regression need to be trained individually. Thus, there are a lot of intermediate data that need to be stored separately during the process. From the perspective of computer architecture, data needs to be repeatedly written to memory and then read back from the memory, which is costly.
(4) Low detection speed. Repeated computation and multistep training may lead to slow R-CNN detection. It may take 13 seconds to process one image on a K40 GPU, and it may take 53 seconds on a CPU [79]. This makes R-CNN far from real-time processing, i.e., 25 frames per second (fps), in video analysis applications.

3.3.2.2 Fast R-CNN

In order to improve the performance of image object detection, Ross Girshick proposed Fast R-CNN [83], which not only improves the processing speed, but also im-

---

by the original R-CNN may lose the box of the person standing behind, but the soft NMS algorithm [86] can retain the boxes of both people.

proves the detection precision. The framework of Fast R-CNN is shown in Fig. 3.26. The main process of Fast R-CNN is described below.

First, Fast R-CNN uses the same region proposal algorithm in R-CNN to extract about 2000 region proposals from the original image.

Second, Fast R-CNN feeds the original image to a CNN to get convolutional feature maps. Unlike R-CNN, which performs CNN 2000 times, Fast R-CNN only needs to do this once.

ROI pooling is proposed in Fast R-CNN. According to the mapping, corresponding feature maps inside region proposals are extracted from the convolutional feature maps and converted into small feature maps with a fixed size by max pooling, as the fully connected layer requires a fixed input size. Since Fast R-CNN only performs the CNN processing once, it greatly reduces computational overhead and improves the processing speed.

Then, these feature maps are sent to the fully connected layer and converted into an ROI feature vector.

Finally, after the fully connected layer, the softmax classifier is used for classification, a bbox regressor is used to correct the position and size of the bounding box, and NMS is performed for each category to remove redundant boxes.

The essential change of Fast R-CNN is to run a CNN on the whole input image once, instead of running a CNN on the 2000 region proposals individually like R-CNN.

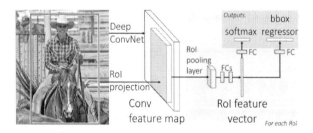

FIGURE 3.26

Fast R-CNN framework.[12]

ROI corresponds to the extracted region proposals. ROI pooling can convert the convolutional feature maps on different ROIs into a set of fixed-size feature maps, such as 7×7. On the one hand, it can reuse feature maps extracted by the convolutional layer to improve the processing speed. On the other hand, it can provide fixed-size feature maps to the fully connected layer. For each feature map channel, ROI pooling divides the input feature maps of size $h \times w$ into multiple blocks according to the output size $H \times W$, so the size of each block is about $h/H \times w/W$, and then takes the maximum value of each block as the output value.

The improvement of Fast R-CNN includes:

(1) Convolutions are performed on the entire image directly instead of performing convolutions on each region proposal separately, thus reducing a lot of redundant computation.

(2) ROI pooling is used to pool feature maps inside ROIs with various sizes into feature maps with a fixed size.

(3) The category-specific bbox regressors and the network are trained jointly.

(4) The softmax layer is used to replace the SVM classifier, thereby merging many small neural networks in R-CNN into one large neural network.

However, Fast R-CNN still uses many traditional computer vision technologies. In particular, the extraction of region proposals uses selective search and consumes most of the object detection time. On a K40 GPU, Fast R-CNN based on VGG16 takes 3.2 seconds [84] to extract the region proposals, while other parts take only 0.32 seconds in total. Therefore, after 2000 CNNs become one large neural network, the extraction of region proposals becomes the bottleneck of Fast R-CNN.

3.3.2.3 Faster R-CNN

In order to solve the bottleneck of region proposal extraction in Fast R-CNN, Faster R-CNN [84] proposes a more efficient region proposal algorithm, RPN, which achieves region proposal extraction using neural networks, therefore further improving the performance of object detection.

Faster R-CNN combines RPN and Fast R-CNN, as shown in Fig. 3.27(a), including the following steps:

(1) The input image passes through a multilayer CNN, such as ZF [56] and VGG16. Feature maps are extracted and fed into RPN and ROI pooling in Fast R-CNN. The shared feature maps of RPN and Fast R-CNN can greatly reduce computational overhead.

(2) RPN processes the feature maps to generate region proposals, uses softmax to determine whether the region proposals are foreground or background (i.e., the cls layer in Fig. 3.27(a)), and selects the foreground region proposals. RPN uses the bbox regressor to adjust the position and size of the bbox (i.e., the reg layer in Fig. 3.27(a)) to find the region proposals.

(3) The ROI pooling layer, like Fast R-CNN, pools the corresponding region proposals on the feature maps at different sizes into maps of the same size.

(4) Like Fast R-CNN, a softmax classifier is used to determine the category, and a bbox regressor is used to correct the position and size of the bounding box.

The core of Faster R-CNN is RPN. The input of RPN is feature maps, and the output is a set of region proposals, including the probability scores that each region proposal belongs to the foreground and background and the coordinates, without any limits of region proposals. RPN adopts an anchor mechanism, which can directly select the features of the region proposal from the feature map. Compared to selective search, it greatly reduces the computational overhead. The whole process is integrated in one network, which is convenient for training and testing. The whole computation process of RPN is shown in Fig. 3.27(b):

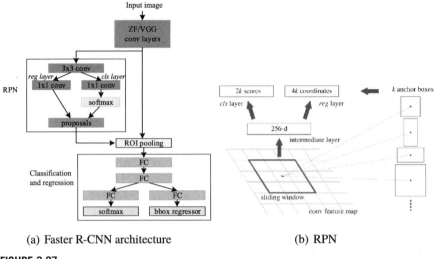

(a) Faster R-CNN architecture   (b) RPN

FIGURE 3.27

Faster R-CNN architecture, which omits the conversion before and after softmax in RPN, that is, transforming 2D feature maps into 1D vectors and transforming 1D vectors into 2D feature maps, respectively.[13]

(1) After a 3×3 convolutional layer, each convolution window outputs a 256-dimensional (ZF model) or 512-dimensional (VGG16) feature vector.
(2) The features go into two branches. One branch is to classify the anchor box into foreground or background. The convolutional features are passed through a 1×1 convolutional layer and a softmax layer to calculate the probability of a box belonging to foreground or background. The other branch is bbox regression to determine the position and size of the region proposals.
(3) After the two-branch processing, foreground region proposals are obtained, the redundant boxes are removed by NMS, and the region proposals are output.

Faster R-CNN does not limit the number of region proposals, e.g., 2000, but proposes anchor boxes (Fig. 3.28). Each position of the feature map has up to $k = 9$ possible anchor boxes, including three kinds of areas and aspect ratios. The three types of areas can be 128×128, 256×256, and 512×512. Each area is divided into three types of aspect ratios, which are $2 : 1$, $1 : 2$, and $1 : 1$, making a total of nine different anchor boxes. In RPN, each position of the feature map outputs $2k$ scores, which represent the probability that these k anchors of the position are foreground/background. Meanwhile, each position outputs $4k$ coordinates, including the center coordinates (x, y) and the width w and height h of the k anchor boxes, which are all computed by the neural network.

---

[13] Fig. 3.27(b): ©2017 IEEE. Reprinted with permission from [84].

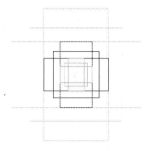

FIGURE 3.28

Anchor boxes in Faster R-CNN.

3.3.2.4 Summary

Several steps in R-CNN use nonneural network technologies. In the real world, the biological vision channel uses a set of biological neural networks to detect all objects. Therefore, in theory, all steps in object detection can be converted into neural networks. This goal is basically achieved through the gradual efforts of Fast R-CNN and Faster R-CNN. Fast R-CNN replaces the SVM classifier in R-CNN with a softmax layer, and Faster R-CNN replaces selective search with RPN. From R-CNN to Fast R-CNN, and then to Faster R-CNN, the four basic steps of object detection (i.e., region proposal extraction, feature extraction, classification, and bbox regression), most of which adopt traditional computer vision technologies, have gradually been unified to the deep learning framework, with performance significantly improved.

3.3.3 YOLO

The aforementioned R-CNN series are two-stage algorithms that first generate region proposals and then perform CNN classification. You Only Look Once (YOLO) pioneers the one-stage detection algorithm, unifying the object classification and localization within one neural network to achieve end-to-end object detection. As shown in Fig. 3.29, the main idea of YOLO is to frame the object detection problem as a single regression problem of extracting the bounding box and category probability, providing the object category and location simultaneously [80]. Therefore, the performance of YOLO is very promising. It can achieve 45 fps on some GPUs, which can meet the demand of real-time applications.

3.3.3.1 Unified detection

The YOLO model is demonstrated in Fig. 3.30. The process of unified detection is as follows.

First, separate the input image into an $S \times S$ grid. Each grid cell predicts B bounding boxes, and each bounding box is represented by five predicted values: x, y, w, h, and confidence, where (x, y) are the center coordinates of the bounding box and w and h are the width and height of the bounding box, respectively. These four values

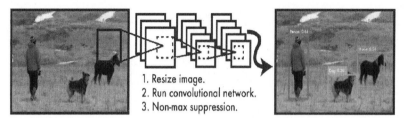

1. Resize image.
2. Run convolutional network.
3. Non-max suppression.

FIGURE 3.29

YOLO detecting system.[14]

are all normalized to the interval [0, 1] for training. The confidence considers the possibility of the existence of the object in the current bounding box $Pr(Object)$ and IoU of the predicted box and ground-truth box IoU_{pred}^{truth} together [80]:

$$confidence = Pr(Object) \times IoU_{pred}^{truth}, Pr(Object) = \begin{cases} 1, & \text{object in the cell,} \\ 0, & \text{object not in the cell.} \end{cases} \tag{3.11}$$

If there is no object in a box, confidence $= 0$; otherwise the confidence equals IoU_{pred}^{truth}. The confidence of each box can be calculated during training.

Then, with the confidence, each grid cell predicts C conditional class probabilities $Pr(Class_i|Object)$, $i = 0, 1, ...C$, where C is the number of object categories in the dataset. In the test, B bounding boxes belonging to a specific grid share the C conditional class probabilities. The class-specific confidence for each bounding box is [80]

$$\begin{aligned} confidence &= Pr(Class_i|Object) \times Pr(Object) \times IoU_{pred}^{truth} \\ &= Pr(Class_i) \times IoU_{pred}^{truth}. \end{aligned} \tag{3.12}$$

At last, the model outputs a tensor with dimension $S \times S \times (B \times 5 + C)$. YOLO uses the PASCAL VOC detection dataset to divide the image into a $7 \times 7 = 49$ grid, and each grid cell has two bounding boxes, namely $S = 7$, $B = 2$. Because there are 20 categories in the VOC dataset, $C = 20$. Thus the final prediction result is a tensor of $7 \times 7 \times 30$.

3.3.3.2 Network architecture

YOLO is inspired by GoogLeNet and consists of 24 convolutional layers and 2 subsequent fully connected layers, as shown in Fig. 3.31. YOLO does not use the Inception module, but instead uses an 1×1 convolutional layer followed by 3×3 convolutional layers. The output of YOLO is a tensor of $7 \times 7 \times 30$. YOLO uses Leaky ReLU as

---

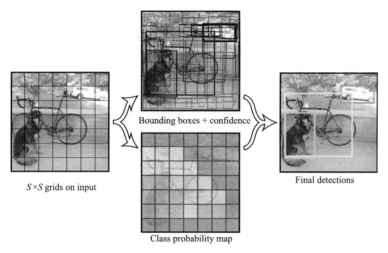

FIGURE 3.30

The YOLO model.[14]

the activation function:

$$f(x) = \begin{cases} x, & x > 0, \\ 0.1x, & \text{otherwise.} \end{cases} \qquad (3.13)$$

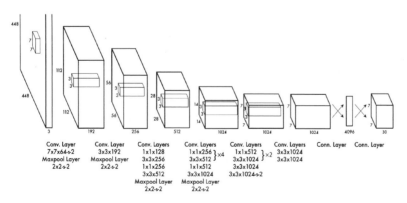

FIGURE 3.31

YOLO network architecture.[14]

3.3.3.3 Summary

YOLO uses a unified detection model. Compared to traditional object detection, YOLO has several significant advantages:

(1) The detection is very fast. YOLO frames the object detection as a single regression problem, directly processes the input image, outputs the bounding box coordinates and class probability at the same time, and only predicts 98 bounding boxes in each image. Therefore, the detection of YOLO is very fast, which can reach 45 fps on a Titan X GPU. The detection speed of Fast YOLO can reach 155 fps [80].

(2) Fewer background mistakes are made. In the past, object detection algorithms based on the sliding window or region proposal extraction can only use local information, thus mistaking the background for the object. While YOLO can see the global information in each grid cell during training and testing, it is not easy to misunderstand the image background as the object.

(3) The generalization is better. YOLO can learn the generalized representation of the object and can be transferred to other fields. For example, when a model is trained on natural images and tested on artworks, the performance of YOLO is much better than that of DPM, R-CNN, etc.

YOLO is fast, but its precision is not very attractive, mainly because of the following aspects:

(1) Each grid cell can only predict two bounding boxes and one object class. YOLO divides an image into 49 grid cells. If the centers of multiple objects are in the same cell, only one category of objects can be predicted in one cell, and other objects are discarded.

(2) The design of the loss function is too simple. The coordinates of the bounding box and classes are different, but YOLO uses both MSE of coordinates and classes as the loss function.

(3) YOLO directly predicts the coordinates of the bounding box, and the model is not easy to train.

To address the problems in YOLO, there have been many improved versions. YOLO v2 [87] draws on the idea of the anchor box in Faster R-CNN, improves the network architecture to form the Darknet-19 network, and replaces the fully connected layer in YOLO with a convolutional layer, which greatly reduces the number of parameters, thus improving the precision and speed of object detection. YOLO v3 [88] adopts a multiscale prediction and draws ideas from ResNet to form a 53-layer Darknet-53 network, using multilabel classifiers instead of softmax and other technologies to further improve the detection precision. Readers can refer to these papers for more details.

3.3.4 SSD

Single Shot Detector (SSD) [81] is another one-stage detection algorithm based on YOLO, borrowing the anchor box design from Faster R-CNN and using multiscale feature map detection. Object detection can be completed with one deep neural network, which greatly improves the detection precision while meeting the detection speed requirements. The network architecture of SSD is shown in Fig. 3.32.

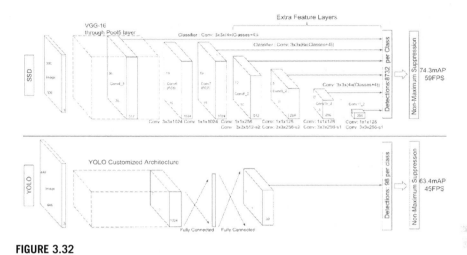

FIGURE 3.32

Comparison of the SSD architecture and the YOLO architecture.[15]

In a CNN, the feature map closer to the input layer is generally larger, while the sizes of further ones are gradually reduced due to stride 2 convolution or pooling layers. For example, if input image size is 224×224, the size of the feature map shrinks to 112×112, 56×56, 28×28, and 14×14 step by step. The size of the objects in the same-sized boxes in the feature maps of different sizes could be different. For example, in a 14×14 feature map, the object in the box could be very large, which is equivalent to locating a large object at a far distance.

The main idea of SSD is to extract default boxes, similar to anchor boxes, on feature maps of different sizes for detection to find the position and size of the most suitable boxes. Thus, one can detect relatively small objects on a relatively large feature map or large objects on a relatively small feature map, as shown in Fig. 3.33. The box on the 8×8 feature map is used to detect a relatively small object, a cat, and the box on the next layer of the 4×4 feature map is used to detect a larger object, a dog.

SSD uses m layers of feature maps for prediction. Each position on each feature map has six default boxes. The default boxes include two squares and four rectangles, with aspect ratios $a_r \in \{1, 2, 3, 1/2, 1/3\}$. The scale of the default box on the kth feature map is

$$s_k = s_{min} + \frac{s_{max} - s_{min}}{m - 1}(k - 1), \quad k \in [1, m], \qquad (3.14)$$

where $s_{min} = 0.2$ and $s_{max} = 0.9$ correspond to the scale of the lowest and highest layers, respectively. The width of each default box is $w_k^a = s_k \sqrt{a_r}$, and the height is

---

[15] Reprinted with permission from Springer Nature: Springer Nature, SSD: single shot multibox detector, by Wei Liu et al. [81] ©2016, https://doi.org/10.1007/978-3-319-46448-0_2.

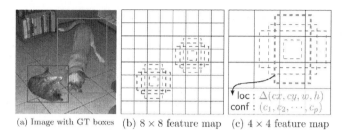

(a) Image with GT boxes   (b) 8×8 feature map   (c) 4×4 feature map

FIGURE 3.33

SSD framework.[16]

$h_k^a = s_k / \sqrt{a_r}$. For the case where the aspect ratio is 1, one more default box with scale $s_k' = \sqrt{s_k s_{k+1}}$ is added. Thus, each position on the feature map has six default boxes with different sizes and shapes.

The IoU is computed for the default boxes on the multilayer feature maps. IoU can help find the closest box to the real object, and thus better precision can be achieved during training. Fig. 3.34 shows an example of the default boxes on different layers.[17] On the low layer, the default box may cover a part of an object, and the IoU is small. On the high layer, the default box may cover a whole object, but the box is too large, and the IoU is also small. On the middle layer, the size and shape of the boxes are the most suitable, with the highest IoU. Through these optimization techniques, SSD achieves higher detection precision compared to YOLO, and it is easier to train.

 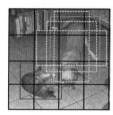 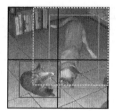

Low-layer feature map   Middle-layer feature map   High-layer feature map

FIGURE 3.34

Default boxes on different layers. The blue (dark gray in print version) boxes and red (light gray in print version) boxes are the ground-truth boxes of cat and dog, respectively.

3.3.5 Summary

Object detection algorithms are roughly divided into one-stage and two-stage algorithms. Two-stage algorithms were proposed earlier, including R-CNN, Fast R-CNN,

---

[16] Reprinted with permission from Springer Nature: Springer Nature, SSD: single shot multibox detector, by Wei Liu et al. [81] ©2016, https://doi.org/10.1007/978-3-319-46448-0_2.
[17] The background picture is from [81].

and Faster R-CNN. After Faster R-CNN, there are many optimization algorithms, including better feature networks, better RPN, more complete ROI classification, sample postprocessing, larger minibatch, etc., becoming today's famous R-FCN and Mask R-CNN algorithms. For the one-stage algorithms, YOLO is a classic model. After YOLO, SSD is another influential work. After SSD, there are works like R-SSD, DSSD, DSOD, and FSSD. Due to the limited space of this chapter, we are not going to introduce all models one by one. Readers can refer to related papers for further reading. In general, with both one-stage and two-stage models, mainstream object detection algorithms can now be completed by neural networks.

3.4 Sequence models: recurrent neural networks

Previous sections have introduced how to use CNNs to process image data. In the real world, sequence data is more common, including text, speech, and video. The size of the image data is fixed, but the length of the sequence data is dynamic. For example, as for the typical sequence data, text, a sentence may be very long and may have dozens of words, and one may not know how many words there are in this sentence before listening to this sentence. The length of a video may be 1000 frames, or it could be hundreds of thousands of frames. In addition, sequence data is data with temporal input in time series. The adjacent data are correlated and not independent from each other.

Taking text as an example, there is a correlation between words, and the meaning of the same word depends on context, tone, expression, and even multimodal information. There is correlation between adjacent data in the sequence data, which requires the neural network to have the ability to store information. CNNs for image recognition introduced earlier in this chapter do not need to store information. The model only needs fixed weights and would not change the internal state according to the previous input. Thus, researchers have proposed RNNs [13]. RNNs can effectively save historical information, so they are more suitable for processing sequence data.

3.4.1 RNNs

RNNs are mainly used for machine translation, image caption, video caption, visual question answering, etc. There are many examples of RNN applications on GitHub. Interested readers can visit "Awesome Recurrent Neural Network" [89] on GitHub for more information.

3.4.1.1 RNN architecture

RNNs use neurons with self-feedback, and thus they can process sequence data of any length. Fig. 3.35 shows an RNN. In this RNN, the input is x, the output is $\hat{y}$, and the hidden layer is h. The hidden layer h is a memory cell, which can store information, i.e., its output affects the next input. Fig. 3.35 is a schematic diagram after unfolding the RNN in time. Suppose the input at time t is $\boldsymbol{x}^{(t)}$, the output is $\hat{\boldsymbol{y}}^{(t)}$, and the hidden state is $\boldsymbol{h}^{(t)}$. Here $\boldsymbol{h}^{(t)}$ is not only related to the current input $\boldsymbol{x}^{(t)}$, but also related to the previous hidden state $\boldsymbol{h}^{(t-1)}$. At each time step, the output $\hat{\boldsymbol{y}}^{(t)}$ and the hidden state are updated as follows:

$$
\begin{aligned}
\boldsymbol{h}^{(t)} &= f(\boldsymbol{W}\boldsymbol{h}^{(t-1)} + \boldsymbol{U}\boldsymbol{x}^{(t)} + \boldsymbol{b}), \\
\boldsymbol{o}^{(t)} &= \boldsymbol{V}\boldsymbol{h}^{(t)} + \boldsymbol{c}, \\
\hat{\boldsymbol{y}}^{(t)} &= softmax(\boldsymbol{o}^{(t)}),
\end{aligned}
\tag{3.15}
$$

where $\boldsymbol{b}$ and $\boldsymbol{c}$ are biases and $\boldsymbol{U}$, $\boldsymbol{V}$, and $\boldsymbol{W}$ are weight matrices of input–hidden layer, hidden–output layer, and hidden–hidden layer, respectively. At different times, the weight matrices $\boldsymbol{U}$, $\boldsymbol{V}$, and $\boldsymbol{W}$ are the same; $f(x)$ is a nonlinear activation function, usually a tanh or ReLU function. Without loss of generality, the following uses $f(x) = tanh(x)$ as an example with only one hidden layer.

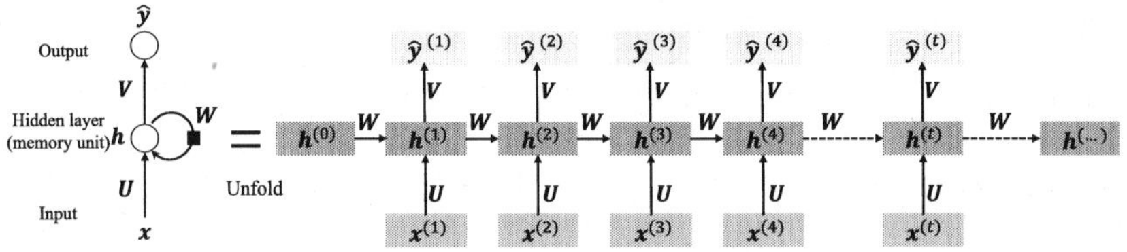

FIGURE 3.35

RNN (left) and time-unfolded RNN (right).

Sequence information can be modeled with such RNN. Neighbor data ($\boldsymbol{x}^{(t)}$, $\boldsymbol{x}^{(t+1)}$) in the sequence are not independent. For example, in text, the next word is related to the previous word and they affect each other. The recurrent characteristics of RNNs are reflected in repeating the same operation on each input, and these same operations can be repeated recurrently. The parameters $\boldsymbol{W}$ and $\boldsymbol{U}$ are identical at each time. The RNN has memory. The hidden layer $\boldsymbol{h}^{(t)}$ captures all the information before time t. In theory, $\boldsymbol{h}^{(2)}$ may contain part of the information of $\boldsymbol{x}^{(2)}$ and $\boldsymbol{x}^{(1)}$; $\boldsymbol{h}^{(t)}$ may contain information of $\boldsymbol{x}^{(t)}, \boldsymbol{x}^{(t-1)}, \ldots, \boldsymbol{x}^{(1)}$. Therefore, in theory, $\boldsymbol{h}^{(t)}$ can contain all information before time t, and its memory can be infinitely long. In practice training, the memory of $\boldsymbol{h}^{(t)}$ is limited because of gradient explosion and so on.

Let us take a look at the Neural Turing Machine. A Neural Turing Machine [90] is an interesting work done by Google DeepMind. The improved version [91] was published in *Nature*. In the original concept of Turing Machine, there is an infinite tape inside the machine, and there is a tape head that can read and write a single cell at a time. The tape head can observe what the value is on the tape, move left or right according to the value on the tape, or modify the value in the current cell of the tape. In a sense, the tape head in the Turing Machine is the computer and program (i.e., hardware and software), and the tape is the memory. The Neural Turing Machine uses a neural network to replace the tape head in the original Turing Machine. The

Turing Machine is a universal machine model. If the tape head is designed, it can complete an arbitrary function, such as sorting, string copying, etc. In theory, if a neural network is trained to perform the functions of a tape head, the neural network can perform any computer function, including sorting and string copying. This is an essential work leading to general artificial intelligence. The tape head should consider that historical information such as left or right is related to other information on the tape. Therefore, RNN can be used as a tape head. DeepMind researchers found that a long-trained neural network for a tape head can finish string copy perfectly if the string length is less than 20. However, with longer strings, like 100 or 200, the neural network tape head is broken. This is because RNN and its improved version LSTM have a limited memory.

RNN is flexible in applications, supporting multiple input-output architectures, including one-to-many, many-to-one, and many-to-many. Fig. 3.36(a) shows a traditional neural network architecture without loops. Dark gray indicates input, light gray indicates output, and gray indicates hidden layers. Fig. 3.36(b) shows a one-to-many RNN architecture, the input is an image, and the output is a sequence. For example, image caption uses a paragraph to describe a given picture. Given an image input, the output is a continuous string. For example, the description of a given picture could be "a cat squatting next to a dog." Fig. 3.36(c) shows a many-to-one RNN architecture, the input is a sequence, and the output may be a word. For example, given a sequence, the neural network outputs "football game" after analysis. Fig. 3.36(d) and Fig. 3.36(e) show many-to-many RNN architectures, and the output and input are both sequences, such as machine translation that translates English into Chinese or Chinese into English or video caption that writes a news report for a long continuous sequence such as a football match: "In the 5th minute, Paul passes to Reno, Reno passes to Rambo, and Rambo shoots." The many-to-many architecture also supports synchronous sequence conversion. For example, video classification labels information for each frame of the video. The application of RNN is very flexible. Depending on training samples, the neural network can train one-to-many, many-to-one, or many-to-many architectures as requested.

3.4.1.2 Back-propagation of RNN

RNN is trained using a variant of back-propagation called back-propagation through time (BPTT) [92]. As shown in Fig. 3.37, the main idea is to unfold RNN in time and then conduct back-propagation. After completing the forward propagation, BPTT uses cross-entropy as the loss function and then computes the gradient descent. The loss function L is the sum of the loss function $L^{(t)}$ at each time:

$$L = \sum_{t=1}^{\tau} L^{(t)} = -\sum_{t=1}^{\tau} \boldsymbol{y}^{(t)} \ln \hat{\boldsymbol{y}}^{(t)}. \tag{3.16}$$

The derivative of the loss function to parameter $\boldsymbol{V}$ is

$$\frac{\partial L}{\partial \boldsymbol{V}} = \sum_t \frac{\partial L^{(t)}}{\partial \boldsymbol{V}} = \sum_t \frac{\partial L^{(t)}}{\partial \hat{\boldsymbol{y}}^{(t)}} \frac{\partial \hat{\boldsymbol{y}}^{(t)}}{\partial \boldsymbol{o}^{(t)}} \frac{\partial \boldsymbol{o}^{(t)}}{\partial \boldsymbol{V}} = \sum_t \frac{\partial L^{(t)}}{\partial \hat{\boldsymbol{y}}^{(t)}} \frac{\partial \hat{\boldsymbol{y}}^{(t)}}{\partial \boldsymbol{o}^{(t)}} \boldsymbol{h}^{(t)\top}. \tag{3.17}$$

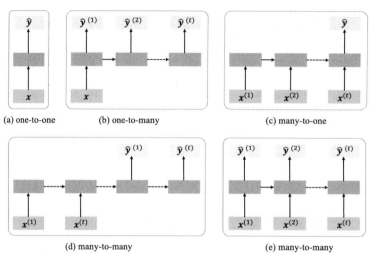

FIGURE 3.36

Types of RNN.

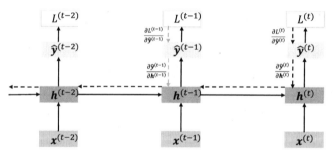

FIGURE 3.37

Back-propagation of RNN.

The derivative of the loss function to parameter W is

$$\frac{\partial L}{\partial W} = \sum_t \frac{\partial L^{(t)}}{\partial W} = \sum_t \frac{\partial L^{(t)}}{\partial \hat{y}^{(t)}} \frac{\partial \hat{y}^{(t)}}{\partial o^{(t)}} \frac{\partial o^{(t)}}{\partial h^{(t)}} \frac{\partial h^{(t)}}{\partial W}. \tag{3.18}$$

According to formula (3.15) and the chain rule of partial derivative, we have

$$\frac{\partial L}{\partial W} = \sum_t \sum_{k=1}^t \frac{\partial L^{(t)}}{\partial \hat{y}^{(t)}} \frac{\partial \hat{y}^{(t)}}{\partial o^{(t)}} \frac{\partial o^{(t)}}{\partial h^{(t)}} \frac{\partial h^{(t)}}{\partial h^{(k)}} \frac{\partial h^{(k)}}{\partial W}, \tag{3.19}$$

$$\frac{\partial \boldsymbol{h}^{(t)}}{\partial \boldsymbol{h}^{(k)}} = \prod_{i=k+1}^{t} \frac{\partial \boldsymbol{h}^{(i)}}{\partial \boldsymbol{h}^{(i-1)}} = \prod_{i=k+1}^{t} \boldsymbol{W}^{\top} diag(1 - (\boldsymbol{h}^{(i)})^2), \qquad (3.20)$$

where $diag(1 - (\boldsymbol{h}^{(i)})^2)$ is a diagonal matrix containing elements $1 - (\boldsymbol{h}_j^{(i)})^2$. The chain process of partial derivative is shown in Fig. 3.37.

Therefore,

$$\frac{\partial L}{\partial \boldsymbol{W}} = \sum_{t} \sum_{k=1}^{t} \frac{\partial L^{(t)}}{\partial \hat{\boldsymbol{y}}^{(t)}} \frac{\partial \hat{\boldsymbol{y}}^{(t)}}{\partial \boldsymbol{o}^{(t)}} \frac{\partial \boldsymbol{o}^{(t)}}{\partial \boldsymbol{h}^{(t)}} \left(\prod_{i=k+1}^{t} \boldsymbol{W}^{\top} diag\left(1 - (\boldsymbol{h}^{(i)})^2\right) \right) \frac{\partial \boldsymbol{h}^{(k)}}{\partial \boldsymbol{W}}. \quad (3.21)$$

Similarly, the partial derivative of the loss function with respect to parameter $\boldsymbol{U}$ is

$$\frac{\partial L}{\partial \boldsymbol{U}} = \sum_{t} \sum_{k=1}^{t} \frac{\partial L^{(t)}}{\partial \hat{\boldsymbol{y}}^{(t)}} \frac{\partial \hat{\boldsymbol{y}}^{(t)}}{\partial \boldsymbol{o}^{(t)}} \frac{\partial \boldsymbol{o}^{(t)}}{\partial \boldsymbol{h}^{(t)}} \left(\prod_{i=k+1}^{t} \boldsymbol{W}^{\top} diag\left(1 - (\boldsymbol{h}^{(i)})^2\right) \right) \frac{\partial \boldsymbol{h}^{(k)}}{\partial \boldsymbol{U}}. \quad (3.22)$$

When $t \gg k$, $\| \prod_{i=k+1}^{t} \boldsymbol{W}^{\top} diag\left(1 - (\boldsymbol{h}^{(i)})^2\right) \|_2$ is easy to transfer a large gradient to a larger one at the next time, and gradually larger along with time. That is, the positive feedback becomes larger and larger, until infinity, resulting in gradient explosion. Another possible result is that the gradient at the next time is small and keeps getting smaller until 0, resulting in gradient vanishing. Since RNNs are prone to gradient vanishing or explosion, RNNs can only learn a short-term dependency, such as dependencies within several recent time steps.

The obvious gradient vanishing or explosion phenomenon in RNNs is mainly caused by the recurrent architecture. A general neural network has many layers, and the weight matrix of each layer is different. But the weight matrix of each layer in the RNN is the same. This leads to a sharp monotonic increase or decrease in the absolute value of the gradient. The following is an example where RNN cannot handle long-term dependencies due to gradient vanishing.

Consider a language model that tries to predict the next word based on previous words. If one wants to predict the last word in "The birds are flying in the _____," one knows that the next word is "sky" without many contexts. The interval between the relevant information ("birds" and "flying") and the predicted position is relatively small. In this case, RNN can learn to use the previous information to predict the word "sky." However, if one wants to predict the last word in "I grew up in Italy. I speak fluent _____," he/she needs to use the preceding text that contains "Italy." Related information ("Italy") could be very far from the predicted position. With this long interval, the gradient of RNN vanishes and cannot find the dependency before or after, thus making a wrong decision.

In order to solve the gradient explosion problem, Pascanu et al. proposed a gradient truncation method [93]. When the gradient $\hat{g} = \frac{\partial L}{\partial \boldsymbol{W}}$ is greater than a predefined threshold, the model truncates at $threshold$ to get $\hat{g} = \frac{threshold}{\|\hat{g}\|} \hat{g}$. In order to solve the gradient vanishing problem, the popular LSTM [61] or gated recurrent unit (GRU) [94] are better choices.

3.4.2 LSTM

LSTM helps the RNN remember the long-term dependencies. LSTM [61] was first proposed in 1997. Through 20 years of development, it has become the most commonly used tool for the processing of temporal sequential information.

The core idea of LSTM is that information from a long time ago may be important and needs to be preserved, but the memory of the neural network is limited. Thus, a way must be found to remember important things in the past and drop the newly learned unimportant information. Therefore, LSTM determines whether new information is important. If it is important, it should enter long-term memory and be kept for a long time. Otherwise, it belongs to short-term memory and should soon be dropped.

To achieve this goal, the LSTM network designs an LSTM cell to replace the hidden-layer cell in RNN. Fig. 3.38 shows the architecture of the LSTM cell unfolded in time. Compared to RNN, the input and output of each LSTM cell remain unchanged, but state and multiple gates are added to control the information transmission, in which the most important is cell state $c^{(t)}$; $c^{(t)}$ is composed of the previous state and current input. The transmission of a previous state and current input is controlled by the forget gate and input gate, respectively. In some cases, if all forget gates are 0, the previous state is ignored, while if all the input gates are 0, the state calculated by the current input is ignored.

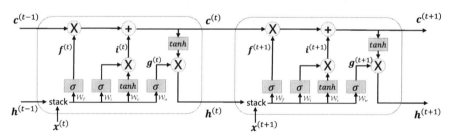

FIGURE 3.38

Time-unfolded LSTM cell.

There are three gates in LSTM, namely, forget gate, input gate, and output gate. The forget gate indicates how much content of the previous state needs to record; the value of the forget gate is limited between 0 and 1 through the sigmoid function. The forget gate $f^{(t)}$ at time step t is

$$f^{(t)} = \sigma \left(U^f x^{(t)} + W^f h^{(t-1)} + b^f \right) = \sigma \left(\mathcal{W}_f \begin{pmatrix} h^{(t-1)} \\ x^{(t)} \end{pmatrix} + b^f \right), \qquad (3.23)$$

where $x^{(t)}$ is the input at the current time step, $h^{(t)}$ is the current hidden state, U^f, W^f, and b^f represent the input weight matrix, recurrent weight matrix, and the bias of the forget gate, respectively, and $\mathcal{W}_f$ is defined by W^f and U^f.

The input gate is used to indicate how much input information is written to the current state. The computation is similar to the forget gate, with its value range limited between 0 and 1. The input gate $i^{(t)}$ at time step t is

$$i^{(t)} = \sigma \left(U^i x^{(t)} + W^i h^{(t-1)} + b^i \right) = \sigma \left(\mathcal{W}_i \begin{pmatrix} h^{(t-1)} \\ x^{(t)} \end{pmatrix} + b^i \right), \qquad (3.24)$$

where U^i, W^i, and b^i represent the input weight matrix, recurrent weight matrix, and the bias of the input gate, respectively. The computation of state $\tilde{c}^{(t)}$ is the same as the hidden state in RNN:

$$\tilde{c}^{(t)} = tanh \left(U x^{(t)} + W h^{(t-1)} + b \right) = tanh \left(\mathcal{W}_c \begin{pmatrix} h^{(t-1)} \\ x^{(t)} \end{pmatrix} + b \right). \qquad (3.25)$$

The internal state of the LSTM cell is updated as follows:

$$c^{(t)} = f^{(t)} c^{(t-1)} + i^{(t)} \tilde{c}^{(t)}. \qquad (3.26)$$

The output gate can control the output of the current cell state. The output gate $g^{(t)}$ at time step t is

$$g^{(t)} = \sigma \left(U^o x^{(t)} + W^o h^{(t-1)} + b^o \right) = \sigma \left(\mathcal{W}_o \begin{pmatrix} h^{(t-1)} \\ x^{(t)} \end{pmatrix} + b^o \right), \qquad (3.27)$$

where U^o, W^o, and b^o represent the input weight matrix, recurrent weight matrix, and the bias of the output gate, respectively. The output of the LSTM cell is

$$h^{(t)} = g^{(t)} tanh(c^{(t)}). \qquad (3.28)$$

There are many variant models of LSTM. One of the most popular LSTM variants is to add a peephole connection between cell states and gate units [95]. The value of the gate unit does not only depend on the previous hidden state $h^{(t-1)}$ and the current input $x^{(t)}$, but also on the previous cell state $c^{(t-1)}$, as shown in Fig. 3.39. The forget gate, input gate, and output gate are updated as follows:

$$f^{(t)} = \sigma \left(U^f x^{(t)} + W^f h^{(t-1)} + M^f c^{(t-1)} + b^f \right),$$
$$i^{(t)} = \sigma \left(U^i x^{(t)} + W^i h^{(t-1)} + M^i c^{(t-1)} + b^i \right), \qquad (3.29)$$
$$g^{(t)} = \sigma \left(U^o x^{(t)} + W^o h^{(t-1)} + M^o c^{(t-1)} + b^o \right),$$

where M^f, M^i, and M^o represent the weight matrix of the cell state of the forget gate, input gate, and output gate, respectively.

Some LSTM variants couple the forget gate and input gate [96]. It no longer uses two gates to determine the forgotten and new information separately, but combines them as $i^{(t)} = 1 - f^{(t)}$, and the internal state is updated as $c^{(t)} = \tilde{f}^{(t)} c^{(t-1)} + (1 -$

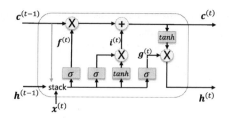

FIGURE 3.39

Adding a peephole connection in LSTM.

$f^{(t)})\tilde{c}^{(t)}$. As illustrated in Fig. 3.40, this LSTM variant only adds new information when forgetting the old state.

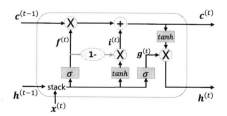

FIGURE 3.40

Coupling the forget gate and input gate in LSTM.

3.4.3 GRU

GRU [94], which is also a variant of LSTM, was proposed in 2014. On the basis of LSTM, GRU merges the cell state and the hidden state, combines the input gate and forget gate into an update gate, removes the output gate, and adds a reset gate, as shown in Fig. 3.41.

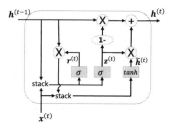

FIGURE 3.41

GRU unit architecture.

The update gate determines how much historical and present information is used to update the current hidden state. The update gate at time step t is

$$z^{(t)} = \sigma\left(U^z x^{(t)} + W^z h^{(t-1)} + b^z\right),\tag{3.30}$$

where b^z, U^z, and W^z represent the bias, input weight matrix, and recurrent weight matrix of the update gate, respectively.

The reset gate determines how much historical information is kept. The reset gate at time step t is

$$r^{(t)} = \sigma \left(U^r x^{(t)} + W^r h^{(t-1)} + b^r \right), \tag{3.31}$$

where b^r, U^r, and W^r represent the bias, input weight matrix, and recurrent weight matrix of the reset gate, respectively.

The hidden state is updated as

$$h^{(t)} = (1 - z^{(t)}) h^{(t-1)} + z^{(t)} \tilde{h}^{(t)}, \tag{3.32}$$

where

$$\tilde{h}^{(t)} = tanh \left(U x^{(t)} + W(r^{(t)} h^{(t-1)}) + b \right). \tag{3.33}$$

There are many LSTM variants. The main underlying idea is to add a variety of gates to choose whether to retain the past knowledge and whether to update the new information into the memory. If the current input is updated into the memory, it inevitably dilutes the existing knowledge. If the past knowledge is supposed to be kept, such as information 1000 words ago, it is recorded in the hidden state.

3.4.4 Summary

RNN can process sequences of any length by using neurons with self-feedback loops. However, there are problems such as gradient vanishing and explosion in RNN training. Especially, the gradient vanishing could cause RNN to lose long-term dependency. The LSTM model can remember long-term dependencies by adding cell states and gate units in the RNN cell. When the gate is opened or closed, the relevant parameters can be obtained through training. GRU is a variant of LSTM. LSTM has hidden states and cell states, as well as forget gates, output gates, and input gates. The representation ability of LSTM is stronger, but it has more parameters, which makes it harder to train. GRU is simpler, with only hidden states, update gates, and reset gates. GRU has fewer parameters, and therefore they are faster to train. Whether LSTM or GRU is better than the other is not conclusive. In practice, they are chosen based on the application. In addition to GRU, there are many other variants of LSTM [96], all of which add some gates to or remove some gates from LSTM. The main idea behind LSTM-like models is to use gates to choose whether to keep past knowledge and whether to update new information into knowledge.

3.5 **Generative adversarial networks**

At present, the two most commonly used types of deep learning algorithms are CNNs for image processing and RNNs for sequence processing. The common feature of these neural networks is that they require a large number of training samples. For example, AlexNet requires tens of thousands of images for training. In order to obtain labeled training samples, a new business of data annotation has appeared.

In contrast to these network models, humans do not need so many samples to learn. Therefore, many researchers are trying to develop few-shot learning techniques, hoping to train an accurate neural network with a few samples. Among these technologies, the most notable technique is that of GANs [71].

Many researchers believe that GAN is the greatest achievement in the field of neural networks since the turn of the millennium. Its core idea is to make the generative network and the discriminative network learn against each other and improve together. In this way, the generative network can generate fake samples, and the discriminative network can accurately determine which samples are real or generated.[18]

3.5.1 GAN modeling

GAN consists of two networks, the generative network (i.e., generator) and the discriminative network (i.e., discriminator). The generator is analogous to the counterfeiter, who finds out the statistical distribution within the observed data and generates samples that look as authentic as possible. The discriminator is analogous to the police, who determine whether a sample comes from a real sample set or a generated sample set. The relationship between the generator and the discriminator is similar to the relationship between the two sides of the debate, through which both sides improve.

For example, the generator first looks at a photo of a real cat and then tries to generate a lot of cat photos. The discriminator tries to determine whether a given photo is fake or real. If the discriminator identifies the fake photo, the generator must improve its strategy to deceive the discriminator. On the contrary, if the discriminator makes a false judgment, the ability of the discriminator needs to be improved. Through a constant confrontation between generation and discrimination, the final generator will generate a photo that fakes a real cat, and the discriminator would be perfect to tell the difference between the real photo and the fake one. GANs have many interesting novel applications, such as face swap videos.

3.5.2 Training in GAN

3.5.2.1 The training process

The training process of GANs is shown in Fig. 3.42. The discriminator D and the generator G are iteratively trained in an alternating way.

The discriminator is trained with a conventional method. The training data includes a minibatch of real samples x and a minibatch of random noise z. The label

---

[18] We believe that GAN has inherited the dialectic of Socrates in ancient Greece, in a sense. Socrates' dialectic was to discover the truth by continuously exposing the contradiction between two people through dialog and debate.

of the real samples is 1, and the label of the fake samples generated by the generator with random noise is 0.

After training with these data, the discriminator trains the generator. When training a generator, it generates fake samples from the input random noise and then feeds them into the discriminator. The discriminator could be deceived. If deceived, the discriminator outputs 1; otherwise, it outputs 0. Next, by performing back-propagation, the parameters of the generator are updated, while the discriminator stays the same.

Then, the training continues to update the discriminator and the generator alternately. After many iterations, the generator is trained to produce realistic fake samples. For example, it can be used in image style transfer to generate a fake Van Gogh-style painting.

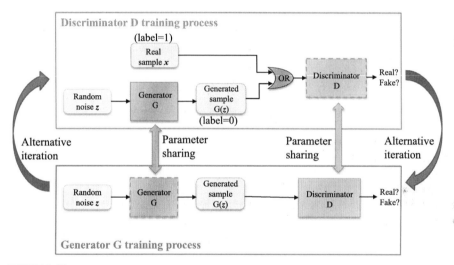

FIGURE 3.42

The training process of GAN.

3.5.2.2 Loss function

The goal of the training of the discriminator is that if the input is a real sample, the output is close to 1; otherwise, if the input is a fake sample, the output is close to 0. Therefore, the loss function of the discriminator D is

$$L^{(D)} = -\mathrm{E}_{x \sim p_{data}(x)}[\log(D(x))] - \mathrm{E}_{z \sim p_z(z)}[\log(1 - D(G(z)))], \qquad (3.34)$$

where $p_{data(x)}$ represents the distribution of real samples x, $p_z(z)$ represents the distribution of input noise z, $D(x)$ represents the probability that x comes from the real sample set judged by the discriminator, and $G(z)$ represents the sample generated by the generator with input z. $L^{(D)}$ is the cross-entropy loss function.

The goal of the training of the generator is to generate fake samples $G(z)$ as real as possible to deceive the discriminator to output 1. Therefore, the loss function of the generator G is

$$L^{(G)} = E_{z \sim p_z(z)}[\log(1 - D(G(z)))].   \qquad (3.35)$$

By minimizing $L^{(G)}$, the generator can deceive the discriminator to treat the generated fake samples as real samples.

Obviously, $L^{(G)}$ and $L^{(D)}$ are closely related. The overall loss function of GAN can be written as

$$V(D, G) = -L^{(D)} = E_{x \sim p_{data}(x)}[\log(D(x))] + E_{z \sim p_z(z)}[\log(1 - D(G(z)))].   \qquad (3.36)$$

The training of GAN is a MiniMax game problem. This is a zero-sum game, and the optimization process includes the maximization of the inner layer and the minimization of the outer layer of the loss function V:

$$\min_G \max_D V(D, G).   \qquad (3.37)$$

Ian Goodfellow et al. [71] proved that when the generator is fixed, the optimal discriminator is

$$D_G^*(x) = p_{data}(x)/(p_{data}(x) + p_g(x)),   \qquad (3.38)$$

where $p_g(x)$ represents the distribution of generated data x. When $p_g(x) = p_{data}(x)$, the generator is optimal.

3.5.2.3 Problems with GAN

In the MiniMax game of GAN, when the discriminator successfully determines with high confidence that the sample generated is fake, the gradient of the generator vanishes. This scenario may often be seen in the early stages of training. When the generator is weak, the generated fake samples are clearly different from the real samples, which can be easily identified by the discriminator with high confidence, so $\log(1 - D(G(z)))$ is saturated. In order to solve the gradient vanishing problem in the early training stage, Ian Goodfellow et al. [71] used the following loss function to train the generator:

$$L^{(G)} = -E_{z \sim p_z(z)}[\log(D(G(z)))].   \qquad (3.39)$$

By minimizing this loss function, the generator can maximize the probability of the discriminator being cheated. This technique can provide stronger gradients in the early stages of training.

However, the above technique may cause mode collapse [97]. Mode collapse means that the generator only generates samples of a few patterns, sometimes a specific pattern, thus lacking diversity. Martin Arjovsky et al. [98] proved that when Eq. (3.39) is used as the generator loss, the generator optimization problem becomes the problem of minimizing the Kullback–Leibler (KL) divergence between the generated and real distribution, while maximizing its Jensen–Shannon (JS) divergence. The two divergences contradict each other, leading to unstable gradients. Moreover, since the KL divergence is asymmetric, the cost of generating fake samples is much higher than the mode reduction. Therefore, the generator converges to samples with a few patterns, which can fool the discriminator with high confidence. At the same time, since the generator only generates samples of a few specific patterns, the discriminator is limited.

To solve the problem of mode collapse, Martin Arjovsky et al. [98] proposed Wasserstein GAN (WGAN). The idea of WGAN is to replace the loss function based on KL divergence and JS divergence with the loss function based on the Wasserstein distance:

$$\min_{G} \max_{D \in \mathcal{D}} E_{x \sim p_{data}(x)}[D(x)] - E_{z \sim p_z(z)}[D(G(z))], \tag{3.40}$$

where $\mathcal{D}$ is the set of 1-Lipschitz continuous functions and the discriminator D (called critic in paper [98]) can provide more reliable gradient information compared to traditional GAN. The loss function of WGAN approximates the Wasserstein distance between the real distribution and the generated distribution. Based on the optimized discriminator, the optimized generator can reduce the Wasserstein distance, that is, converge the generated distribution to the real distribution. Moreover, compared to KL divergence and JS divergence, the Wasserstein distance is differentiable almost everywhere. Therefore, WGAN effectively solves the problem of GAN mode collapse and unstable training.

3.5.3 The GAN framework

Since first proposed, GAN has received extensive attention from both academia and industry. There are already hundreds of GAN-related papers [99]. In the original GAN, both the discriminator and generator use fully connected neural networks. Later, for different application demands, many GAN variants appeared. These variants can be roughly divided into several categories [100]: convolutional GANs, conditional GANs (CGANs), GANs with inference models, adversarial autoencoders, etc.

Convolutional GAN extends the fully connected neural network in GAN to a CNN, thereby expanding the applicability of GAN, supporting image restoration, superresolution, image conversion, etc. Representative works include deep convolutional GAN (DCGAN) [101], LapGAN [102], ResGAN [103], SRGAN [104], CycleGAN [105], and other architectures.

CGAN adds class conditions to the GAN generator and discriminator to provide a better representation of multimodal data generation. Representative works include CGAN [106], InfoGAN [107], etc.

GANs with inference models add inverse mapping learning from real data to a noise vector in latent space, such as BiGAN [108], which can support unsupervised feature learning.

Adversarial autoencoders, such as VAE-GAN [109], can use a variational autoencoder (VAE) [110] to learn the deterministic mapping from the data space to the latent space. The VAE decoder maps the latent space back to the data space (known as the sample reconstruction) and combines the decoder and the GAN generator into one. The discriminator is used to decide the similarity between the original sample and the reconstructed sample, which can be used for signal/image reconstruction.

Due to space limitations, we only introduce DCGAN and CGAN in this book.

3.5.3.1 Deep convolutional GAN

DCGAN replaces the fully connected network in GAN with a CNN. DCGAN's discriminator and generator use strided convolutions and fractionally strided convolutions (sometimes called deconvolutions or transposed convolutions, respectively) to replace pooling layers and to do spatial downsampling and upsampling to support the mapping between high-dimensional data space and low-dimensional latent space. BN is used in both the generator and the discriminator to facilitate the training and to prevent the generator from mode collapse. The generator uses the tanh function as the activation function of the output layer and uses ReLU as the activation function of other layers to accelerate learning. The discriminator uses Leaky ReLU as the activation function, which is effective in application, especially when processing high-resolution images. Fig. 3.43 shows the generator architecture trained on the LSUN bedroom dataset.

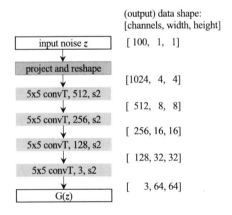

FIGURE 3.43

DCGAN generator architecture. convT denotes fractionally strided convolution.

3.5.3.2 Conditional GAN

The input of the original GAN generator is random noise, so the pattern of the output data is uncontrollable. By adding class conditions to the input, expected output can be obtained. For example, we input the array {0, 1, 2, 3}, hoping to output handwritten numbers. In the image style transfer, we input a picture of outer space, hoping to output a picture of outer space in Van Gogh style. In a gender swap, we input a picture of a female and expect the output to be a picture of a male with a similar appearance. Besides the input z, CGAN feeds auxiliary information y as additional input into the generator, such as class labels or data from other modalities. CGAN also feeds additional information y into the discriminator, besides the input x. The objective function of CGAN training becomes [106]

$$\min_{G} \max_{D} V(D, G) = E_{x \sim p_{data}(x)}[\log(D(x|y))] + E_{z \sim p_z(z)}[\log(1 - D(G(z|y)))].$$

(3.41)

The network architecture is illustrated in Fig. 3.44. The discriminator not only distinguishes the authenticity of the input sample but also makes sure that the input sample is consistent with the auxiliary information.

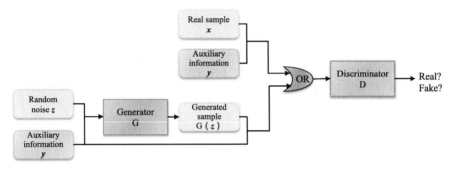

FIGURE 3.44

CGAN architecture [106].

Similar to CGAN, InfoGAN can also complete the image style transfer task. InfoGAN decomposes the input noise vector into two parts: incompressible noise z and latent code c. By maximizing the mutual information between the latent code c and the generator output $G(z, c)$, the latent code can be learned in an unsupervised manner. Latent code is used to represent salient structured semantic features of data distribution including location, lighting, and so on. The objective function of InfoGAN [107] becomes

$$\min_{G} \max_{D} V_I(D, G) - \lambda I(c; G(z, c)),$$

(3.42)

where $I(c; G(z, c))$ is the mutual information between c and $G(z, c)$. The architecture of InfoGAN is illustrated in Fig. 3.45. The auxiliary distribution network Q shares the convolutional layers of the discriminator and only adds one extra fully connected layer with limited overhead. InfoGAN not only requires that the generated image is indistinguishable from the real image but also can learn the conditional probability distribution $Q(c|x)$ from the generated image.

3.6 Driving example

The driving example in this section is to transfer a photo, such as a photo of outer space, into a photo of Van Gogh-style outer space. In later chapters and experiments

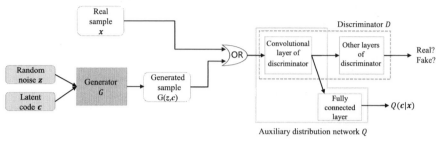

FIGURE 3.45

InfoGAN architecture.

of this book, we mainly introduce how to directly use CNN to complete image style transfer, as CNN is intuitive and simple. For sure, the aforementioned CGAN or InfoGAN can also do the job but in a complicated way. Readers who are interested may refer to related papers.

3.6.1 **CNN-based image style transfer**

Leon Gatys et al. [111] proposed a CNN-based approach to realize the image style transfer. The main idea is shown in Fig. 3.46. First, CNN inputs the content image p and the style image a, where the style image a is "Starry Night" painted by Van Gogh and the content image p is a photo of outer space. There are unique features in Van Gogh's paintings as well as the outer space image. The image style transfer needs to combine these two features together. In order to obtain the feature map, the content image and the style image are passed through CNN to generate their own feature maps to form the content features P and the style features A, respectively. Then, a random noise image x is fed into the CNN, and content features F and style features G are obtained. The loss function is then calculated using P, A, F, and G. Based on the loss function, the image x is updated to make content features F closer to P and make style features G closer to A. After several iterations, the content of the image x can be consistent with the content image, while the style is consistent with the style image.

Paper [111] uses 16 convolutional layers and 5 pooling layers in a pretrained VGG19 for the image style transfer. The image style transfer requires two loss functions: a content loss function and a style loss function. The content loss function is the Euclidean distance between the random noise image x and the content image p on the content feature [111]:

$$L_{content}(p, x, l) = \frac{1}{2} \sum_{i,j} (F_{ij}^l - P_{ij}^l)^2, \tag{3.43}$$

where P_{ij}^l represents the feature value at position j on the ith feature map in layer l of the content image p and F_{ij}^l represents the feature value at position j on the ith

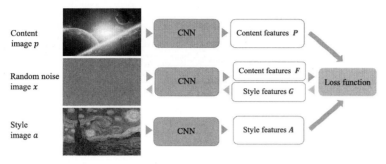

FIGURE 3.46

Image style transfer.

feature map in layer l of the generated image x. When matching content features on a higher network layer, the image content and texture of the artwork can be appropriately merged together without overretention of detailed pixel information. Thus, content features in layer conv4_2 are used to calculate the content loss. By minimizing the content loss function, the gap between the generated image and the content image can be narrowed. The partial derivative of content loss to F_{ij}^l is [111]

$$\frac{\partial L_{content}}{\partial F_{ij}^l} = \begin{cases} (F^l - P^l)_{ij}, & \text{if } F_{ij}^l > 0, \\ 0, & \text{if } F_{ij}^l < 0. \end{cases} \tag{3.44}$$

The style loss function uses features in layers conv1_1, conv2_1, conv3_1, conv4_1, and conv5_1 to calculate the style loss. First, the style feature of the image is calculated with the inner product of the ith and jth feature maps in layer l. The style feature of the generated image is

$$G_{ij}^l = \sum_k F_{ik}^l F_{jk}^l. \tag{3.45}$$

In the same way, the style feature A of the style image can be obtained. Second, the style loss in layer l is calculated as

$$E_l = \frac{1}{4N_l^2 M_l^2} \sum_{i,j} (G_{ij}^l - A_{ij}^l)^2, \tag{3.46}$$

where N_l is the number of feature maps in layer l and M_l is the size of feature maps in layer l. Finally, the style loss function is the weighted sum of each layer's style loss:

$$L_{style}(a, x) = \sum_l w_l E_l, \tag{3.47}$$

where w_l is the weighting factor, which can be user-defined. The partial derivative of E_l with respect to F_{ij}^l is [111]

$$\frac{\partial E_l}{\partial F_{ij}^l} = \begin{cases} \frac{1}{N_l^2 M_l^2}((F^l)^\top (G^l - A^l))_{ji}, & \text{if } F_{ij}^l > 0, \\ 0, & \text{if } F_{ij}^l < 0. \end{cases} \qquad (3.48)$$

The total loss function is defined as the weighted sum of the content loss function and the style loss function:

$$L_{total}(\boldsymbol{p}, \boldsymbol{a}, \boldsymbol{x}) = \alpha L_{content}(\boldsymbol{p}, \boldsymbol{x}) + \beta L_{style}(\boldsymbol{a}, \boldsymbol{x}), \qquad (3.49)$$

where α and β are the weight factors. As shown in Fig. 3.47, by calculating the partial derivative of the loss function to the input pixel $\frac{\partial L_{total}}{\partial \boldsymbol{x}}$, the gradient can be obtained. Then, back-propagation is performed to update the input pixel value. After a number of iterations, the generated image is obtained. For example, a random white noise image is fed into the network. Forward propagation is performed, loss is calculated with convolutional feature maps, and then the pixel values of the image are updated through back-propagation. Repeating this process, the loss could converge close to zero, and the generated image simultaneously matches both the content and style features.

The parameters α and β could affect the loss function, which eventually affects the training process. The larger the α/β ratio, the less stylized the generated image. In theory, if $\alpha = 1$, $\beta = 0$, the generated image is the same as the input content image. Conversely, if β is large and α is small, the generated image may look texturized.

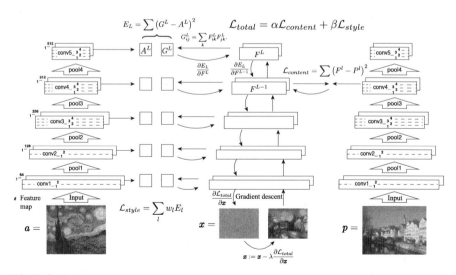

FIGURE 3.47

Image style transfer algorithm flow.[19]

3.6.2 **Real-time style transfer**

The aforementioned image style transfer process is a complicated training process requiring multiple iterations. It is difficult to achieve real-time transfer. The experiment in this book uses a real-time and fast image-style transfer method proposed in [112]. This method divides the image style transfer into two steps, the training process and the real-time transform process, as shown in Fig. 3.48. The purpose of the training process is to train an image transform network. Once the image transform network is trained, one only needs to perform the forward propagation of the image transform network once instead of doing heavy neural network training for each input image [111].

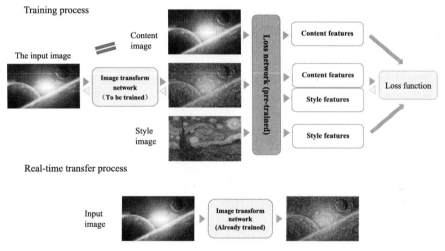

FIGURE 3.48

Real-time image style transfer.

The specific process of real-time image style transfer is shown in Fig. 3.49. The process includes two networks, the image transform network and the loss network. In the process of training the image transform network, the input image x is sent to the image transform network for processing, and a generated image $\hat{y}$ is output. Then, the generated image, style image y_s, and content image $y_c = x$ are fed separately into the loss network to extract features and the loss is calculated. The image transform network f_W is a deep residual network to facilitate training. Specifically, this deep residual network roughly follows the architecture design of DCGAN, replacing pooling layers with strided convolutions and fractionally strided convolutions. Except for the output layer, all nonresidual convolutional layers are followed by BN and ReLU. The output layer uses a scaled tanh function to limit the output pixel value to the range of [0, 255]. The first and last convolutional layers use 9×9 convolution kernels, and the other convolutional layers use 3×3 convolution kernels.

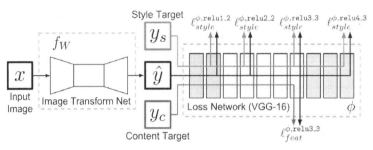

FIGURE 3.49

Real-time image style transfer algorithm flow.[20]

The loss network uses the VGG16 network pretrained on the ImageNet dataset. The perceptual loss function defined in the loss network is composed of feature reconstruction loss $L_{feature}$ and style reconstruction loss L_{style} [112] as

$$L = \mathrm{E}_{\boldsymbol{x}, \boldsymbol{y}_c, \boldsymbol{y}_s} \left[\lambda_1 L_{feature}(f_W(\boldsymbol{x}), \boldsymbol{y}_c) + \lambda_2 L_{style}(f_W(\boldsymbol{x}), \boldsymbol{y}_s) \right], \tag{3.50}$$

where λ_1 and λ_2 are weighting factors. Feature reconstruction loss is calculated as follows [112]:

$$L^j_{feature}(\hat{\boldsymbol{y}}, \boldsymbol{y}) = \frac{1}{C_j H_j W_j} \|\phi_j(\hat{\boldsymbol{y}}) - \phi_j(\boldsymbol{y})\|_2^2, \tag{3.51}$$

where C_j, H_j, and W_j represent the number of channels, height, and width of output feature maps in layer j, respectively; $\phi_j(\boldsymbol{y})$ is the feature map of layer j in the loss network. In practice, the feature reconstruction loss is computed at layer relu3_3 of the loss network. The style reconstruction loss at layer j is the squared Frobenius norm of the difference between the Gram matrices of the output image and the target image [112]:

$$L^j_{style}(\hat{\boldsymbol{y}}, \boldsymbol{y}) = \|G_j(\hat{\boldsymbol{y}}) - G_j(\boldsymbol{y})\|_F^2, \tag{3.52}$$

where the Gram matrix $G_j(\boldsymbol{x})$ is a $C_j \times C_j$ matrix and the matrix elements are [112]

$$G_j(\boldsymbol{x})_{c,c'} = \frac{1}{C_j H_j W_j} \sum_{h=1}^{H_j} \sum_{w=1}^{W_j} \phi_j(\boldsymbol{x})_{h,w,c} \phi(\boldsymbol{x})_{h,w,c'}. \tag{3.53}$$

The style reconstruction loss is the sum of the style reconstruction loss at layers relu1_2, relu2_2, relu3_3, and relu4_3.

---

[20] Reprinted with permission from Springer Nature: Springer Nature, Perceptual losses for real-time style transfer and super-resolution, by Justin Johnson et al. [112] ©2016, https://doi.org/10.1007/978-3-319-46475-6_43.

Compared to the work in [111], the real-time image style transfer algorithm [112] has a slightly poorer effect on generated images, but the speed is increased 200–1000-fold. Readers can visit GitHub [113] to find the reference code of the real-time image style transfer algorithm.

3.7 Summary

This chapter introduces the cutting-edge work on the development of deep learning algorithms, including the basic ideas of CNNs, image classification deep learning algorithms, image object detection deep learning algorithms, RNNs for sequence information processing, and the very popular GANs. Finally, we introduce the driving example of the image style transfer algorithms based on CNN. Readers can download codes from relevant websites to learn more about deep learning.

Exercises

3.1 Calculate the number of neurons and the number of trainable parameters in the three networks of AlexNet, VGG19, and ResNet152.

3.2 Calculate the number of multiplications and the number of additions required by the three networks in Exercise 3.1 to complete a forward process.

3.3 Briefly describe the relationship between error rate and IoU and mAP.

3.4 Briefly describe the relationships among convergence, training accuracy, and test accuracy.

3.5 Give the requirements for the amount of computation of SVM and AlexNet in solving ImageNet image classification problems, and describe the reasons briefly.

3.6 Briefly describe the differences between R-CNN, Fast R-CNN, and Faster R-CNN.

3.7 Briefly describe the main functions of the three gates in the LSTM cell, and write the calculation formula.

3.8 Briefly describe the training process of GAN.

3.9 Briefly describe the basic process of the image style transfer application.

*3.10 Train a multilayer perceptron network on the MNIST dataset. The scale and architecture of the network can be customized, and the model accuracy is required to be greater than 95%.

*3.11 Improve the standard back-propagation algorithm, increase the training speed, and calculate the acceleration ratio of the training improvement (in the case of convergence).

*3.12 Apply the new algorithm you designed in Exercise 3.11 to the ImageNet dataset. Has the accuracy obtained been affected? How big is the impact? Adjust your algorithm to ensure accuracy.

Fundamentals of programming frameworks

4

With more and more deep learning applications appearing in image recognition, speech processing, natural language processing, and other related fields, various deep learning algorithms are proposed one after another. These deep learning algorithms are often introduced in various forms and have increasingly complex architectures. Therefore, to embrace the diversity of the algorithms, many different kinds of computing devices and chips are designed, including CPU, GPU, deep learning processors, FPGA, and so on, for which many corresponding programming languages have also been developed. To efficiently implement deep learning algorithms, programmers need to make considerable effort to balance the application demands, algorithm efficiency, hardware architecture, and programming language. Such efforts make the implementation extremely difficult and also increase the learning costs for programmers. To solve this problem, programming frameworks are proposed. On the one hand, a programming framework can encapsulate common operations in algorithms into a direct operator call, such as convolution, pooling, etc. On the other hand, as the programming interface between hardware and software, the programming framework can encapsulate the hardware architecture, thus reducing the complexity and difficulty of programming or applying deep learning algorithms.

The programming framework plays a middleware role in the whole intelligent computing system, which is similar to the operating system in the information industry. An operating system is the interface between software and hardware and is used to manage the computer's hardware and software resources. Programmers or users can use the hardware through the operating system. In the intelligent computing system, the programming framework provides the programmer with the interface to leverage the hardware and the computing system and therefore is the critical part of the intelligent computing system. Google's TensorFlow is one of the most popular deep learning programming frameworks available today, allowing users to use it without taking the underlying CPU and GPU hardware or deep learning processor into account.

This chapter first introduces the concept and function of the deep learning programming framework. Then, the widely used basic concepts and programming model of TensorFlow are discussed. Finally, the inference and training implementation method of deep learning based on TensorFlow is presented through some code examples.

AI Computing Systems. https://doi.org/10.1016/B978-0-32-395399-3.00010-X

4.1 Necessities of programming frameworks

At present, deep learning algorithms have attracted wide attention from both research and industry. More and more companies and programmers need to deploy task-related deep learning algorithms. However, the theory behind the deep learning algorithm is very complex, as it involves the calculation of various partial derivatives, loss functions, activation functions, etc. This complexity undoubtedly increases the learning costs for programmers. Even if the mathematics behind deep learning algorithms is well understood, the implementation of the code is still complex. For example, programming gradient descent in Python requires nearly a hundred lines of code, while gradient descent is only one of the many steps in the deep learning algorithm implementation. To complete a full algorithm, the total lines of code may reach tens of thousands or even hundreds of thousands of lines. In addition, even if a deep learning algorithm can be coded based on the ideas from some paper references, the performance of the implementation could be undesirable. In many cases, such as image classification, the training accuracy of the proposed deep learning algorithm in a paper could be 87%, but the reproduction of the proposed algorithm may drop to 57%. The reason is twofold. First, some details cannot be well demonstrated due to the limited length of the chapter. Second, one may reproduce the proposed algorithm with incorrect codes. Specifically, the accuracy of a training result is averaged over a large number of test samples. Therefore, if the reproduction is conducted with incorrect codes, the debugging of the deep learning algorithm is extremely difficult.

An important way to solve the problem mentioned above is code reuse. Among different deep learning algorithms, there are some common operations, such as convolution, pooling, full connection, and other operators. The code of these common operations can be reused in the implementation. Therefore, encapsulating some basic or common operations for different algorithms is of great significance. The benefit is twofold. First, such encapsulation of the common or basic operators can effectively avoid unnecessary coding and thus improve implementation efficiency. Second, the encapsulation can bring in better computing performance. The main reason is that the number of encapsulated operators may be only a few hundred or even a thousand. Hardware programmers can fully optimize these encapsulated operators to better support the application users, thus achieving the best performance. As such, the programming framework plays a key role within the intelligent computing system.

4.2 Fundamentals of programming frameworks

4.2.1 Generic programming frameworks

As stated above, basic operations of deep learning algorithms can be encapsulated into a series of components to help programmers implement existing algorithms or design new ones. Here, a deep learning programming framework can be constituted with the series of components. Users can further use these components to build neural networks such as AlexNet or ResNet in way that resembles the use of LEGO bricks.

This technique effectively reduces the huge effort that is required to implement deep learning algorithms.

Until 2013, each programmer in the deep learning community wrote their own neural network programs independently. This independent manner made most of the programs unscalable and unportable. In 2014, Yangqing Jia, at the time a student at the Berkeley Vision and Learning Center (BVLC), launched the programming framework Caffe [46]. Caffe was easy to use, robust, efficient at that time, and therefore widely used in the training and inference of deep learning algorithms. At the end of 2015, Google released the open source programming framework TensorFlow [114] [26]. The released framework performs numerical computations based on computational graphs, supports automatic differentiation, finishes the gradient calculation without manual work, and is scalable and portable. The trained model can be easily deployed on a variety of hardware and operating system platforms, so it has attracted wide attention after its release. Since then, there have been other deep programming frameworks such as MXNet [47], PyTorch [27], and PaddlePaddle [115]. These frameworks make it easy for programmers to develop deep learning algorithms and actively promote the development of deep learning algorithms.

4.2.2 TensorFlow basics

There are more than a dozen deep learning programming frameworks in practice, including TensorFlow, Caffe2 [116], PyTorch, and MXNet. TensorFlow is currently one of the most mainstream and widely used programming framework. One of its best-known applications is helping AlphaGo Master defeat the Go world champion Jie Ke in 2017. TensorFlow and its variants can be easily deployed and used on various types of heterogeneous systems, including mobile devices such as phones and tablet PCs, as well as large-scale distributed systems with hundreds of machines and thousands of computing devices. In this book, TensorFlow is chosen as the representative to introduce the deep learning programming framework.

The development of TensorFlow did not happen overnight. Before releasing TensorFlow, Google designed the first generation of the distributed deep learning platform DistBelief in 2011 [117]. This platform, which can be used for the training and inference of deep neural networks, is an early result of the Google Brain project. The Google team has carried out a variety of studies based on DistBelief, including unsupervised learning, image classification, video classification, speech recognition, sequence prediction, pedestrian detection, reinforcement learning, etc. The platform has established the image search function in Google Photos and promoted the experiment of Google's automated image captioning. Based on DistBelief, Google also carried out the famous "cat recognition" experiment, which selected 10 million images from YouTube videos and self-learned to recognize the cat face without any external interference [29].

DistBelief is a successful first-generation, production-level framework. However, due to its close relationship with the underlying products within Google, it has considerable reuse limitations in practice. To address this problem, Google launched the second generation of the large-scale machine learning system—TensorFlow.

TensorFlow is a deep learning programming framework developed by Google and open sourced in November 2015 for implementing and deploying large-scale machine learning models. Compared to DistBelief, it has many advantages in function, performance, flexibility, etc. This framework can support the deployment of deep learning algorithms on a wider range of heterogeneous hardware platforms and supports a wider range of neural network models. In this chapter, the TensorFlow programming model and its usage are briefly introduced. Those who are interested in TensorFlow can also visit the TensorFlow official website [118] and related course websites [119] [120] for further information.

4.3 TensorFlow: model and tutorial

In the process of program development, different methodologies are usually adopted based on different ideas of solving problems. There are two common types of programming, imperative and declarative. Most interactive interfaces or operating systems use imperative programming, in which the computer performs specific operations step by step according to the sequence of code instructions. Declarative programming tells the computer what it wants to express, but does not specify specific steps to achieve. The model only describes the relationships between data through functions, inferential rules, etc. Declarative programming is suitable for the implementation of deep learning algorithms and is now used in TensorFlow.

In TensorFlow, **Computational Graph** is used to describe the computational process of the machine learning algorithm, showing all the computation and states in a machine learning algorithm. In this graph, the various types of computation are defined as **Operations**, and all the data is modeled as **Tensors**, which connect between nodes in the computational graph. The actual operation is not performed when the computational graph is built. It is performed by defining **Session**. For state parameters such as model parameters in the computational graph, they are stored as **Variable**. In contrast to variables, TensorFlow also provides **Constant** for immutable parameters. In addition, tensors are passed to the session via **Placeholder**. TensorFlow also provides functionality **Queue** for handling data reading and asynchronous execution of computed graphs. In this section, the concepts of computational graphs, operations, tensors, sessions, variables, placeholders, and queues are introduced.

4.3.1 Computational graph

TensorFlow describes computation in terms of a directed graph which contains a set of nodes and edges. This directed graph is called a computational graph. Fig. 4.1 describes the computational process of multiplying two matrices x and w to get y.

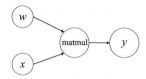

FIGURE 4.1

An example of a computational graph.

The essence of a computational graph is the relationship between nodes and edges, where the nodes can represent input, output, and model parameters, etc. (x, y, and w in Fig. 4.1, respectively). It can also represent various kinds of processing, including mathematical operations, variable reading and writing, data filling, etc., as the matrix multiplication (matmul) shown in Fig. 4.1. Edges represent input/output relationships between nodes. There are two types of edges. One is an edge that passes specific data, which is called a tensor. The other one represents the control dependency between nodes. This kind of edge does not transfer data but only represents the order of node execution. After the preorder node completes its computation, the postorder node can start its computation.

The execution of the computational graph follows the order of the directed graph. Every time a tensor passes through a node, it is calculated as the input of the operation node, and the output result keeps flowing along the output edge to the following node.

The TensorFlow program consists of two parts, building a computational graph and executing this graph. TensorFlow supports building computational graphs in a variety of high-level languages, including C++, Python, and more. A code example is shown in Fig. 4.2.

```
1   import tensorflow as tf
2
3   # Define two constants
4   x = tf.constant([[3.,3.]])
5   w = tf.constant([[2.],[2.]])
6
7   y = tf.matmul(x,w)
8
9   with tf.Session() as sess:
10      result = sess.run(y)
11      print(result)
```

FIGURE 4.2

TensorFlow code example.

As shown in line 1 of Fig. 4.2, when building the computational graph, the TensorFlow library is first loaded and named tf. Then, the two constants x and w are defined,[1] and finally the matrix multiplication operation is conducted, as shown in lines 4–7 of the code. Based on this code, TensorFlow constructs the computational graph in Fig. 4.1. The computational graph is static, and TensorFlow does not actually perform the computation at this point. To compute the value y, one shall create a session to execute the computational graph. This is done by first creating a session with the tf.Session() function and then passing the compiled graph to the session. TensorFlow performs the relevant operations and returns results, as shown in lines 9–11 in Fig. 4.2.

Describing deep learning algorithms through computational graphs has many advantages. First, the complex computation with multiple algorithm inputs is expressed as a directed graph composed of several basic operations, which is simple, intuitive, and convenient to process. Second, by computing through the graph, it is convenient to retain the intermediate results of all inner nodes, which helps the back-propagation, enables the chain rule for automatic differentiation, and thus achieves automatic gradient computation.

4.3.2 Operations

Each node in the computational graph represents one operation, which is a local computation. Each node receives 0 or more tensors as inputs and produces 0 or more tensors as outputs. Lines 4 and 5 of the code example in Fig. 4.2 are the constant definitions and assignment operations, which create the input x and w nodes, respectively, in Fig. 4.1. Line 7 is the matrix multiplication operation of x and w, with an output of y, which creates the matmul operator node and the output y node in Fig. 4.1.

Each operation has parameters that identify information about the execution. These parameters are determined when building the computational graph. Common parameters include name, type (e.g., add), inputs, outputs, control_inputs, device, graph, traceback, etc.

The common operations in TensorFlow are shown in Table 4.1. For scalar operations, TensorFlow provides operations such as addition, subtraction, multiplication, division, logarithm, and exponentiation, etc. For matrix operation, TensorFlow supports matrix multiplication, matrix inversion, etc. For neural network operations, TensorFlow has convolution, maximum pooling, bias, softmax, sigmoid, ReLU, etc. Moreover, it also provides logical operations, save, restore, initialization, and random operations. Using these basic operations, it is easy to design on-demand programs and implement deep learning algorithms.

---

[1] In this chapter, the symbolic representations of matrices, tensors, variables, etc., are consistent with their definition forms in the programming code; that is, they are denoted using normal font as in the code, rather than using black italic or italic as in Chapters 2 and 3.

Table 4.1 Some common operations in TensorFlow.

Operation type	Common operations
Scalar operations	add, subtract, multiply, div, greater, less, equal, abs, sign, square, pow, log, sin, cos
Matrix operations	matmul, matrix_inverse, matrix_determinant, matrix_transpose
Logical operation	logical_and, is_finite
Neural network operations	convolution, max_pool, bias_add, softmax, dropout, sigmoid, relu
Store and restore	save, restore
Initialization operation	zeros_initializer, random_normal_initializer, orthogonal_initializer
Random operations	random_gamma, multinomial, random_normal, random_shuffle

4.3.3 Tensors

TensorFlow uses tensors to represent all data in the computational graph. The tensors flow between nodes in the graph, but they do not contain data and only serve as references to the results of operations.

A tensor is an array of N dimensions, and the dimension of the array is the rank of the tensor. Rank-0 tensors equal to scalar data. A rank-1 tensor is a 1D array, or a vector. A rank-2 tensor is a 2D array, which is a matrix. Similarly, a rank-N tensor is equivalent to an N-dimensional array. For example, an RGB image can be represented as a rank-3 tensor, and a dataset composed of multiple RGB images can be represented as a rank-4 tensor.

As shown in Table 4.2, each tensor has some common parameters, including data type (dtype), shape, name, op, device, graph, and so on. These parameters are described in more detail below.

Table 4.2 Common parameters of tensors.

Parameter name	Meaning
dtype	Tensor data type
shape	Tensor shape
name	The name of the tensor in the computational graph
op	The operation that calculates the tensor
device	The name of the device used to calculate the tensor
graph	The computational graph that contains the tensor

4.3.3.1 Tensor data type

The dtype parameter of a tensor represents the data type. TensorFlow supports a variety of data types, including signed integers, unsigned integers, float pointing numbers, complex numbers, Booleans, strings, and quantized integers, as shown in Table 4.3. In this table, bfloat16 [121] is a data format between float16 and float32, consisting of 1 symbol bit, 8 exponential bits, and 7 decimal bits, where float16 has

5 exponential bits and 10 decimal bits and float32 has 8 exponential bits and 23 decimal bits. This data type is widely used in deep learning by tuning down accuracy requirements to obtain a larger numerical representation space.

Table 4.3 Supported tensor data types in TensorFlow.

TensorFlow data type	Description
int8/int16/int32/int64	8-bit/16-bit/32-bit/64-bit signed integers
uint8/uint16/uint32/uint64	8-bit/16-bit/32-bit/64-bit unsigned integers
float16/float32/float64	Half-precision/single-precision/double-precision floating point numbers
bfloat16	Trimmed half-precision floating-point numbers
bool	Boolean
string	String
complex64/complex128	64-bit single-precision complex numbers/128-bit double-precision complex numbers
qint8/qint16/qint32	Quantized 8-bit/16-bit/32-bit signed integers
quint8/quint16	Quantized 8-bit/16-bit unsigned integer

The code example that contains the data type definition of tensor is shown in Fig. 4.3. The code defines a rank-1 tensor of constant type, whose data type is float32, and thus TensorFlow will treat the constant elements 2 and 3 of tensor a as float32.

```
1    a=tf.constant([2,3],dtype=tf.float32)
```

FIGURE 4.3

TensorFlow declares a constant of data type float32.

In the tensor definition, the data type is an optional parameter. If the dtype is not explicitly defined, the program will automatically determine its data type based on the input format. For example, if the data is read without a decimal point, it defaults to int32. If there is a decimal point, the default is float32. The program checks the data type syntax of all tensors during execution and reports an error if the data types do not match.

4.3.3.2 Tensor shape

The tensor shape is the shape parameter of the tensor, which represents the length of each rank of the tensor. A tensor can be regarded as an array of N dimensions. The rank of the tensor is the dimension of the array, and the length of each rank in the tensor is expressed in shape. Fig. 4.4 illustrates the concept of shape. A rank-0 tensor is a scalar with an empty shape. A rank-1 tensor is a 1D vector, and its shape value is the length of the vector. Therefore, the shape of the rank-1 tensor in the example is (3). A rank-2 tensor is a matrix. In Fig. 4.4, the shape of the rank-2 tensor is (3, 3). A rank-3 tensor is a 3D array, and its shape value contains three elements, where each element represents the length of one rank, so the shape of the rank-3 tensor in the example is (2, 3, 3).

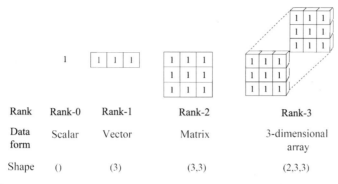

Rank	Rank-0	Rank-1	Rank-2	Rank-3
Data form	Scalar	Vector	Matrix	3-dimensional array
Shape	()	(3)	(3,3)	(2,3,3)

FIGURE 4.4

The shape of tensor.

The shape of the tensor is an optional parameter in TensorFlow. If the shape of a tensor is not explicitly declared in the program, TensorFlow will make shape predictions based on the input tensor values to ensure that the operation will be executed correctly.

4.3.3.3 *Tensor device*

TensorFlow uses the tf.device() function to specify the name of the device on which the tensor is computed. The official version of TensorFlow calculates the tensor on both CPU and GPU devices. At the same time, users can manually add devices of the deep learning processor. TensorFlow does not discriminate between CPUs, so all CPUs use /cpu:0 as the device name. Instead, TensorFlow specifies which GPU to run by using /gpu:n for the *n*th GPU device. In Fig. 4.5, line 3 specifies the CPU that lines 4–5 run on and line 7 specifies the GPU 0 that line 8 runs on.

4.3.3.4 *Tensor operations*

Table 4.4 lists all common operations for tensors in TensorFlow. Refer to the TensorFlow website [118] for more details.

To check the parameters of a tensor, users can invoke the print() function. Lines 3–14 assign values to each constant. The program in Fig. 4.6 defines four constants, t0, t1, t2, and t3, where t0 is a constant of type int32, t1 is a vector of type float32, t2 is an array of strings of 2×2, and t3 is a tensor of rank-3 int32. A direct call to the function print() on t0, t1, t2, and t3 prints out the three parameters of each tensor: name, shape, and dtype. To check the value of a tensor, one may need to create a session in which the run() function is executed. Fig. 4.7 shows a code example to obtain tensor values and outputs.

```
1  import tensorflow as tf
2
3  with tf.device('/cpu:0'):
4      a = tf.constant([[3.,3.]])
5      b = tf.constant([[2.],[2.]])
6
7  with tf.device('/gpu:0'):
8      y = tf.matmul(a,b)
9
10  with tf.Session() as sess:
11      result = sess.run(y)
12      print(result)
```

FIGURE 4.5

TensorFlow specifies the device for the operation.

Table 4.4 Common operations on tensors.

Operation name	Functions
tf.shape(tensor)	Return the shape of *tensor*
tf.to_double(x, name='ToDouble')	Convert *x* to a 64-bit floating point type
tf.to_float(x, name='ToFloat')	Convert *x* to a 32-bit floating point type
tf.to_int32(x, name='ToInt32')	Convert *x* to a 32-bit integer
tf.to_int64(x, name='ToInt64')	Convert *x* to a 64-bit integer
tf.cast(x, dtype)	Convert data type of *x* to *dtype*
tf.reshape(tensor, shape)	Modify the shape of *tensor* to *shape*
tf.slice(input, begin, size)	Extract a slice of size *size* from the *input* starting at the position specified by *begin*
tf.split(value, num_or_size_splits, axis)	Cut *value* along the rank of *axis* into *num_or_size_splits* parts
tf.concat(values, axis)	Concatenate *values* along the rank of *axis*

4.3.4 Tensor session

The computational graph in TensorFlow only describes the computational process. It does not assign values to the input and perform the computation. The computation needs to be defined and performed in TensorFlow sessions. The session provides a running environment in which the program evaluates tensors, performs operations, and translates the computational graph into execution paths on different devices.

A typical procedure of a session consists of three steps: (1) create a session; (2) execute the session; and (3) close the session. Fig. 4.8 shows a code example.

4.3.4.1 Session creation

TensorFlow uses the tf.Session() function to create a session, as shown in Fig. 4.9.

The input parameters of tf.Session() and their meanings are shown in Table 4.5. The parameter config describes the session-related configurations. With this parame-

```
1   import tensorflow as tf
2
3   #Create an integer tensor of rank-0
4   t0 = tf.constant(9,dtype=tf.int32)
5
6   #Create a tensor of rank-1 floating point numbers
7   t1 = tf.constant([3.,4.1,5.2],dtype=tf.float32)
8
9   #Create a 2*2 rank-2 string tensor
10  t2 = tf.constant([['Apple','Pear'],['Potato','Tomato']],
11                   dtype=tf.string)
12
13  #Create a 2*3*1 rank-3 integer tensor
14  t3 = tf.constant([[[2],[2],[1]],[[7],[3],[3]]])
15
16  print(t0)
17  print(t1)
18  print(t2)
19  print(t3)
```

```
1   Tensor("Const:0",shape=(),dtype=int32)
2   Tensor("Const_1:0",shape=(3,),dtype=float32)
3   Tensor("Const_2:0",shape=(2,2),dtype=string)
4   Tensor("Const_3:0",shape=(2,3,1),dtype=int32)
```

FIGURE 4.6

Tensor parameters code example printed by TensorFlow (top) and the printed result (bottom).

ter, one can define the number of devices in computation, the number of threads, the GPU configuration, etc. For detailed configurations, refer to [122].

4.3.4.2 Session execution

A session execution is the tensor solving or computing based on the computational graph and input. The session is executed in TensorFlow using the run() function, whose parameters and meanings are shown in Table 4.6.

The first two parameters, *fetches* and *feed_dict*, are more commonly used. The tensor or operation to be calculated is specified through *fetches*. *feed_dict* lists the tensor or operation needed for processing *fetches*, along with the data.

Fig. 4.10 shows a specific example of the run() function. In the code, lines 2–6 first define tensors a and b without assignment. Tensor c is equal to the product of tensors a and b. The session *sess* is then created and performed by the *sess.run()* function. *sess.run()* specifies that the target tensor is c, which requires values of a and b. Therefore, the function fills tensors a and b with *feed_dict={a:100,b:200}*, where tensors a and b are filled with 100 and 200, respectively. In this way, $c = 20,000$

```
1   with tf.Session() as sess:
2           print(sess.run(t0))
3           print(sess.run(t1))
4           print(sess.run(t2))
5           print(sess.run(t3))
```

```
1    9
2    [3.   4.1  5.2]
3    [['Apple'  'Pear']
4    ['Potato'  'Tomato']]
5    [[[2]
6    [2]
7    [1]]
8
9    [[7]
10   [3]
11   [3]]]
```

FIGURE 4.7

Code example of printing the actual value of Tensor using session (top) and the printed result (bottom).

```
1    #Create session
2    sess = tf.Session()
3
4    #Execute session
5    sess.run(...)
6
7    #Close the session
8    sess.close()
```

FIGURE 4.8

TensorFlow session API.

```
1    sess = tf.Session(target='',graph=None,config=None)
```

FIGURE 4.9

Create TensorFlow session.

is calculated by the *sess.run()* function. Similarly, lines 8–13 illustrate the process of filling a rank-2 tensor with a value through *feed_dict* for matrix multiplication. *feed_dict* is one of the most commonly used parameters in TensorFlow, which is also used later in the *tensor.eval()* function and placeholders.

Table 4.5 Input parameters of tf.Session().

Parameter	Function description
target	The execution engine of the session; the default is the in-process engine
graph	The computational graph loaded when the computation is performed. The default value is the only computational graph in the current code. When multiple computational graphs are defined in the code, use *graph* to specify the computational graph to be loaded
config	Specify related configuration items, such as the number of devices, the number of parallel threads, GPU configuration parameters, etc.

Table 4.6 Input parameters of session execution.

Parameter	Function description
fetches	The tensor or operation to be calculated in this session
feed_dict	Specify the tensor or operation to be filled when the session is executed and the corresponding filling data
options	Set the control options when the session is running, such as tracing
run_metadata	Set the nontensor information when the session is running

```
1   import tensorflow as tf
2   a = tf.placeholder(tf.int32)
3   b = tf.placeholder(tf.int32)
4   c = tf.multiply(a,b)
5   with tf.Session() as sess:
6           print(sess.run(c,feed_dict={a:100,b:200}))
7
8   x1 = tf.placeholder(tf.float32,[2,3])
9   x2 = tf.placeholder(tf.float32,[3,2])
10  x3 = tf.matmul(x1,x2)
11  with tf.Session() as sess:
12          print(sess.run(x3,feed_dict={x1:[[1,2,3], [4,5,6]],\
13                              x2:[[1,2],[3,4],[5,6]]}))
```

```
1   20000
2   [[22.  28.]
3    [49.  64.]]
```

FIGURE 4.10

TensorFlow executes a session function.

4.3.4.3 Session close

The session is responsible for managing all running resources and needs to be closed when the execution finishes. TensorFlow provides two ways to close the session and release resources:

1) Explicitly close the session with the *close()* function. The code example is shown in Fig. 4.11.

2) Use the *with* statement to implicitly close the session. Create a session with the context manager *with tf.Session() as sess* and execute the session with *sess.run()*,

```
1   #Create session
2   sess = tf.Session()
3   #Execute session
4   sess.run(...)
5   #Close the session using close()
6   sess.close()
```

FIGURE 4.11

An example of closing the session explicitly in TensorFlow.

which automatically closes the session and frees resources when the context exits. A code example is shown in Fig. 4.12.

```
1   #Create session
2   with tf.Session() as sess:
3     #Execute session
4     sess.run(...)
5   #Automatically close the session when the context exits
```

FIGURE 4.12

An example of closing the session implicitly in TensorFlow.

4.3.4.4 Tensor evaluation

The tensor value needs to be solved in the session, which can be calculated in two ways:

1) Calling the *run()* function, which is shown in the code example in Fig. 4.10.

2) Using the *tensor.eval()* function to calculate the tensor. The code example is shown in Fig. 4.13.

```
1   import tensorflow as tf
2
3   a = tf.constant([[1.0,2.0]])
4   b = tf.constant([[3.0],[4.0]])
5   c = tf.matmul(a,b)
6
7   with tf.Session():
8       print(a.eval())
9       print(c.eval())
```

```
1   [[1. 2.]]
2   [[11.]]
```

FIGURE 4.13

A code example of using tensor.eval() to calculate tensor values (top) and output result (bottom).

Both *tensor.eval()* and *run()* can be used to calculate values of the tensors. The function takes two input parameters, *feed_dict* and *session*. The *feed_dict* parameter is used to specify the tensor to be populated and its corresponding data. The *session* parameter specifies the session.

The main difference between *tensor.eval()* and *run()* is that *tensor.eval()* can only handle a single tensor at a time, whereas *session.run()* can handle multiple tensors at once. The code example in Fig. 4.14 contrasts their differences. When calculating the tensors *y*1 and *y*2, the *tensor.eval()* function calls a tensor-by-tensor computation twice, as shown in lines 11–12. The *run()* function is only called once, as shown in line 13.

```
1   import tensorflow as tf
2
3   a = tf.constant([[1.0,2.0]])
4   b = tf.constant([[3.0],[4.0]])
5   c = tf.constant([[5.0],[6.0]])
6
7   y1 = tf.matmul(a,b)
8   y2 = tf.matmul(a,c)
9
10  with tf.Session() as sess:
11      y1.eval()
12      y2.eval()
13      sess.run([y1,y2])
```

FIGURE 4.14

Comparison between eval() and run() for calculating tensors.

4.3.5 Variable

A variable is a state node in the computational graph, which stores and updates a specified tensor when the same computational graph is executed multiple times. The variable is often used to represent model parameters in machine learning. As a state node, its output is jointly determined by the input, node operations, and the stored state.

The common parameters of variables are similar to tensors, as shown in Table 4.7.

Like other tensors, a variable represents the input to an operation in a computational graph, but in a more complex way. The variable must be created and explicitly initialized before using it. The creation, initialization, and update of variables are discussed in the following sections.

4.3.5.1 Variable creation

The *tf.Variable()* function is used to create variables. The main functionality is to determine the basic parameters, including initial value, shape, data type, etc. The initial value of a variable can be of any type and shape. Concretely, there exist three ways to create a variable:

Table 4.7 Common parameters of the variable.

Parameter name	Meaning
dtype	Variable data type
shape	Shape of the variable
name	Name of the variable in the computational graph
op	Operation that produced this variable
device	Name of the device used to store this variable
graph	Computational graph containing this variable
initial_value	Initial value of the variable
initializer	Initialization operation for variable assignment
trainable	Whether to be updated by the optimizer during training

1) Use the *tf.Variable()* function to define the initial value, shape, data type, and other information of the variable directly. The process is the same as the constant definition. A code example is shown in Fig. 4.15.

```
1  a = tf.Variable([1,2])
2  b = tf.Variable([[1,2,3],[4,5,6],[7,8,9]],dtype=tf.float32)
```

FIGURE 4.15

Define the initial value of the variable directly.

2) Use the built-in TensorFlow function to define the initial value. Programmers can use the built-in *tf.zeros()*, *tf.random_normal()*, and other functions[2] to define the initial value of a variable, either a constant or a random value. The code example is shown in Fig. 4.16.

```
1  #Create a normal distribution random number with a shape
2  #of (20, 40) and a standard deviation of 0.35 as the initial
3  #value of the variable
4  c = tf.Variable(tf.random_normal([20,40],stddev=0.35))
5
6  #Create a constant whose shape is (2,3) and all elements
7  #are 0 as the initial value of the variable
8  d = tf.Variable(tf.zeros([2,3]))
```

FIGURE 4.16

Use the built-in function of TensorFlow to define the initial value of the variable.

---

[2] Here, they are called *functions* for programmers. However, in TensorFlow, these functions are treated as operators (op).

3) Use the initial values of other variables to define new variables. Programmers can use other variables to define a current variable as shown in Fig. 4.17. The *tf.Variable()* generates the initial value of the variable *weights*. The *weights* can be used to define new variables *w2* and *w_twice*.

```
1    #Create a normal distribution random number with a shape of
2    #(30, 60) and a standard deviation of 0.35 as the initial value
3    #of the variable, and the variable is named weights
4    weights = tf.Variable(tf.random_normal([30,60],stddev=0.35),
5        name="weights")
6
7    #Use the initial value of the variable weights as the initial
8    #value of the current variable w2
9    w2 = tf.Variable(weights.initialized_value(),name="w2")
10
11   #Use the initial value of the variable weights*2 as the
12   #initial value of the current variable w\_twice
13   w_twice = tf.Variable(weights.initialized_value()*2,
14       name="w_twice")
```

FIGURE 4.17

Use other variables to define variables.

Common operations to define variable are shown in Table 4.8, which are used to initialize variables.

Table 4.8 TensorFlow operations often used to define the initial value of a variable.

Operation	Description
tf.zeros()	Construct a tensor with all 0 values
tf.ones()	Construct a tensor with all 1 values
tf.random_normal()	Construct a normally distributed random number
tf.truncated_normal()	Output random numbers from truncated normal distribution
tf.random_uniform()	Construct an evenly distributed random number
tf.random_gamma()	Construct random numbers from gamma distribution
tf.fill()	Construct a tensor of all given values
tf.constant()	Construct a constant
variable.initialized_value()	Generate the initial value of a variable

4.3.5.2 Variable initialization

When creating a variable using the *tf.Variable()* function, the function simply defines the basic information about the initial value, shape, and data type of the variable. If actually assigning an initial value to the variable, programmers are required to start initialization on the variable within a session. The most common way to initialize a variable is to use the function *tf.global_variables_initializer()* to set up all the variables previously defined as the initialization within a session.

```
1   import tensorflow as tf
2
3   a = tf.Variable(tf.constant(0.0),dtype=tf.float32)
4
5   #Using tf.global\_variables\_initializer() to initialize
6   #all variables in session
7   with tf.Session() as sess:
8       sess.run(tf.global_variables_initializer())
9       print(sess.run(a))
```

```
1   0.0
```

FIGURE 4.18

Initialize variables (top) and output results (bottom).

Fig. 4.18 shows an example for initializing variables. Line 3 creates a variable *a* and defines the initial value as 0.0. To pass the initial value to *a*, programmers need to first create a session and then run the function *tf.global_variables_initializer()* in the session to initialize the variable *a*. Next, line 9 is used to print the initial value of the variable *a*.

4.3.5.3 Variable updating

A variable is a state node in a computational graph. The variable is affected by the input, node operations, and the stored state. Variables are mainly used to represent model parameters in the deep learning algorithm. TensorFlow automatically updates the value of variables in the training process. TensorFlow does not support the direct update of variables. However, if programmers would like to set a variable manually, they can reinitialize this variable using the *tf.assign()* function or add/subtract values to the variable using the *tf.assign_add()* or *tf.assign_sub()* functions.

Fig. 4.19 shows a code example for updating. First, a variable *f* is created. Then, *tf.assign()* is called to initialize *f* + 2.0 to *f*, *tf.assign_add()* is called to increase 3.0 to *f*, and *tf.assign_sub()* is called to decrease 1.5 from *f*. Next, a session is created and all codes are executed. Finally, the variable *f* is updated and printed.

4.3.6 Placeholders

As mentioned earlier, TensorFlow uses computational graphs to represent the network topology of a deep learning algorithm. In deep learning training, there is a training sample as the input of the graph. If each training sample is represented as a constant, all training samples need to be added as constants to the computational

```
1   f = tf.Variable(1.0)
2   f2 = tf.assign(f,f+2.0)
3   f3 = tf.assign_add(f,3.0)
4   f4 = tf.assign_sub(f,1.5)
5   with tf.Session() as sess:
6     sess.run(tf.global_variables_initializer())
7     print(sess.run(f))
8     print(sess.run(f2))
9     print(sess.run(f3))
10    print(sess.run(f4))
```

FIGURE 4.19

An example of updating variable.

graph, which makes the final graph too large to compute. To address this problem, a placeholder mechanism is provided in TensorFlow.

A placeholder is a data structure in TensorFlow that has no initial value and only allocates memory in the program. A placeholder represents a training sample of the model, which is created by adding a node to the graph and only needs to be initialized when the session is executed.

tf.placeholder() is used in TensorFlow to create placeholders, with a specification on the data type *dtype*. Other placeholder parameters include *shape*, i.e., the shape of the to-be-filled data, and *name*, i.e., the name of the placeholder. Among these parameters, *dtype* is required, while *shape* and *name* are optional. While used in the session, placeholder needs to work with the parameter *feed_dict*, which passes the data to be populated to the placeholder.

```
1   import tensorflow as tf
2
3   #Create variable
4   w1 = tf.Variable(tf.random_normal([1,2],stddev=1,seed=1))
5
6   #Create a placeholder
7   x = tf.placeholder(tf.float32,shape=(1,2))
8   a = tf.add(x,w1)
9
10  with tf.Session() as sess:
11    sess.run(tf.global_variables_initializer())
12    #Placeholder x needs to be filled when calculating a
13    y_1=sess.run(a,feed_dict={x:[[0.7,0.9]]})
14    print(y_1)
```

FIGURE 4.20

An example of using placeholders in TensorFlow.

Fig. 4.20 shows an example of placeholders. First, a placeholder x is defined and a computational graph that contains the placeholder operations is built. Then, a session is created with the tensor a. When computing the tensor a, the value of the placeholder x needs to be obtained, so *feed_dict* is used to fill the placeholder x with data $[0.7, 0.9]$, thus helping to finish the computation of the tensor a.

4.3.7 Queue

Queue is another state operation. TensorFlow provides a variety of queue mechanisms. For example, FIFOQueue is one of the simplest queues in which tensors are executed in a first-in first-out (FIFO) order. FIFOQueue supports enqueue and dequeue operations. The enqueue operation puts the input to the end of FIFOQueue, and the dequeue operation takes the first element out of FIFOQueue. The enqueue operation is blocked when the queue is full, and the dequeue operation is blocked when the queue is empty. In addition to FIFOQueue, TensorFlow also provides random shuffle queue and priority queue. Queues process the current data while prefetching the next input batch (see Section 4.5.1 for details), which can also be used to complete the asynchronous computation of different subgraphs.

4.4 Deep learning inference in TensorFlow

In this section, image style transfer is introduced as a driving example to describe how to use a pretrained deep learning model in TensorFlow.

The image style transfer algorithm [111] uses 16 convolutional layers and 5 pooling layers from VGG19 [72]. Its network architecture is shown in Fig. 4.21. Programmers can use TensorBoard [123], a visualization tool provided by TensorFlow, to draw the computational graph, as shown in Fig. 4.22(a). The generated computational graph maps to the actual network architecture, where multiple convolution layers and pooling layers are alternately stacked. TensorFlow uses namespaces to represent a logical subgraph. For example, Fig. 4.22(b) demonstrates a pooling subgraph node *pool1* in the namespace. In *pool1*, the input data is pooled through MaxPool, and the output results are directly fed into the next node, *conv2*. The second set of convolution nodes, *conv2* in the namespace, is shown in Fig. 4.22(c). The output of *pool1* and corresponding weights are computed through the Conv2D operation, along with the input of biases through the BiasAdd operation for the offset. Finally, the output of *conv2_1* is computed by a ReLU operation, which is the input of *conv2_2*. In this procedure, the input data is convolved through a stack of convolutional layers until the final output is produced.

TensorFlow supports various formats of pretrained model file, including h5 from Keras [124], npy or npz from NumPy [125], and the default formats ckpt and pb. For simplicity, the example here uses a model in the uncompressed npy file format by leveraging NumPy.

The basic process of implementing the neural network inference mainly consists of four steps: (1) load all input samples; (2) define the basic operations of the neural network with the core functions of TensorFlow; (3) build the network model with the predefined computation unit; and (4) execute the built neural network in a session

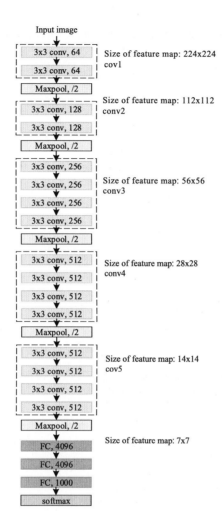

FIGURE 4.21

Network architecture of VGG19 for image style transfer.

to compute the final output. To better understand the prediction process, each of the above steps is described in detail.

4.4.1 Load input

The input samples should be read and preprocessed accordingly, as shown in Fig. 4.23. For example, programmers can use OpenCV [126] to read an image and resize it to 224×224, as required by VGG19. All images are normalized and returned in NHWC format, which is the default data format used in TensorFlow to store 4D tensors, including [batch, height, width, channel] elements.

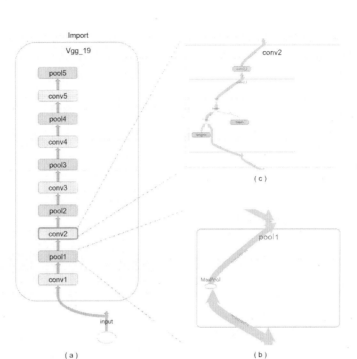

FIGURE 4.22

(a) Computational graph generated by TensorFlow. (b) Pooling node namespace. (c) Convolution node namespace.

```
1   import cv2
2   import numpy as np
3
4   def load_image(path):
5       img = cv2.imread(path, cv2.IMREAD_COLOR)
6       resize_img = cv2.resize(img, (224, 224))
7       norm_img = resize_img / 255.0
8       return np.reshape(norm_img, (1, 224, 224, 3))
```

FIGURE 4.23

Load input image.

4.4.2 Define the basic operations

Next, the *basic_calc* function is defined, which describes basic operations that might be used in VGG19, such as convolution, pooling, and so on. A code example is illustrated in Fig. 4.24.[3] If the current layer is a convolutional layer, it convolves the input

---

[3] Code examples in Sections 4.4.2, 4.4.3, and 4.5.4 are referenced from https://blog.csdn.net/aaronjny/article/details/79681080, https://blog.csdn.net/qq_29462849/article/details/80442839, and https://github.

nin and the weight *inwb[0]*, adds *inwb[1]* as the bias, and finally outputs through the ReLU function. If the current layer is a pooling layer, it outputs the pooling result of the input *nin*.

```
1   def basic_calc(caltype, nin,inwb=None):
2       if caltype=='conv':
3           #nin:This layer input;inwb:inwb[0],
4           #inwb[1] == weights,bias
5           return tf.nn.relu(tf.nn.conv2d(nin,inwb[0],
6                   strides=[1,1,1,1], padding='SAME')+ inwb[1])
7       elif caltype=='pool':
8           return tf.nn.max_pool(nin, ksize=[1,2,2,1],
9                   strides=[1,2,2,1], padding='SAME')
```

FIGURE 4.24

Define basic operation.

When using a neural network to make the prediction, first, the model parameters are loaded from VGG19, i.e., the *inwb* in Fig. 4.24. These model parameters are stored in the array of *data_dict*, which also provides weights and biases for computation by the layer *name*. The code in Fig. 4.25 implements the function of reading weights and biases from *data_dict*.

```
1   import numpy as np
2
3   def read_wb(vgg19_npy_path,name):
4       #Read model parameters from vgg19_npy_path path to array
5       #data_dict
6       data_dict = np.load(vgg19_npy_path,encoding='latin1').item()
7       weights = data_dict[name][0]
8       weights = tf.constant(weights)
9       bias = data_dict[name][1]
10      bias = tf.constant(bias)
11      return weights,bias
```

FIGURE 4.25

Load model parameters.

The *tf.nn* module is used to define the basic operations in *basic_calc()*. This module is the core module for deep learning computation in TensorFlow and provides functions for a large number of operations of neural networks, such as convolution, pooling, activation, and loss computation.

com/machrisaa/tensorflow-vgg. The former two are under a CC BY-SA 4.0 license; see https://creativecommons.org/licenses/by-sa/4.0/.

Table 4.9 Part of the convolution, pooling, activation, and loss functions provided by the tf.nn module.

Function	Description
Convolution function	
tf.nn.conv2d(input, filter, strides, padding)	Calculate the convolution of tensor *input* and *filter*
tf.nn.depthwise_conv2d(input, filter, strides, padding)	Depthwise convolution: each input channel is independently convolved with a different convolution kernel, and all convolution results are concatenated as output
tf.nn.separable_conv2d(input, depthwise_filter, pointwise_filter, strides, padding)	Separable convolution: after depthwise convolution, do pointwise convolution
tf.nn.bias_add(value, bias)	Add bias to the input
Pooling function	
tf.nn.avg_pool(value, ksize, strides, padding)	Average pooling of inputs
tf.nn.max_pool(value, ksize, strides, padding)	Max pooling of input
tf.nn.max_pool_with_argmax(input, ksize, strides, padding)	Max pooling of input, maximum output, and index
Activation function	
tf.nn.relu(features)	Calculate the ReLU function
tf.nn.elu(features)	Calculate the exponential linear function ELU
Loss function	
tf.nn.l2_loss(t)	Use the L^2 norm of the input tensor t to calculate the error value of the tensor, where $output = \sum t_i^2/2$

Table 4.9 lists the convolution, pooling, activation, and loss computation provided by *tf.nn*. Regarding the convolution operation, *tf.nn* provides a commonly used convolution function *tf.nn.conv2d( )*, as well as the commonly used depthwise convolution function *tf.nn.depthwise_conv2d( )* and the separable convolution function *tf.nn.separable_conv2d( )*. For pooling, *tf.nn* provides common pooling functions, including average pooling *tf.nn.avg_pool( )* and max pooling *tf.nn.max_pool( )*. As for activation operation, *tf.nn* provides functions like ReLU that are commonly used in deep learning. Moreover, the commonly used L^2 norm *tf.nn.l2_loss( )* is provided as a loss function, which takes the sum of the square of all the elements in the input tensor and then divides it by 2. The result is added back to the total loss function as a penalty term multiplied by a coefficient to prevent overfitting during training.

4.4.3 **Create neural network models**

After defining these basic operations, a neural network model can be built. According to the network architecture of VGG19, starting from the image input, the operation is implemented layer by layer. The output of one layer is fed as the input of the next layer until the final result is obtained through all these forwarding operations. The output of each layer is stored in *models*, as shown in Fig. 4.26. After the network model is built, TensorFlow automatically generates a computational graph similar to Fig. 4.22(a).

```
1   def build_vggnet(vgg19_npy_path):
2       models = {}
3       models['input'] = tf.Variable(np.zeros((1, 224, 224,
4               3)).astype('float32'))
5       models['conv1_1'] = basic_calc('conv',models['input'],
6               read_wb(vgg19_npy_path, 'conv1_1'))
7       models['conv1_2'] = basic_calc('conv',models['conv1_1'],
8               read_wb(vgg19_npy_path, 'conv1_2'))
9       models['pool1']   = basic_calc('pool',models['conv1_2'])
10      models['conv2_1'] = basic_calc('conv',models['pool1'],
11              read_wb(vgg19_npy_path, 'conv2_1'))
12      models['conv2_2'] = basic_calc('conv',models['conv2_1'],
13              read_wb(vgg19_npy_path, 'conv2_2'))
14      models['pool2']   = basic_calc('pool',models['conv2_2'])
15      models['conv3_1'] = basic_calc('conv',models['pool2'],
16              read_wb(vgg19_npy_path, 'conv3_1'))
17      models['conv3_2'] = basic_calc('conv',models['conv3_1'],
18              read_wb(vgg19_npy_path, 'conv3_2'))
19      models['conv3_3'] = basic_calc('conv',models['conv3_2'],
20              read_wb(vgg19_npy_path, 'conv3_3'))
21      models['conv3_4'] = basic_calc('conv',models['conv3_3'],
22              read_wb(vgg19_npy_path, 'conv3_4'))
23      models['pool3']   = basic_calc('pool',models['conv3_4'])
24      models['conv4_1'] = basic_calc('conv',models['pool3'],
25              read_wb(vgg19_npy_path, 'conv4_1'))
26      models['conv4_2'] = basic_calc('conv',models['conv4_1'],
27              read_wb(vgg19_npy_path, 'conv4_2'))
28      models['conv4_3'] = basic_calc('conv',models['conv4_2'],
29              read_wb(vgg19_npy_path, 'conv4_3'))
30      models['conv4_4'] = basic_calc('conv',models['conv4_3'],
31              read_wb(vgg19_npy_path, 'conv4_4'))
32      models['pool4']   = basic_calc('pool',models['conv4_4'])
33      models['conv5_1'] = basic_calc('conv',models['pool4'],
34              read_wb(vgg19_npy_path, 'conv5_1'))
35      models['conv5_2'] = basic_calc('conv',models['conv5_1'],
36              read_wb(vgg19_npy_path, 'conv5_2'))
37      models['conv5_3'] = basic_calc('conv',models['conv5_2'],
38              read_wb(vgg19_npy_path, 'conv5_3'))
39      models['conv5_4'] = basic_calc('conv',models['conv5_3'],
40              read_wb(vgg19_npy_path, 'conv5_4'))
41      models['pool5']   = basic_calc('pool',models['conv5_4'])
42      return models
```

FIGURE 4.26

Build a VGG19 network model.

4.4.4 Output prediction

The computational graph generated in the previous step is a static graph, which does not perform any computation. In order to get the output, *tf.Session()* is used to create a session, instantiate the *build_vggnet()* function in the session, perform the output prediction through *sess.run()*, and output the calculated results. A code example is shown in Fig. 4.27.

```
1   #Model file path needs to be loaded
2   vgg19_npy_path = './vgg_models.npy'
3   #Get the input content image
4   img_content = load_image('./content.jpg')
5
6   with tf.Session() as sess:
7       sess.run(tf.global_variables_initializer())
8       models = build_vggnet(vgg19_npy_path)
9
10
11      sess.run(models['input'].assign(img_content))
12      res = sess.run(models['pool5'])
13
14      # other process
15      ...
```

FIGURE 4.27

Computation and output of the neural network.

4.5 Deep learning training in TensorFlow

Compared to prediction, deep learning training is more complex. The process of implementing deep learning training based on TensorFlow is shown in Fig. 4.28. The basic process can be divided into three parts [26]:

(1) Load and then preprocess the input data sample.

(2) Iteratively train the model. The framework starts the session to initialize the computational graph and specify the loaded input data and output result nodes for forward computation, backward gradient computation, and parameter updating. Model training usually takes a long time. When the training result is not satisfactory, programmers can tune the training strategy or model architectures and adjust the preprocessing technique. This procedure may be repeated for many times until the training result is satisfactory.

(3) Save checkpoints during the process. During the training process, TensorFlow has a checkpoint mechanism to save the model's parameters in real time.

4.5.1 Data loading

Loading the input data and preprocessing is the first step in the model training. TensorFlow supports four methods to load data:

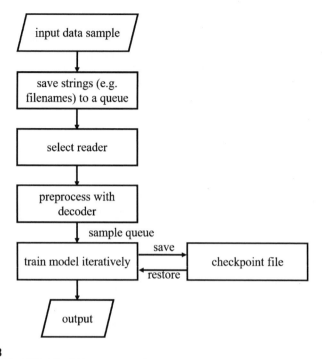

FIGURE 4.28

Diagram of the training process in TensorFlow.

- Feeding: get the input data using *feed_dict*.
- Prefetching: use constants and variables to read the input data.
- Queue-based API: build an input pipeline based on queue-related APIs.
- *tf.data* API: use the *tf.data* API to build the input pipeline.

4.5.1.1 Feeding

When the input data is in NumPy array format, programmers can populate the data directly with *feed_dict*, as shown in Fig. 4.29.[4]

4.5.1.2 Prefetching

If the dataset is small, the better choice is to use a constant or a variable to read all input directly into memory, which is called data prefetching, and can improve execution efficiency.

---

[4] Codes in Sections 4.5.1.1, 4.5.1.2, and 4.5.1.3 are referenced from the TensorFlow official documentation. Please refer to *https://github.com/tensorflow/tensorflow/blob/r1.10/tensorflow/docs_src/api_guides/python/reading_data.md*, under Apache License Version 2.0; see https://www.apache.org/licenses/LICENSE-2.0.

```
1    with tf.Session():
2      input = tf.placeholder(tf.float32)
3      classifier = ...
4      print(classifier.eval(feed_dict={input: one_numpy_ndarray}))
```

FIGURE 4.29

Data feeding code example.

Fig. 4.30 shows a code example of data prefetching. Although reading all input by a constant is simple to use, the constant is inline in the computational graph, and thus the internal data will be copied multiple times if the constant is called more than once, which results in a waste of memory. Thus, TensorFlow also provides the user with the possibility of storing data as a variable.

```
1    training_data = ...    #some data like numpy array
2    training_labels = ...
3    with tf.Session():
4      input_data = tf.constant(training_data)
5      input_labels = tf.constant(training_labels)
6      ...
```

FIGURE 4.30

Use constants for data prefetching.

Fig. 4.31 shows a code example that uses variables to prefetch data. This approach initializes the variable before the graph is evaluated. The *trainable* parameter of the variable is set to False so that the value will not be updated during training. Also, *collections* = [] is set to guarantee that the variable will not be saved or restored.

4.5.1.3 Build input pipeline based on queue API

Due to the limited memory of the computing devices (i.e., GPU, Cambricon, etc.), large-scale data cannot be fully read into memory. Hence, batch reading is needed. If the execution mode of "Read Batch1 - Compute Batch1 - Read Batch2 - Compute Batch2" is adopted, the computation and memory access are processed sequentially. Because the processing time of the two does not overlap, its computing can be inefficient. Therefore, TensorFlow provides a set of queue-based APIs to enable an efficient read pipeline to achieve simultaneous reading while computing.

Queues in TensorFlow support enqueue, dequeue, and synchronization. When the queue is full, the enqueue thread is suspended. On the contrary, when the queue is empty, the dequeue thread hangs and waits. A typical queue-based input pipeline is shown in Fig. 4.28. It contains the following elements:

```
1    training_data = ...    #some data like numpy array
2    training_labels = ...
3    with tf.Session() as sess:
4      data_initializer = tf.placeholder(dtype=training_data.dtype,
5                             shape=training_data.shape)
6      label_initializer = tf.placeholder(dtype=training_labels.dtype,
7                             shape=training_labels.shape)
8      input_data = tf.Variable(data_initializer, trainable=False,
     collections=[])
9      input_labels = tf.Variable(label_initializer, trainable=False,
     collections=[])
10     ...
11     sess.run(input_data.initializer,
12             feed_dict={data_initializer: training_data})
13     sess.run(input_labels.initializer,
14             feed_dict={label_initializer: training_labels})
15     ...
```

FIGURE 4.31

Use variables for data prefetching.

- a list of file names,
- a FIFO queue that holds the file names,
- a file format reader,
- a decoder,
- ShuffleQueue.

Fig. 4.32 shows a code example for queue-based data loading. Line 2 uses *tf.train.string_input_producer* to generate the FIFO queue for the file. After calling this function, the program creates the queue and the enqueue operation. By default, it invokes the *QueueRunner* operation to create an enqueue thread. Lines 7–8 select the corresponding reader according to the file format. Lines 12–15 preprocess the data file with the decoder. In the case of image data, the preprocessing generally includes unifying data type, normalizing pixel values between 0 and 1, chopping size, etc. In the case of textual data, the preprocessing contains text alignment, text encoding, and so on. Line 22 uses *start _queue _runners* to start executing the created queue, which is a shuffle queue after processing, providing a dataset for training.

Giving two files, file0.csv and file1.csv, as shown in Fig. 4.33, the sample queue randomly generated by the code example is shown in Fig. 4.34. Of course, the results may not be the same each time.

Programmers can further create multiple threads for batch processing, as shown in Fig. 4.35. The key function is *tf.train.shuffle_batch*, which is responsible for creating (1) a RandomShuffleQueue to hold the sample data; (2) multiple queue threads using the *QueueRunner* class; and (3) a dequeue operation, *dequeue_many*.

```
1   #FIFO queue used to save file names
2   filename_queue = tf.train.string_input_producer(["file0.csv",
3       "file1.csv"])
4
5   #Depending on the reader selected for the csv file,
6   #readers for different file types are different
7   reader = tf.TextLineReader()
8   key, value = reader.read(filename_queue)
9
10  #The default value set to handle the occurrence of null
11  #values,and the type of output of a given decoder
12  record_defaults = [[1], [1], [1], [1], [1]]
13  col1, col2, col3, col4, col5 = tf.decode_csv(
14      value, record_defaults=record_defaults)
15  features = tf.stack([col1, col2, col3, col4])
16
17  with tf.Session() as sess:
18      #Create a coordinator
19      coord = tf.train.Coordinator()
20      #Before calling run or eval to perform reading,
21      #tf.train.start_queue_runners must be used to fill the queue
22      threads = tf.train.start_queue_runners(coord=coord)
23
24      for i in range(10):
25          #Get the result of each reading
26          example, label = sess.run([features, col5])
27          print "example_=_", example, ",_label_=_", label
28
29      coord.request_stop()
30      coord.join(threads)
```

FIGURE 4.32

Code example for loading data based on the queue API.

4.5.1.4 tf.data API

The *tf.data* API, like queue-based input pipelining, is suitable for efficient reading of large datasets. This *tf.data* API is simpler to use with two basic classes, *Dataset* and *Iterator*.

First, *Dataset* is created for the input data. A *Dataset* is a sequence consisting of elements with the same type and each element consists of one or more tensors. There are two ways to create *Dataset*.

(1) Read different types of data through different APIs and return a *Dataset*, such as

- *Dataset.from_tensor_slices()*: read data directly from memory.
- *tf.data.TextLineDataset()*: read the CSV file.
- *tf.data.FixedLengthRecordDataset()*: read a binary file.
- *tf.data.TFRecordDataset()*: read the data of TFRecord.

```
1   #file0.csv
2   111,222,333,444,555
3   222,333,444,555,666
4   333,444,555,666,777
5   444,555,666,777,888
6
7   #file1.csv
8   555,444,333,222,111
9   666,555,444,333,222
10  777,666,555,444,333
11  888,777,666,555,444
```

FIGURE 4.33

Contents in file0.csv and file1.csv.

```
1   example = [111   222   333   444], label  = 555
2   example = [222   333   444   555], label  = 666
3   example = [333   444   555   666], label  = 777
4   example = [444   555   666   777], label  = 888
5   example = [555   444   333   222], label  = 111
6   example = [666   555   444   333], label  = 222
7   example = [777   666   555   444], label  = 333
8   example = [888   777   666   555], label  = 444
9   example = [555   444   333   222], label  = 111
10  example = [666   555   444   333], label  = 222
```

FIGURE 4.34

Randomly generated sample queue.

(2) Get a new Dataset based on the existing Dataset with transformation, including map, shuffle, batch, repeat, etc. Fig. 4.36 shows an example of reading the TFRecord dataset from MNIST and performing transformation.[5]

After the Dataset is created, programmers can use the *Iterator* class to read the data in the created Dataset. There are four commonly used types of *Iterators*:

- one-shot iterator,
- initializable iterator,
- reinitializable iterator,
- feedable iterator.

---

[5] This code is referenced from the official documentation of TensorFlow. Refer to the website *https://github.com/tensorflow/tensorflow/blob/r1.10/tensorflow/examples/how_tos/reading_data/fully_connected_reader.py*, under Apache License Version 2.0; see https://www.apache.org/licenses/LICENSE-2.0.

```
1   #Similar to the previous example, read the samples one by one
2   def read_my_file_format(filename_queue):
3       reader = tf.SomeReader()
4       key, record_string = reader.read(filename_queue)
5       example, label = tf.some_decoder(record_string)
6       processed_example = some_processing(example)
7       return processed_example, label
8
9   def input_pipeline(filenames, batch_size, num_epochs=None):
10      filename_queue = tf.train.string_input_producer(
11          filenames, num_epochs=num_epochs, shuffle=True)
12      example, label = read_my_file_format(filename_queue)
13      #The minimum number of the remaining data after the
14      #dequeue operation
15      min_after_dequeue = 10000
16      #Queue capacity
17      capacity = min_after_dequeue + 3 * batch_size
18      example_batch, label_batch = tf.train.shuffle_batch(
19          [example, label], batch_size=batch_size,
20          capacity=capacity, min_after_dequeue=min_after_dequeue)
21      return example_batch, label_batch
```

FIGURE 4.35

Data batch processing code example.

The one-shot iterator is the simplest, with all elements being read only once, as shown in line 36 of Fig. 4.36. Other iterators are more complex. The reader interested in this part can refer to the TensorFlow website for more information.

4.5.2 Training models

After reading the input data successfully, the neural network model is constructed. The construction method is consistent with the one used in the prediction. After that, programmers define the loss function, create the optimizer, and define the model training method. Finally, the training process is iteratively executed.

4.5.2.1 Define loss function

TensorFlow provides several basic operation functions to help programmers define loss functions using different computational methods, including basic arithmetic operations, scientific computations, conditional judgment operations, and dimensionality reduction operations, as shown in Table 4.10.

Note that operations *tf.reduce_sum()* and *tf.reduce_mean()*, listed in the table above, convert the output to a scalar by summing or averaging the higher-dimensional tensor elements, respectively. Fig. 4.37 shows a code example that calls *tf.reduce_mean()* to calculate the mean squared error loss function, which converts

```
1   def decode(serialized_example):
2       #Grab images and labels from serialized_example
3       features = tf.parse_single_example(
4           serialized_example,
5           features={
6               'image_raw': tf.FixedLenFeature([], tf.string),
7               'label': tf.FixedLenFeature([], tf.int64),
8           })
9
10      #Use the decoder to preprocess the data
11      image = tf.decode_raw(features['image_raw'], tf.uint8)
12      image.set_shape((mnist.IMAGE_PIXELS))
13      label = tf.cast(features['label'], tf.int32)
14      return image, label
15
16  def inputs(train, batch_size, num_epochs):
17      filename = os.path.join(FLAGS.train_dir, TRAIN_FILE
18                              if train else VALIDATION_FILE)
19
20      with tf.name_scope('input'):
21          dataset = tf.data.TFRecordDataset(filename)
22
23          #What map loads is a function that performs the same
24          #operation on each sample
25          dataset = dataset.map(decode)
26          #Some other preprocessing functions
27          dataset = dataset.map(augment)
28          dataset = dataset.map(normalize)
29          ...
30          dataset = dataset.shuffle(1000 + 3 * batch_size)
31          dataset = dataset.repeat(num_epochs)
32          dataset = dataset.batch(batch_size)
33          #At this time, these data are shuffled into batches
34          #of batch_size, and repeated num_epochs times
35
36          iterator = dataset.make_one_shot_iterator()
37      return iterator.get_next()
```

FIGURE 4.36

Read data in TFRecord format from the MNIST dataset and preprocess.

the high-dimensional output to a scalar by squaring and averaging the difference between the true value y and the predicted value y_data.

In addition to the customized loss function, TensorFlow has four built-in cross-entropy loss functions:

1) Softmax cross-entropy

The definition of the softmax cross-entropy loss function is given in Fig. 4.38. The loss function has two parameters: "labels" and "logits." The "logits" parameter repre-

Table 4.10 Some basic operations of customized loss functions.

Type	Basic functions and functional description
Arithmetic operations	tf.add(), tf.subtract(), tf.multiply()
Scientific computations	tf.abs(), tf.square(), tf.sin()
Comparison operations	tf.greater(): return True or False
Conditional judgment operations	tf.where(condition, x, y): return x when condition is True, otherwise return y
Dimensionality reduction operations	tf.reduce_sum(), tf.reduce_mean(): to sum or average the high-dimensional tensor elements to output a scalar value

```
1   #Calculate the mean square error loss
2   loss = tf.reduce_mean(tf.square(y-y_data))
```

FIGURE 4.37

Calculate the mean squared error.

sents the predicted output of the neural network, and the "labels" are true artificially provided values.

```
1   tf.nn.softmax_cross_entropy_with_logits(labels, logits)
```

FIGURE 4.38

Softmax cross-entropy.

2) Sparse softmax cross-entropy

The sparse softmax cross-entropy loss function is similar to the softmax cross-entropy. Their parameters, which are "labels" and "logits," as shown in Fig. 4.39, are the same.

```
1   tf.nn.sparse_softmax_cross_entropy_with_logits(labels, logits)
```

FIGURE 4.39

Sparse softmax cross-entropy.

3) Sigmoid cross-entropy

The definition of the sigmoid cross-entropy loss function is similar to the softmax cross-entropy loss function, as shown in Fig. 4.40:

ı tf.nn.sigmoid_cross_entropy_with_logits(labels,logits)

FIGURE 4.40

Sigmoid cross-entropy.

According to the definition of cross-entropy in Section 2.3.3.2, the sigmoid cross-entropy loss function is the sigmoid cross-entropy of *labels* and *logits*:

$$loss = -labels \times log(sigmoid(logits)) - (1 - labels) \times log(1 - sigmoid(logits)).$$
$$(4.1)$$

If $x = logits$ and $z = labels$, then we have [127]

$$
\begin{aligned}
loss &= -z \times log(sigmoid(x)) - (1 - z) \times log(1 - sigmoid(x)) \\
&= -z \times log(\frac{1}{1 + e^{-x}}) - (1 - z) \times log(\frac{e^{-x}}{1 + e^{-x}}) \\
&= z \times log(1 + e^{-x}) + (1 - z) \times log(\frac{1 + e^{-x}}{e^{-x}}) \\
&= z \times log(1 + e^{-x}) + (1 - z) \times (log(1 + e^{-x}) - log(e^{-x})) \\
&= log(1 + e^{-x}) + x(1 - z) \\
&= x - xz + log(1 + e^{-x}).
\end{aligned}
\qquad (4.2)
$$

When $x < 0$, to prevent e^{-x} overflowing, the *loss* is transformed as

$$loss = log(e^x) - xz + log(1 + e^{-x}) = -xz + log(1 + e^x). \qquad (4.3)$$

By the aforementioned transformation, e^{-x} is removed. Thus, when $x < 0$, e^x would not overflow in Eq. (4.3). When $x > 0$, e^{-x} would not overflow in Eq. (4.2). Combining these two above, the loss function can be expressed as

$$
loss = \begin{cases} x - xz + log(1 + e^{-x}), & \text{if } x >= 0, \\ -xz + log(1 + e^x), & \text{if } x < 0. \end{cases}
\qquad (4.4)
$$

Therefore, in practice, to ensure program stability and prevent overflow, the following unified expression is used to deal with the sigmoid cross-entropy loss function:

$$loss = \max(x, 0) - xz + log(1 + e^{-|x|}). \qquad (4.5)$$

4) Weighted sigmoid cross-entropy

The weighted sigmoid cross-entropy loss function calculates the sigmoid cross-entropy with weights. When the number of positive and negative examples in the training samples is not balanced, weights can be added to increase or decrease the loss

```
1   tf.nn.weighted_cross_entropy_with_logits(targets,logits,
2                  pos_weight)
```

FIGURE 4.41

Weighted sigmoid cross-entropy.

value of positive examples in cross-entropy. The added weight is the third parameter in the function, *pos_weight*, as shown in Fig. 4.41.

The realization principle of this function is very simple: on the basis of the traditional sigmoid cross-entropy, the positive example is multiplied by the weight *pos_weight* as

$$loss = -pos\_weight \times targets \times log(sigmoid(logits)) - \\ (1 - targets) \times log(1 - sigmoid(logits)). \tag{4.6}$$

To prevent overflow, this function should be transformed. With $x = logits$, $z = targets$, $q = pos\_weight$, by inserting the weighted sigmoid cross-entropy function, we get [128]

$$
\begin{aligned}
loss &= -q \times z \times log(sigmoid(x)) - (1 - z) \times log(1 - sigmoid(x)) \\
&= -qz \times log(\frac{1}{1 + e^{-x}}) - (1 - z) \times log(\frac{e^{-x}}{1 + e^{-x}}) \\
&= qz \times log(1 + e^{-x}) + (1 - z) \times log(\frac{1 + e^{-x}}{e^{-x}}) \\
&= qz \times log(1 + e^{-x}) + (1 - z) \times (log(1 + e^{-x}) - log(e^{-x})) \\
&= (qz + 1 - z)log(1 + e^{-x}) + x(1 - z) \\
&= x - xz + (1 + (q - 1)z)log(1 + e^{-x}).
\end{aligned}
\tag{4.7}
$$

The above equation contains the term e^{-x}, and adopting the same idea as sigmoid cross-entropy, we have

$$loss = max(x, 0) - xz + l \times log(1 + e^{-|x|}), \tag{4.8}$$

where $l = (1 + (q - 1)z)$. With this equation, overflow could be eliminated in the computation of the loss function.

4.5.2.2 Create an optimizer

The optimizer implements the optimization algorithm that automatically calculates the gradient of the model parameters. TensorFlow provides a number of optimizer functions, including:

- tf.train.Optimizer: the optimizer,
- tf.train.GradientDescentOptimizer: gradient descent optimizer,

- tf.train.AdadeltaOptimizer: Adadelta algorithm optimizer,
- tf.train.AdagradOptimizer: Adagrad algorithm optimizer,
- tf.train.AdagradDAOptimizer: Adagrad dual averaging algorithm optimizer,
- tf.train.MomentumOptimizer: Momentum gradient descent optimizer,
- tf.train.AdamOptimizer: Adam algorithm optimizer,
- tf.train.FtrlOptimizer: FTRL algorithm optimizer,
- tf.train.ProximalGradientDescentOptimizer: proximal gradient descent algorithm optimizer,
- tf.train.ProximalAdagradOptimizer: proximal Adagrad algorithm optimizer,
- tf.train.RMSPropOptimizer: RMSProp algorithm optimizer,

where *tf.train.optimizer* is the base class of the optimizers. Common optimizer functions include the gradient descent optimizer (*tf.train.GradientDescentOptimizer*), momentum gradient descent optimizer (*tf.train.MomentumOptimizer*), and Adam algorithm optimizer (*tf.train.AdamOptimizer*).

The parameter of the gradient descent optimizer is *learning_rate*, which is shown Fig. 4.42.

```
train = tf . train . GradientDescentOptimizer ( learning_rate )
```

FIGURE 4.42

Gradient descent optimizer.

The Adam optimizer can dynamically adjust the learning rate for each parameter. The traditional stochastic gradient descent method adopts the same learning rate for all parameters, so it may take a long time to reach the minimum of the loss function. In order to improve the training performance to support a deeper and more complex network, it is necessary to use an algorithm that can adjust the learning rate adaptively. The Adam algorithm combines the momentum gradient descent method and the RMSProp algorithm, which dynamically adjusts the learning rate of each parameter, according to the first and second moment estimation of each gradient in the loss function. The definition of the Adam optimizer is shown in Fig. 4.43.

```
train = tf . train . AdamOptimizer ( learning_rate )
```

FIGURE 4.43

Adam algorithm optimizer.

4.5.2.3 *Define the training method*

Model training generally adopts the method of minimizing the loss function. Tensor-Flow provides the function *minimize()* for this purpose. The definition is shown in Fig. 4.44.

```
1    train_op = tf.train.Optimizer.minimize(loss, global_step=None,
2                       var_list=None)
```

FIGURE 4.44

Minimize the loss function.

The *minimize()* function calls *tf.train.Optimizer.compute_gradients()* and *tf.train.optimizer.apply_gradients()*, which compute gradients in models and update the calculated gradients, respectively. These two functions are shown in Table 4.11.

Table 4.11 Common training operations in TensorFlow.

Operation	Description
tf.train.Optimizer.compute_gradients (loss,var_list=None)	Calculate the gradient of the model parameters listed in *var_list* and return a list of (gradient, model parameters)
tf.train.Optimizer.apply_gradients (grads_and_vars)	Update the calculated gradient to the model parameters and return to the operation of updating the parameters

The *minimize()* function consists of *compute_gradients()* and *apply_gradients()* for model training. However, for a multilayer neural network, gradient explosion or vanishing may occur due to illegal input data or the limitation of derivation accuracy, which prevents the model training from convergence. In this case, the gradient calculated by *compute_gradients()* needs to be processed to keep the gradient within a certain range and then updated to the model [93]. The process is as follows:

(1) Calculate the gradient using the *compute_gradients()* function.
(2) Process the gradient according to demand, such as clipping, normalization, etc.
(3) Update the processed gradient value to the model parameters using the *apply_gradients()* function.

TensorFlow has a series of built-in gradient processing functions, as shown in Table 4.12, including the gradient L^2 norm clipping function *tf.clip_by_norm()*, the gradient average L^2 norm clipping function *tf.clip_by_average_norm()*, the gradient global L^2 norm clipping function *tf.clip_by_global_norm()*, and a function that clips the gradient to a given range *tf.clip_by_value()*. By clipping, the gradient can be controlled within a certain range, so as to alleviate the gradient explosion or vanishing.

In Table 4.12, the *tf.clip_by_norm(t,clip_norm)* function clips the gradient L^2 norm so that its value never exceeds *clip_norm*. The gradient L^2 norm is defined as the square root of the sum of squares of all the gradients, namely $\|t\|_2 = \sqrt{\sum_i grad(w_i)^2}$, where w_i represents model parameters and $grad(w_i)$ represents the gradient of parameter w_i. In order to clip the gradient L^2 norm, the clipping threshold *clip_norm* is defined. If the gradient L^2 norm is less than or equal to the threshold, the gradient remains unchanged; otherwise it is multiplied by

Table 4.12 Gradient processing functions in TensorFlow.

Function	Description
tf.clip_by_value (t, clip_value_min, clip_value_max)	Clip the gradient t to the interval of [clip_value_min, clip_value_max]
tf.clip_by_norm (t, clip_norm)	Clip the gradient t so its L^2 norm is less than clip_norm
tf.clip_by_average_norm (t, clip_norm)	Clip the gradient t so its average L^2 norm is less than clip_norm
tf.clip_by_global_norm (t_list, clip_norm)	Perform global L^2 norm clipping for all gradients in t_list, clip_norm is the clipping threshold

$\frac{clip\_norm}{\|t\|_2}$ [129]:

$$grad(w_i) = \begin{cases} \frac{clip\_norm}{\|t\|_2} grad(w_i), & \text{if} \quad \|t\|_2 > clip\_norm, \\ grad(w_i), & \text{otherwise.} \end{cases} \quad (4.9)$$

A code example that defines the model training method is shown in Fig. 4.45. An Adam optimizer is used to compute the gradient using *compute_gradients()*, clip the gradient L^2 norm, and call *apply_gradients()* to update the processed gradient values.

```
1  #Create Adam optimizer
2  optimizer = tf.train.AdamOptimizer(learning_rate)
3
4  #Calculate the gradient
5  grads = optimizer.compute_gradients(loss)
6
7  #Clip the L2 norm of the gradient
8  grads = tf.clip_by_norm(grads,clip_norm)
9
10 #Update model parameters
11 train_op = optimizer.apply_gradients(grads)
```

FIGURE 4.45

The code example that defines the model training method.

4.5.3 Model checkpoint

During training, TensorFlow uses the checkpoint mechanism to periodically save model parameters in the file system, so that the data can be recovered later to continue training or prediction. The checkpoint mechanism is implemented by the *saver* object, whose main functions are listed as follows:

- save,
- restore.

4.5.3.1 Save model

If programmers want to save variable values during or after model training, the function *tf.train.saver()* can be used to save all variables in the model.

```
import tensorflow as tf
weights = tf.Variable(tf.random_normal([30,60],stddev=0.35),
                name="weights")
w2 = tf.Variable(weights.initialized_value(),name="w2")

#Instantiate saver object
saver = tf.train.Saver()

with tf.Session() as sess:
    sess.run(tf.global_variables_initializer())
    for step in xrange(1000000):
        #Perform model training
        sess.run(training_op)
        if step % 1000 == 0:
            #Save the training variable values to the checkpoint file
            saver.save(sess, './ckpt/my-model')
```

FIGURE 4.46

Save the model.

Fig. 4.46 shows a code example of the *tf.train.saver()* function. First, two variables *weights* and *w2* are created. At the same time, *tf.train.saver()* is used to create a *saver* instance that manages all variables in the model. Next, a session is created and all the variables are initialized to start the iterative training. Every 1000 iterations of training, *saver.save()* saves the value of the variable at this time to a binary checkpoint file under the specified path on the disk. Checkpoint files are binary files that map variable names to tensor values in a specific format. In our case, the file name of checkpoint is *my-model. saver* has the ability to automatically number the checkpoint filename using built-in counters. In this way, multiple checkpoint files can be saved by different indices while training. In addition, *saver* can manage the number of checkpoint files to avoid running out of disk memory. For example, a programmer can keep only *n* of the latest files, or one checkpoint for every *n* hours of training, etc.

4.5.3.2 Restore model

When restoring model parameters to continue training or prediction, one can use the *restore()* function to recover the saved variables from the checkpoint file.

To restore the model from the checkpoint file saved in Fig. 4.46, first, the to-be-restored variables *weights* and *w2* are re-created, the saver object is instantiated again, and then the session is created. As shown in Fig. 4.47, unlike the model saving process, there is no need to initialize the variables in the session. Instead, the variables are recovered directly from the checkpoint file by calling *restore()*.

```
1   import tensorflow as tf
2
3   weights = tf.Variable(tf.random_normal([30,60],stddev=0.35),
4                name="weights")
5   w2 = tf.Variable(weights.initialized_value(),name="w2")
6
7   #The folder path where the checkpoint file is saved
8   model_path = "./ckpt"
9
10  #Instantiate saver object
11  saver = tf.train.Saver()
12
13  with tf.Session() as sess:
14    #Find the filename of the latest saved checkpoint
15    #file in model_path folder
16    ckpt = tf.train.latest_checkpoint(model_path)
17    #Restore variable
18    saver.restore(sess,ckpt)
19    print(sess.run(weights))
20    print(sess.run(w2))
```

FIGURE 4.47

Restore the model.

4.5.4 Image style transfer training

Sections 4.5.1–4.5.3 describe how to load data, train models, and save models using TensorFlow. The following section describes how to implement an image style transfer training based on TensorFlow.

First, according to the introduction in Section 3.6, the loss function of style transfer includes two parts, a content loss function and a style loss function. The code example is shown in Fig. 4.48.

After the definition of the loss function, the training process is defined for a VGG19 network. In the implementation, first, a random noise image is used as input, and the image is fine tuned by iteratively optimizing the loss function. Finally, a style transferred image is obtained which is consistent with the content image in contents and the style image in styles. The code example is shown in Fig. 4.49.

4.6 Summary

This chapter mainly introduces the usage of a deep learning programming framework. First, the basic concept and connotation of deep learning programming frameworks are introduced. Then TensorFlow, one of the most widely used programming frameworks, is presented, including its history, programming model, and basic concepts. On this basis, by using image style transfer as a driving example, the usage of TensorFlow for deep learning prediction and training is introduced.

```
1   import tensorflow as tf
2   import numpy as np
3   STYLE_LAYERS = [('conv1_1', 0.2), ('conv2_1', 0.2),
4       ('conv3_1', 0.2), ('conv4_1', 0.2), ('conv5_1', 0.2)]
5   #Define loss function
6   def loss(sess, models, img_content, img_style):
7       #Calculate the content loss function
8       sess.run(models['input'].assign(img_content))
9       #The feature matrix of the content image in the
10      #conv4_2 layer
11      p = sess.run(models['conv4_2'])
12      #The feature matrix of the input image in the
13      #conv4_2 layer
14      x = models['conv4_2']
15      M = p.shape[1] * p.shape[2]
16      N = p.shape[3]
17      content_loss = (1.0 / (4 * M * N)) * tf.reduce_sum
18          (tf.pow(p - x, 2))
19
20      #Calculate the style loss function
21      sess.run(models['input'].assign(img_style))
22      style_loss = 0.0
23      for layer_name, w in STYLE_LAYERS:
24          #The feature matrix of the style image in layer
25          #of layer_name
26          a = sess.run(models[layer_name])
27          #The feature matrix of the input image in layer
28          #of layer_name
29          x = models[layer_name]
30          M = a.shape[1] * a.shape[2]
31          N = a.shape[3]
32          A = gram_matrix(a, M, N)
33          G = gram_matrix(x, M, N)
34          style_loss += (1.0 / (4 * N ** 2 * M**2))*
35              tf.reduce_sum(tf.pow(G - A, 2)) * w
36
37      total_loss = ALPHA * content_loss + BETA * style_loss
38      return total_loss
39  def gram_matrix(x, M, N):
40      x = tf.reshape(x, (M, N))
41      return tf.matmul(tf.transpose(x), x)
```

FIGURE 4.48

Define the loss function of the image style transfer algorithm.

Exercises

4.1 Define a constant which can print "Hello, TensorFlow!" on the screen.

```
1    def get_random_img(img_content):
2        #Generate a noisy image img_random, the generation
3        #method is to superimpose random noise on the content image
4        noise_image = np.random.uniform(-20, 20, [1, 224, 224, 3])
5        img_random = noise_image * NOISE + img_content * (1 - NOISE)
6        return img_random
7    def train_vgg():
8        sess = tf.Session()
9        #Build the model, using the same network architecture as
10        #the model inference
11       models = build_vggnet(vgg19_npy_path)
12       #Load the input content image, style image
13       img_content = load_image('./content.jpg')
14       img_style = load_image('./style.jpg')
15       #Generate noisy image img_random
16       img_random = get_random_img(img_content)
17       sess.run(tf.global_variables_initializer())
18       #Define loss function
19       total_loss = loss(sess, models, img_content, img_style)
20       #Create an optimizer
21       optimizer = tf.train.AdamOptimizer(2.0)
22       #Define the model training method
23       train_op = optimizer.minimize(total_loss)
24       sess.run(tf.global_variables_initializer())
25       #Use noisy image img_random for training
26       sess.run(models['input'].assign(img_random))
27       ITERATIONS = 3000
28       for i in range(ITERATIONS):
29           #Complete a back-propagation
30           sess.run(train_op)
31           if i % 100 == 0:
32               #Print the intermediate results every 100
33               #training iterations to monitor the training effect
34               img_transfer = sess.run(models['input'])
35               print('Iteration %d' % (i))
36               print('cost: ', sess.run(total_loss))
37
38       #The training is over, save the training results
39       #and display the image
40       ...
41   if __name__ == '__main__':
42       train_vgg()
```

FIGURE 4.49

Train the VGG19 network.

4.2 Implement the addition of two tensors, that is, evaluate $A + B$ and print the result, where A is a constant, B is a placeholder, and the data types are customized by you but need to be consistent.

4.3 Implement a matrix multiplication, customize its data type and size, and execute it using CPU and GPU.

4.4 Reconstruct the *build_vggnet*, *read_wb*, and *basic_calc* functions in this chapter so that you only need to open the weight file once during the network building process.

4.5 Investigate the Python hierarchical interfaces of image processing libraries such as OpenCV, Skimage, and PIL. Use these libraries to load image data. After loading regular color images with default parameters, what is the order of stored data in the channel dimension, RGB or BGR? What should be paid attention to in data preprocessing?

4.6 Investigate commonly used image data preprocessing methods and data augmentation methods. Implement a function that selects an image file from the ImageNet2012_Val dataset, reads the data, resizes the image to (256, 256, 3), and then center crops it into a (224, 224, 3) image. Next, implement a function that reads the data, center crops the image into an (0.875 × width, 0.875 × height, 3) image, and then resizes it to (224, 224, 3).

4.7 Investigate the TFRecord format, build an image dataset (e.g., the ImageNet2012_Val dataset) into a file in this format, and then read the data from it.

4.8 A learning rate schedule is sometimes needed in network training. Suppose the initial learning rate is 0.1, and every 10,000 iterations, the learning rate becomes 0.9 times the previous rate. Use the gradient descent optimizer and other APIs to implement this.

4.9 Calculate the shape and size of the tensor after each pooling layer in the VGG19 network with single batch and an input of (224, 224, 3). Investigate how to use TensorBoard, use TensorBoard to visualize the VGG19 network to check the network information, and verify the previous computations.

*4.10 Use TensorFlow to realize linear regression, k-nearest neighbor, and other algorithms. Realize the handwriting digit recognition function on the MNIST dataset. First investigate relevant materials.

*4.11 Use TensorFlow to implement a LeNet-5 neural network for digit recognition on the MNIST dataset.

*4.12 Design a convolutional neural network for image classification on ImageNet data. Improve the top five accuracy to 85%.

Programming framework principles

The previous chapter used TensorFlow as an example to introduce the use of a deep learning programming framework. In this chapter, the principles and mechanisms of TensorFlow are introduced in detail to help readers understand how large-scale heterogeneous systems work in processing deep learning tasks. Specifically, Section 5.1 introduces the design principles of TensorFlow and clarifies several goals in TensorFlow, such as high performance, easy development, and portability. Section 5.2 introduces the core computational graph mechanism of TensorFlow, including automatic differentiation, the checkpoint mechanism, complex control flow, and the two operation modes of the computational graph, i.e., local and distributed mode. Section 5.3 discusses the architecture and implementation of TensorFlow, which supports efficient programming and execution on various devices. Section 5.4 compares mainstream programming frameworks from multiple aspects. Section 5.5 summarizes this chapter.

5.1 TensorFlow design principles

TensorFlow draws on the basic ideas of the high-level programming model of the data flow system [130,131]. Programmers are expected to achieve efficient programming and execution on different (heterogeneous) devices through a simple data flow programming model. Specifically, the design principles of TensorFlow are mainly concentrated on three aspects: *high performance*, *easy development*, and *portability*.

5.1.1 High performance

The operators integrated in TensorFlow have been fully optimized for the underlying hardware architecture during the design process, and thus can well support upper-level user applications and achieve better runtime performance. At the same time, for computational graphs, TensorFlow provides a series of optimization operations to improve operational efficiency. In addition, the TensorFlow scheduler issues nodes without data dependencies concurrently based on characteristics of the network architecture. The dependency satisfied nodes are issued asynchronously without waiting for the intermediate results of each node synchronously.

AI Computing Systems. https://doi.org/10.1016/B978-0-32-395399-3.00011-1

The code in Fig. 5.1 shows an example of concurrent execution. Since there is no dependency between the computation of tensor c and the computation of tensor d, they can be executed concurrently, resulting in a high implementation performance.

```
1   import tensorflow as tf
2
3   a = tf.constant(1,0)
4   b = tf.constant(2,0)
5   c = tf.sin(a)
6   d = tf.cos(b)
7   e = tf.add(c,d)
8
9   with tf.Session() as sess:
10      sess.run(e)
```

FIGURE 5.1

An example of concurrent execution.

5.1.2 Easy development

TensorFlow extracts a large number of common operators for a variety of existing deep learning algorithms, such as convolution, max pooling, ReLU, etc. When programmers use TensorFlow for algorithm development, they are able to directly call these operators to easily build neural network architectures and implement deep learning algorithms.

5.1.3 Portability

TensorFlow achieves cross-platform portability by defining general abstractions for different devices, including CPUs, GPUs, deep learning processors, etc. Specifically, for a new hardware device, the following must be implemented for its abstract execution model:

1) the method of starting the operator to be executed on the device;
2) the allocation method of input and output data address space;
3) the data transmission method between the host and the device.

For each operator, such as matrix multiplication, different low-level implementations on different devices will be provided. Through the above mechanism, a unified user program can be executed on different hardware platforms.

5.2 TensorFlow computational graph mechanism

The computational graph is the core of TensorFlow, covering various functions including computation, data access, logic control, and device communication [114,26]. This section first introduces the core mechanism of the computational graph and then specifically describes the two execution modes of the computational graph, local and distributed mode.

5.2.1 Computational graph

This section focuses on the core mechanism of the computational graph, including the automatic differentiation and checkpoint mechanism during model training, control flow, and the main execution modes of the computational graph.

5.2.1.1 Automatic differentiation

In deep learning, *gradient descending* is usually used to update the model parameters. According to the result of forward computing and the loss, each parameter should be tuned with an offset derived from the gradient and thus update the model. Generally speaking, there are several ways to compute the derivation [132]:

- Manual differentiation

  Manual differentiation uses the chain rule to solve the gradient equation, writes the code based on the equation, and substitutes a numerical value for calculation to obtain the gradient. The disadvantage is that it cannot be used universally or reused. Every time the model is modified, the gradient equation and the related code need to be reimplemented.

- Numerical differentiation

  Numerical differentiation uses the original definition of the derivative, like Eq. (5.1). When h takes the minimum value, the derivative can be calculated directly. The advantage is that it can hide calculation details. However, the disadvantages are also obvious. First, the computational overhead is large and thus is slow. Second, it introduces roundoff error and truncation error. Some approximate approaches can be used to reduce the error, yet the error cannot be eliminated. The derivative is defined as follows:

$$f'(x) = \lim_{h \to 0} \frac{f(x+h) - f(x)}{h}. \tag{5.1}$$

- Symbolic differentiation

  Symbolic differentiation automatically calculates expressions following the differentiation formulas, but it also encounters the problem of expression swell. Take a simple expression, $l_{n+1} = 4l_n(1 - l_n)$, $l_1 = x$, as an example, as shown in Table 5.1.[1]

---

[1] Data source of Table 5.1: Atilim Gunes Baydin et al., Automatic Differentiation in Machine Learning: a Survey, Table 1. Journal of Machine Learning Research, 18(153): 1–43, 2018. Under a CC-BY 4.0 license; see https://creativecommons.org/licenses/by/4.0/.

When $n = 3$, the symbolic differentiation has the problem of expression swell compared to the manual differentiation, thus resulting in a slower computation.

Table 5.1 Expression swell, taking $l_{n+1} = 4l_n(1 - l_n)$, $l_1 = x$ as an example.

n	l_n	$\frac{d}{dx}l_n$	$\frac{d}{dx}l_n$ (Simplified form)
1	x	1	1
2	$4x(1-x)$	$4(1-x) - 4x$	$4 - 8x$
3	$16x(1-x)(1-2x)^2$	$16(1-x)(1-2x)^2 - 16x(1-2x)^2 - 64x(1-x)(1-2x)$	$16(1 - 10x + 24x^2 - 16x^3)$
4	$64x(1-x)(1-2x)^2$ $(1-8x+8x_2)^2$	$128x(1-x)(-8+16x)(1-2x)^2(1-8x+8x^2) + 64(1-x)(1-2x)^2(1-8x+8x^2)^2 - 64x(1-2x)^2(1-8x+8x^2)^2 - 256x(1-x)(1-2x)(1-8x+8x^2)^2$	$64(1 - 42x + 504x^2 - 2640x^3 + 7040x^4 - 9984x^5 + 7168x^6 - 2048x^7)$

- Automatic differentiation

   Mainstream deep learning programming frameworks all use automatic differentiation methods to automatically compute gradients. Programmers only need to describe the process of forward computation, and the programming framework automatically derives the computational graph to complete the differentiation. This is a method between symbolic differentiation and numerical differentiation. The core of symbolic differentiation is to first establish an expression and then substitute it into the numerical calculation, while the numerical differentiation begins with the actual data. Between these two, the automatic differentiation first realizes the differentiation expressions of a batch of commonly used basic operators, such as constants, power functions, and trigonometric functions, then substitutes them into numerical calculations and retains the intermediate results, and finally finds the differentiation of the function. The automatic differentiation is not only flexible, but it can completely hide the differentiation process. This differentiation naturally fits the computational graph model used by TensorFlow. The computational graph expresses the complex paths of multiple inputs as a directed graph composed of multiple basic binary operations, and all intermediate results are retained. This helps to automatically use the chain rule for differentiation.

   Automatic differentiation in TensorFlow implements forward inference and backward differentiation for each operator. The code in Fig. 5.2 registers the backward differentiation operation for $Sinh(x)$, where *grad* is the gradient passed by the upstream node and *op* refers to the current operator, which can be used to obtain the inputs and outputs of the corresponding operator from forward pass.

   TensorFlow automatically generates the backward derivative node and adds it to the computational graph. This node is a local subgraph, generated by the back-differentiation function. The minimum back-propagation computational granularity

```
1  @ops.RegisterGradient("Sinh")
2  def _SinhGrad(op, grad):
3    """Returns grad * cosh(x)."""
4    x = op.inputs[0]
5    with ops.control_dependencies([grad]):
6      x = math_ops.conj(x)
7      return grad * math_ops.cosh(x)
```

FIGURE 5.2

Register the backward derivative method of the *Sinh*(*x*) function in TensorFlow.[2]

of the entire neural network is backward derivative nodes. Take the code in Fig. 5.3 as an example. The obtained graph is shown in Fig. 5.4.[3]

```
1  v1 = tf.Variable(0.0, name="v1")
2  v2 = tf.Variable(0.0, name='v2')
3  loss = tf.add(tf.sin(v1), v2)
4  sgd = tf.train.GradientDescentOptimizer(0.01)
5  grads_and_vars = sgd.compute_gradients(loss)
```

FIGURE 5.3

Back-propagation calculation code example.

After the differentiation function of each operator has been implemented, the chain rule is applied to calculate the final gradient of the computational graph. For each parameter, the corresponding part of the entire computational graph executes only once.

5.2.1.2 Checkpoint

The model training process inevitably involves the preservation and restoration of the model. As shown in Fig. 5.5, TensorFlow completes the mode preservation by inserting the *Save* node and associated nodes into the computational graph. The associated nodes include the *Const* and *tensor_names* nodes, which indicate the checkpoint file name and to-be-saved tensor lists, respectively. Similarly, model restoration is achieved by inserting the *Restore* node and associate nodes. The *Restore* node uses an *Assign* node to fill the to-be-filled variables.

5.2.1.3 Control flow

TensorFlow uses different combinations of basic control flow operators to realize various complex control scenarios [133]. In order to support different programming

---

[2] Source: https://github.com/tensorflow/tensorflow/blob/master/tensorflow/python/ops/math_grad.py, under Apache License Version 2.0; see https://www.apache.org/licenses/LICENSE-2.0.
[3] Fig. 5.4 and Fig. 5.5 are generated by TensorBoard.

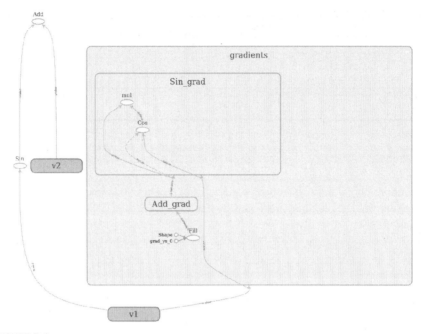

FIGURE 5.4

Derivation node generated by back-propagation in TensorFlow.

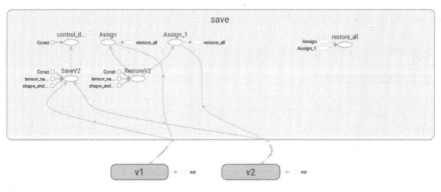

FIGURE 5.5

An example of a computational graph for saving and restoring models in TensorFlow.

languages with this control flow back-end, these basic operators should be flexible and powerful in representation. At the same time, the control flow operator shall suit the computational graph, the distributed execution, and automatic differentiation in TensorFlow. The principle of control flow design in TensorFlow refers to the data flow design from Arvind and Culler [134]. This design provides five basic control flow operators, as shown in Fig. 5.6, including *Switch*, *Merge*, *Enter*, *Exit*, and *NextIteration*. The combination of *Switch* and *Merge* can realize the function of conditional branching, and these five operators can be put together to realize the loop function.

Before introducing these five control flow operators in detail, the concept of execution frames needs to be discussed. Each operator in TensorFlow is executed in an execution frame, which is created and managed by some special control flow logic. For example, for each while loop, the control flow logic creates an execution frame, and all operators in the while loop are executed in this frame. The execution frame works like a function stack and supports functions such as nesting. Operators in different execution frames can be executed in parallel if there is no data dependency.

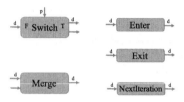

FIGURE 5.6

Typical control flow operators in TensorFlow.

The specific functions of these basic operators are introduced as follows:

- *Switch*. Based on the given condition, the *Switch* operator chooses to pass the input to one of the two different ports, true port/false port. When the input data and the condition are both valid, the *Switch* operator is executed.
- *Merge* operator. The *Merge* operator has two inputs, and at most one input data is valid at a given time. Once an input data is valid, the *Merge* operator gets executed and passes valid input data to the output port. In practice, the two inputs of the *Merge* operator cannot be both valid at the same time.
- *Enter* operator. The *Enter* operator passes the input data into the execution frame called *name*. It is mainly used to transfer input data from the current parent execution frame to the child frame. Each child frame may have multiple *Enter* operators, and each of them is executed asynchronously. The *Enter* operator is executed immediately once its input is valid. For each execution frame, when the first *Enter* operator is executed, the execution frame is established. The *Enter* operator works as the argument passing in functions.
- *Exit* operator. The *Exit* operator passes its input to the parent execution frame. It is used to return the result of the child execution frame to the parent frame. Each execution frame can have multiple *Exit* operators, and each *Exit* operator is executed asynchronously. The *Exit* operator is executed immediately once its input is valid. It works as the return value of a function.
- *NextIteration* operator. The *NextIteration* operator passes the input to the iterator of the execution frame. The TensorFlow runtime system tracks the iteration of the execution frame. Each operator in the execution frame has an iteration ID,

which is used to describe the iteration of the operator. The *NextIteration* operator gets executed immediately once the input is valid. Since there may exist multiple *NextIteration* operators in one execution frame, the execution frame in TensorFlow adds the iterator count when it encounters the first *NextIteration* at the beginning of the execution. During the Nth loop execution, TensorFlow starts the $(N + 1)$th loop when the first *NextIteration* is encountered. As more and more *NextIteration* executions end, many nodes following the *NextIteration* operator become executable.

Based on the above operators, TensorFlow can implement various complex control flows, such as conditional branching and looping. At the same time, TensorFlow further encapsulates the two control flow APIs of conditional operation *cond* and loop operation *while_loop*, which are translated into a control flow during execution. The concrete implementation principle is detailed here.

- Conditional operation: *cond*

The format of calling the conditional operation API is *cond(pred, true_fn, false_fn)*. It means that if *pred* is true, it returns *true_fn*; otherwise it returns *false_fn*. The code in Fig. 5.7 describes the main process of converting the conditional operation API to the TensorFlow computational graph. For each branch of *cond*, a conditional data flow context is created, and then *true_fn* or *false_fn* is called in the context to construct a computational graph. The conditional data flow context can automatically capture the input tensors and insert *Switch* and *Merge* operators at the appropriate position. The *Switch* operator guarantees that only branches that meet the input conditions can be executed in the data stream. Due to the asynchronous execution mechanism, a *Switch* node is inserted after each input tensor to maximize the parallelism of the computational graph. Different branches return the calculated output tensors (*res_t* and *res_f*), and then the *Merge* operator is added to return the valid result of the execution frame. Similarly, since each branch outputs their results asynchronously, the concurrency can be achieved by adding the *Merge* operators.

Take Fig. 5.8 as an example to introduce the conversion process. This conditional statement has two input variables: *x* and *y*. The control flow inserts a *Switch* operator after *x* and *y*. Only one of them is valid. When $x > y$ is true, only the *Sub* operator is executed. When $x > y$ is false, only the *Add* operator is executed. Finally, the *Merge* operator has only one valid output to the execution frame. There are multiple implementations of *Switch* and *Merge* operators to support the conditional operation. The current approach of TensorFlow is mainly to implement the automatic differentiation simply.

- *Loop operation: while_loop*

The API format of loop operation is *while_loop(pred, body, loop_vars)*. It repeatedly executes the *body* argument under the loop condition *pred*, and *loop_vars* is a list of input tensors, passed from the parent execution frame to the loop control execution

```
1   # Add Switch node
2   switch_f, switch_t = Switch(pred, pred)
3   # Create execution context when Switch is true
4   ctx_t = MakeCondCtx(pred, switch_t, branch=1)
5   # Create a computational graph when Switch is true
6   res_t = ctx_t.Parse(true_fn)
7   # Create execution context when Switch is false
8   ctx_f = MakeCondCtx(pred, switch_f, branch=0)
9   # Create a computational graph when Switch is false
10  res_f = ctx_f.Parse(false_fn)
11  # Merge the results of the two branches
12  rets = [Merge([f, t]) for (f, t) in zip(res_f, res_t)]
```

FIGURE 5.7

Implementing the conditional operation with the control flow operators.

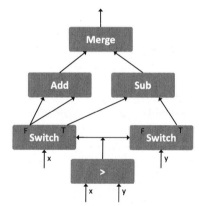

tf.cond(x>y, lambda: tf.subtract(x,y), lambda: tf.add(x,x))

FIGURE 5.8

Computational graph generated by the *cond* operation.

frame. Fig. 5.9 describes the conversion from the *while_loop* high-level API to the computational graph of TensorFlow.

Similar to the implementation process of *cond*, the *while_loop* operation first establishes the execution context. Then, for each tensor in *loop_vars*, the corresponding *Enter*, *Merge*, and *Switch* operators are added successively. The subgraph for condition *pred* is built based on the output of the *Merge* operator to determine the termination condition of the loop. Next, the subgraph for the loop body *body* is constructed based on the output of the *Switch* operator. Since the loop body requires to be executed iteratively, the *NextIteration* operator is added and its output is connected to the second input of the *Merge* operator. In this way, the output of the *Enter* operator is used for the first iteration, and the output of the *NextIteration* operator is used for

```
1  # Create the execution context
2  while_ctx = WhileContext()
3  while_ctx.Enter()
4  # Add an Enter node for each loop variable
5  enters = [Enter(x, frame_name) for x in loop_vars]
6  #Add a Merge node, the second input of the Merge node
7  #will be updated later
8  merges = [Merge([x, x]) for x in enters]
9  # Build loop subgraph
10 pred_results = pred(*merges)
11 # Add Switch node
12 switchs = [Switch(x, pred_result) for x in merges]
13 # Build the loop body
14 body_res = body(*[x[1] for x in switchs])
15 # Add NextIteration node
16 nexts = [NextIteration(x) for x in body_res]
17 # Build loop iteration
18 for m, n in zip(merges, nexts):
19   m.op.update(1, n)
20 # Add Exit node
21 exits = [Exit(x[0]) for x in switchs]
22 while_context.Exit()
```

FIGURE 5.9

Implementing the loop operation with the control flow operators.

the remaining iterations. Finally, the loop result is returned to the parent execution frame by adding the *Exit* operator.

Similarly, the constructed context automatically captures the external variables in the condition subgraph and the loop body subgraph. Then, the context adds the corresponding *Enter* operator for each external variable to be included as part of the loop and accessible.

Fig. 5.10 shows the computational graph when there is only one loop variable. If there are multiple loop variables, the corresponding *Enter*, *Merge*, *Switch*, *NextIteration*, and *Exit* operators need to be added in the computational graph. In this way, both interloop parallelism and intraloop parallelism can be realized.

The above-mentioned conditional operation and loop operation also support arbitrary nesting. For example, the loop body of the *while_loop* can call a new *while_loop*. The conversion mechanism in TensorFlow can recursively implement loop nesting and ensure that a unique frame name is assigned to each loop.

5.2.1.4 Execution mode

Computational graph execution in TensorFlow typically involves a client, a master, and one or more worker processes. Each worker process can access one or more computing devices (e.g., CPU cores, GPU cards, etc.) and execute the computational graph on them. TensorFlow provides both local and distributed execution methods.

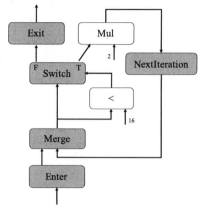

tf.while_loop(lambda i : i < 16, lambda i:tf.mul(i, 2), [4])

FIGURE 5.10

Computational graph generated by the while_loop operation.

Local execution means that the client, master, and worker processes run on a single physical machine with a single operating system, while distributed execution allows the client, master, and worker processes to execute on different machines [114], as shown in Fig. 5.11. For local execution, each worker process can include a single device or multiple devices.

Overall, the nodes in the computational graph are executed in the order of their dependencies. The TensorFlow scheduler continuously monitors the unexecuted nodes. Once the number of predecessor nodes on which a node depends is 0 (i.e., when in-degree is 0), the node is in the ready state and will be immediately placed in the preexecution queue. The executor then takes out the node from the preexecution queue. Based on the node information, the executor will assign the appropriate device to execute the corresponding operator node. After the execution of a node, all the dependencies that depend on that node will be updated.

5.2.2 Local execution of a computational graph

The computational graph has experienced a multistage process from its creation to execution. Specifically, the process includes the following four steps:

1) Pruning: Pruning is performed on the complete computational graph according to the input and output list to obtain the minimum dependency computational graph required for local execution.

2) Placement: Based on the minimum dependency computational graph, the device is assigned to each graph node according to specific device allocation rules and constraints of the operation.

3) Optimization: TensorFlow performs a series of optimization operations on the computational graph to improve its efficiency.

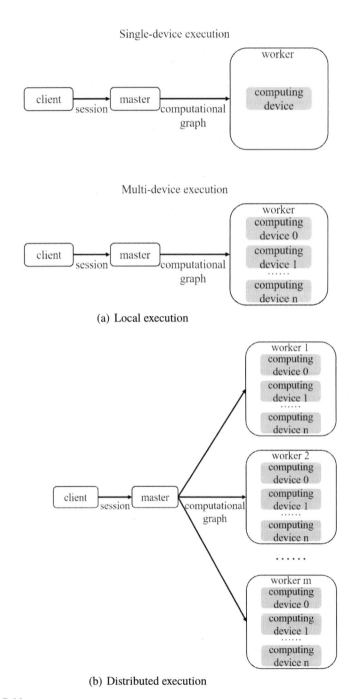

(a) Local execution

(b) Distributed execution

FIGURE 5.11

Local execution and distributed execution of a computational graph.

4) Partition: Based on placement, the computational graph is partitioned to create its own computational subgraph for each device.

5.2.2.1 Computational graph pruning

The purpose of computational graph pruning is to obtain the minimum dependency subgraph required for local operation. The pruning process includes two parts. The first part is to remove the edges and nodes in the computational graph that are not directly related to the final output node. The second part is to establish the external interactions for the input and output nodes. Taking the code in Fig. 5.12 as an example, six nodes $(a-f)$ are defined. Since the f node only depends on a, b, c, and f, other irrelevant nodes can be removed. Other problems solved in the pruning stage include passing the input of a and b from feed_dict to the corresponding nodes in the computational graph and returning the value of the f node to *res*.

```
1    import tensorflow as tf
2
3    a = tf.placeholder(dtype=tf.float32)
4    b = tf.placeholder(dtype=tf.float32)
5
6    c = tf.add(a, b)
7    d = tf.sin(a)
8    e = tf.multiply(c, d)
9    f = tf.cos(c)
10
11   with tf.Session() as sess:
12           res = sess.run(f, feed_dict={a:2, b:3})
13   print "res = ", res
```

FIGURE 5.12

An example of computational graph pruning.

In the local execution mode, TensorFlow uses the *FunctionCallFrame* function to deal with the input and output value transfer. Specifically, this function inserts an *Arg* node before each input node and adds a *RetVal* node after each output node to facilitate parameter and result passing using *FunctionCallFrame*. Finally, all inputs are connected to the *Source* node through the control-dependent edge. Similarly, all the outputs are connected to the *Sink* node through the control-dependent edge to build a complete computational graph.

The process of removing irrelevant nodes and edges starts from the output node, performs a breadth first search (BFS), and deletes nodes and edges that are not touched during the search process. After the BFS is completed, multiple connected graphs could be generated. Thus it is necessary to connect all nodes with 0 in-degree of each connected graph to the *Source* node and connect all nodes with 0 out-degree to the *Sink* node. Finally, the computational graph pruning is completed.

By setting the logging level of TensorFlow to 3, as shown in Fig. 5.13, programmers can view the detailed log and obtain information such as the execution node and execution sequence of runtime.

```
export  TF_CPP_MIN_VLOG_LEVEL=3
```

FIGURE 5.13

Set TensorFlow log verbose level to 3.

5.2.2.2 *Computational graph placement*

Computational graph placement solves the problem of which device the graph node executes on in a multidevice system. The user can specify the computing device for a certain operation or which computing nodes colocate on the same device. After TensorFlow guarantees these determined allocation rules, for unspecified computing nodes, they use specific algorithms to automatically allocate nodes to different devices to improve computing efficiency.

In order to obtain the most suitable device allocation schedule, a corresponding cost model is designed in TensorFlow to support the partition. In the cost model, there are data volumes of input and output and the computational overhead of each node, where the computational cost can be estimated through models or obtained through historical operating information.

The basic allocation algorithm uses a greedy strategy to allocate each node. Starting from the Source node, the algorithm simulates each node execution on all devices that support the node and obtains the execution overhead of the node on each device. This algorithm not only considers the computational cost of the current node in the cost model, but also includes the communication cost of copying the input data to the node. The device allocation algorithm selects the device with the lowest cost to execute the node and then performs subsequent node allocation. Obviously, because the device allocation algorithm only pays attention to the current node each time, the result obtained is only a local optimum and the global optimum cannot be guaranteed. To solve this problem, TensorFlow provides an additional interface that allows users to provide additional helpful information or restriction information to the device allocation algorithm to achieve efficient device allocation.

5.2.2.3 *Computational graph optimization*

Graph optimization in TensorFlow is implemented by the Grappler module. Users can use this module to implement customized optimizations. The main reason why the optimization is chosen at the graph level is because it is independent of each back-end, e.g., CPU or GPU, as shown in Fig. 5.14, so the optimization result can be shared by these back-ends. Through optimization, the scheduling strategy can be adjusted according to different hardware architectures, thus faster computation and higher hardware utilization can be obtained. Graph optimization can reduce the peak memory required in the inference process, thereby running larger models.

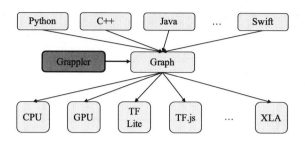

FIGURE 5.14

The level of the graph optimization module Grappler.

Various optimization methods have been implemented in Grappler. Typical optimization methods include *ConstFold* (including constant folding and other optimizations), *Arithmetic* (including arithmetic simplification, etc.), *Layout* (including layout optimization, etc.), and *Remapper* (including operator fusion, etc.). These optimization methods are uniformly called by *MetaOptimizer*.[4] The following is a detailed introduction to these methods.

ConstFold optimization

ConstFold optimization is a method that detects which constant nodes can be calculated in advance in graph static analysis. Thus, this precomputation can generate new nodes to replace the original constant nodes, thereby reducing the amount of computation at runtime.

The *ConstFold* optimization in TensorFlow is mainly composed of three key functions:

- *MaterializeShapes*: *MaterializeShapes* processes shape-related nodes, such as *Shape, Size, Rank, ShapeN, TensorArraySize*, etc. With the shape information, the result can replace the original node.
- *FoldGraph*: *FoldGraph* detects the inputs of each node. If the detected inputs are all constant nodes, the value is calculated in advance to completely replace the current node.
- *SimplifyGraph*: *SimplifyGraph* focuses on simplifying constant operations in nodes. For example, Mul(c1, Mul(tensor, c2)), where $c1$ and $c2$ are constant tensors, is simplified to Mul(tensor, $c1 \times c2$), Concat([tensor1, c1, c2, tensor2]) is simplified to Concat([tensor1, Concat([c1, c2]), tensor2]), and Zeros(tensor_shape)-tensor1 is simplified to Neg(tensor1).

Arithmetic optimization

Arithmetic optimization mainly consists of two parts: common subexpression elimination and arithmetic simplification. Some examples follow:

- tensor + tensor + tensor + tensor is converted into $4 \times$ tensor;

---

[4] For more optimization methods, please refer to [135].

- AddN(tensor × c1, c2 × tensor, tensor × c3) is converted to tensor × AddN(c1+ c2+c3);
- (mat1 + s1) + (mat2 + s2) is converted to (mat1 + mat2) + (s1 + s2), where s1 and s2 are scalars;
- redundant calculations can be removed: g(g(h)) is converted to h, when g refers to operations such as negation or reciprocal.

Layout optimization

The *Layout* optimization is mainly for GPUs, since the default data format of tensor is NHWC in TensorFlow and it is more efficient to use NCHW in GPUs. So it is necessary to insert NHWC2NCHW and NCHW2NHWC nodes in the computational graph to converse between these two data formats. After adding the conversion nodes of NHWC2NCHW and NCHW2NHWC before and after the node, the continuous NCHW2NHWC and NHWC2NCHW conversion nodes between two consecutive GPU computing nodes should cancel each other out, as shown in Fig. 5.15.

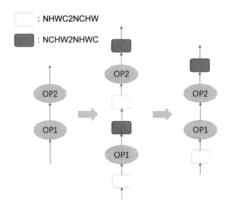

FIGURE 5.15

Layout optimization diagram.

Remapper optimization

Remapper optimization generally refers to the fusion of operators, meaning that subgraphs appearing at a higher frequency can be replaced by a single operator to improve efficiency. Typical examples of single operator substitutions include:

- Conv2D + BiasAdd + Activation,
- Conv2D + FusedBatchNorm + Activation,
- MatMul + BiasAdd + Activation.

Operator fusion has many benefits. After fusion, the scheduling overhead is completely eliminated, which provides space for improving the underlying optimization of instruction-level parallelism or vectorization. In addition, when calculating Conv2D + BiasAdd, the data processing of Conv2D is loop tiled. Then the fused operator performs while the current data is still in on-chip storage, making full use of the time and space locality of the memory access.

5.2.2.4 Computational graph partitioning and device communication

Computational graph partitioning is performed to place the computational graph on multiple devices after a series of optimizations. Each device corresponds to a partition subgraph. At this time, the communication problem between devices needs to be solved.

In the new subgraph, all cross-device edges are replaced with a pair of nodes composed of *send* and *recv*. In the example shown in Fig. 5.16, the graph on the left shows a cross-device edge from node Y to node X, indicating that cross-device data communication is required during execution. In the graph on the right, the cross-device edges are removed, and a pair of *send/recv* nodes are added to each edge, where the output of Y is connected to the *send* node and the output of the *recv* node is connected to X.

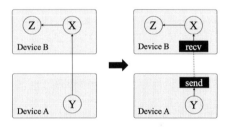

FIGURE 5.16

Cross-device data communication example and send/receive node insertion.

At runtime, *send/recv* nodes cooperate to complete cross-device communication. Meanwhile, they shield the communication details and reduce the runtime complexity. For performance, all nodes that use the same target tensor are restricted to a single *recv* node, instead of each node that uses one target tensor corresponding to a *recv* node. This ensures that each tensor that needs to be transmitted only communicates once across devices.

This communication strategy naturally assigns nodes on different devices to different worker processes. The *send/recv* node transmits data communication requirements to different devices or worker processes. Until *recv* gets valid data, the operation in the graph is blocked. The master process only needs to transmit requests to different worker processes and is not responsible for the synchronization. This allows TensorFlow to have good scalability and a more efficient execution strategy.

5.2.3 Distributed execution of computational graphs

The distributed execution of the computational graph is similar to the local execution of multidevice computational graphs. After the computational graph placement, a subgraph is created for each device. *send/recv* nodes communicate between worker processes using a remote communication mechanism, such as TCP or RDMA, for data transmission. For distributed execution, distributed communication and fault tolerance mechanisms are discussed below.

5.2.3.1 Distributed communication

The communication between parallel tasks is generally divided into two categories, point-to-point communication and collective communication. Compared to point-to-point communication, collective communication is slightly more complicated to implement, yet it has higher communication efficiency. The basic operators in TensorFlow include:

- all_sum: Accumulate all input tensors and broadcast the accumulation results to all output tensors.
- all_prod: Multiply all input tensors and broadcast the multiplication results to all output tensors.
- all_min: Take the minimum value of all input tensors and broadcast the result to all output tensors.
- all_max: Take the maximum value of all input tensors and broadcast the result to all output tensors.
- reduce_sum: Accumulate all input tensors and return this result.
- broadcast: Broadcast the input tensor to all devices.

5.2.3.2 Fault tolerance mechanism

For complex models, even if a large-scale distributed system is used, it may still need a long time to accomplish training. During long-term operation, TensorFlow may encounter errors. In order to ensure the stability of a distributed system, error checking and fault tolerance mechanisms have been added to TensorFlow. On the one hand, TensorFlow checks the correctness of the *send* and *recv* nodes. On the other hand, the master process regularly checks the status of each working machine. When an error occurs in the system, the entire computational graph execution stops immediately and is then restarted by the programmer. TensorFlow saves the intermediate state during the training process, and thus it later can restore the state before the error.

5.3 TensorFlow system implementation

This section introduces the implementation of TensorFlow, including the architecture, core logic, computational graph execution module, device abstraction and management, network and communication, and specific operator implementation.

5.3.1 Overall architecture

Fig. 5.17 shows the overall architecture of TensorFlow. The whole system can be divided into three main parts. The first part is language packs for various languages.

The kernel of TensorFlow is based on the C/C++ API and encapsulated in multiple high-level language packs, which is convenient to use. The second part is the C/C++ API. Based on the kernel code of TensorFlow, two sets of APIs are encapsulated in C and C++, mainly for higher performance requirements. The third part is the back-end code of TensorFlow. It is implemented by C/C++ to ensure portability and performance. TensorFlow supports a variety of mainstream operating systems, such as Linux, Windows, macOS, Android, and iOS. The implementation also supports a variety of mainstream hardware, such as x86, ARM, and GPU.

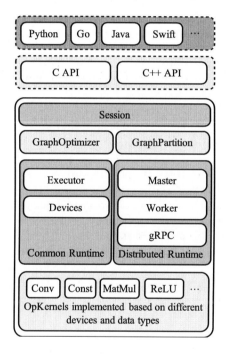

FIGURE 5.17

Overall architecture diagram implemented by TensorFlow.

The core back-end code can be roughly divided into the following parts from the code architecture:

- core/common_runtime and core/distributed_runtime. This part is divided into local runtime (*common_runtime*) and distributed runtime (*distributed_runtime*). The local runtime includes executor logic and device management, and the distributed runtime includes the master process, worker process, and remote communication.
- core/framework. This part includes the definition of the basic data structure of TensorFlow, such as the definition of Graph, Node, function, OpKernel, etc.
- core/graph. This part includes the construction and partition of computational graphs.

- core/grappler. This part includes the optimization of computational graphs and the establishment of computational graph cost models.
- core/kernels. This part includes the specific implementation of computing kernel functions, such as Conv, MatMul, ReLU, etc.
- core/ops. This part includes the registration logic of computing nodes, and so on.

5.3.2 Computational graph execution module[5]

5.3.2.1 Session execution

A Session is the interface between the user and the TensorFlow runtime. Once the input is received, the Session starts running. Each device has an executor, which is responsible for the subgraph execution on the device. The executor optimizes for large computational graphs. Based on the multithreading mode on the CPU or the multistreaming mechanism on the GPU, the executor can maximize the goal of reducing latency and increasing throughput.

The *run* function is the core logic of session execution. The execution includes argument passing, program running, and results returning. The specific code logic can be found in the *run* function of file tensorflow/core/common_runtime/direct_session.cc.

The code in Fig. 5.18 describes the process of passing arguments before the execution of the computational graph. The *FunctionCallFrame* is the window between the session and the executor, with *feed* and *fetch* as input and output, respectively. The executor obtains input from the *feed* and writes the execution result to the *fetch*.

After the argument passing process, the session calls the *RunInternal* function to start the process. The process invokes multiple parallel executors. The barrier of the executors is also created to ensure the completion of all executors. The key code of the *RunInternal* function is shown in Fig. 5.19. After the *RunInternal* function, the process returns to the *run* function to continue and process the computational graph for the final results.

5.3.2.2 Executor logic

For the executor, the concept of stream is introduced in TensorFlow. The stream is defined as a queue that can store computational tasks. These tasks are executed following the order in which they enter the queue. To achieve parallelism, there exist different streams in the device for performing tasks. These computational tasks are executed by the streams in parallel, and the tasks in a stream are executed serially. For each node in the graph, the executor performs stream allocation. The principle is that nodes with data dependencies are allocated to the same stream and nodes without data dependencies are allocated to different streams. The purpose is to minimize the number of synchronizations of streams

---

[5] Codes in Sections 5.3.2, 5.3.4, and 5.3.5 are referenced from https://github.com/tensorflow/tensorflow/tree/master/tensorflow/core, under Apache License Version 2.0; see https://www.apache.org/licenses/LICENSE-2.0.

```
1   Status  DirectSession::Run(const  RunOptions& run_options,
2       const NamedTensorList& inputs, const std::vector<string>&
3       output_names, const std::vector<string>& target_nodes,
4       std::vector<Tensor>* outputs, RunMetadata* run_metadata){
5           // Extract input name
6           std::vector<string> input_tensor_names;
7           input_tensor_names.reserve(inputs.size());
8           size_t input_size = 0;
9           for (const auto& it : inputs) {
10                  input_tensor_names.push_back(it.first);
11                  input_size += it.second.AllocatedBytes();
12          }
13          metrics::RecordGraphInputTensors(input_size);
14          // Create or get an executor
15          ExecutorsAndKeys* executors_and_keys;
16          RunStateArgs run_state_args(run_options.debug_options());
17          run_state_args.collective_graph_key=run_options.
18              experimental().collective_graph_key();
19          TF_RETURN_IF_ERROR(GetOrCreateExecutors(
20            input_tensor_names,output_names,
21            target_nodes,&executors_and_keys,&run_state_args));
22          {
23                  mutex_lock l(collective_graph_key_lock_);
24                  collective_graph_key_ =
25                      executors_and_keys->collective_graph_key;
26          }
27          /* Set the functioncallframe argument. TensorFlow uses
28          feed and fetch dictionaries to interact with the executor.
29          Feed can be thought as input, and fetch is output. */
30          FunctionCallFrame call_frame(executors_and_keys->
31              input_types,executors_and_keys->output_types);
32          gtl::InlinedVector<Tensor, 4> feed_args(inputs.size());
33          for (const auto& it : inputs) {
34                  if (it.second.dtype() == DT_RESOURCE) {
35                  Tensor tensor_from_handle;
36                  TF_RETURN_IF_ERROR
37                          (ResourceHandleToInputTensor(it.second,
38                          &tensor_from_handle));
39                  feed_args[executors_and_keys->
40                          input_name_to_index[it.first]]
41                          = tensor_from_handle;
42          }
```

FIGURE 5.18

The argument passing process before the execution of the computational graph.

and maximize the parallelism between streams. After the stream allocation, the executor starts the *ScheduleReady* function to start the asynchronous execution of the nodes in the graph. After the executor calls the *RunAsync* function, it

```
43                    else {
44                        feed_args[executors_and_keys ->
45                            input_name_to_index[it.first]]
46                            = it.second;
47                    }
48                }
49            const Status s = call_frame.SetArgs(feed_args);
50            ... ...
51        }
```

FIGURE 5.18

(*continued*)

returns to the main logic and waits for the execution to end. The logic executed by the executor can be found in the *RunAsync* function in file tensorflow/core/common_runtime/executor.cc.

The logic of the *ScheduleReady* function is simple, as shown in Fig. 5.20. The function calls the *Process* method for each node in the queue. There are mainly two queues. The ready queue is a preexecution queue; inline_ready is the queue to be processed by the current thread. If inline_ready is empty (inline_ready is empty at the beginning of the executor), a new thread is used to process each node in ready queue. When inline_ready is not empty and all nodes are low overhead, they are fed into the inline_ready queue one by one. If the node is expensive and the inline_ready queue is empty, the first expensive node is put in the inline_ready queue. Otherwise, new threads are used to execute expensive nodes.

The *Process* function performs the computation of the node, including the following steps: setting the operating parameters for OpKernel, preparing the input for the OpKernel, setting the calculation parameters, calling the device execution, processing the output, propagating the output, updating the dependencies between nodes, completing postprocessing, and possibly starting a new *ScheduleReady* function, as shown in Fig. 5.21.

It is worth noting that the *Process* function has two operating modes, synchronous and asynchronous. Most of the nodes are executed in the synchronous mode, while the *send/recv* nodes are executed in the asynchronous mode. The main reason is that the execution time of *send* and *recv* nodes is nonnegligible and uncertain. If the *Process* waits for *send/recv* to complete the execution, it will lower the overall execution efficiency. In fact, for devices like GPUs with streaming mechanism, the kernel function does not actually run synchronously. Executing the *Compute* function only means that the computing task has been sent to the execution stream.

5.3.3 Device abstraction and management

The device is the operation entity of TensorFlow execution. Each device is responsible for the operation of one subgraph. TensorFlow uses a registration mechanism to

```
1    Status  DirectSession :: RunInternal ( int64  step_id ,
2        const RunOptions& run_options , CallFrameInterface* call_frame ,
3        ExecutorsAndKeys* executors_and_keys ,
         RunMetadata* run_metadata ,
4        const  thread :: ThreadPoolOptions& threadpool_options ) {
5            run_state . rendez  =  new
6                    IntraProcessRendezvous ( device_mgr_ . get ());
7
8            /* Start parallel executor.
9            Since the executor is executed asynchronously ,
10           barrier is created to detect the end state of the
11           executor . */
12           const  size_t  num_executors  =
13                    executors_and_keys –>items . size ();
14           ExecutorBarrier* barrier  =  new  ExecutorBarrier (
15                    num_executors ,  run_state . rendez ,  [& run_state ]
16                    ( const  Status& ret ) {
17                        {
18                                mutex_lock  l ( run_state . mu_ );
19                                run_state . status . Update ( ret );
20                        }
21                        run_state . executors_done . Notify ();
22                    } );
23
24           // Start executor asynchronously
25           for ( const  auto& item  :  executors_and_keys –>items ) {
26                    thread :: ThreadPool* device_thread_pool  =
27                    item . device –>tensorflow_device_thread_pool ();
28                    if (! device_thread_pool ) {
29                            args . runner  =  default_runner ;
30                    } else {
31                            args . runner  =  [ this ,  device_thread_pool ]
32                                ( Executor :: Args :: Closure  c ) {
33                                device_thread_pool –>Schedule ( std :: move ( c ));
34                            };
35                    }
36                    if ( handler != nullptr ) {
37                            args . user_intra_op_threadpool  =
38                            handler –>AsIntraThreadPoolInterface ();
39                    }
40                    item . executor –>RunAsync ( args ,  barrier –>Get ());
41           }
42           // Wait for the executor to end
43           WaitForNotification (& run_state ,  & step_cancellation_manager ,
44           run_options . timeout_in_ms ()> 0? run_options . timeout_in_ms ():
45              operation_timeout_in_ms_ );
46              ... ...
47   }
```

FIGURE 5.19

RunInternal function.

```
1   void ExecutorState :: ScheduleReady (const TaggedNodeSeq& ready ,
2   TaggedNodeReadyQueue* inline_ready ) {
3           if (ready.empty ()) return ;
4
5       if (inline_ready == nullptr ) {
6               /* Schedule to run all ready nodes in
7               the thread pool. */
8               for (auto& tagged_node : ready ) {
9                       runner_ ([=]() { Process (tagged_node ,
10                      scheduled_nsec ); });
11              }
12              return ;
13      }
14      const TaggedNode* curr_expensive_node = nullptr ;
15      for (auto& tagged_node : ready ) {
16              const NodeItem& item = *tagged_node.node_item ;
17              if (tagged_node.is_dead ||
18                      !item.kernel ->IsExpensive ()) {
19                      inline_ready ->push_back (tagged_node );
20              } else {
21                      if (curr_expensive_node ) {
22                      /* Start a new thread to execute for
23                      expensive nodes. */
24                      runner_ (std :: bind (
25                      &ExecutorState :: Process , this ,
26                      *curr_expensive_node , scheduled_nsec ));
27                      }
28                      curr_expensive_node = &tagged_node ;
29              }
30      }
31      if (curr_expensive_node ) {
32              if (inline_ready ->empty ()) {
33                  inline_ready ->push_back (*curr_expensive_node );
34              } else {
35              /* inline_ready is not empty, put expensive
36              nodes into other threads for execution. */
37                  runner_ (std :: bind(&ExecutorState :: Process ,
38                  this , *curr_expensive_node , scheduled_nsec ));
39              }
40      }
41      ... ...
42  }
```

FIGURE 5.20

ScheduleReady function.

manage devices. Customized devices, such as deep learning processors, can also be supported through the registration interface.

In order to support the registration mechanism, TensorFlow defines an abstract device class. The local device base class *Device* is defined based on the *DeviceBase*

```
1   void ExecutorState::Process(TaggedNode tagged_node,
2   int64 scheduled_nsec) {
3           /*Prepare inputs and parameters
4           for OpKernel::Compute.*/
5           TensorValueVec inputs;
6           DeviceContextVec input_device_contexts;
7           AllocatorAttributeVec input_alloc_attrs;
8           OpKernelContext::Params params;
9           params.step_id = step_id_;
10          Device* device = impl_->params_.device;
11          ... ...
12          bool completed = false;
13          inline_ready.push_back(tagged_node);
14          /*Loop through each node in inline_ready
15          until inline_ready is empty.*/
16          while (!inline_ready.empty()) {
17                  tagged_node = inline_ready.front();
18                  inline_ready.pop_front();
19                  ... ...
20                  /*Prepare input data, make sure
21                  the input is valid.*/
22                  s = PrepareInputs(item, first_input, &inputs,
23                  &input_device_contexts,
24                  &input_alloc_attrs, &is_input_dead);
25                  ... ...
26                  /*Most nodes are in synchronous calculation
27                  mode, but Send/Recv is in asynchronous
28                  calculation mode.*/
29                  if (item.kernel_is_async) {
30                  // Asynchronous calculation.
31                          ... ...
32                  } else {
33                          // Synchronous calculation.
34                          device->Compute(op_kernel, &ctx);
35                          // Process the output.
36                          s = ProcessOutputs(item, &ctx,
37                          &outputs, stats);
38                          // Propagate the output.
39                          PropagateOutputs(tagged_node, &item,
40                          &outputs, &ready);
41                          // Postprocessing.
42                          completed = NodeDone(s, item.node,
43                          ready, stats, &inline_ready);
44                  }
45          }
46  }
```

FIGURE 5.21

Process function.

class in *tensorflow/core/common_runtime/device.h*. Based on the *Device* class, the *LocalDevice* class is designed. Local devices such as CPU and GPU can create their own device classes based on the *LocalDevice* class. For deep learning processors, programmers can also create their own device classes based on *LocalDevice*. Using the deep learning processor as an example, the class of deep learning processor devices needs to be implemented, named *BaseDLPDevice*. The code in Fig. 5.22 shows the class definition of *BaseDLPDevice*.

After the definition of *BaseDLPDevice*, the device needs to be registered to the TensorFlow runtime. Then the system can use the deep learning processor when needed.

5.3.4 Network and communication

The communications between different devices and machines in TensorFlow are carried out by *send* and *recv* nodes, which use the Rendezvous mechanism to complete data interaction. Rendezvous is an abstract class designed based on the producer–consumer model, where producers and consumers both correspond to different devices in TensorFlow. Each Rendezvous instance has a channel table, which records the relationship and status of each *send/recv* pair. Different channels have unique key–value pairs, which are generated using the information of producers and consumers. The producer uses *send* to transmit data to a specific channel, and the consumer uses *recv* to obtain data from the specific channel. The producer can transmit multiple consecutive sets of data through the channel, and the consumer can obtain this set of data in the sending order. Consumers call the *recv* method to obtain data at any time and use callback or blocking methods to obtain data. In this way, consumers can get the data as soon as it is valid. The producer is not blocked at any time.

The Rendezvous abstract class is defined in file *tensorflow/core/framework/rendezvous.h*. The key code is shown in Fig. 5.23.

The Rendezvous class has various specifically implemented methods. However, the sending- and receiving-related functions are virtual functions.

- *Send*: The producer of a tensor calls the *send* method from Rendezvous to transmit data such as tensor value (*val*) and state (*is_dead*) to a specific key–value channel. *is_dead* is a variable set by control flow-related operators. *args* passes some information to *recv* by *send*. Usually, this information is only valid when *send* and *recv* are in the same worker process.
- *Recv*: The *recv* node runs in asynchronous callback mode. Once it reads a valid tensor, the callback function is invoked to complete the subsequent operations of *recv*.

5.3.4.1 Local communication: LocalRendezvousImpl

LocalRendezvousImpl is the Rendezvous class for local execution implemented in *tensorflow/core/framework/rendezvous.cc*. It mainly implements the *send* and *recv* functions.

```
1   class BaseDLPDevice : public LocalDevice {
2     public:
3           BaseDLPDevice(const SessionOptions& options,
4               const string& name,
5                   Bytes memory_limit, const DeviceLocality&
6                   locality, const int device_id,
7                   const string& physical_device_desc,
8                   Allocator* dlp_allocator,
9                   Allocator* cpu_allocator,
10                  bool sync_every_op, int32 max_streams);
11
12          /*Whether it is necessary to record
13          the accessed tensor.*/
14          bool RequiresRecordingAccessedTensors() const override;
15
16          /*Allocate the execution stream for the
17          computational graph of the current device,
18          and use hardware resources as much as possible.*/
19          Status FillContextMap(const Graph* graph,
20          DeviceContextMap* device_context_map) override;
21
22          /*Synchronization: wait until all computing tasks
23          in the execution stream are completed.*/
24          Status Sync() override;
25
26          /*Calculation: Send the calculation task to the
27          execution stream.*/
28          void Compute(OpKernel* op_kernel,
29                  OpKernelContext* context) override;
30
31          /* Asynchronous calculation, the callback function
32          is executed until the end of the actual
33          calculation. Only Send and Recv are asynchronous
34          kernel functions.*/
35          void ComputeAsync(AsyncOpKernel* op_kernel,
36              OpKernelContext* context,
37              AsyncOpKernel::DoneCallback done) override;
38          ... ...
39      /*The system may contain multiple intelligent
40          devices.This function is used to return the current
41          intelligent device ID.*/
42          int dlp_id() const { return dlp_id_; }
43          /*The deep learning processor executor is used to
44          manage the device and control the execution stream of
45          the deep learning processor.*/
46          DLPStreamExecutor* executor()
47                          const {return executor_; }
48          ... ...
```

FIGURE 5.22

BaseDLPDevice definition.

```
49
50      protected:
51              // Memory allocator
52              Allocator* dlp_allocator_; // not owned
53              Allocator* cpu_allocator_;  // not owned
54
55              // Executor of deep learning processor
56              DLPStreamExecutor* executor_;  //not owned
57
58      private:
59              // Execution stream array
60              vector<DLPStream*> streams_;
61              // Device context
62              std::vector<DLPDeviceContext*> device_contexts_;
63              // Device Information
64              DLPDeviceInfo* dlp_device_info_ = nullptr;
65              ... ...
66      };
```

FIGURE 5.22

(*continued*)

The implementation of the *send* function is simple, as shown in Fig. 5.24. If the queue, i.e., the key–value channel, is empty or there is only *send* information in the queue, the code continues to put new data into the queue. If there exists *recv* information in the queue, the *send* function is directly passed to *recv* through the callback function.

The main logic of the *recv* function is *RecvAsync*, and the processing logic is similar to *send*, as shown in Fig. 5.25. If there already exists *send* information in the queue, the *send* information is processed directly. If the queue is empty or there is only *recv* information, the code continues to put this *recv* information into the queue.

5.3.4.2 Remote communication: RemoteRendezvous

RpcRemoteRendezvous is defined in *tensorflow/core/distributed_runtime/rpc/rpc_rendezvous_mgr.cc* and is mainly used for remote data interaction. *RpcRemoteRendezvous* and *LocalRendezvousImpl* follow the same implementation logic. They both use *send* and *recv* to interact. In TensorFlow, the RPC communication mechanism is used to realize remote communication.

The *RpcRemoteRendezvous* class inherits from *BaseRemoteRendezvous*. The implementation of *RecvAsync* is defined in *BaseRemoteRendezvous*, and the specific code logic is shown in Fig. 5.26. If the source and destination are in the same worker process, the code calls a local *RecvAsync*. Otherwise, the code calls the remote *recv* method.

RpcRemoteRendezvous uses the RPC to obtain remote data. The code in Fig. 5.27 shows the specific implementation of *RecvFromRemoteAsync*. The core of *RecvFromRemoteAsync* is to prepare and start a procedure call of *RpcRecvTensorCall*

```
 1   class Rendezvous : public core::RefCounted {
 2      public:
 3         struct Args {
 4            DeviceContext* device_context = nullptr;
 5            AllocatorAttributes alloc_attrs;
 6            CancellationManager* cancellation_manager
 7               = nullptr; // not owned.
 8         };
 9
10         // Create a rendezvous key value.
11         static string CreateKey(const string& src_device,
12            uint64 src_incarnation,const string& dst_device,
13            const string& name,const FrameAndIter& frame_iter);
14
15         /*Analyze the rendezvous key value to obtain information
16         such as source and destination devices.*/
17         struct ParsedKey {
18            StringPiece src_device;
19            DeviceNameUtils::ParsedName src;
20            uint64 src_incarnation = 0;
21            StringPiece dst_device;
22            DeviceNameUtils::ParsedName dst;
23            StringPiece edge_name;
24
25            ParsedKey() {}
26            ParsedKey(const ParsedKey& b){*this = b;}
27            ... ...
28         };
29
30         // The Send function is a virtual function
31         virtual Status Send(const ParsedKey& key,const Args& args,
32            const Tensor& val,const bool is_dead) = 0;
33         typedef std::function<void(const Status&,const Args&,
34            const Args&,const Tensor&,const bool)>
35            DoneCallback;
36         // RecvAsync function is virtual function
37         virtual void RecvAsync(const ParsedKey& key,
38            const Args& args, DoneCallback done) = 0;
```

FIGURE 5.23

The core code implemented by Rendezvous.

for obtaining remote tensors, which eventually calls *RecvTensorAsync* in the worker process to initiate the request.

5.3.5 Operator definition

Operators are the basic components of TensorFlow. Each operator has its properties, which can be set by the programmer or derived from the context when the compu-

```
44
45        // Synchronous  Recv  function  encapsulated  using  RecvAsync
46        Status Recv(const ParsedKey& key, const Args& args, Tensor* val,
47          bool* is_dead, int64 timeout_ms);
48        Status Recv(const ParsedKey& key, const Args& args, Tensor* val,
49          bool* is_dead);
50        ... ...
51    };
```

FIGURE 5.23

(*continued*)

tational graph is created. The most common attribute is to set the data type of the operator. *OpKernel* is the specific execution of the operator and depends on the underlying hardware. Operators can be implemented by different opkernels on different devices and data types by using the high-performance library from the underlying hardware or by using a specific programming language. For example, the *OpKernel* function on the CPU is usually implemented with Eigne, which provides an optimized high-performance library for multicore CPUs. For quantized data types, some low-bit-width libraries, such as gemmlowp, can achieve runtime acceleration [136]. On GPU, *OpKernel* is implemented using the CUDA C programming language. On a deep learning processor, some novel programming languages, which will be introduced later in this book, can be used to implement and optimize the operators. TensorFlow supports different operators and OpKernel functions through a registration mechanism.

In order to support the OpKernel registration mechanism, TensorFlow defines the *OpKernel* abstract class. The basic *OpKernel* class is defined in *tensorflow/core/framework/op_kernel.h*. Fig. 5.28 gives a basic definition of OpKernel.

OpKernel computation can be synchronous or asynchronous. The *Compute* methods of the OpKernels must ensure thread safety because the same graph could be executed with multiple copies at the same time. Most OpKernels are executed in a synchronous computing mode. These OpKernels should inherit the OpKernel class and override the *Compute* method. After completing the required work in *Compute* method, results are immediately returned to indicate that the work has been accomplished. Communication-related OpKernels, such as *send* and *recv*, are executed asynchronously. These OpKernels need to inherit the *AsyncOpKernel* class and override the *ComputeAsync* method. All OpKernels above obtain input and output information from *OpKernelContext* when implementing *Compute* or *ComputeAsync* methods and set the running state to *OpKernelContext*.

Take the *MaxPool* operator as an example to introduce the process of adding a deep learning processor operator. First, the OpKernel class of deep learning processors is implemented based on OpKernel, as shown in Fig. 5.29.

```
1   Status Send(const ParsedKey& key, const Args& send_args,
2       const Tensor& val, const bool is_dead) override {
3           uint64 key_hash = KeyHash(key.FullKey());
4           ItemQueue* queue = &table_[key_hash];
5           if (queue->empty() || queue->front()->IsSendValue()) {
6                   /* If the queue is empty or the first item in
7                   the queue is Send information, continue to put
8                   Send information in the queue. */
9                   Item* item = new Item;
10                  item->value = val;
11                  item->is_dead = is_dead;
12                  item->send_args = send_args;
13                  if (item->send_args.device_context) {
14                          item->send_args.device_context->Ref();
15                  }
16                  queue->push_back(item);
17                  mu_.unlock();
18                  return Status::OK();
19          }
20          /* There is information that has been placed
21          by Recv in the queue, meaning that this Send is
22          exactly what this Recv needs, so this Send
23          information can be processed directly. */
24          Item* item = queue->front();
25          /* If there is only one item in the queue,
26          delete this key from the table. */
27          if (queue->size() == 1) {
28                  table_.erase(key_hash);
29          } else {
30                  queue->pop_front();
31          }
32          mu_.unlock();
33
34          /* Notify the waiter to execute the callback
35          function. */
36          item->waiter(Status::OK(), send_args, item->recv_args,
37          val, is_dead);
38          delete item;
39          return Status::OK();
40  }
```

FIGURE 5.24

Send function in LocalRendezvousImpl.

After implementing DLPMaxPoolOp, programmers also need to register deep learning processor *OpKernel* in TensorFlow. As shown in Fig. 5.30, the macro REGISTER_KERNEL_BUILDER is used to register *OpKernel*.

```
1    void RecvAsync(const ParsedKey& key, const Args& recv_args,
2    DoneCallback done) override {
3            uint64 key_hash = KeyHash(key.FullKey());
4            ItemQueue* queue = &table_[key_hash];
5            ... ...
6            if (queue->empty() || !queue->front()->IsSendValue()){
7                    /* If the queue is empty or there is only
8                    Recv information, continue to put the Recv
9                    information in the queue. */
10                   Item* item = new Item;
11                   ... ...
12                   item->waiter = std::move(done);
13                   item->recv_args = recv_args;
14                   item->cancellation_token = token;
15                   if (item->recv_args.device_context) {
16                           item->recv_args.device_context->Ref();
17                   }
18                   queue->push_back(item);
19                   mu_.unlock();
20                   return;
21           }
22           /* The Send information has already been in the
23           queue, so the Recv can be processed immediately. */
24           Item* item = queue->front();
25           ... ...
26           // Call done function
27           done(Status::OK(), item->send_args, recv_args,
28           item->value, item->is_dead);
29           delete item;
30   }
```

FIGURE 5.25

RecvAsync function in LocalRendezvousImpl.

5.4 Programming framework comparison

The deep learning programming framework provides some basic components for deep learning design, training, verification, and other functions. Using the high-level API provided by the framework, users can easily and conveniently implement various deep learning and machine learning algorithms. At present, there are many popular open source frameworks on the market, each with its own advantages and disadvantages. Almost all frameworks support CPU and GPU devices and use common device-based acceleration libraries, such as BLAS, cuBLAS [137], NCCL [138], etc. In this section, four representative frameworks, TensorFlow, PyTorch, Caffe, and MXNet, are picked for a comprehensive comparison.

```
1    void BaseRemoteRendezvous :: RecvAsync ( const ParsedKey& parsed ,
2         const Rendezvous :: Args& recv_args , DoneCallback done ) {
3         ... ...
4         if ( IsSameWorker ( parsed . src , parsed . dst )) {
5              /* If the source and destination are in the
6              same worker process . */
7              local_ ->RecvAsync ( ... ... );
8         } else {
9         /* RecvFromRemoteAsync function to call
10        RpcRemoteRensezvous . */
11        RecvFromRemoteAsync ( parsed , recv_args , std :: move ( done ));
12        }
13        ... ...
14   }
```

FIGURE 5.26

RecvAsync function in BaseRemoteRendezvous.

First, the activity level of each framework in the community is collected,[6] as shown in Fig. 5.31. From the open source community GitHub, the number of Stars, the number of Forks, the number of Issues, and the number of Pull Requests from each framework are taken into account. These four indicators roughly reflect the popularity and activity of a framework. TensorFlow has obvious advantages in all three items. PyTorch ranks first in the number of Pull Requests, indicating that it is a framework with many active users.

Table 5.2 lists other comparison items of these frameworks, including main maintenance groups, front-end language support, operating system platforms, programming models, and current auxiliary tools. Each framework is discussed separately from these perspectives below.

5.4.1 TensorFlow

TensorFlow is a large-scale framework that was widely used within Google before it was open sourced. Afterwards, it quickly became one of the most popular frameworks in the community.

TensorFlow has a wide coverage. It supports many common front-end languages, covering almost all platforms from the cloud to the terminal. At the same time, there are many auxiliary tools to support multiple platforms and devices. For example, the computational graph visualization tool TensorBoard allows users to view the architecture of the graph and also allows users to track the training process, such as convergence loss. TFLite can export the trained model as a lightweight model for terminal devices, which is convenient for mobile phones or embedded equipment.

---

[6] The collection ended on October 26, 2019.

```
1    void RpcRemoteRendezvous :: RecvFromRemoteAsync (
2    const Rendezvous :: ParsedKey& parsed ,
3           const Rendezvous :: Args& recv_args , DoneCallback done ){
4           CHECK( is_initialized ());
5           Status s;
6           // Prepare a RecvTensor procedure call
7           RpcRecvTensorCall* call = get_call_freelist ()->New ();
8           ... ...
9           WorkerSession* sess = session ();
10          WorkerInterface* rwi =
11                 sess ->worker_cache ()->GetOrCreateWorker
12                 ( call ->src_worker_ );
13          Device* dst_device ;
14          if (s.ok ()) {
15                 s = sess ->device_mgr ()->LookupDevice (
16                        parsed . dst_device , &dst_device );
17          }
18          ... ...
19          // Initializing procedure call
20          call ->Init (rwi , step_id_ , parsed . FullKey (),
21                 recv_args . alloc_attrs , dst_device ,
22                        recv_args , std :: move (done ));
23
24          // Begin procedure call
25          Ref ();
26          call ->Start ([ this , call ]() {
27                 call ->ReleaseWorker (session ()->worker_cache ());
28                 call ->done ()(s , Args (), call ->recv_args (),
29                        call ->tensor (), call ->is_dead ());
30                 get_call_freelist ()->Release (call );
31                 Unref ();
32          });
33   }
```

FIGURE 5.27

RecvFromRemoteAsync implementation in RpcRemoteRendezvous.

Profiler is a performance analysis tool that can help users analyze and optimize model performance.

The TensorFlow community is open, well documented, and friendly to beginners. As shown in Fig. 5.31, there are many programmers working with TensorFlow who have written a lot of TensorFlow tutorials on community websites such as GitHub, StackOverflow, CSDN, and Medium. Beginners can easily find problems encountered before. In addition, TensorFlow also provides a wealth of tutorials and open source model libraries (tensorflow/models) to help users learn and use them conveniently.

TensorFlow also has some limitations that are widely criticized by users, such as confusing APIs and inconvenient debugging for declarative programming. Therefore,

```
1   class OpKernel {
2     public:
3       explicit OpKernel(OpKernelConstruction* context);
4       virtual ~OpKernel();
5       // Synchronous operation method.
6       virtual void Compute(OpKernelContext* context) = 0;
7       // Asynchronous calculation method.
8       virtual AsyncOpKernel* AsAsync() { return nullptr; }
9       // Is current OpKernel high-overhead?
10      virtual bool IsExpensive() { return expensive_; }
11      // Some methods of accessing data.
12      const NodeDef& def() const { return *def_; }
13      const string& name() const;
14      const string& type_string() const;
15      const string& requested_device() const;
16      bool is_internal() const { return is_internal_; }
17      int num_inputs() const { return input_types_.size(); }
18      DataType input_type(int i) const { return input_types_[i]; }
19      const DataTypeVector& input_types() const
20                  { return input_types_; }
21      ... ...
22    private:
23      const std::unique_ptr<const NodeDef> def_;
24      const DataTypeVector input_types_;
25      const MemoryTypeVector input_memory_types_;
26      const DataTypeVector output_types_;
27      const MemoryTypeVector output_memory_types_;
28      const int graph_def_version_;
29      const bool is_internal_;
30      NameRangeMap input_name_map_;
31      NameRangeMap output_name_map_;
32      bool expensive_;
33      ... ...
34  };
```

FIGURE 5.28

OpKernel class definition.

in the latest version of TensorFlow 2.0, many APIs have been systematically deteriorated and some redundant ones have been removed. More importantly, TensorFlow adopts imperative programming, i.e., Eager mode, suitable for rapid development and debugging by default in TensorFlow 2.0. Programmers can execute commands line by line without starting a session. Imperative programming cannot globally optimize the entire computational graph, and the performance is low. Therefore, it is recommended to use Session-based declarative programming to develop large-scale applications based on TensorFlow 2.0. By providing two programming modes, TensorFlow 2.0 not only meets the flexibility for academic researchers to write code, debug, and ver-

```
1   class DLPMaxPoolOp : public OpKernel {
2     public:
3       explicit DLPMaxPoolOp(OpKernelConstruction* context) :
4       OpKernel(context) {
5         /* Perform arguments initialization and
6         checks according to context information.*/
7         ... ...
8       }
9       void Compute(OpKernelContext* context) override {
10        /* Use deep learning processor programming language to
11        realize the MaxPool operation. */
12        ... ...
13      }
14      ... ...
15  };
```

FIGURE 5.29

OpKernel for deep learning processors to realize MaxPool.

```
1   REGISTER_KERNEL_BUILDER(Name("MaxPool")// Operator name
2                   .Device(DEVICE_DLP)        // Device type
3                   .TypeConstraint<T>("T"),   // Data type
4                   DLPMaxPoolOp<T>);          // OpKernel object
```

FIGURE 5.30

Registration of DLPMaxPoolOp.

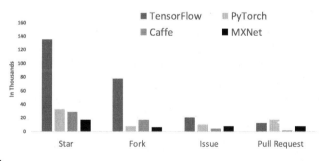

FIGURE 5.31

Community activity of the four frameworks.

ify ideas but also continues to provide the high efficiency and reliability required by large-scale industrial projects.

Table 5.2 Comparison of mainstream open source programming frameworks.

Name	Primary maintenance group	Front-end support language	Support platform	Programming mode	Auxiliary tool ecology
TensorFlow	Google	Python, C/C++, Java, Go, JavaScript, R, Julia, Swift	Linux, macOS, Windows, iOS, Android	Graph: declarative; Eager: imperative	TensorBoard, Profiler, TFLite, TF-serving, tfdbg, Official model library
PyTorch	Facebook	Python, C++	Linux, macOS, Windows	Imperative	TorchVision, Official model library, ONNX model exchange format
MXNet	Amazon	Python, C++, Go, Julia, MATLAB®, R, JavaScript, Scala, Perl, Clojure	Linux, macOS, Windows, iOS, Android	MXNet: declarative; Gluon: Imperative	MXboard, Official model library
Caffe	Officially no longer maintained, launch Caffe2	Python, C++, MATLAB	Linux, macOS, Windows	Declarative	Official model library

5.4.2 PyTorch

PyTorch is currently mainly maintained by Facebook. Compared to TensorFlow, PyTorch appears small but flexible.

The PyTorch front-end supports Python and C++ and is especially friendly to Python users. The automatic derivation supported by PyTorch is different from TensorFlow. The latter needs to implement the derivation function when adding a new operator, while PyTorch does not. In addition, PyTorch's modular programming method is particularly suitable for multiplexing network architectures, which can significantly improve development efficiency. PyTorch has always supported the imperative programming mode. Although the imperative programming mode sacrifices efficiency, it is more user friendly (such as for complex recurrent networks) and convenient for debugging (such as Python's debugging tool pdb), so it is widely accepted.

PyTorch also has many auxiliary tools. In addition to its own visualization tool TorchVision, it also supports the visualization of models on TensorBoard with a rich model library. With the increase in the number of users, the content of the community has become more and more complete. Based on the above advantages, in small-scale scenarios and academia, the number of Pytorch users has increased rapidly, with a trend to catch up with TensorFlow.

In addition, PyTorch cannot fully support various platforms, which means that the trained model cannot be easily transferred to other platforms or devices. Therefore, PyTorch is not the first choice for production.

5.4.3 MXNet

MXNet is a deep learning framework designed for efficiency and flexibility. Like TensorFlow, it supports both declarative programming and imperative programming (MXNet Gluon). Users can mix declarative and imperative programming to maximize development efficiency. MXNet supports a wide range of languages, such as R, Julia, and Go. The overall framework of MXNet is similar to TensorFlow, but the back-end code is much lighter. MXNet is based on a dynamically dependent scheduler and can efficiently support multiple devices and multiple machines.

5.4.4 Caffe

Caffe is one of the earliest frameworks. It was originally developed by the University of California, Berkeley, and maintained by the open source community.

Compared to TensorFlow's computational graph with an operator as a unit, computation in Caffe uses Layer as the basic unit, which corresponds to the layers in the neural network. Caffe provides forward and backward implementations for each layer and uses the prototxt format to represent the hierarchical stack of the network architecture. Compared to the scattered operators presented in TensorBoard, where without an organized Namespace it is difficult to understand the network architecture and functions, the prototxt in Caffe is intuitive and simple. These features enable users to quickly grasp the internal nature and implementations of basic deep learning algorithms and thus develop their own Caffe variants to complete customized functions.

However, as Caffe uses the layer to describe a network, it lacks flexibility, scalability, and reusability. At the same time, because Caffe was designed for convolutional neural networks in the early days, it has many limitations in functions, resulting in limited support for RNN-type networks. Caffe does not support multidevice and multimachine usage scenarios. Although the early version of Caffe is no longer maintained and updated, Caffe still provides a tool and platform for deep learning beginners to understand the nature of deep learning computing.

5.5 Summary

This chapter mainly uses TensorFlow as an example to introduce the mechanism of a programming framework. In order to meet the design goals of programming frameworks such as high performance, easy development, and portability, mainstream programming frameworks have adopted mechanisms based on computational graphs. These include the automatic derivation of the computational graph, the checkpoint mechanism of the model, and the control flow on the graph. In order to support large-scale model training, the computational graph also supports both local and distributed operations. For the specific implementation of TensorFlow, the main architecture includes the execution modules of the computational graph, device abstraction and management, network and communication, and the implementation of operators. Finally, the mainstream programming frameworks, including TensorFlow, PyTorch, Caffe, and MXNet, are compared from multiple perspectives.

Exercises

5.1 Investigate and learn the use of Eager API. Use Eager API to realize the addition of two numbers and matrix multiplication.

5.2 There are several common programming frameworks, including static graph mode and dynamic graph mode. What are the advantages and disadvantages of these two execution modes?

5.3 Analyze the difference in the process of training convolutional neural networks under single-machine single-card, single-machine multicard, and multimachine multicard equipment when using GPU computing. Which steps can be parallelized and which steps must be serialized?

5.4 Check the TensorFlow source code. In python/keras, find the code related to data preprocessing of the ImageNet dataset, learn several commonly used data preprocessing methods, and list the data preprocessing methods implemented in keras.

5.5 Check the TensorFlow source code. In python/ops, find the code related to registering the gradient calculation of the sin operator and the gradient calculation of the maxpool operator, check the code of other operators registered in the relevant files, and learn to understand the registration of Python layer operators.

5.6 Check the TensorFlow source code. In core/ops, find the code related to the conv operator. Briefly describe the operator registration process.

5.7 Check the TensorFlow source code. In core/kernel, find the code related to the conv operator. Briefly describe the specific implementation of convolution.

5.8 TensorFlow uses Simplified Wrapper and Interface Generator (SWIG) to make the Python language call the underlying C/C++ interface. Learn to understand the basic principles of SWIG. Find SWIG-related parts in the source code. List a use case of SWIG.

5.9 Several common machine learning frameworks now support the mixed-precision training method. Mixed-precision training uses half-precision floating points for forward propagation calculation and single-precision floating points for back-propagation calculation. It is necessary to store both half-precision and single precision during training. Investigate the specific implementation method of mixed precision and briefly describe how to implement the training of the sparse convolutional neural network model based on mixed precision. Note: The sparse convolutional neural network model generally refers to a model in which the weights of the convolution layer and the fully connected layer have many 0 elements. The sparse model can be stored in a dense matrix or a sparse matrix.

*5.10 Use the TF_CPP_MIN_VLOG_LEVEL environment variable and set it to 3. Run the computational graph pruning-related program in the textbook. Analyze the output log.

*5.11 Try to analyze the reason why operator fusion improves computational efficiency compared to nonfusion. In the commonly used classification network, which characteristics of the network of operator fusion will bring greater speedup?

*5.12 On the MNIST dataset, instead of using common machine learning frameworks, computing libraries such as NumPy can be used to implement the prediction and training of a three-layer fully connected network. Use the method in Exercise 5.9 to implement the training of a sparse fully connected network. It is recommended that the sparsity of each layer is 50%, and the sparsity can be increased gradually from 0 to 50% during the training process. Note: The sparsity of the convolution layer and the fully connected layer refers to the proportion of 0 elements in the parameters.

Deep learning processors

6

Deep learning processors (DLPs) are designed to execute deep learning operators with high performance and energy efficiency. In deep learning programming works, users' programs of deep learning algorithms are converted into a combination of deep learning operators, which are provided by the programming frameworks. Therefore, accelerating deep learning operators is the key to accelerating deep learning algorithms.

As programming frameworks like TensorFlow contain thousands of operators that have different patterns in computation, memory accesses, and control, designing a full-featured industrial-level DLP that can widely support various deep learning algorithms is very complicated. Fortunately, for the image style transfer algorithm, we need no more than 20 operators. Thus, in this chapter, we introduce the basic design principles of DLPs, while only considering to support the image style transfer for simplicity. Specifically, this chapter includes the following parts: an overview of DLPs, a presentation of algorithm analysis, a discussion of DLP architecture, a discussion on optimization design, and a comparative performance evaluation.

6.1 Deep learning processors (DLPs)

6.1.1 The purpose of DLPs

Since the 1950s, neural network algorithms have evolved rapidly, from perceptrons with only one input and one output layer to multilayer perceptrons with one hidden layer and deep neural networks with multiple hidden layers. Both the depth (i.e., number of layers) and the scale of neural networks keep increasing. The earliest perceptron, which was a single neuron that has one input, one output, and no activation function, could not solve nonlinear classification problems. To address nonlinear problems, the multilayer perceptron was later proposed, which contained multiple layers in a network and each layer contains dozens of neurons. The latest deep neural network contains far more layers and neurons in a network. Some deep neural networks contain hundreds or even thousands of layers, where each layer may contain millions of neurons and billions of synapses.

With the continuously growing number of layers, neurons, and synapses in deep neural networks, conventional chips such as CPUs and GPUs cannot meet the ever-increasing requirement of performance and energy efficiency. For example, in 2016,

Google used 1202 CPUs and 176 GPUs [30] to run AlphaGO to play against Lee Sedol in the game of Go. While each game consumed thousands of dollars of electrical power, the human brain consumed only ~20 W. Therefore, DLPs with high performance and low energy consumption are urged to support a wide range of artificial intelligence (AI) applications. In the future of the AI era, every computing device may require its own DLP, ranging from cameras, cell phones, and cloud servers to supercomputers.

6.1.2 The development history of DLPs

The predecessors of DLPs were the neural network computers/chips. In the First Wave of AI, not long after Donald Hebb proposed the Hebb learning law, Marvin Minsky developed the first neural network simulator, SNARC, in 1951. Just after Frank Rosenblatt proposed the perceptron model, the world's first neural network computer for perceptron models, Mark-I, was developed in 1960. Mark-I could perform simple tasks with a single-layer perceptron and could be connected to a camera for image processing. In the Second Wave of AI, important breakthroughs were made in the neural network research. For example, the back-propagation algorithm was proposed to train shallow neural networks more effectively than previous algorithms. Due to such algorithm advancements in the field of AI, neural network computers/chips were widely developed in the 1980s and early 1990s. Many large companies, startups, and research institutions, including Intel, Motorola, IBM, Texas Instruments, the Institute of Semiconductors of the Chinese Academy of Sciences, and the University of Science and Technology of China, developed various neural network computers/chips, including ETANN [139] (as shown in Fig. 6.1), CNAPS [140], MANTRAI [141], and CASSANDRA-I [142]. In 1989, the National Intelligent Computer Research and Development Center was established as the general technical unit by the National Science and Technology Commission of China (now the Ministry of Science and Technology of the People's Republic of China), with the Institute of Computing Technology of the Chinese Academy of Sciences as the support organization, to develop AI computers in China.

However, these early neural network computers/chips, which could only handle small-scale, shallow neural networks, were not widely used in industry with great success. The main reason was threefold. First, a killer application for small-scale, shallow neuron networks and an efficient training algorithm for large-scale, deep neural networks was lacking. Second, the technology of integrated circuits limited the hardware capability of neural network computers/chips. In comparison to today's mainstream 7-nm technology (0.007 μm), the mainstream technology at that time was 1 μm. Therefore, only a few computation logic units could be placed on one chip, e.g., 64 hardware neurons in Intel's ETANN chip. Third, a mature architecture design to support large-scale algorithm neurons with limited hardware neurons was lacking.

Along with the failure of Japan's Fifth Generation Computer Systems (FGCS), the second wave of AI went over and the development of AI was almost at a standstill. Under these circumstances, starting from the mid-1990s, startups focusing on

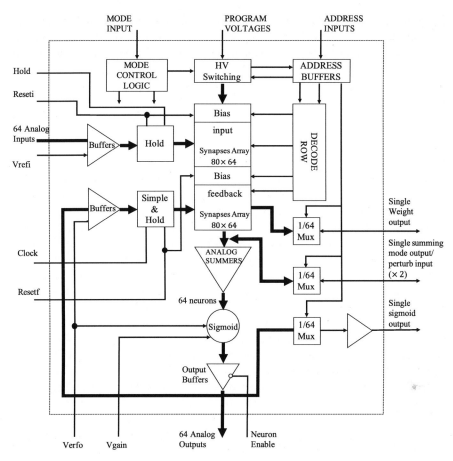

FIGURE 6.1

Intel's analog circuit neural network chip ETANN.[1]

neural network computers/chips went bankrupt, branches in large companies were dissolved, and funding was suspended in countries all over the world.

In 2006, the Third Wave of AI started, with the advanced deep learning promoted by Yann LeCun, Yoshua Bengio, Geoffrey Hinton, and other researchers. Shortly thereafter, in 2008, Yunji Chen, Tianshi Chen, and other researchers from the Institute of Computing Technology, Chinese Academy of Sciences (ICT team, also known as the "Cambricon" team[2]) started the cross-research of AI and chip design. In 2013, the joint research of the ICT team and Olivier Temam from Inria, France, proposed

[1] ©1989 IEEE. Reprinted with permission from [139].

[2] The Cambrian was a geological period during which life forms rapidly evolved into significant diversification and the first representatives of all modern animal phyla were produced, which is also known as

the world's first DLP architecture, i.e., DianNao [33]. DianNao is different from previous neural network chips. It can be flexible and efficient with hundreds of layers, tens of millions of neurons, and hundreds of millions of synapses, without limitation on the size of neural networks. Compared to traditional general-purpose CPUs, DianNao can achieve at least two orders of magnitude higher energy efficiency. Subsequently, the joint team of ICT and Inria designed the world's first multicore DLP architecture, i.e., DaDianNao [34], and the world's first machine learning processor architecture, i.e., PuDianNao [35]. Later, Cambricon [37], the first deep learning instruction set in the world, was proposed by the ICT team. "Cambricon-1," the world's first DLP chip, was developed by the ICT team. Nowadays, the series of Cambricon processors have been used in nearly 100 million devices, including smartphones and servers, promoting the research of DLPs and the subsequent development of practical products from which all people benefit.

The work of the ICT team and its collaborators promoted the direction of DLP architecture research from scratch, which has become a hot academic topic in the entire international field of computer architecture. For example, in the International Symposium on Computer Architecture (ISCA) from 2016 to 2018, nearly a quarter of the published papers cited the ICT team's works, on which the related research of DLPs was based. At present, the papers published by the ICT team have been widely cited by researchers from 200 institutions in 30 countries on 5 continents, including Harvard, Stanford, MIT, Princeton, the University of California Berkeley, Columbia, Google, Intel, Nvidia, etc. Therefore, *Science* Magazine reported that the ICT team is "pioneering in terms of specialized chip architecture [...] by all accounts among the leaders" and added that the team has achieved "groundbreaking advances" [32].

Compared to the earlier neural network chips, the reason for the booming development of DLPs is threefold.

(1) The wide range of applications of deep learning. Deep learning has been applied in many applications such as image recognition, speech recognition, and natural language processing, which are the major workloads on mainstream computing devices. Therefore, devices ranging from supercomputers to data centers and from smartphones to computers, urge for DLPs.

(2) The slowdown of integrated circuit technology advancement. As Moore's law is gradually approaching stagnation, the performance gain of general-purpose CPUs keeps decreasing. While the demand for deep learning processing keeps increasing rapidly, customized design of DLPs, which can achieve high performance and energy efficiency, is expected.

(3) The fast development of computer architecture. Earlier neural network chips maped each neuron in the algorithm to a hardware neuron independently, and thus they could support current large-scale neural networks. Today's DLPs are no longer limited by the scale of neuron networks, where a time-division mul-

---

the Cambrian explosion. The name of the team, "Cambricon," represents the expectation for the explosion of AI.

tiplexing mechanism is adopted. Therefore, one hardware operation unit can process different neurons in an algorithm at different times controlled by instructions, and the DLPs can be both flexible and efficient enough to support the large number of fast-evolving deep learning applications [33].

6.1.3 The design motivation

The DLP has become the most popular research topic in the field of computer architecture internationally. Since the very early von Neumann machine, energy efficiency and versatility are the two major concerns in computer architecture design. The former refers to how many computations can be performed per watt. The latter refers to the application scope that can be covered by the design.

Two trends have emerged in computer architecture research: application-specific integrated circuits (ASICs) and general-purpose CPUs. ASICs have extremely high energy efficiency, e.g., 1000 tera operations per second (TOPS)/W (i.e., more than 1×10^{15} operations per second can be performed with only 1 W of power) for some specific applications, which is several orders of magnitude higher than the typical energy efficiency of a CPU. But a general-purpose CPU could process all computational tasks, even with an energy efficiency of 0.1 TOPS/W, which is about 10,000 times lower than that of ASIC chips, as shown in Fig. 6.2. The main reason is that for general processing purposes, the CPU uses a heavy and complex instruction pipeline, functional components, and cache hierarchy, whereas the arithmetic units only take $<10\%$ of the total chip area. GPUs make another trade-off. GPUs achieve energy efficiencies that are 10–100 times higher than that of CPUs and maintain a certain degree of versatility. Earlier GPUs could only perform graphics processing. However, with the continuous development of GPUs by manufacturers such as Nvidia and AMD, modern GPUs can also perform scientific computing operations, such as matrix multiplication, efficiently. Moreover, many researchers try to leverage GPUs for deep learning. Yet, there is still a large gap between GPU and specialized DLPs in energy efficiency.[3]

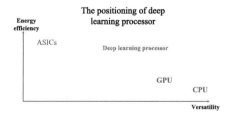

FIGURE 6.2

Energy efficiency and versatility of different types of processors.

---

[3] Nvidia began to integrate DLPs such as Tensor Core into the GPU.

DLP manufacturers must find a balance between versatility and flexibility, achieving high energy efficiency for a wide range of deep learning applications. On one hand, deep learning is not a specific algorithm but a collection of thousands of deep neural network algorithms. It is unrealistic to build a chip for each deep neural network algorithm like traditional ASIC does. On the other hand, deep learning algorithms are evolving rapidly. An ASIC chip developed for a certain deep learning algorithm, which usually takes about two years, may be out of date even before its tape-out. Therefore, DLPs should provide energy efficiency close to that of ASICs, with a degree of versatility that can better support existing and future deep learning algorithms. A similar idea holds for the development of computer architecture. The core feature of the classic von Neumann machine is to store programs; that is, the hardware does not need to be changed when the application changes, and only the software program is changed. DLPs will also follow the same principle of programmability, providing support to various existing and future deep learning operators in programming frameworks such as TensorFlow, Caffe, and MXNet.

Therefore, when designing a DLP, programmers must first analyze the computation and memory access patterns of the algorithm and accordingly determine the microarchitecture of DLP, taking into account instruction sets, pipelines, computing components, and memory access components.

6.2 Deep learning algorithm analysis

In this chapter, using image style transfer as the driving example, we analyze the used deep neural network, VGG19 [111], which has been well discussed in previous chapters, for architecture design. We first analyze the computation patterns and then the memory access patterns.

6.2.1 Computational characteristics

In this section, we only analyze the forward pass of VGG19 and leave the backward pass to readers for practice, as the backward pass in convolutional neural networks is similar. Our analysis focuses on the computation patterns, i.e., the fixed and repeated computations in neural networks. Once the computation patterns can be found, we can design corresponding instructions and hardware arithmetic units for acceleration.

Three typical types of layers exist in VGG19, which is a typical convolutional neural network, including a convolutional layer, the pooling layer, and the fully connected layer.

6.2.1.1 Fully connected layer

In a fully connected layer, the input and output are both vectors, where each output in the output vector is determined by all inputs. The specific operation can be expressed as inner products between the input vector and a set of synaptic weight vectors (with bias normally). Then the results of inner products are sent to the activation function to get the final output. Formally, in the fully connected layer, output vector $y[]$ can be computed as

$$y[j] = G \left(b[j] + \sum_{i=0}^{N_i-1} W[j][i] \times x[i] \right), \tag{6.1}$$

where x is the input vector, W is the set of weight vectors, b is the bias vector, and G is the activation function.

Fig. 6.3 shows the C code of the fully connected layer, where $x[i]$ is the ith input neuron, $y[j]$ is the jth output neuron, $W[j][i]$ is the synaptic weight between the input $x[i]$ and output neuron $y[j]$, $b[j]$ is the bias of the jth output neuron, and G is the activation function. In such implementation, one output neuron is obtained by input vector with N_i neurons performing inner product with weights, addiction with biases, and activation functions; N_o output neurons can be obtained by repeating the same process. It can be observed that the key computations are the inner product to input vector and weight matrix, which is a vector operation, and the nonlinear activation function applied to each output neuron, which is an elementwise operation.

```
1    //x is the input neuron,y is the output neuron,W is the weight
2    y(all) = 0; //Initialize all output neurons
3    for (j=0; j<No; j++)
4            for (i=0; i<Ni; i++){
5                    y[j]+=W[j][i]*x[i];
6                    if (i==Ni)
7                            y[j]=G(y[j]+b[j]);
8            }
```

FIGURE 6.3

Code implementation of the fully connected layer.[4]

6.2.1.2 Convolutional layer

A convolutional layer can be viewed as a set of local filters designed for identifying certain characteristics of input feature maps by performing convolution operations with a sliding window. Different from the fully connected layer, output neurons are connected to a part of the input neurons (inside a sliding window), rather than all input neurons. Convolution takes the highest proportion of computational overhead in the convolutional neural network. For example, in VGG19, a 19-layer neural network with 16 convolutional layers, the total execution time of the convolution on the general-purpose CPU accounts for more than 90% of the total processing time. There are 16 convolutional layers in VGG19.

Assuming that the size of the convolution kernels is $K_r \times K_c$, the N_{if} input features X have a size of $N_{ir} \times N_{ic}$, and the N_{of} output feature maps Y have a size of

---

[4] Minor revision of [35], https://doi.org/10.1145/2775054.2694358.

$N_{or} \times N_{oc}$. Formally, the output features maps can be computed as

$$Y[nor][noc][j] = G\left(b[j] + \sum_{n_i \in N_{if}} \sum_{k_c=0}^{K_c-1} \sum_{k_r=0}^{K_r-1} W[k_r][k_c][j][i] \times X[r+k_r][c+k_c][i]\right).$$

(6.2)

Fig. 6.4 shows the C code implementation of the convolutional layer, where $X[r][c][i]$ is the input neuron at position (c, r) on the ith input feature map, $Y[nor][noc][j]$ is the output neuron at the (noc, nor) position on the jth output feature map, $W[kr][kc][j][i]$ is the synapse weight between the two neurons, and G represents the activation function. Computing one output neural requires performing N_{if} inner products between $K_r \times K_c$ input neurons and corresponding kernels, where their results are summed up and fed to the activation function. By repeating the same process, all $N_{of} \times N_{or} \times N_{oc}$ output neurons can be obtained. It can be observed that the key computation is the inner product between input neurons and kernels, and other computations such as the elementwise activation function are the same as the fully connected operator.

```
1   nor = 0;
2   for (r=0; r<Nir; r+=sr) {
3       //sr is the vertical convolution stride
4           noc = 0;
5           for (c=0; c<Nic; c+=sc){
6           //sc is the convolution stride in the horizontal
7           direction
8                   for (j=0; j<Nof; j++)
9                       sum[j]=0;
10                  for (kr=0; kr<Kr; kr++)
11                      for (kc=0; kc<Kc; kc++)
12                          for (j=0; j<Nof; j++)
13                              for (i=0; i<Nif; i++)
14                                  sum[j]+=W[kr][kc][j][i]*
15                                      X[r+kr][c+kc][i];
16                  for (j=0; j<Nof; j++)
17                      Y[nor][noc][j]=G(sum[j]+b[j]);
18              noc++;}
19          nor++;
20  }
```

FIGURE 6.4

Code implementation of the convolutional layer.[5]

6.2.1.3 Pooling layer

A pooling layer directly downsamples an input feature map by performing maximum or average operations to nonoverlapping windows of input neurons (i.e., pooling window, each with $k_r \times k_c$ neurons) in the feature map. Formally, each output neuron with

---

[5] Minor revision of [33], https://doi.org/10.1145/2541940.2541967.

maximum pooling can be computed as

$$Y[nor][noc][i] = \max_{0 \le kc < K_c, 0 \le kr < K_r} (X[r+kr][c+kc][i]), \qquad (6.3)$$

and the output neuron with average pooling can be computed as

$$Y[nor][noc][i] = \frac{1}{K_c \times K_r} \sum_{kc=0}^{K_c-1} \sum_{kr=0}^{K_r-1} X[r+kr][c+kc][i], \qquad (6.4)$$

where X are the input neurons on the ith input feature map and Y are the output neurons at position (noc, nor) on the ith output feature map.

Fig. 6.5 shows the C code of the pooling layer. Similar to the convolutional layer, each output neuron is decided by all the input neurons in the pooling window. It can be observed that the major computation is the elementwise operation.

```
1   nor = 0;
2   for (r=0; r<Nir; r+=sr) {
3         //sr is the vertical pooling stride
4             noc = 0;
5             for (c=0; c<Nic; c+=sc){
6   //sc is the pooling stride in the horizontal direction
7                     for (i=0; i<Nif; i++)
8                         value[i]=0;
9                     for (kr=0; kr<Kr; kr++)
10                        for (kc=0; kc<Kc; kc++)
11                            for (i=0; i<Nif; i++) {
12                                //for average pooling
13                                value[i]+=X[r+kr][c+kc][i];
14                                //for max pooling
15                                value[i] =max(value[i],
16                                    X[r+kr][c+kc][i]);}
17
18              for (i=0; i<Nif; i++)
19                  //for average pooling
20                        Y[nor][noc][i]=value[i]/Kr/Kc;
21                  //for max pooling
22                        Y[nor][noc][i]=value[i];
23              noc++;}
24          nor++;
25  }
```

FIGURE 6.5

Code implementation of the pooling layer.[5]

Table 6.1 summarizes features of operations in the convolutional layer, pooling layer, and fully connected layer. The primary fact is that all the three layers are working with either vector or matrix data, i.e., *vectorizable* operations. For example, in the fully connected layer, when the bias is taken as a synapse connected to an input neuron with "1" as constant output, the fully connected layer can be simplified as a matrix operation, $y = Wx$. Similarly, both the convolutional layer and the pooling layer can be converted into vector and matrix operations. In fact, deep neural networks are mainly composed of operations of vector and matrix data. For mainstream neural networks, matrix and vector operations account for more than 99% of the total execution time. More importantly, these vector matrix operations provide a high degree of data parallelism but with simple control flows. In summary, the main operations used in the image style transfer algorithm are matrix and vector operations with a high degree of data parallelism. Thus, we can design specific instructions and hardware acceleration optimization.

Table 6.1 Computational characteristics of different layers.

Layer	Operation	Number of multiply-accumulate (MAC) operations	Number of activation function operations
Convolutional	Matrix inner product, vector elementwise operation	$N_{if} \times N_{of} \times N_{or} \times N_{oc} \times K_r \times K_c$	$N_{of} \times N_{or} \times N_{oc}$
Pooling	Vector elementwise operation	$N_{if} \times N_{or} \times N_{oc} \times K_r \times K_c$ Additions/comparisons $+N_{if} \times N_{or} \times N_{oc}$ Division operations (average pooling)	0
Fully connected	Matrix-multiply-vector, vector elementwise operation	$N_o \times N_i$	N_o

6.2.2 Memory access patterns

Providing specialized and powerful computing modules and instructions for DLP based on computation patterns does not necessarily bring about a significant increase in processing speed. This is because in addition to computing power, memory access capabilities may also limit speed. Intuitively, the arithmetic unit that can be placed in a chip increases in proportion to the chip area, and the memory access bandwidth of a chip increases in proportion to the chip circumference. Their growth rates are mismatched. That is to say, with the enhancement of computing power, memory access will definitely become a new bottleneck. Therefore, it is necessary to analyze the memory access patterns of deep learning algorithms and improve the locality of data access to reduce the requirement of memory access bandwidth for matching the computing power of DLPs.

Two important characteristics of memory access, *decomposability* and *reusability*, exist in deep learning networks. Decomposability means that the memory access of weights, input neurons, and output neurons in a neural network can be decomposed into independent data streams. Reusability means that the weights, input neurons, and output neurons (intermediate results) in a neural network are used multiple times during computation.

Regarding decomposability, we use the fully connected layer as an example, whose C code implementation is shown in Fig. 6.3. After traversing the input neurons to calculate the jth output neuron, computing the $j + 1$ output neurons would traverse all the input neurons again. Therefore, only when the next output neuron is calculated, the 0th input neuron $x[0]$ will be read in and reused, where the reuse distance is very long. During this calculation, weights (synapses) are not reused, but output neuron $y[j]$ can be reused well. In the inner loop, the reuse distance of $y[j]$ is very short: $y[j]$ is reused once every cycle until the end of the inner loop. It can be observed that input neurons need to be repeatedly and continuously accessed (traversing all input neurons), while the output neurons are calculated continuously in each inner loop and do not need to be accessed again after that inner loop. The weights are not reused. Therefore, leveraging the decomposability, these three types of data can be fetched separately without interference.

Regarding the reusability, due to limited on-chip data storage, the memory access bandwidth required for data that is not reusable or has a large reuse distance[6] would be high. Fig. 6.6(b) depicts the required memory bandwidth of synaptic weights, input neurons, and output neurons when running on a general-purpose CPU. Because the weights are accessed multiple times, the required memory access bandwidth is very high. As the input neurons have long reuse distances with nonreuse basically, the required memory access bandwidth is also high. As the output neurons have very short reuse distances with high reusability, the required memory access bandwidth is low.

To reduce the memory bandwidth requirement, program transformation is proposed to change the reusability of the data. One common technique is loop tiling, which can change the reuse distance of data without increasing the amount of calculations and changing the semantics of the program. The basic idea is to divide the input neurons (and output neurons) into small blocks and take one block each time to calculate the intermediates of multiple output neurons. Therefore, we can leverage the reusability of the data in the neural network to maximize the number of data reused as often as possible, thus reducing the frequency of invalid and repeated memory accesses.

Leveraging the decomposability and reusability together with the loop tiling technique, we analyze the memory access patterns of fully connected layers, convolutional layers, and pooling layers.

6.2.2.1 Fully connected layer

Fig. 6.6(a) shows the code implementation of the fully connected layer where loop tiling is applied to the input neurons. In the outer loop, input neurons are split into

---

[6] Memory accesses between two accesses to same data in memory.

multiple blocks with a size of T_i. Input neurons participate in the calculation of all N_o output neurons block by block. Without loop tiling, as shown in Fig. 6.3, the input neuron $x[i]$ would be reused only once every N_i multiply-accumulate (MAC) operations. Such a reuse interval would be longer if the size of input neurons N_i became larger. When the on-chip buffer cannot hold N_i input neurons due to limited space, each neuron needs to be fetched into the on-chip buffer N_o times. Therefore, it would totally need $N_o \times (N_i + 1)$ fetches for all input neurons (and biases), which puts a large pressure on the memory access bandwidth. Such problem can be solved by loop tiling because the reuse interval is reduced to the size of one block and the on-chip buffer can easily hold a block of neurons in general. Thus, each input neuron would not be repeatedly fetched, and it would only need $N_i + 1$ accesses to memory. Assuming $N_i = 16,384$, the input neuron needs a total of 64 kB of storage space, and 46.7% of memory access can be reduced by using loop tiling, as shown in Fig. 6.6(b). Moreover, as there is no reuse for weights, the required bandwidths for memory access are the same.

```
1    //T is the size of the loop block
2    y(all) = 0; //Initialize all output neurons
3    for (ii=0; ii<Ni; ii+=Ti)
4         for (j=0; j<No; j++)
5              for (i=ii; i<ii+Ti; i++){
6                   y[j]+=W[j][i]*x[i];
7                   if (i==Ni)
8                        y[j]=G(y[j]+b[j]);
9              }
```

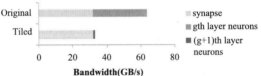

FIGURE 6.6

Pseudocode of the fully connected layer with loop tiling (top) and the effect on memory access bandwidth ($N_i = 16,384$) (bottom).[4]

Multilevel tiling can be applied further to leverage the locality of multilevel memory hierarchy. When output neurons in a fully connected layer are too large to be held in on-chip buffers, both the output neurons and input neurons can be tiled multiple times. Fig. 6.7 shows an example of a two-level loop tiling for input/output neurons. First, output neurons and input neurons are tiled into multiple blocks of size T_{jj} and T_{ii}, respectively. Each output neuron block of size T_{jj} is further tiled into subblocks of size T_j. Each input neuron block of size T_{ii} is further tiled into subblocks of size T_i, where each T_i-sized input neuron block will be used to compute a T_j output neuron block. Therefore, each subblock of T_i input neurons is reused T_j times after being loaded to on-chip buffers. Such loop tiling can be partially performed by modern compilers.

```
1   for (jjj=0; jjj<No; jjj+=Tjj) {
2   //Tiling the output neurons into blocks, Tjj and Tj
3   are the two-layer block size
4           for (jj=jjj; jj<jjj+Tjj; jj+=Tj) {
5               for (j=jj; j<jj+Tj; j++)
6                   y[j]=0;
7               for (iii=0; iii<Ni; iii+=Tii) {
8   //Tiling the input neurons into blocks, Tii and Ti are two-layer block sizes
9               for (ii=iii; ii<iii+Tii; ii+=Ti)
10                  for (j=jj;j<jj+Tj; j++)
11                      for (i=ii; i<ii+Ti; i++)
12                          y[j] +=
13                                  W[j][i]*x[i];}
14          for (j=jj;j<jj+Tj;j++)
15              y[j]=G(sum[j]+b[j]);
16  }}
```

FIGURE 6.7

Pseudocode of the fully connected layer with two-level loop tiling.[5]

6.2.2.2 Convolutional layer

For convolutional layers, the input/output neurons and weights can all be reused. Assuming that a convolutional layer has N_{if} input feature maps with a size of $N_{ir} \times N_{ic}$, N_{of} output feature maps with a size of $N_{or} \times N_{oc}$, and $N_{if} \times N_{of}$ convolution kernels with a size of $K_c \times K_r$, we analyze their reusability during computation. As each input feature map is used to compute N_{of} output feature maps, it will be reused N_{of} times. As each output feature map is computed with N_{if} input feature maps, it needs to be reused at least N_{if} times. When performing the convolution with the ith input feature map for the jth output feature map, the convolution kernels are shared among different convolutional windows and thus are reused many times. With a loop tiling technique similar as in fully connected layers, the convolutional layer can also be transformed as the pseudocode shown in Fig. 6.8. In the outermost loop, each input feature map is first tiled into multiple blocks with a size of $T_c \times T_r$. Each block can reuse a $K_c \times K_r$ convolution kernel and can be reused by N_{of} output feature maps. Because a convolutional layer may be too large to be put in the on-chip buffer such as the L1 cache (see Appendix A.2), $N_{if} \times N_{of} \times K_c \times K_r$ parameters in total, other references in the loop nest can also be tiled with multilevel tiling. The channel dimension of the output feature maps is tiled into blocks (each block in size T_{jj}), where each block needs $N_{if} \times T_{jj} \times K_c \times K_r$ convolution parameters. If N_{if} and T_{jj} are still too large for L1 cache, second-level tiling can be applied to N_{if} and T_{jj} blocks, where each block needs T_i input neurons and T_j output neurons. In the inner loop, T_i input feature maps are used to compute the result of the T_j output feature maps on the same position. Therefore, it can be observed that multilevel loop tiling can improve the data reusability and reduce the memory bandwidth requirement in convolutional layers.

```
1   for (rr=0; rr<Nir; rr+=Tr) {
2   // Tiling the vertical direction of the input feature map
3     for (cc=0; cc<Nic; cc+=Tc){
4     // Tiling the vertical direction of the input feature map
5       for (jjj=0; jjj<Nof; jjj+=Tjj){
6       // Tiling the channels of the output feature map, Tjj is
7       // the size of the outer loop block
8         nor = 0;
9         for (r=rr; r<rr+Tr;r+=sr){
10          noc = 0;
11          for (c=cc; c<cc+Tc; c+=sc){
12            for (jj=jjj; jj<jjj+Tjj; jj+=Tj){
13            // The channel of the output feature map is further
14            // divided into tiles, and Tj is the size of tiling loop
15              for (j=jj; j<jj+Tj; j++)
16                sum[j]=0;
17              for (kr=0; kr<Kr; kr++)
18                for (kc=0; kc<Kc; kc++)
19                  for (ii=0; ii<Nif; ii+=Ti)
20                  // Tiling the channels of the input feature map
21                    for (j=jj; j<jj+Tj; j++)
22                      for (i=ii; i<ii+Ti; i++)
23                        sum[j]+=W[kr][kc][j][i]*X[r+kr][c+kc][i];
24              for (j=jj; j<jj+Tj; j++)
25                Y[nor][noc][j]=G(sum[j]+b[j]);}
26            noc++;}
27          nor++;
28   }}}}
```

FIGURE 6.8

Pseudocode of the convolutional layer with loop tiling.[5]

6.2.2.3 Pooling layer

Compared to the convolutional layer, the pooling layer is relatively simple. Note that during the computation of the pooling layer, if the pooling window is larger than the stride, part of the input neurons can be reused. Fig. 6.9 shows the pseudocode of the pooling layer with loop tiling, where inputs in the sliding windows can be reused.

Table 6.2 summarizes the data reusability in the convolution layer, fully connected layer, and pooling layer. Note that with batch processing,[7] the weight of the fully connected layer can also be reused inside the batch, further reducing the memory bandwidth requirement.

In summary, for the image style transfer application, loop tiling can significantly reduce the memory bandwidth requirements. Therefore, DLP should support loop tiling in design. Different from CPUs and GPUs,[8] DLP should support separate data access to avoid interference because the reuse patterns of input neurons, output neurons, and synaptic weights are different.

---

[7] Batch processing computes multiple input samples at the same time, where the batch size is the number of input samples.

[8] The CPU and GPU provide a unified channel for different data. For example, when processing deep learning on the CPU, all kinds of different data go through the same register–L1 cache–L2 cache–memory path.

```
1    for (rr=0; rr<Nir; rr+=Tr) {
2    //Tiling the vertical direction of the input feature map
3      for (cc=0; cc<Nic; cc+=Tc){
4    //Tiling the horizontal direction of the input feature map
5        for (iii=0; iii<Ni; iii+=Tii){
6    /*Tiling the input feature map channel, Tjj is the size of
7       the outer loop block*/
8          nor = 0;
9          for (r=rr; r<rr+Tr; r+=sr){
10           noc = 0;
11           for (c=cc; c<cc+Tc; c+=sc){
12             for (ii=iii; ii<iii+Tii; ii+=Ti){
13    /*The channel of the input feature map is further divided
14    into blocks, and Tj is the block size of the inner loop*/
15               for (i=ii;i<ii+Ti;i++)
16                 value[i]=0;
17               for (kr=0; kr<Kr; kr++)
18                 for (kc=0; kc<Kc; kc++)
19                   for (i=ii; i<ii+Ti; i++) {
20                     //for average pooling
21                     value[i]+=X[r+kr][c+kc][i];
22                     //for max pooling
23                     value[i] = max(value[i], X[r+kr][c+kc][i]);}
24                   for (i=ii; i<ii+Ti; i++) {
25                     //for average pooling
26                     Y[noc][nor][i]=value[i]/Kx/Ky;
27                     //for max pooling
28                     Y[noc][nor][i]=value[i];}}
29               noc++;}
30           nor++;
31  }}}}
```

FIGURE 6.9

Pseudocode for the pooling layer with loop tiling.[5]

Table 6.2 Reuse characteristics of different layers.

Layer	Reusable	Not reusable
Convolutional layer	Input neurons, output neurons, synaptic weights	None
Pooling layer	When the pooling window is greater than the stride, some input neurons can be reused.	When the pooling window is less than or equal to the stride, neither the input neuron nor the output neuron can be reused.
Fully connected layer	Input neurons, output neurons	Synaptic weights

6.3 DLP architecture

This section describes how to design the instruction set, pipeline, arithmetic components, and memory access components of DLP based on the above analysis about computation and memory access patterns.

6.3.1 **Instruction set architecture**

Two solutions, the hardwired solution and the instruction set solution, are mainly used in practice to enable a chip to support different operators (or layers) in deep learning algorithms. The hardwired solution could provide dedicated hardware control logic for each neural network layer, but it cannot support newly emerged neural network layers. The instruction set solution decomposes various neural network layers or operators into some basic operations, where each operation is completed by one instruction. If the instruction set covers all the basic deep learning operators, newly emerged neural network layers can be assembled from these instructions (similar to all scientific calculations that are performed with basic operations such as addition, subtraction, multiplication, division, and jump concatenation). In other words, the instruction set solution can balance energy efficiency and versatility.

Therefore, the instruction set solution is adopted for DLPs. The instruction set is the core of DLP architecture, the abstraction of DLP to programmers, and the interface between software and hardware.

Improving the parallelism is the most critical part in designing the instruction set of DLP. As analyzed in the previous section, the main operations are *vectorizable* in loop nested deep learning algorithms suitable for parallelization. Parallelization in instruction set design mainly includes data-level parallelism and instruction-level parallelism. Data-level parallelism refers to the simultaneous processing of multiple data by one instruction. One example is vector instructions, in which the data are statically specified during programming for parallel processing. The advantage of data-level parallelism is that the number of instructions is small, leading to a low power consumption and area overhead of the instruction pipeline. The disadvantage of data-level parallelism is its inflexibility. Instruction-level parallelism is a common technique in general-purpose CPU design. Each instruction only performs computation for one output, but the CPU can dynamically schedule dozens of instructions to execute simultaneously in the CPU at runtime. For this part of the CPU instruction set, please refer to Appendix A.1. The advantage of instruction set parallelism is the flexibility, and the disadvantage is that the control path of the instruction pipeline would be complex, leading to a high power consumption and area overhead. Since deep learning mainly consists of regular vector and matrix operations, especially the convolutional layer and fully connected layer, the control flow is relatively simple. Because DLPs require high efficiency, data-level parallelism should be considered in DLP design.

Fig. 6.10 shows the designed instruction set in this book. This instruction set adopts the load/store architecture that the main memory can only be accessed through the load/store instructions. The instruction set mainly includes four types of instructions, computational, logical, control, and data transfer. Data transfer and computational instructions include instructions for matrices, vectors, and scalars, respectively. Logical instructions involve vector and scalar logic instructions. There are 64 32-bit scalar general-purpose registers for the control purpose. The instruction bit-width is fixed to be 64 bits, but the sizes of matrix/vector operands are variable. For example, one instruction can support the matrix multiplication between a 1000×1000 matrix and a 1000×1000 matrix or the matrix multiplication between a 100×100 matrix and a 100×100 matrix. Because the operand size of each instruction is variable, the execution time of each instruction is variable. In this way, the instruction set is flexible and concise to realize large-scale deep learning applications.

Instruction Type		Examples	Operands
Control		jump, conditional branch	register (scalar value), immediate
Data Transfer	Matrix	matrix load/store/move	register (matrix address/size, scalar value), immediate
	Vector	vector load/store/move	register (vector address/size, scalar value), immediate
	Scalar	scalar load/store/move	register (scalar value), immediate
Computational	Matrix	matrix multiply vector, vector multiply matrix, matrix multiply scalar, outer product, matrix add matrix, matrix subtract matrix	register (matrix/vector address/size, scalar value)
	Vector	vector elementary arithmetics (add, subtract, multiply, divide), vector transcendental functions (exponential, logarithmic), dot product, random vector generator, maximum/minimum of a vector	register (vector address/size, scalar value)
	Scalar	scalar elementary arithmetics, scalar transcendental functions	register (scalar value), immediate
Logical	Vector	vector compare (greater than, equal), vector logical operations (and, or, inverter), vector greater than merge	register (vector address/size, scalar)
	Scalar	scalar compare, scalar logical operations	register (scalar), immediate

FIGURE 6.10

DLP instruction set.[9]

Control instruction

Control instructions include jump instruction (JUMP) and conditional branch (CB) instruction, as shown in Fig. 6.11. Jump instruction uses immediate or general-purpose registers to specify offset. Conditional branch instruction uses general-purpose registers to store conditions and general-purpose registers or immediate to specify branch address offsets.

Data transfer instructions

Data transfer instructions support variable-length data in order to support matrix and vector computational or logical instructions flexibly. The data transfer instruction specifies the data size through the operand. Fig. 6.11 shows a vector load instruction (VLOAD). It can load the vector from the main memory to the on-chip buffer, where the address of the source data is the sum of the base address and the immediate value. Other instructions like vector store (VSTORE) and matrix load/store instructions (MLOAD, MSTORE) work in a similar way to VLOAD instruction.

Computational instruction

Most computations in neural networks are operations on vectors or matrices, as discussed previously. For example, 99.992% of arithmetic operations in GoogLeNet are vector operations, and 99.791% of vector operations are matrix operations, such as vector-matrix multiplication. For example, as in the VGG19 network used in this

---

[9] ©2016 IEEE. Reprinted with permission from [37].

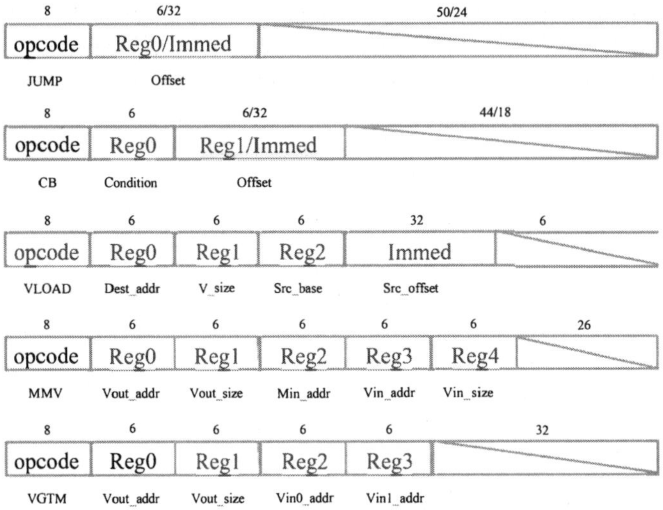

FIGURE 6.11

Some examples of instructions.[9]

book, the computation of a single output neuron in the fully connected layer is a vector inner product; combining these inner products, it becomes a matrix multiplication. Therefore, computational instructions for deep learning mainly include matrix, vector, and scalar instructions.

Matrix instructions are designed to perform matrix operations like matrix-vector multiplication ($\mathbf{y} = \mathbf{W}\mathbf{x}$) operations in convolution and fully connected layers. Fig. 6.11 shows the matrix-multiply-vector (MMV) instruction in the designed instruction set. In MMV, Reg0 specifies the base address where the output vector is stored on the chip. Reg1 specifies the size of the output vector. Reg2, Reg3, and Reg4 specify the base addresses of the input matrix and the input vector and the size of the input vector, respectively. The MMV instruction supports matrix-vector multiplication of any size as long as the input and output data can be stored in on-chip memory. The MMV instruction also needs some variants. For example, when using the back-propagation to train a neural network, calculating the gradient vector requires multiplying a vector with a matrix. If using MMV instructions, additional instructions are needed to perform matrix transposition. To avoid such additional data movements, DLPs also provide a vector-multiply-matrix (VMM) instruction, following a similar design principle.

Vector instructions are mainly designed to perform vector operations such as $\mathbf{y} + \mathbf{b}$ in convolutional and fully connected operations. For this reason, DLP instruction set has designed inner product, vector-add-vector (VAV), vector-multiply-vector (VMV), vector-subtract-vector (VSV), and vector-divide-vector (VDV) instructions. In order to support activation functions, such as the sigmoid function, the DLP instruction set also contains vector-exponent (VEXP) and vector-logarithm (VLOG) instructions. In addition, when the neural network does dropout or random sampling, it needs to use random vector generation. The DLP instruction set contains a random vector instruction to generate random vectors with uniform distributions in the [0, 1] interval.

Scalar instructions are mainly designed for completeness; for neural networks like GoogLeNet, only 0.008% of arithmetic operations require scalar instructions. Scalar instructions include basic arithmetic operations and scalar transcendental functions, as shown in Fig. 6.10.

Logical instruction

In order to support comparison in maximum pooling, the DLP instruction set provides the vector-greater-than-merge (VGTM) instruction. As shown in Fig. 6.11, this instruction compares each element in vectors $Vin0$ and $Vin1$ and stores the larger one in the output vector $Vout$, or $Vout[i] = (Vin0[i] > Vin1[i])?Vin0[i] : Vin1[i]$. In addition, the DLP instruction set provides vector-greater-than (VGT), vector-equal (VE), and vector AND/OR/NOT (VAND/VOR/VNOT) instructions, scalar comparison, and scalar logic instructions to handle branch conditions.

Code example

Using the DLP instruction set, the representative convolutional layers, fully connected layers, and pooling layers in neural networks can be easily implemented. Fig. 6.12 shows a code example of a fully connected layer and a max pooling layer. Specifically, when calculating the maximum pooling layer, values in the same position of all input feature maps (N_i) are placed in the same input vector, and each VGTM instruction performs the corresponding element comparison of the two N_i-dimensional vectors in parallel. The convolutional layer and fully connected layer are calculated similarly.

In contrast, the instruction set of a CPU is not specially designed for neural networks, thus a large number of instructions are required to construct a neural network. As shown in Fig. 6.12, to construct the same neural network, the lines of code with the DLP instruction set are only 10.15% of the lines with the X86 instruction set.

6.3.2 Pipeline

The instruction execution pipeline of DLP contains seven stages: fetching, decoding, transmitting, reading registers, executing, writing back, and submitting, as shown in Fig. 6.13. After fetching and decoding, an instruction is sent to the in-order issue queue. After successfully fetching operands (scalar data, address/size of vector/matrix data) from the scalar register file, the instruction is issued to different function units. Similar to general-purpose CPUs, control instructions and scalar computation/logic instructions are sent to the scalar function unit (Scalar FU) for direct processing.

Data transfer, vector/matrix computational, and vector logical instructions may access different on-chip memories. Thus, these instructions will be sent to the address generation unit (AGU) to calculate the specific memory access addresses. These instructions are placed in an in-order memory queue to resolve potential memory access dependencies with earlier instructions in the queue. Then the load/store requests from the scalar data transfer instruction will be sent to the L1 cache, the vector data

```
1   MLP code:
2   //$0: input size, $1: output size, $2: matrix size
3   //$3: input address, $4: weight address
4   //$5: bias address, $6: output address
5   //$7–$10: temp variable address
6
7   VLOAD    $3, $0, #100          //load input vector from address (100)
8   MLOAD    $4, $2, #300          //load weight matrix from address (300)
9   MMV      $7, $1, $4, $3, $0    //Wx
10  VAV      $8, $1, $7, $5        //tmp = Wx + b
11  VEXP     $9, $1, $8            //exp(tmp)
12  VAS      $10, $1, $9, #1       //1 + exp(tmp)
13  VDV      $6, $1, $9, $10       //y = exp(tmp)/(1 + exp(tmp))
14  VSTORE   $6, $1, #200          //store output vector to address(200)
15
16  Pooling code:
17  //$0: feature map size, $1: input data size,
18  //$2: output data size, $3: pooling window size −1
19  //$4: x−axis loop num, $5: y−axis loop num
20  //$6: input addr, $7: output addr
21  //$8: y−axis stride of input
22
23      VLOAD  $6, $1, #100 //load input neurons from address (100)
24      SMOVE  $5, $3       //init y
25  L0: SMOVE  $4, $3       //init x
26  L1: VGTM   $7, $0, $6, $7
27      //∀ feature map m, output[m]=(input[x][y][m]>output[m])? input[x][y][
                m]: output[m]
28      SADD   $6, $6, $0   //Update input address
29      SADD   $4, $4, #−1  // x——
30      CB     #L1,$4       // if(x>0) goto L1
31      SADD   $6, $6, $8   //update input address
32      SADD   $5, $5, #−1  // y——
33      CB     #L0, $5      // if(y>0) goto L0
34      VSTORE $7, $2, #200 // store output neurons to address (200)
```

FIGURE 6.12

Code examples of the fully connected layer and maximum pooling.[9]

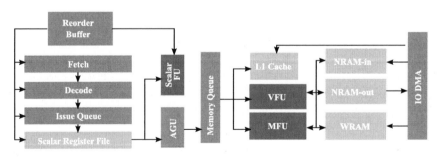

FIGURE 6.13

The DLP architecture.

transfer/computational/logical instructions will be sent to the vector functional unit (VFU), and the matrix data transfer/computational instructions will be sent to the

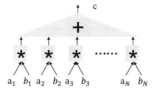

FIGURE 6.14

Vector MAC computing unit.

matrix functional unit (MFU). After an instruction is executed and written back, if it is the oldest uncommitted instruction in the reorder buffer, it will be committed from the reorder buffer and retired from the execution pipeline.

6.3.3 Computing unit

To perform the various vector and matrix operation instructions in the instruction set, the functional components VFU and MFU are designed. In DLPs, the VFU and MFU are mainly designed based on vector MAC, as shown in Fig. 6.14.

6.3.3.1 Vector MAC

The function of a basic scalar MAC is to complete a multiply-add operation. Its inputs are two scalars a and b, and its output is the product of the two scalars plus the original accumulated value c, i.e., $a \times b + c$.

Different from the scalar MAC, the inputs of a vector MAC are two vectors $\boldsymbol{a} = [a_1; a_2; a_3; ...; a_N]$ and $\boldsymbol{b} = [b_1; b_2; b_3; ...; b_N]$, and the output is the inner product of the two vectors plus the original accumulated value c:

$$\sum_{i=1}^{N} a_i \times b_i + c. \qquad (6.5)$$

The vector MAC with two N-dimensional vector inputs can complete the computation of a fully connected layer with N inputs and one output every clock cycle (activation functions excluded). If integrating M such vector MACs, DLP can finish the computation of a fully connected layer with N inputs and M outputs every clock cycle. Therefore, vector MAC is suitable for neural network operations.

6.3.3.2 Extensions to vector MAC

Simply organizing multiple vector MAC units together is not sufficient to support deep learning. One single vector MAC unit essentially completes a vector inner product operation, the inner product instruction in Fig. 6.10, thus multiple vector MAC units only complete the function of matrix vector multiplication, namely the MMV instruction. Although the computation in deep learning is mainly based on vector inner products, it also needs other operations. If these operations are not fully supported by the arithmetic component, DLPs cannot perform complete deep learning processes. For example, the activation function cannot be performed without the basic vector operations (e.g., the VAV instruction), and the pooling layer cannot be performed without the comparison operations (e.g., Vector-Max [VMAX] and Vector-Min [VMIN] instructions). Therefore, it is necessary to enhance the vector MAC unit in Fig. 6.14 to support the deep learning instruction set as previously designed.

We use the three typical operators (convolutional, pooling, and fully connected) of the convolutional neural network as examples to analyze how the vector MAC unit could be enhanced for the design of the VFU and MFU in DLPs. Specifically, for the fully connected layer operation in Eq. (6.1), it contains vector inner product, bias addition, and an activation function. Among all instructions in Fig. 6.12 for the fully connected layer, the MMV instruction can be directly supported by the vector MAC, but the remaining VAV, VEXP, VAS, and VDV cannot be directly implemented in the vector MAC unit. For the convolutional layer operation in Eq. (6.2), similar to the fully connected layer operation, the same instructions cannot be performed. For the pooling operation in Eq. (6.3), it only contains the maximum value operation without vector inner product operation. Among all instructions in the pooling layer in Fig. 6.12, the VGTM instruction cannot be supported by the vector MAC unit.

Therefore, to support the entire convolutional neural network in our driving example, we need to enhance the vector MAC with additional functionalities.

First, an activation function processing unit is needed. In Section 2.3.2, we have introduced several typical activation functions. The computations of these activation functions are different and sometimes complicated. For example, the standard ReLU activation function is relatively simple, i.e., if the input is less than 0, the output is 0, otherwise the output is equal to the input. Therefore, the standard ReLU activation function is easy to implement in hardware. However, activation functions, such as *sigmoid* and *tanh*, are more complicated. The sigmoid function needs to compute $1/(1 + e^{-x})$, and the tanh function needs to compute $(e^x - e^{-x})/(e^x + e^{-x})$, requiring complicated exponential calculation. Without calling the mathematical function library, it is complicated to use the C program directly to calculate exponential functions with Taylor expansion. When designing a dedicated DLP, the hardware implementation should not be too complicated; otherwise it may result in poor performance and efficiency. In DLPs, we leverage a lookup table to calculate the activation function [33] with a piecewise approximation. In this method, the activation function curve is divided into many small pieces, each approximated with a line segment. Therefore, given an x, the lookup table decides which line segment $[x_i, x_{i+1})$ this x falls into, and the result is computed using linear interpolation ($f(x) = a_i \times x + b_i$). In general cases, dividing the activation curve into 16 line segments for linear interpolation delivers negligible accuracy loss. In this way, integrating a lookup table with an interpolation circuit in hardware can perform the activation functions like sigmoid without computing e^{-x} precisely. Besides the sigmoid function, many other activation functions (such as tanh, etc.) are also often required in practice. Thus, the lookup table should be configurable. In other words, each interval of the lookup table is configurable, such as $[0, 0.3)$, $[0, 0.2)$, or $[0, 0.1)$, and the interpolation for a certain interval should be also configurable. In a nutshell, the activation function can be realized through a lightweight configurable lookup table.

Second, pooling operations should be supported. The commonly used pooling operations, average pooling and maximum pooling, are simple and easy to be implemented. For example, a 2×2 average pooling calculates the average for the four input numbers, and a 2×2 maximum pooling selects the maximum value from the four input numbers. The previous proposed geometric average, which is more complex, is seldom used in today's mainstream deep neural networks.

Finally, a local accumulator is added to support the operation of adding a bias after the vector inner product.

With the three enhancements to the vector MAC unit, it can support all the operators of the forward computation in the VGG19 network. Fig. 6.15 shows the DLP arithmetic unit designed accordingly. Specifically, the arithmetic unit has made the following improvements based.

(1) Adding a reconfigurable arithmetic component for the nonlinear activation function. The number of arithmetic components is consistent with the number of vector MACs.
(2) Adding a local accumulator to support the operation of bias addition.
(3) Adding exit paths of MFU-1/MFU-2/MFU-3 to support pooling. The maximum pooling only needs comparison rather than matrix multiplication. Thus it does not need to enter the multiplication part in MFU-1. Average pooling multiplies the sum of neurons in pooling by the reciprocal of the number of neurons (i.e., dividing by the number of neurons). Thus it requires the multiplication part in MFU-1. Both of the pooling operations do not require the remaining part and can exit the MFU early.

By enhancing the original vector MAC unit, adding activation functions, local accumulators, and additional exit paths of MFU-1/MFU-2/MFU-3, DLPs can preform all operations in the convolutional, pooling, and fully connected layers.

6.3.3.3 VFU and MFU

MFU and VFU are the arithmetic units designed in DLPs and support matrix and vector instructions, respectively. The MFU in Fig. 6.15 is based on the expansion of the vector MAC unit. To support the loop tiling with a length of T_n, $T_n \times T_n$ 16-bit multipliers are required in MFU-1 to support fully connected and convolutional layers. T_n addition trees (each addition tree has $T_n - 1$ adders) are designed in the MFU-2 stage to support the average pooling layer, the fully connected layer, and the convolutional layer. A 16-input shifter and a max comparator are integrated into MFU-2 to support the pooling layer. T_n 16-bit multipliers and 16 adders are designed in MFU-3 to support computation in the fully connected layer, the convolutional layer, and the pooling layer. In addition, MFU supports instructions including MMV, VMM, matrix-multiply-scalar, outer product, matrix-add-matrix, and matrix-subtract-matrix.

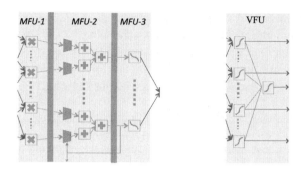

FIGURE 6.15

VFU and MFU.

VFU is designed to support 1D vector operation instructions, including complex instructions like VEXP. If these operations are supported by MFU as well instead of using a specific VFU, the complexity of the MFU will greatly increase, resulting in a large overhead. Meanwhile, the flexibility of vector operations will be sacrificed. Therefore, the VFU built based on a single vector MAC is retained in DLPs. VFU supports vector operations, such as VAV, VSV, VMV, VDV, VEXP, VLOG, inner product, random vector, VMAX, and VMIN.

6.3.4 Memory access unit

DLPs have to address the issue of data access. Today's general-purpose CPU cores contain dozens of arithmetic units, e.g., the most advanced Intel CPU supporting 32 16-bit MACs in one instruction. But DLPs contain thousands of MACs in one core, which are dozens or even hundreds of times more operators than the Intel CPU. When the computational capacity increases, the arithmetic units may not be provided with enough data, which has been the issue of memory wall[10] for CPUs in the recent two decades. DLPs face the same issue. In this section, we discuss how to address or alleviate the memory wall issue in DLPs.

The common solution used in CPU is cache. However, due to different access patterns and reusability of input neurons, output neurons, and weights, the cache solution may lead to a low efficiency for their interference. DLPs adopt scratchpad memory to allocate these three types of data to different on-chip memories (decomposability). Therefore, all three types of data can be accessed independently to achieve high efficiency for data access.

Integrating the aforementioned designed arithmetic unit and on-chip memories, the basic DLP architecture is achieved, as shown in Fig. 6.13. Specifically, on-chip memories include $NRAM$-in (Input Neuron RAM), $NRAM$-out (Output Neuron RAM), and $WRAM$ (Weight RAM) to store input neurons, output neurons, and

---

[10] For memory access on the general-purpose CPU, please refer to Appendix A.2.

weights, respectively. The VFU and MFU read input data from the on-chip memory $NRAM\text{-}in$ and $WRAM$ and write the computation results to $NRAM\text{-}out$.[11]

The loop tiling is implemented by basic deep learning operators. In the fully connected layer operation, each subblock has T_n input data, T_n output data, and $T_n \times T_n$ weights. If the vector MAC computation uses 16 bits per data (i.e., 2 bytes), the bit-width of the on-chip memory $NRAM\text{-}in$ and $NRAM\text{-}out$ should be $T_n \times 2$ bytes, and the bit-width of $WRAM$ should be $T_n \times T_n \times 2$ bytes.

6.3.5 Mapping from algorithm to chip

Input/output neurons may have various numbers, e.g., 100, 10,000, hundreds of thousands, or even hundreds of millions. It means the size of the algorithm could be infinite. But the hardware is always limited in size. It is impossible to design one single chip that can hold 1 million multipliers (hardware neurons). Thus, the hardware computing unit must be reused, i.e., *time-division multiplexed*. Roughly, DLPs compute a small block of output neurons with a small block of input neurons in one cycle repetitively. Thus, by repeatedly computing a small part of the neural network, a small-scale DLP could support large-scale neural networks.

Fully connected layer. For a fully connected layer, each time T_i input neurons and $T_i \times T_j$ weights are loaded to a row of the on-chip memory $NRAM\text{-}in$ and $WRAM$, respectively. DLPs perform the vector MAC operations, and the results are stored in the on-chip memory $NRAM\text{-}out$. Next T_i input neurons and $T_i \times T_j$ weights are loaded to compute the same outputs, and the above process is repeated until all N_i input feature data are processed. The resulting data are sent to VPU for nonlinear activation function computation, and the final T_j output results are obtained. The whole process is shown in Fig. 6.16(a).

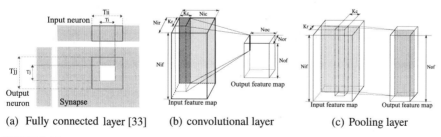

(a) Fully connected layer [33]   (b) convolutional layer   (c) Pooling layer

FIGURE 6.16

Mapping from algorithm to hardware.[12]

Convolutional layer. For a convolutional layer, the innermost loop of the algorithm in Fig. 6.8 can be mapped to the MFU for computation, as shown in

---

[11] As the input neurons and output neurons do not belong to the same layer, reading and writing these data do not interfere with each other. $NRAM\text{-}in$ and $NRAM\text{-}out$ can also be merged into one NRAM in DLPs.

[12] Fig. 6.16(b): ©2017 IEEE. Reprinted with permission from [143].

Fig. 6.16(b). First, each time T_i channels of data at the (c, r) position in the input feature maps are loaded. That is, T_i data along the N_i directions are loaded. Then, these data are convolved with $T_i \times T_j$ weights, where T_j intermediate results *sum* are calculated. In practice, T_i and T_j are usually the same, and T_i data fits into one row of on-chip memory $NRAM$-*in* or $NRAM$-*out*. $T_i \times T_j$ convolution weights can be prestored in the on-chip memory $WRAM$. T_i input data and the corresponding weights are sent to MFU. Then, the next T_i input neurons along the N_i direction in the input feature maps are loaded. Convolution results are added to the intermediate result *sum*. This process is repeated until all N_i input feature maps are visited. Third, move to a new position $(c + sc, r)$ in the input feature map and repeat the above process until all $K_c \times K_r$ input features are calculated. After performing a nonlinear activation function, the final T_j output neurons at the (noc, nor) position in the output feature maps are obtained. In order to compute all outputs, we only need to move along the T_j direction, the horizontal direction, and the vertical direction in turns and repeat the above process.

Pooling layer. The computation of the pooling layer is similar to that of the convolutional layer, as shown in Fig. 6.16(c). Each time, $K_c \times T_i$ inputs are loaded to the on-chip memory $NRAM$-*in*. Then, MFU performs pooling to obtain the intermediate results of T_i outputs. By moving K_r times in the vertical direction, the final result of T_i outputs can be obtained. We keep sliding along the N_i direction, horizontal direction, and vertical direction to have all output feature maps.

6.3.6 Summary

The simple but complete DLP has been built by combining the instruction set design, pipeline, computing units, and memory units. Different network layers (including the convolutional, fully connected, and pooling layers) can be mapped to DLP with the loop tiling for full data reuse.

This section uses a convolutional neural network as an example to introduce how to design a DLP. DLPs support forward propagation in convolutional neural networks such as VGG19. However, it is difficult to accomplish complex operations such as ROI pooling in Faster R-CNN. Readers can follow the basic design principles to carry out their own DLP design. For designing computing systems or processors for new applications in the future, readers can also follow the basic principle to analyze the common computation and memory access patterns; design the corresponding computing units, memory access units, and instruction sets; and map the algorithm to hardware.

6.4 *Optimization design

On the basis of a straightforward DLP design as illustrated above, researchers proposed a series of optimization designs from various perspectives, such as computing units, sparsity, and low bit-width.

6.4.1 Scalar MAC-based computing unit

Compared with vector MAC-based computing units introduced in Section 6.3.3, scalar MAC-based computing units could reduce the off-chip data accesses by leveraging data reuse in convolutions. This section introduces the scalar MAC, the principle of data reuse, and the implementation of the scalar MAC-based computing unit.

For a scalar MAC, two scalars are input and multiplied at a time, then the multiplication result is added to the value originally stored in this scalar MAC. To provide sufficient parallelism of data access and computation, multiple scalar MACs are combined into a 2D or 3D MAC array to support large-scale parallel operations, e.g., convolutions.

The convolution operation provides many opportunities for data reuse across multiple convolution windows. There are three common types of data reuse, namely bilateral reuse, feature map reuse, and kernel reuse. In bilateral reuse, only one output feature map with only one corresponding set of kernels exists, as shown in Fig. 6.17(a). For each input feature map, multiple convolution windows share the same convolution kernel, and adjacent convolution windows can share part of the neurons in the input feature map. So neurons and weights can be bilaterally reused in convolution operations by leveraging convolution reuse. Neuron reuse is the case where multiple output feature maps with multiple corresponding sets of convolution kernels exist, as shown in Fig. 6.17(b). In each convolution window, multiple sets of kernels share the same input feature map. So neurons can be reused in this case. Weight reuse is usually adapted to batch processing. Multiple samples (input feature maps) are processed in parallel by the same set of kernels, as shown in Fig. 6.17(c). So weights can be reused in this case [144][145].

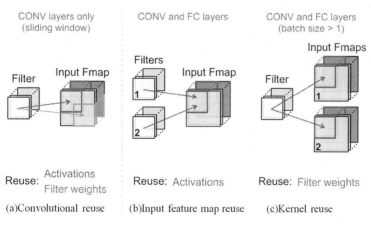

CONV layers only (sliding window)   CONV and FC layers   CONV and FC layers (batch size > 1)

Reuse: Activations / Filter weights   Reuse: Activations   Reuse: Filter weights

(a)Convolutional reuse   (b)Input feature map reuse   (c)Kernel reuse

FIGURE 6.17

Data reuse in convolutions.[13]

---

[13] ©2017 IEEE. Reprinted with permission from [145].

When implementing computing units with scalar MACs, it is necessary to make effective use of this data reuse. Fig. 6.18(a) computes a 4×4 input feature map with a 3×3 convolution kernel to obtain a 2×2 output feature map. Different convolution windows are marked with boxes with a gray solid frame, a black solid frame, a black dashed frame, and a gray dashed frame in Fig. 6.18(a). For example, there are six overlapping weights for reusing between the convolution in the box with a gray solid frame and the convolution in the box with a black solid frame: $X_{1,0}$, $X_{2,0}$, $X_{1,1}$, $X_{2,1}$, $X_{1,2}$, and $X_{2,2}$. When designing a 2D computing unit composed of 2×2 scalar MACs, as shown in Fig. 6.18(a), each processing element (PE), which contains one scalar MAC, is responsible for processing one convolution window. For example, $PE_{0,0}$ processes the convolution operation in the box with a gray solid frame, $PE_{1,0}$ processes the convolution operation in the box with a black solid frame, $PE_{0,1}$ processes the convolution operation in the box with a black dashed frame, and $PE_{1,1}$ processes the convolution operation in the box with a gray dashed frame.

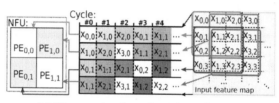

(a) The mapping from algorithm to hardware

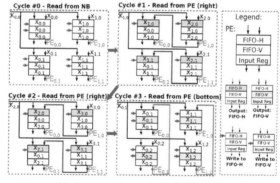

(b) A computing unit implementation

FIGURE 6.18

Scalar MAC-based computing units.[14]

The computation flow in the implemented computing unit is shown in Fig. 6.18(b). In the first cycle, each PE gets the first input neuron in its corresponding convolution window, i.e., $X_{0,0}$, $X_{1,0}$, $X_{0,1}$, and $X_{1,1}$, and performs the first MAC operation

---

[14] ©2015 IEEE. Reprinted with permission from [36].

in its corresponding 3×3 convolution. In the second cycle, each PE gets the second input in its convolution window. At this time, the neuron required by $PE_{0,0}$ is $X_{1,0}$, which has been acquired by $PE_{1,0}$ in the first cycle. Therefore, $PE_{0,0}$ sends a request to $PE_{1,0}$ for transferring the input neuron $X_{1,0}$, instead of acquiring the data from off-chip memory. Obtaining the required data through the data transfer among PEs can effectively reduce the off-chip data accesses. After several cycles of repeating the aforementioned inter-PE data fetching and computation, operations in one convolution window, as well as a convolutional layer, could be finished.

Table 6.3 compares features of the scalar MAC-based computing unit to a same-scale vector MAC-based computing unit. With the same 256 multipliers, the vector MAC-based computing unit requires fewer adders. It is because every 16-dimensional vector MAC unit only needs $8+4+2+1 = 15$ adders to compute 16 inputs.[15] While the scalar MAC-based computing unit is usually built with an organization like a systolic array, the bandwidth requirement is significantly reduced. But flexibility is inevitably sacrificed. Such sacrifice of flexibility for scalar MAC-based computing units is reflected in the low performance of performing some operations, such as computing the activation function, or the inability of some features, such as leveraging the sparsity in convolution. In general, both implementations have their own pros and cons. This requires architects to carefully consider the application scenario for an appropriate implementation.

6.4.2 Sparsity

In previous examples, both convolutional layers and fully connected layers are computed as dense matrices. However, neural networks have a lot of redundancy. For example some neurons or weights having zero or very small values can be deleted from networks as they have (almost) no effect on the network outputs. The sparsity could significantly reduce computations in neuron networks while not affecting the network accuracy. Fig. 6.19(b) and Fig. 6.19(c) show the static weight sparsity and neuron sparsity, respectively. In addition, Fig. 6.19(d) shows the dynamic sparsity, which indicates that the sparsity is related to the network inputs and the topology of networks could vary during runtime. For example, in ReLU activation, the output would be 0 when the input is less than 0. Assuming that the neurons are uniformly distributed such that 50% of neurons are less than 0, 50% of outputs would be 0 and all links around these zero nodes could be removed without affecting the final results. These zero nodes do not participate in computations, so MAC operands are reduced and the efficiency is improved.

To leverage the sparsity, researchers proposed sparsity-aware architecture designs [38]. There are two straightforward ways for adapting sparsity. One way is to only compute the nonsparse part, and the other is to skip the sparse part directly. The

---

[15] There is an equivalent statement. In the real circuit implementation, it may use a more efficient implementation method to add 16 numbers, such as the Wallace tree, instead of an addition tree composed of a two-input adder.

Table 6.3 Comparison of a vector MAC-based computing unit (16 16-dimensional vector MACs) and a scalar MAC-based computing unit (256 MACs, 16×16).

	Vector MAC-based computing unit	Scalar MAC-based computing unit
Size	16 16-dimensional vector MACs	256 MACs, 16×16 array
Number of multipliers	256	256
Number of adders	240 (16×15)	256
Number of external operands required per cycle	512	32
Operation granularity	Vector, matrix	Vector, matrix
Convolutional layer mapping	Input neuron reuse, output neuron reuse	Input neuron reuse, output neuron reuse, weight reuse
Advantages	Efficient support for matrix vector mapping, high flexibility	Dedicated data stream for supporting convolution efficiently, reduced bandwidth requirements
Disadvantages	Rely on external data arrangement, high bandwidth requirements	Poor flexibility, difficult to support other operators and other features

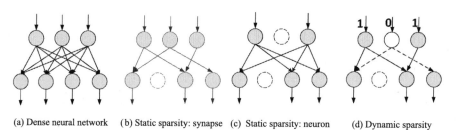

(a) Dense neural network   (b) Static sparsity: synapse (c) Static sparsity: neuron   (d) Dynamic sparsity

FIGURE 6.19

Different types of sparsity.[16]

former requires preprocessing the sparse data, removing all zero values to compress the sparse data into dense data such that all computations in the hardware unit are valid. It could make efficient use of data sparsity, improving the computation performance and energy efficiency. However, it requires some major modifications to the hardware, which may also affect the entire computing process [38]. The latter needs less hardware modification. It only needs to add a conditional logic in front of the computing unit to judge whether the input contains zeros. Using a two-input multiplication unit as an example, if any input is zero, the result would be zero, and the

---

multiplier can be turned off and output zero directly. The advantage of this approach is that developers make fewer changes to the hardware and gain the benefits of energy efficiency without affecting the entire computing process.

Moreover, to further reduce the requirements for storage and memory bandwidth, sparsity and data compression can be combined to optimize the entire computing process, as shown in Fig. 6.20. By leveraging the sparsity, the number of needed neurons and weights is reduced, and quantization can be further applied. Roughly, quantization is using several values to represent original continuously distributed synaptic weights. Furthermore, such quantized weights can be further compressed with entropy-coding. Weights occurring with higher probability are encoded with fewer bits. Otherwise, they are encoded with more bits. For some given benchmarks, the storage and memory bandwidth can be reduced about 10 times after sparsity and compression [146].

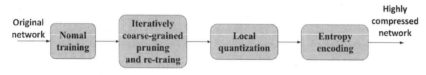

FIGURE 6.20

Compression flow after sparsity.[16]

6.4.3 Low bit-width

Many neural networks use 32-bit floating-point (FP32) data originally, while recent research proved that for many widely used neural networks, low bit-width (16-bit or 8-bit) fixed-point data can fully meet accuracy requirements. Therefore, low-bit-width computing units, together with corresponding low-bit-width storage units, can be used in processor design to improve efficiency. This section introduces the low-bit-width fixed-point data format and the implementation of low-bit-width computing units.

Unlike the 32-bit floating-point data format, which is composed of a 1-bit sign bit, an 8-bit exponent, and a 23-bit mantissa, the low-bit-width fixed-point data format can be designed in a variety of formats. For example, the 8-bit fixed-point number in Fig. 6.21(b) left consists of a 1-digit symbol s and a 7-digit mantissa x. The mantissa is divided into two parts, a $(7 - f)$-digit integer and an f-digit fraction, where the value of each number is $n = (-1)^s 2^{-f} m$. For data in neural networks that may have different ranges, f needs to be tuned dynamically. If the data value is relatively small, the mantissa can all be fractions, as shown in Fig. 6.21(b)(right). In this case, the 8-bit dynamic fixed-point number is composed of one sign bit s and nine fractional bits (including two zero digits).

For the implementation of low-bit-width computing units, one approach is to directly modify traditional compute units (e.g., parallel multipliers) to support low-bit-width fixed-point data. Another approach is to use serial operations, such as a

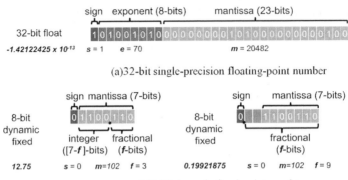

(a) 32-bit single-precision floating-point number

(b) 8-bit dynamic fixed-point number

FIGURE 6.21

Data formats of different precision.[13]

bit-serial multiplier [147]. Taking the multiplier as an example, in the formal approach, the 8-bit fixed-point multiplier only needs to process an 8-bit multiplication, while the original 32-bit floating-point multiplier has to add the 8-bit exponent bits and multiply the 23-bit mantissa bits. As expected, the hardware overhead of an 8-bit fixed-point multiplier is about one-eighth of that in a 32-bit floating-point multiplier. However, such parallel multipliers only support a specific bit-width, thus losing flexibility for processing data of various bit-widths.

In the latter approach, such a problem could be resolved by a bit-serial multiplier [147]. The calculation flow in a serial multiplier is as follows. For the multiplication of two 16-bit data, A and B, the bit-serial multiplier obtains the operator A from the most significant bit (MSB) to the least significant bit (LSB) in a bit-serial manner. If the input bit of A is 0, the intermediate at this cycle is 0; otherwise, the intermediate is B. Then, the multiplier accumulates the nonzero intermediate to the current partial sum after a left-shift operation. Repeating such process for 16 clock cycles can complete the 16-bit fixed-point multiplication, i.e., $A \times B$. Formally, the computation of the ith clock cycle is $C = A[15 - i] \times B + (C << 1)$. If A is represented by lower-bit-width fixed-point data, such as 4 bits, the bit-serial multiplier only needs four cycles to complete the multiplication.

To further compare the parallel multiplier and the serial multiplier, we provide examples of using those two multipliers to process an inner product, $C = A_0 \times B_0 + A_1 \times B_1$, in Fig. 6.22. For the serial multiplier, as shown in Fig. 6.22(b), A_0 and A_1 are serially fed from MSB to LSB. The serial multiplications, i.e., $A_0 \times B_0$ and $A_1 \times B_1$, are processed cycle by cycle. For parallel multiplier, as shown in Fig. 6.22(a), all digits of A_0, A_1, B_0, and B_1 are fed and processed in one cycle. For example, for an 8-bit multiplication, the parallel multiplier requires 64 full adders, which are calculated in one cycle. The serial multiplier requires 8 full adders, and the calculation is completed in 8 cycles. Compared to parallel multipliers, serial multipliers usually have simpler arithmetic logic but more complicated control circuits. Therefore, a more practical approach is to support only a limited number of bit-widths. Such compromise takes into account the advantages of the two schemes with a certain degree of flexibility and does not introduce more control overhead.

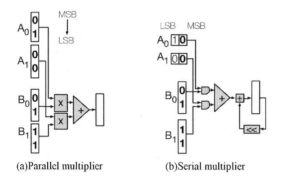

(a)Parallel multiplier　　　　(b)Serial multiplier

FIGURE 6.22

Vector inner product using a serial multiplier.[17]

6.5 **Performance evaluation**

From the perspective of architecture, the performance evaluation criteria of DLPs include computing capability, memory access capability, and power consumption. From the perspective of application, the performance evaluation of DLP can be performed with public test benchmark programs of machine learning.

6.5.1 **Performance metrics**

Similar to general-purpose processors, the common performance metric for DLPs is how many operations are performed per second (measured in TOPS). Since neural network computation may use data in different formats, such as floating-point, 32-bit fixed-point, and 16-bit fixed-point formats, the number of operations is uniformly measured by operands. TOPS reflects the peak computing capability of the processor, which is positively correlated with the number of multipliers and adders in the processor and the main frequency f_c:

$$TOPS = f_c \times (N_{mul} + N_{add})/1000, \qquad (6.6)$$

where the unit of processor frequency (f_c) is GHz and N_{mul} and N_{add} indicate how many multiplications and additions are performed in each cycle, respectively. For example, to analyze the MFU in DLPs, assuming $T_n = 16$ and each data is in the

16-bit fixed-point format, the widths of $NRAM$-in and $NRAM$-out are both 256 bits. For the fully connected layer and the convolutional layer, all arithmetic units of MFU-1 and MFU-2 totally process $256 + 16 \times 15 = 496$ fixed-point operations in each cycle. When the processor frequency is 1 GHz, the computing capability is 496 GOPS. If the activation calculation is required at the end of each layer, MFU-3 would work at the same time. In this case, all MFUs totally process $496 + 2 \times 16 = 528$ fixed-point operations in each cycle, and the computing capability is 528 GOPS.

The real performance of the processor is not only affected by the peak computing capability but also by the memory bandwidth (BW), including the bandwidth for accessing off-chip memories and accessing multilevel on-chip memories. In recent years, the performance bottleneck of DLPs and general-purpose processors is mainly memory access bandwidth. BW is related to the main frequency f_m of memory, storage bit-width b, and memory access efficiency η:

$$BW = f_m \times b \times \eta, \tag{6.7}$$

where the unit of the memory main frequency f_m is GHz, b is the digit number of load/store data in each cycle, and η is related to storage structures and application behaviors. When designing a processor, it is necessary to balance computing capabilities and memory access capabilities. For example, in DLPs, the processor performance reaches the peak when the memory access capability matches the computing capability. Therefore, the memory $NRAM$-in and $NRAM$-out will provide $T_n = 16$ data per cycle, and $WRAM$ will provide $T_n \times T_n = 256$ data per cycle. If we process 16-bit fixed-point data in DLPs under 1 GHz, the off-chip memory bandwidth requires a minimum of 1 GHz $\times ((256 + 16) \times 16$ bits$) \times 1 = 544$ GB/s (assuming the efficiency η is 1), which is much higher than the bandwidth of common memories, such as DDR.

Moreover, whether it is a power-sensitive terminal or a large-scale cloud server, both have requirements for the power consumption of DLP. The power consumption of an intelligent system may come from the memory, processor, hard disk, or cooling system. For example, one chess game between AlphaGo and Lee Sedol costs thousands of dollars in electricity bills. The power consumption in the chip mainly includes switching power, short-circuit power, and electricity power consumption. To reduce power consumption, the chip can be optimized from the system level, algorithm level, gate circuit level, etc.

6.5.2 Benchmarking

TOPS and BW reflect the peak capacity of the processor, e.g., computation and memory access. The actual performance of the processor still depends on the time it takes to run a program and the power consumption. To evaluate the performance of DLPs more comprehensively and reasonably, Google, Baidu, Intel, AMD, Harvard University, and Stanford University jointly released the benchmark program MLPerf [148] in 2018. MLPerf includes training [149] and prediction benchmarks [150] to measure the performance of the system in training a machine learning model and in predicting a trained model (Table 6.4), respectively. At present, MLPerf only evaluates the runtime of executing different applications and does not measure power consumption, which may be addressed in the future.

Table 6.4 MLPerf inference benchmark.[18]

Reference model	Dataset	Quality target	Task
Resnet-50 v1.5	ImageNet (224 × 224)	99% of FP32 (76.46%) Top one accuracy	Image classification
MobileNet-v1 224	ImageNet (224 × 224)	98% of FP32 (71.68%) Top one accuracy	Image classification
SSD-ResNet-34	COCO (1200 × 1200)	99% of FP32 (0.20 mAP)	Object detection
SSD-MobileNet-v1	COCO (300 × 300)	99% of FP32 (0.22 mAP)	Object detection
GNMT	WMT16	99% of FP32 (23.9 SACREBLEU)	Machine translation

6.5.3 **Factors affecting performance**

The performance of a DLP is the time used to complete a deep learning task. Performance is obtained by dividing the total cycles of all operations (including multiplication and addition) by the main frequency. The number of operations required by the task depends on the deep learning algorithm. The number of cycles required by each operation depends on the operator type, microarchitecture design, etc. The main frequency of the processor depends on the processor structure, circuit, and physical technology. The runtime of a deep learning task can be written as

$$T = \sum_i N_i \times C_i / f_c, \tag{6.8}$$

where N_i represents the number of the ith operation in the task, C_i represents the number of cycles required to complete the ith operation, and f_c represents the main frequency of the processor. These operations include arithmetic operations such as multiplication and addition, as well as memory access operations.

To reduce the processing time of deep learning tasks, programmers can start from the following aspects. First, they can reduce the number of execution cycles of frequent operations. For example, multiply/add operations frequently appear in deep learning. Assuming that multiply and add operations totally account for 80% of the runtime and the execution performance of these operations is doubled, the overall performance can be increased by $1/(20\% + 80\%/2) = 1/0.6 = 1.67$ times.

Second, programmers can exploit data locality, which includes temporal and spatial locality. Temporal (time) locality indicates how long it takes to visit the same

---

[18] ©2020 IEEE. Reprinted with permission from [150].

address again. If the time interval between visits to the same address A is only one cycle, the time locality is ideal. Spatial locality means how often adjacent addresses (e.g., A+1, A+2, and A+3) are accessed after accessing address A. Designing the storage structure according to the memory access behavior and fully exploiting the data locality can improve the efficiency of memory access.

Finally, programmers can adopt multilevel parallelism. For deep learning, optimization can be performed from the level of computing device, data, and task to improve performance. Device-level parallelism can explore time parallelism through pipelines and realize spatial parallelism by designing multiple concurrent functional components. Data-level parallelism in general-purpose processors mainly refers to the single-instruction multiple-data (SIMD) architecture, and similar ideas can also be adapted in the DLP design. Task-level parallelism includes parallelism between multiple batches of image processing, parallelism between multiple application tasks, etc.

6.6 Other accelerators

Other than DLPs discussed in this chapter, there exist other accelerators that can be used for deep learning, mainly including GPU and FPGA.

6.6.1 The GPU architecture

GPU is a single-instruction multiple-threads (SIMT) matrix acceleration device. In the past, GPU was mainly used to accelerate graphic computation tasks, such as 3D graphics rendering and game image rendering. However, because of its higher parallel processing capability, GPU is gradually being used by developers in deep learning.

We briefly introduce the architecture adopted by GPU from three aspects: computation, storage, and control. From the viewpoint of the computation unit, a GPU is composed of hundreds of simple computing cores. These cores usually do not have complex program flow control units or support some complex control scheduling behaviors such as branch prediction, so the efficiency of programs with more branches and complex control requirements would be lower. From the perspective of architecture, a GPU actually has a SIMD architecture. Compared to the SIMD unit of the CPU, a GPU has multiple SIMD processing units which support a large number of SIMD threads, namely the SIMT programming model. Moreover, multiple GPU SIMD units share the same storage, thus simplifying the complexity of control.

From the perspective of storage, a GPU has a multilevel storage hierarchy. For example, an independent GPU usually has a large-capacity and high-bandwidth device memory (such as GDDR), a global memory for all SIMT units to access, a local memory for individual SIMT, and a shared memory for SIMT unit threads. In particular, a GPU used in deep learning usually has a large device memory to reduce data access between the CPU and GPU, thus providing sufficient bandwidth for a large number of computing units in GPU. When the program starts, the GPU needs to transfer data from the host memory in the CPU to the device memory. Thus, subsequent operations can take advantage of the high-speed data access brought about by the device memory. For example, Nvidia GPU V100 has a DRAM device memory of up to 32 GB, which can provide a bandwidth of up to 900 GB/s.

From the perspective of control, since the GPU uses the SIMD architecture, the control is also based on fixed-length vector/matrix instructions. To ensure efficiency, GPU conceals the average memory access latency on a single thread by scheduling and executing multiple threads on a SIMD unit. In fact, for deep learning tasks, GPU developers spend a lot of manpower and resources to optimize parallel programming libraries. For example, GPU manufacturer Nvidia released the acceleration library cuDNN at the end of 2014, which has been continuously updated.

6.6.2 The FPGA architecture

FPGA is a general-purpose programmable acceleration device with a wide range of uses. In deep learning acceleration, FPGAs are often used to implement a variety of different architectural designs, and they are often used for preverification of architectural design.

We also briefly introduce FGPA from three aspects, namely computation, storage, and control. For computation, FPGA adopts a large number of basic configurable logic blocks (CLBs). These modules implement various functions through a lookup table. The basic idea of a lookup table is to store all output conditions associated with all input combinations in a lookup table, then scan the table according to the input to find the designated output. For example, to implement the basic logic of an XOR, the lookup table stores the entire truth table, e.g., four rows with input combinations 00, 01, 11, and 10. In practice, due to the limited computing capability of a single CLB, FPGA needs to determine the CLB functions and mutual interconnections through programming, thus completing the complex functions by combining multiple CLBs together.

In terms of storage, for flexibility considerations, FPGAs usually provide many on-chip storage resources, which can be configured in different forms for different uses. For example, Xilinx's FPGA integrates numerous of BlockRAMs inside, which are dedicated to implementing the data temporary storage function, and each clock domain is arranged with several BlockRAMs. By organizing and configuring these BlockRAMs into the required storage modules, FPGAs can provide functions such as single-port ROM/RAM or dual-port ROM/RAM.

In terms of control, FPGA requires designers to control and use on-chip resources by configuration. In practice, FPGA development tools could help users divide the circuit programmed by the user into small modules and then map these modules to CLBs. By configuring programmable wiring resources in FPGA, these CLBs can be organically organized and combined into a complete circuit, including the sequential circuit.

Table 6.5 Comparison of DLP and other accelerators.

Type	Goal	Speed	Energy efficiency	Flexibility
DLP	Deep learning dedicated	High	High	General in deep learning field
FPGA	General programmable circuit	Low	Medium	General
GPU	SIMD architecture matrix acceleration	Medium	Low	General use of matrix applications

6.6.3 Comparison of DLPs, GPU, and FPGA

In Table 6.5, in the field of intelligent computing, we compare the performance, energy efficiency, and flexibility of DLP, FPGA, and GPU. Compared to the GPU, the deep learning-dedicated DLP architecture achieves better performance, especially in terms of energy efficiency. For example, the energy efficiency of the Tesla V100, a 12-nm product of Nvidia from 2017, is less than 500 GOPS/W in 16-bit floating-point computation. The energy efficiency of the 65-nm DianNao architecture from 2014 is 932 GOPS/W [33] in 16-bit fixed-point computation. The energy efficiency of some of the latest DLPs is even close to 100 TOPS/W. One of the important underlying reasons is that GPU's SIMT computing architecture is designed for matrix operations. As analyzed in Section 6.3.3, deep learning processing is not just matrix operations. Deep learning-oriented computing units in DLPs can better adapt to deep learning applications. Another very important issue is that GPU hardware does not design dedicated data paths for the memory access streams (input neurons, output neurons, and weights) of different features in deep learning, and the access efficiency is relatively low. In DLPs, the on-chip memory resources are divided for different memory access streams, and the on-chip data control is completely managed by the programmer. This design significantly reduces the mutual interference between different memory access streams and greatly improves the memory access effectiveness. Compared to FPGA, in addition to flexibility, DLPs are superior in performance and energy efficiency. This is mainly because FPGA is configurable in each basic CLB to pursue flexibility, which is unnecessarily high for deep learning applications, resulting in much redundancy and undermining efficiency.

6.7 Summary

This chapter takes the forward computation of a convolutional neural network (VGG19) used in image style transfer as an example, introduces how to design a basic DLP, and presents some optimization techniques and performance evaluation methods for DLPs.

Exercises

6.1 What are the differences between DLP and the early neural network chips of the 1980s?

6.2 If a DLP can accelerate the convolutional layer tenfold and the fully connected layer twofold compared to a CPU (without accelerating other layers), what is the overall speedup for AlexNet when compared to the same CPU?

6.3 If a DLP is designed to have a bandwidth of 12.8 GB/s between a DLP chip and DDR3 memory, what is the ideal overall speedup ratio of the fully connected layer compared to a DLP with one ALU?

6.4 Briefly describe why instruction-level parallelism is generally ineffective in DLPs. Under what circumstances can instruction-level parallelism play a role in DLPs?

6.5 Design a depth-specific instruction set and implement a convolutional neural network using the designed instruction set.

6.6 Design the working logic of the decoding unit for the instruction set designed in Exercise 6.5 (a state transition diagram will be enough).

6.7 Assuming that the decoding unit designed in Exercise 6.6 is used, is the load of each instruction balanced? How could you improve it if it is unbalanced? Redo Exercises 6.5 and 6.6 according to the improved instruction set or working logic.

6.8 For DLP designed in this chapter, assuming that the on-chip bandwidth is given as 12.8 GB/s (ignoring the off-chip bandwidth limit), take AlexNet as an example to calculate the utilization rate of its computing unit (nonidle time) and calculate the utilization rate when changing the size of computing units. A plot graph is welcomed.

6.9 Under the same conditions as in Exercise 6.8 and assuming that the calculation architecture based on scalar MAC in Section 6.4.1 is used, recalculate the above question.

*6.10 Roofline is a commonly used method to evaluate hardware capabilities. Draw a Roofline diagram for DLP designed in this chapter.

*6.11 For a convolutional layer, write the code of its loop representation and provide at least three different tiling methods (codes). Draw a figure to show the calculation process corresponding to the three different tilings you proposed.

*6.12 Regarding the loop representation in Exercise 6.11, what are the shortcomings in your designed DLP? How can it be improved? Propose a new convolution representation method that can be better used by the design of DLPs and explain why.

*6.13 Design and implement a cycle-accurate simulator for DLP in this chapter, which is required to support at least three different types of networks. Mark the data of the three networks on the Roofline diagram completed in Exercise 6.10.

Architecture for AI computing systems

7

Chapter 6 introduced the design of a simple but complete deep learning processor (DLP) architecture. Such a basic DLP needs to be further optimized in order to meet the actual needs of the industry. This chapter first introduces a single-core DLP (DLP-S) architecture for AI applications in mobile ends. On the basis of DLP, DLP-S further optimizes the control components, computing components, and on-chip storage components to improve performance and energy efficiency for mobile AI applications in practice. In order to meet the needs of AI applications in cloud scenarios, a multicore DLP (DLP-M) architecture is further introduced. DLP-M extends the DLP-S into a multicore architecture, where multiple DLP-S cores are interconnected through network-on-chip (NoC). Protocols such as unicast, multicast, and intercore synchronization are supported for intercore communication to complete deep learning tasks in the cloud.

7.1 Single-core deep learning processor

With the increasing maturity of artificial intelligence theory and technology, its application in mobile scenarios such as smartphones, tablet computers, smart TVs, and smart electrocardiographs is becoming more and more pervasive. Two prominent features have emerged: low latency and high energy efficiency. However, previously designed DLPs have shortcomings, including lack of supporting instruction-level parallelism, lack of supporting low-bit-width operations, lack of supporting sparse neural network models, and large memory access delay. Therefore, DLPs cannot fully meet the two features, low latency and high energy efficiency, in mobile scenarios. DLP-S is optimized on the basis of DLP to meet such needs. The specific optimizations are mainly reflected in the following four aspects:

(1) The multiissue queue is designed in the control module. Therefore, instructions without dependencies can be issued in parallel, thus supporting instruction-level parallelism.

(2) Affluent operation combinations are supported in the vector functional unit (VPU) to improve performance and flexibility.

(3) A low-bit-width operator is used in the matrix functional unit (MFU), and the sparse model is supported to reduce energy consumption.

AI Computing Systems. https://doi.org/10.1016/B978-0-32-395399-3.00013-5

(4) Fast translation cache (translation lookaside buffer [TLB]) and cache (last-level cache [LLC]) are introduced into the memory module to reduce the delay of memory accesses.

In this section, we will introduce first the overall architecture of DLP-S, then the control module, computing module, and storage module. In each we will focus mainly on optimization techniques for high performance and energy efficiency.

7.1.1 Overall architecture

Fig. 7.1 shows a system diagram of the DLP-S architecture. DLP-S includes three primary modules: the control module, computing module, and on-chip storage module. The control module coordinates the computing and on-chip storage modules to complete the deep learning task. The computing module computes in the deep learning process. The on-chip storage module stores or moves related data.

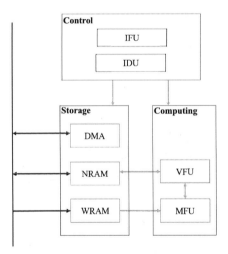

FIGURE 7.1

The DLP-S architecture.

The control module includes an instruction fetching unit (IFU) and an instruction decoding unit (IDU). IFU obtains instructions from off-chip dynamic RAMs (DRAMs). IDU decodes the instructions and sends them to the computing and storage modules for execution.

The computing module includes VFU and MFU. VFU performs vector operations and supports complex operations such as vector multiplication, addition, and nonlinear transformation. MFU manages the core functions of deep learning algorithms—matrix multiplication and convolution.

The on-chip storage module includes neuron RAM (NRAM), weight RAM (WRAM), and direct memory access (DMA). NRAM stores data like input neurons, output neurons, and temporal results of a deep learning network. WRAM stores the weights of deep learning networks. DMA connects the internal high-speed cache and chips via buses and accounts for their data communications.

The execution process of DLP-S can be divided into the following seven steps:

(1) IFU reads instructions from DRAM through DMA. Then IDU decodes them and finally distributes them to DMA, VFU, and MFU.
(2) Upon instructions, DMA reads neurons from DRAM to NRAM and weights to WRAM.
(3) VFU reads neuron data from NRAM after receiving the instruction, performs preprocessing on the neuron data, such as boundary expansion, and sends it to MFU.
(4) MFU receives the data from VFU, reads the weights from WRAM, and sends the computed results to VFU.
(5) VFU performs postprocessing on output neurons, such as activation functions and pooling.
(6) VFU writes the computation result back to NRAM.
(7) NRM writes output neurons to DRAM through the DMA.

In the entire DLP-S execution, neurons flow as DRAM -> NRAM -> VFU -> MFU -> VFU -> NRAM -> DRAM, and the weights flow as DRAM -> WRAM -> MFU. Note that when performing vector operations, for example, adding two vectors, MFU will not be involved.

7.1.2 Control module

The control module serves as the brain of the entire DLP-S, and it coordinates all the other modules to complete the computations. The control module supports two basic functions, instruction fetching from DRAM and instruction translating. These two functions are completed by IFU and IDU in the control module. IFU retrieves the instructions from the off-chip DRAM according to the sequence of the program's instruction flow and sends the retrieved instructions to the IDU. IDU decodes the instructions for distribution. Specifically, after receiving an instruction from IFU, IDU decodes the instruction to obtain its instruction type and distributes the instruction to the corresponding execution unit accordingly. Control instructions and scalar operation instructions are sent to the arithmetic logic unit (ALU). Vector operation instructions are sent to the VFU. Matrix operation instructions are sent to the MFU, and the memory access instructions are sent to the DMA. We detail the IFU and IDU in the rest of this section.

7.1.2.1 Instruction fetching unit

Fig. 7.2 shows the architecture of IFU, which consists of an address generator unit (AGU), an instruction cache (ICache), a refill buffer (RB), and an instruction queue (IQ).

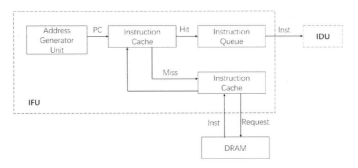

FIGURE 7.2

A system view of IFU.

The AGU is designed to generate a program counter (PC), which points to the address of instructions in the memory. PC values are mainly come from three sources:

(1) Software configuration. When initiating DLP-S, the address of the first instruction configured by the software is used as the first PC value.
(2) The sequentially self-increment of PC. For example, for $PC = PC + 1$, the address of the next instruction is derived as the address of current instruction plus 1, where 1 is the bit-width of the instruction.
(3) IDU. When IDU parses a jump instruction, it returns the destination address to AGU as the next PC value.

ICache is designed to buffer instructions loaded from DRAM, thereby speeding up the instruction fetching speed of IFU. When ICache hits, the instruction will be read out from the ICache directly; when missed, the PC and the number of prefetched instructions will be sent to the RB. The RB receives the prefetch request from the ICache and sends the instruction backfill request to the DMA. The DMA reads the instruction from the address correspondingly in the DRAM and backfills it into the ICache according to the PC. IQ is designed to buffer PC and instructions. IQ decouples the pipeline of IFU and IDU, where the control logic of IFU and IDU are separated to avoid interference.

7.1.2.2 Instruction decoding unit

Fig. 7.3 shows the abstract view of IDU. IDU includes an IDU (decoder), an instruction issue queue, and an ALU.

Decoder. The decoder receives instructions from IFU and decodes the instruction type for distributing to the corresponding instruction issue queues. The instructions can be classified into three categories: control instructions, computing instructions, and memory access instructions. Control instructions include scalar computing instructions and jump instructions. Operation instructions include vector computing instructions and matrix computing instructions. Memory access instructions include LOAD, STORE, MOVE, etc. Instructions from different categories can be executed

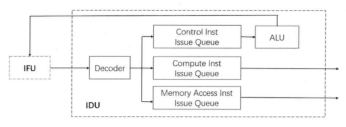

FIGURE 7.3

An abstract view of IDU.

in parallel if independent. After the decoding, the control instruction is sent to the control instruction issue queue, the computing instruction is sent to the compute instruction issue queue, and the memory access instruction is sent to the memory access instruction issue queue.

Issue queue. Three instruction issue queues are designed in IDU to buffer the three different types of instructions. Instructions in these three queues can be issued in parallel, and thus all instructions are issued in an out-of-order manner. But instructions inside each queue are issued sequentially and executed sequentially, i.e., in an in-order manner.

As instructions are issued in an out-of-order manner, dependencies among instructions may cause errors in execution. Here we discuss two cases of instruction dependencies:

- In the first case, two instructions of the same type have dependency. As the two instructions will be sent to the same issue queue where they are issued sequentially, there will be no error in the program execution result. For example, instructions A1 and A2 are two consecutive instructions, and A2 depends on A1. Since both A1 and A2 belong to same class, A1 and A2 will be sent to the same issue queue, where A1 and A2 will be issued and executed in their correct order. In such a case, the correctness of program execution is ensured.
- In the second case, dependency exists between two different types of instructions. These two instructions are sent to two different instruction issue queues. In this case, instructions are executed out of order, which may cause errors in program execution. For example, instruction A1 and instruction B1 are two consecutive instructions, and B1 depends on A1. After decoding, A1 is sent to the A issue queue, and B1 is sent to the B issue queue. Since the instructions in A and B issue queues can be issued in parallel, we cannot predict the execution order of A1 and B1. It is possible that B1 is issued and executed first and thus the program execution result will be wrong.

To ensure the correctness of the execution in the second case, we add a synchronization instruction (SYNC) to the original DLP instruction set. When there is a dependency between two different types of instructions, SYNC will be inserted to ensure the correctness, e.g., SYNC(A1, B1) must be inserted if A1 and B1 have dependency. When the SYNC instruction is detected, it waits and only sends the B1 instruction to the B issue queue when instructions in the A issue queue are all issued.

Fig. 7.4 shows an example of dependencies between instructions, where the arrows indicate the dependencies between instructions. For example, instruction B and instruction C depend on the result of instruction A, while instruction E depends on the result of instruction D. There is no dependency between instruction E and instruction F. In a single queue, all instructions are executed sequentially, from A to B, from C to D, and from E to F. Therefore, dependencies between A and B and between C and D can be ignored, as they are in the same issue queue. We need to focus on how to solve the dependencies between A and C and between D and E, as they are in different issue queues. For such purpose, the synchronization instruction S (i.e., SYNC instruction) is inserted, as shown in Fig. 7.5. Instruction A in the control instruction issue queue will be issued and executed when the compute instruction issue queue is empty. Instruction D in the compute instruction issue queue will be issued and executed when the memory access instruction issue queue is empty. Therefore, the program can be guaranteed an order-preserving execution among different instruction queues. Together with the in-order manner inside each issue queue, the correctness of the whole program can therefore be guaranteed. Inserting synchronization instructions can reduce hardware overhead without sacrificing performance, only requiring adding a few more synchronization instructions by programmers (synchronization instructions can be automatically inserted by a modern compiler or assembler).

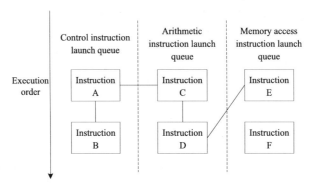

FIGURE 7.4

Dependencies between directives.

ALU. ALU is designed to perform functions like scalar operations and branching. ALU supports standard scalar operations including the basic arithmetic operations, comparison operations, and transcendental functions. Branch operations supported by ALU have three types: direct jump, indirect jump, and conditional jump. Here we detail these three types of branch instructions:

- When executing a direct jump, ALU obtains the corresponding destination address from the register or immediate and sends the destination address to the AGU as the PC of the next instruction.

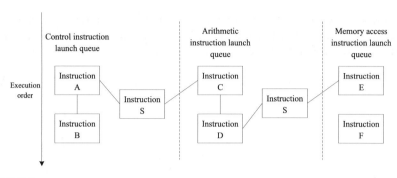

FIGURE 7.5

Schematic diagram of a stream that is synchronized by inserting the synchronization instruction S.

- When executing an indirect jump, ALU obtains the operands (usually the base address and offset) from the register or immediate to calculate the destination address. ALU adds the obtained operands, e.g., base address and the offset, to get the destination address. The destination address is then sent to the AGU.
- When executing a conditional jump, ALU obtains the destination address, same as the direct jump or indirect jump. The difference is that this instruction requires conditional judgment, such as comparing the two operands (from the immediate Or register), to decide whether or not to send the destination address to the AGU.

7.1.3 Arithmetic module

DLP-S includes two arithmetic modules, VFU and MFU, to perform vector and matrix operations, respectively.

7.1.3.1 VFU

VFU is an indispensable computing module in DLP-S. VFU is mainly responsible for the preprocessing of input neurons, such as boundary expansion, and the postprocessing of output neurons, such as activation and pooling. The vector pipeline unit in VFU supports multiple operations, including table lookup, addition, multiplication, pooling, sampling, edge expansion, vector comparison, vector maximization, and data format conversion. VPU supports different data types, including INT8, INT16, INT32, FP16, and FP32.

Vector pipeline

The vector pipeline divides the processing flow into eight steps and adopts an eight-stage pipeline structure. Fig. 7.6 shows the basic structure of the unit, where the intermediate results between two adjacent stages are written into the registers. Stage1 and stage2 in the pipeline perform the lookup table operation. Stage3 and stage4 complete the multiplication operation. Stage5 and stage6 complete the addition operation. Stage7 and stage8 complete the data format conversion operation (data format conversions between data with two different data types, such as FP32 to FP16). Stage1, stage3, stage5, and stage7 can receive input data, and stage2, stage4, stage5, stage6, stage7, and stage8 can send output data.

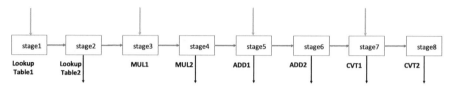

FIGURE 7.6

Vector pipeline.

An important feature of the vector pipeline is that it can be configured to achieve different functions by combing multiple stages. For example, activating stage1–stage6 in turn, which performs table lookup, multiplication, and addition operations sequentially, the activation operation is achieved. In addition, for reducing latency of functions that do not require all the stages, data are allowed to skip over stages and registers among stages. For example, vector addition on floating-point data only needs pipeline stages, i.e., stage5 and stage6, and thus other stages are skipped.

The designed vector pipeline may have instruction overtaking, i.e., an instruction issued later is finished faster than an instruction issued early. Fig. 7.7 shows an example of instruction overtaking. Three instructions, op1–op3, are continuously fed into the vector pipeline. Instruction op1 goes through stage1–stage5, instruction op2 goes through stage5–stage7, and instruction op3 goes through stage3–stage4. Two instructions overtakings occur here if no further action is taken.

- Op2 is finished before op1.
- Op2 and op3 are finished at the same time.

  To avoid instruction overtaking, two rules are applied.

- *rule*1　When an instruction needs to input data from the nth stage, it waits until the input registers of the first–nth stages are cleared and then allows the input data to be fed into the target pipeline stage.
- *rule*2　When an instruction needs to output data from the mth stage, it waits until the registers in the $(m + 1)$st–8th stages are cleared and then allows the data to be sent out.

When applying the above strategy to Fig. 7.7, according to *rule*1, before the input of op2 enters stage5, it waits for the input register of the stage1–stage5 pipeline to be empty. That is, op1 sends the input of op2 after stage5 is executed. To avoid overtaking between op1 and op2, according to *rule*2, before op3 outputs from stage4, it waits for the register of stage5–stage8 to be cleared. It ensures that op2 outputs at stage7 before op3 outputs at stage4, thus solving the problem between op2 and op3.

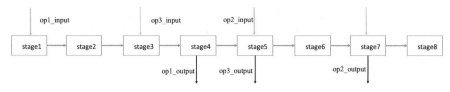

FIGURE 7.7

Examples of vector operation instruction overtaking.

7.1.3.2 MFU

Fig. 7.8 shows the architecture of the MFU. MFU is composed of M processing elements (PEs) connected with an H-tree, where each PE is a leaf node and each edge represents a data path. PEs are built based on vector MACs and each PE unit has N multipliers and an N-input addition tree. The H-tree broadcasts the input neuron to all PEs. Each PE receives different weights for computing different output neurons.

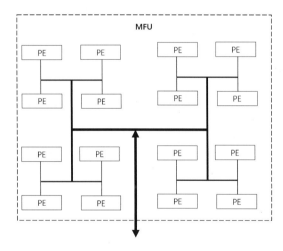

FIGURE 7.8

MFU schematic.

MFU computes the convolutional and fully connected layers in deep learning, whose computations occupy more than 90% of the total computation in the model. Therefore, the energy consumption of MFU becomes the bottleneck of the entire DLP-S. Improving the energy efficiency of MFU becomes the major consideration. In this chapter, MFU adopts a low-bit-width technique to address such issue.

As mentioned in Section 6.4.3, INT16 or INT8 can be used for neural networks with satisfying accuracy. Thus, MFU can adopt such data type in the arithmetic unit design. The multiplier adopts a parallel design, supporting three modes: $int16 \times int16$, $int8 \times int8$, and $int8 \times int4$. Based on the accuracy requirements from neural network applications, programmers can select different modes accordingly. Compared to a 32-bit floating-point arithmetic unit, low-bit-width arithmetic units can significantly reduce the design area and energy consumption. Moreover, as in Section 6.4.2, sparsity widely exists in neural networks. Thus, MFU further optimizes the unit to support sparsity, which can significantly reduce the energy consumption.

7.1.4 Storage unit

The DLP-S storage unit mainly includes three parts: NRAM, WRAM, and DMA. NRAM and WRAM store the weights of neurons and synapses in the neural network, respectively. The DMA converts the memory access instruction into a memory access request and sends it to the data bus for data movement between on-chip memory and off-chip memory.

Storage management

The storage resources in DLP-S usually include a variety of physical memories in terms of media, performance, power consumption, space size, access methods, and access latency. If designing specific instructions for different storage resources, the overall complexity of the instruction set could increase significantly. Therefore, DLP-S adopts a virtual address (VA) to access different storage in a uniform address space, including the SRAM (including NRAM and WRAM) space inside the DLP-S and external storage outside the DLP-S. The VA achieves high-speed direct access to the internal SRAM and indirect access to the external DRAM. Specifically, SRAM inside DLP-S's VA is the same as its physical address (PA), i.e., no address translation. DRAM outside the DLP-S's VA is different from its PA, thus requiring translation, which is achieved by the memory management unit (MMU). MMU maintains an address translation table (i.e., page table) to store the mapping between VA and PA.

Memory access latency reduction

DLP-S has a fixed memory access latency for internal SRAMs but an uncertain access latency to off-chip DRAMs. Thus, the DRAM access can easily become the performance bottleneck. To reduce the overhead of DRAM access, DLP-S adopts two approaches:

(1) **TLB** caches frequently used page tables. During the address translation, the TLB page table will be first visited for VA matching. The frequently used page tables could be directly used without comparing from a large number of page tables. Therefore, TLB reduces the overhead of page table looking and VA–PA translation.

(2) **LLC** caches frequently accessed DRAM data. Memory requests hit in LLC are processed directly without accessing to the slow and unstable DRAM, reducing the frequency of direct accesses to the DRAM and overhead of data accesses.

7.1.5 Summary of single-core deep learning processor

DLP-S is designed for AI applications in mobile scenarios. In order to meet the requirements of low latency and high energy efficiency, DLP-S optimizes both performance and power consumption based on DLP. To improve performance, DLP-S adopts multiple issue queues in the control module so that instructions without dependencies can be issued in parallel, thus supporting instruction-level parallelism. Moreover, DLP-S supports a richer set of operations in the vector operation unit so that the neural network operation of complex operations such as convolution-activation can be completed with one instruction, which reduces the interactions with the storage system. Finally, DLP-S uses TLB and LLC in the memory module to reduce the overhead of DRAM access. To reduce the energy consumption, DLP-S adopts low-bit-width arithmetic units in the matrix operation unit and leverages sparsity in hardware.

7.2 The multicore deep learning processor

Deep learning technology has also been widely used in AI applications in cloud scenarios, such as video reconstruction, advertisement recommendation, and language translation. A notable feature of cloud applications is the huge amount of input data, requiring high storage and high computing capability. Therefore, the processor for cloud applications shall have a large off-chip storage (e.g., a 100–1000-GB DRAM), an on-chip storage (e.g., a 100–1000-MB SRAM), and a powerful computation capability (e.g., a peak performance of 100–1000 trillion floating-point operations per second). Obviously, previous DLP-S cannot meet these demands from cloud applications.

To further improve the computation capability of DLP-S, a straightforward approach is to stack more computation and storage units in DLP-S. However, such an approach would cause a significant increase in the processor area and in the distance of data movement. It eventually leads to additional wiring area and longer transmission latency, which increase the setup time between two adjacent registers and thus decrease the frequency of DLP. Therefore, the simple chip stacking method is not feasible. To break the scalability constraint in a single DLP, multiple DLPs can be integrated in one chip to provide higher computation capability.

In this section, we introduce the multicore deep learning architecture, DLP-M. DLP-M is not a simple stack of multiple DLP-Ss. Instead, DPL-M reconsiders the interconnection and communication among DLP-Ss. In short, DLP-M advances in the following two features:

(1) DLP-M adopts a hierarchical on-chip storage structure to cache data at multiple levels for reducing data access latency.
(2) DLP-M defines a complete framework of synchronization and communication among cores to match the communication requirement in the deep learning algorithm.

In this section, we introduce first the DLP-M architecture, then the communication and synchronization framework, and finally, the interconnection architecture.

7.2.1 The DLP-M architecture

DLP-M adopts a hierarchical multicore design, as shown in Fig. 7.9. DLP-M consists of three layers: *Chip*, *Cluster*, and *Core*. A DLP-M Chip contains multiple DLP clusters (DLP-Cs), and a DLP-C contains multiple DLP-Ss.

As shown in Fig. 7.9(a), at the *Chip* layer, a DLP-M consists of five components: an external memory controller, a peripheral communication module, an on-chip interconnection module, a global barrier controller, and four DLP-Cs. The external storage controller receives the memory access request issued by the DLP cores (i.e., DLP-S) and then visits the external storage device, such as DRAM, for data load/store. The peripheral communication module receives external control information and controls the DLP-M to start or stop. The on-chip interconnection module connects the external storage controller, peripheral communication module, and four DLP-Cs for intercommunication. The synchronization module is designed for synchronizing all modules. DLP-Cs serve as the core computation unit for executing deep learning algorithms efficiently.

At the *Cluster* layer, one DLP-C contains four DLP-Ss and a memory core (MEMCORE), as shown in Fig. 7.9(b). MEMCORE does not have arithmetic functions and is designed for store and communication only. MEMCORE stores the shared data among the four DLP-Ss and performs the communications between DLP-C and off-chip DRAM, between DLP-C and DLP-C, and among multiple DLP-Ss.

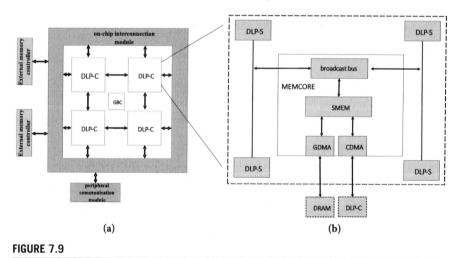

(a)   (b)

FIGURE 7.9

(a) DLP-M overall architecture. (b) DLP-C architecture.

7.2.2 The cluster architecture

Fig. 7.9 shows the architecture of DLP-C, which includes four DLP-Ss and one MEMCORE. MEMCORE is the centered unit, mainly designed for store and communication. MEMCORE contains a shared memory (SMEM), a broadcast bus, cluster

DMA (CDMA), and global DMA (GDMA). SMEM is designed to store shared data, and the other three components respectively solve the three key problems of DLP-C:

- communication among DLP-Ss inside a DLP-C,
- data movement among DLP-Cs,
- data movement between DLP-C and external DRAM.

In the following subsections, we introduce the broadcast bus, CDMA, GDMA, and the multicore synchronization model that solves the problem of memory access conflicts.

7.2.2.1 Broadcast bus

The broadcast bus is designed to perform the high-speed communication between DLP-Ss in DLP-C, supporting broadcast and multicast. We first briefly introduce the concept and motivation of broadcast and multicast. From the perspective of data path, we introduce the intercore communication for unicast read, unicast write, and multicast, as well as the supporting architecture. At last, we introduce the implementation of broadcast and multicast and analyze their advantages and disadvantages, using an example of a DLP-C performing a large-scale convolution operation.

Motivation and basics

The main task for the cloud DLP usually focuses on large-scale deep neural networks. Due to the intensive computation and storage requirements, large-scale deep neural networks need to load data from off-chip constantly, leading to a demand for high off-chip bandwidth. In addition, neural networks have a high data reusability. To leverage such reusability, software needs to partition the computation task to adapt to the deep learning hardware, where each DLP-S only computes part of the operations. Therefore, efficiently sending the reused data to each DLP-S core is a prerequisite for the efficiency of parallel processing. In summary, to ensure the overall performance, it is important and necessary to reduce off-chip memory access and intrachip data communication.

To reduce the off-chip memory accesses, SMEM in MEMCORE serves as an interstation for data transfer with high performance. The reused data in different DLP-Ss is not directly obtained from the off-chip DRAM by each DLP-S but transferred through SMEM. In such way, repeated load data is avoided and MEMCORE can distribute the reused data from SMEM to multiple DLP-Ss quickly and efficiently. Hence, a new broadcast bus architecture with broadcast and multicast support is required and designed. Specifically, both multicast and broadcast happen inside a DLP-C, where multicast refers to a communication that transfers data from SMEM to multiple DLP-Ss and broadcast refers to a communication that transfers data from SMEM to all DLP-Ss. For simplicity, we refer to both broadcast and multicast as multicast in the following parts.

Principles

The broadcast bus is a part of the data path of the communication among the DLP-C cores. It is located inside the SMEM and is responsible for arbitrating and scheduling the communication requests sent by the four DLP-Ss. If the inter-core communication requests are likened to express packages, the broadcast bus acts as a package sorting center, which is responsible for sending each package to the correct destination in an efficient and orderly way. It is worth noting that due to the existence of multicast, multiple copies of a package taken from the sorting center are allowed to be sent to different destinations. When we introduce the function of the broadcast bus, we will also clarify the delivery route of the express package, i.e., the data path of the intercore communication, and what services the express sorting center has for the customers (four DLP-Ss), i.e., the intercore communication initiated by DLP-Ss.

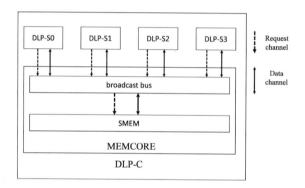

FIGURE 7.10

The data path of DLP-C intercore communication.

Fig. 7.10 shows the communication path among DLP-C cores, including the request channel and data channel that connect the broadcast bus to each DLP-S, and the request channel and data channel that connect the broadcast bus to the SMEM. Note that the data channel is a bidirectional channel, including a read data channel and a write data channel. For simplicity, the read and write requests sent by DLP-S to the broadcast bus are roughly divided into three types: unicast write, unicast read, and multicast.

In Fig. 7.11(a), the unicast write request w_req with the data w_data are sent to the broadcast bus, using the request and data channel. The broadcast bus can receive four DLP-S w_req and w_data simultaneously. The broadcast bus can send a write request write_req through the request channel that connects to SMEM to ask writing data w_data to SMEM through the data channel.

In Fig. 7.11(b), the unicast read request r_req reaches the broadcast bus via the request channel. The broadcast bus first generates a read request read_req sent to SMEM according to the read address in r_req, then reads data from SMEM, and finally writes r_data back to DLP-S via the write data channel.

In Fig. 7.11(c), the multicast request m_req reaches the broadcast bus via the request channel. The broadcast bus reads data from SMEM and sends the read data m_data to the same write address of all DLP-Ss through the write data channel.

Note that the bit-width of the data path between the DLP-S and the broadcast bus is one-fourth of that between the broadcast bus and SMEM.

Normally, taking unicast writing as an example, the broadcast bus combines four unicast write requests from the same DLP-S into one write request and sends it to SMEM. This setup is designed to ensure full utilization of the bandwidth.

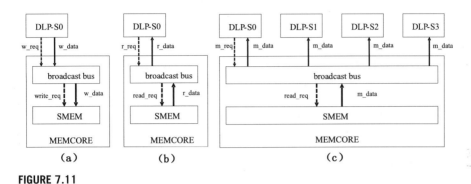

FIGURE 7.11

(a) Unicast write. (b) Unicast read. (c) Multicast.

Applications of multicast

This section takes a DLP-C performing a large-scale convolution operation as an example to introduce the application multicast.

For a convolution layer in a large-scale neural network, input neurons are stored in the NRAM of each DLP-S and weights are stored in the off-chip DRAM. DLP-C needs to load the same weight into the WRAM in all DLP-Ss, so that the four DLP-Ss can perform convolution operations on different input neurons in parallel. Since DLP-Ss need to finish the weight loading before computation, the memory access time could dramatically affect the efficiency of the entire DLP-C.

In the above case, the configuration of instructions and the execution process in DLP-C are as follows:

- First, SMEM drives the DMA to load the weights from off-chip DRAMs into the SMEM using memory access instructions.
- Then, one DLP-S executes the broadcast instruction to drive the DMA to send a multicast request to the broadcast bus. The broadcast bus reads the weight from the SMEM and writes it to the WRAM in all DLP-Ss through broadcast.
- Finally, after the broadcast is completed, four DLP-Ss execute convolution operation instructions.

Without SMEM, DLP-C must repeatedly read the same weight data four times, increasing the amount of off-chip data accesses fourfold. If SMEM is used without broadcast, the same weight data need to be read four times from SMEM, and the total amount of data fetched increases fourfold. As a results, when the memory access bandwidth is limited, the broadcast and multicast save the overhead of weight accesses, thus reducing the runtime of the entire neural network.

7.2.2.2 CDMA

CDMA is designed to communicate among DLP-Cs. In Fig. 7.12, the solid black line marks the data flow. When DLP-S0 in DLP-C0 writes data to DLP-S0 in DLP-C1, there are three steps:

(1) DLP-S0 sends a unicast write request and writes the data into the local SMEM0.
(2) DLP-C0 sends the data in the local SMEM0 to SMEM1 through CDMA0.
(3) DLP-S0 in DLP-C1 sends a unicast read request and read the data from SMEM1.

In Step 2, CMDA0 in DLP-C0 serves as the master, and CDMA1 in DLP-C1 serves as the slave. The master pushes write requests to the slave, including the write address (i.e., AW) and the write data (i.e., W). The slave gives the write response (i.e., B).

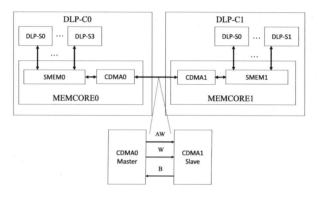

FIGURE 7.12

DLP-C access data flow diagram.

If DLP-C0 transfers data to DLP-C1, DLP-C0 serves as the master and its received memory access instruction should include:

(1) the target cluster index, i.e., DLP-C1;
(2) the source address, i.e., the address in SMEM0 of DLP-C0;
(3) the destination address, i.e., the address in SMEM0 of DLP-C1;
(4) the data size, i.e., the size of transferring data.

Based on the above instructions, CDMA0 in DLP-C0 decodes some memory access requests and pushes multiple AW and W requests to CDMA1 in DLP-C1. The total size of requested data is the data size. DLP-C1 returns the write response signals after finishing. Then data transfer between two DLP-Cs is completed.

7.2.2.3 GDMA

GDMA is responsible for the off-chip memory access of DLP-Cs. It has the following features:

(1) Each DLP-C may correspond to multiple DRAM controllers, so the request address sent by GDMA requires routing.
(2) The request address sent by GDMA is a VA and needs the MMU for VA–PA translation.
(3) GDMA uses TLB to accelerate address translation from virtual to physical.
(4) GDMA uses LLC to reduce the average latency of off-chip memory access.

7.2.2.4 Multicore synchronization model

A multicore system must be synchronized to work in practice. If two cores access the same address simultaneously, a memory access conflict may occur. For example, if two cores run independently and write data to the same address on the off-chip DRAM, the "write-after-write" memory access conflict occurs. To solve the conflict problem, we add a BARRIER instruction, which serves as a lock, to the DLP-S instruction set. Whenever a core executes this instruction, the execution suspends. After all to-be-synced cores have executed the BARRIER instruction, the lock on these cores is released and the execution continues.

Fig. 7.13 illustrates that the BARRIER instruction contains the following instruction fields:

- *Barrier_ID* identifies indices of BARRIER instructions in the same task. Because more than one synchronization may occur in one task, each synchronization must be identified by *Barrier_ID* to prevent the synchronization processing module from confusing different synchronization events.
- *Task_ID* identifies indices of to-be-synced tasks. In a multicore architecture, cores that perform the same task need to be synchronized, and multiple cores may perform multiple tasks simultaneously. Thus, the *Task_ID* is needed to clarify different tasks.
- *Sync_Count* records the number of to-be-synced cores. If *Sync_Count* is less than or equal to 1, the synchronization module would not block the execution. Otherwise, the module suspends the execution of the current core and waits for the BARRIER instruction with the same *Barrier_ID* and *Task_ID* until the cumulative number reaches *Sync_Count*.

BARRIER	Barrier_ID	Task_ID	Sync_Count

FIGURE 7.13

The BARRIER instruction domain.

We take the instruction flow of two cores as an example to illustrate the behavior when multiple cores cooperate to complete a deep learning task. As shown in Fig. 7.14, DLP-S0 and DLP-S1 start to execute instructions simultaneously. DLP-S0 has executed a DMA instruction and finished writing to DRAM address 0. At the same time, DLP-S1 executes the BARRIER instruction. As such, DLP-S1 needs to wait for a matching BARRIER instruction in DLP-S0 to continue. If there is no BARRIER instruction, DLP-S0 writing to DRAM address 0 could conflict with DLP-S1 reading DRAM address 0. Similarly, DLP-S1 writing to DRAM address 1 would conflict with DLP-S0 reading DRAM address 1. The BARRIER instruction can solve the problem of memory access conflicts.

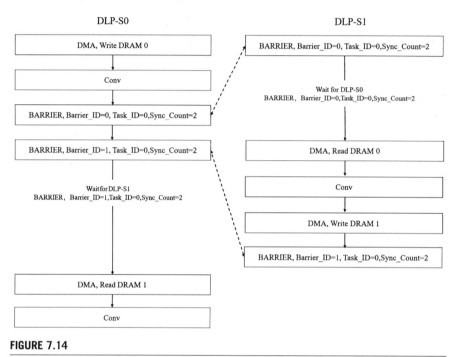

FIGURE 7.14

Dual core collaborative instruction flow.

7.2.3 Interconnection architecture

In the multicore deep learning architecture, each core has functional completeness to handle deep learning tasks, i.e., ability to process deep learning tasks independently. However, in practice, collaborative execution between multiple cores is necessary. The reason is twofold. (1) On one hand, data sharing among multiple cores can reduce data accesses to off-chip memory, thereby improving performance under bandwidth constraints. (2) On the other hand, the multicore coordination can improve the computation capability of the entire processor when processing a single task, thereby reducing computing latency.

The coordination of multiple cores requires real-time data transfer during task execution. One straightforward approach is that all cores access the shared off-chip DRAM. There are two steps for data transfer from core A to core B: (1) First, core A writes the data to the off-chip DRAM. (2) After that, core B reads data from the previously written address on the off-chip DRAM. It can be seen that each data transfer requires two extra data accesses, i.e., one read and one write operation, to the off-chip DRAM. Therefore, such approach suffers from long data access latency and high pressure of memory bandwidth requirements. To achieve efficient data access, it is necessary to add data paths for direct data transfer between cores, i.e., to implement the interconnection among multiple cores.

7.2.3.1 The topology of multicore interconnections

Similar to the interconnection between multiple processors in any parallel system, many possible topologies could be implemented for the on-chip interconnection. In Fig. 7.15, we present some typical topologies.

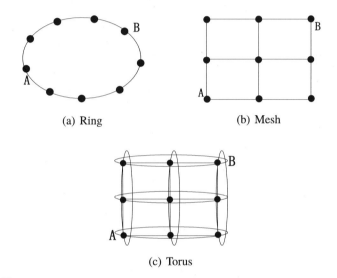

(a) Ring   (b) Mesh

(c) Torus

FIGURE 7.15

Multicore processor on-chip interconnection topology.

Design goals of the interconnection topology are:

(1) All cores are symmetrical, i.e., the latency of data transfer is the same between any two cores. On one hand, this symmetry can provide an equivalent programming model for all cores. On the other hand, it also enables arbitrary task scheduling.
(2) The interconnection paths between cores are as dense as possible, which can reduce the load of a single path and the data access latency.

In theory, only a symmetrical and fully connected topology between cores can meet the above requirements.

7.2.3.2 Interconnection implementation

There are two main approaches to interconnect multiple cores: bus interconnection and NoC.

Bus interconnection

The traditional bus interconnection is that all cores are connected to a common data bus, and the bus connects all the senders and receivers internally.

The main pro of bus interconnection is that each pair of ports is independent, thus avoiding deadlock problems. However, with the increase of core numbers, the bus interconnection is challenged in communication performance, global clock synchronization, and physical implementation.

Network-on-chip

NoC comprises communication nodes and interconnection paths between them. The connection between cores is realized through routing and grouping. NoC adopts a hierarchical and scalable architecture, supporting complex user-defined network topologies and realizing arbitrary point-to-point connections logically. Compared to bus interconnection, NoC has advantages in performance and energy consumption. NoC can significantly lower the complexity of physical links, thus reducing implementation costs. Meanwhile, NoC has better scalability and reusability, thus reducing development costs.

7.2.3.3 Interconnection between DLP-Cs

A DLP-M, which consists of multiple DLP-Cs, is a complex system-on-chip, so that a global synchronous bus is no longer applicable and may even cause some performance and power consumption problems. Thus bus interconnection is not suitable for DLP-M, while the NoC architecture has a globally asynchronous but locally synchronous clock mechanism, which can significantly improve performance. Therefore, DLP-M implements the on-chip interconnection based on NoC, as shown in Fig. 7.16.

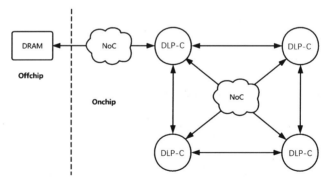

FIGURE 7.16

The interconnection of DLP-C.

7.2.4 Summary of multicore deep learning processors

DLP-M is mainly for intelligent cloud applications. Compared to DLP-S, DLP-M has two notable features: a hierarchical architecture and a novel communication model. DLP-M has a three-layer structure: from top to bottom, Chip, Cluster, and Core.

The main purpose of the hierarchical design is to reduce the data access latency. In the Cluster layer, SMEM is used to cache data from the off-chip memory and to communicate with DLP-Ss. This hierarchical storage structure can significantly reduce the data access latency and improve the performance.

A fundamental problem in DLP-M is how to realize the communication among DLP-Ss, DLP-Cs, and off-chip memories. We have designed MEMCORE to address this problem. MEMCORE has a complete mechanism of multicore communication and synchronization so that it can meet the requirements in deep learning algorithms and reduce the data transfer overhead between the DLP-Ss, DLP-Cs, and off-chip memories.

7.3 Summary

This chapter introduces the architecture of DLP-S and DLP-M.

DLP-S is the basic component of an AI computing system, determining the performance of the entire AI computing system in terms of functionality, executing performance, and energy consumption. To design a general-purpose processor in the field of deep learning, the single-core architecture in this chapter borrows many ideas from the general-purpose CPU. The entire core is divided into a control subsystem, a computation subsystem, and a memory access subsystem. The control subsystem includes components such as the IFU and the IDU. The definition of basic control and scalar instructions also refers to the instruction set in the CPU. Furthermore, while ensuring domain versatility, it is also necessary to consider the energy efficiency of the processor architecture. This feature is mainly reflected in the design of the computation and memory access subsystem. The computation subsystem includes scalar, vector, and matrix units. The memory access subsystem also fully considers the memory access patterns of deep learning algorithms for a customized design. In fact, the designing process of a DLP is to find the balance between versatility, like general-purpose processors, and energy efficiency, like application-specific integrated circuits.

The DLP-M architecture mainly solves the scalability problem of DLPs. Its motivation is similar to that of a multicore CPU. A multicore CPU is proposed when the performance of a single-core CPU cannot be easily improved by increasing the frequency. The motivation of DLP-Ms follows the same intuition. When a DLP-S cannot accumulate more arithmetic units with higher efficiency, DLP-M is proposed. Unlike DLP-S, the main design issues in DLP-M are data communication and synchronization. To address the scalability issue, the common hierarchy design is adopted. The multicore architecture of DLP-M introduced in this chapter includes the Cluster layer, or DLP-C, and uses different interconnection topologies among multiple DLP-Ss inside a DLP-C and between DLP-Cs. Unicast, multicast, and broadcast communication are provided within DLP-C, and the scalability is further enhanced through the flexible NoC topologies among DLP-Cs.

Exercises

7.1 List the peak performance, bandwidth, and power consumption of three commercial DLPs.

7.2 What are the differences between the on-chip storage in DLP-S and the on-chip cache in traditional CPUs?

7.3 What are the differences between the memory access behavior of DLP-S and that of traditional CPUs?

7.4 What are the differences between the instruction decoding process of DLP-S and traditional CPUs?

7.5 To support out-of-order execution, what should be done to modify the DLP-S? From an application perspective, is it necessary for DLPs to support out-of-order execution functions?

7.6 Briefly describe the working process of DMA and its key points.

7.7 Suppose there is a DLP-D with the following features: (1) a total of 256 kB on-chip storage WRAM for storing weights, (2) a total of 128 kB on-chip storage NRAM for storing input/output neurons, (3) a matrix operation unit that can complete 256 32-bit floating-point multiplication and accumulation operations in each clock cycle, (4) the DLP is running at 1 GHz, (5) the total bandwidth of off-chip memory access is 64 GB/s, (6) we assume that the utilization rate of the arithmetic unit is 100% and delay can be ignored, and (7) the utilization rate of memory access bandwidth is 100% and delay can be ignored.

The following simplified instructions can be used:

move ram_type1 ram_type2 size, for transferring *size* bytes of data from *ram_type1* to *ram_type2*, where *ram_type* can be DRAM, NRAM, and WRAM.

compute compute_type num, for computing of *compute_type* operations with a total amount of *num*, where *compute_type* can be MAC_32, MAC_16, ADD_32, ADD_16, SUB_32, SUB_16, MUL_32, MUL_16, DIV_32, DIV_16, etc.

loop loop_time....endloop, for representing the *loop_time* times execution of the loop body.

sync, a synchronous instruction, meaning that all previous instructions must be executed before the subsequent instructions can be executed.

Use the above instructions to complete the following task and estimate the execution time.

Task: Perform a fully connected layer computation. The number of input neurons is 1×256, the size of the weight matrix is 256×1, and all data are in the 32-bit floating-point format.

7.8 Use the processor and instructions described in Exercise 7.7 to complete the following task and estimate the execution time.

Task: Perform a fully connected layer computation. The number of input neurons is 32×256, the size of the weight matrix is 256×128, and all data are in the 32-bit floating-point format.

7.9 Use the processor and instructions described in Exercise 7.7 to complete the following task and estimate the execution time.

Task: Perform a fully connected layer computation. The number of input neurons is 1024×256, the size of the weight matrix is 256×128, and all data are in the 32-bit floating-point format.

7.10 For Exercise 7.9, assuming that the weight and input data have a certain degree of sparsity, the weight can be compressed to one-fourth of the original size through sparse coding, and the input neuron data can be compressed to one-half of the original size. Reestimate the execution time of Exercise 7.9.

*7.11 Suppose there is a quadcore neural network processor, where each core is the same as the single-core neural network processor in Exercise 7.7 (except for off-chip memory access bandwidth). The cluster consists of these four identical cores and includes an on-chip storage of 2 MB SharedRAM shared by the four cores. The total off-chip memory access bandwidth is 128 GB/s and the bandwidth between SharedRAM and each single-core processor is 1 TB/s. The instructions supported by the chip are the same as in Exercise 7.7, and SharedRAM is added as a new ram_type on the basis of it. Use the instructions to complete the following task and estimate the execution time.

Task: Perform a fully connected layer computation. The input neuron is 32×256, the size of the weight matrix is 256×128, and all data are in the 32-bit floating-point format.

*7.12 Use the multicore processor and instructions described in Exercise 7.11 to complete the following task and estimate the execution time.

Task: Perform a fully connected layer computation. The number of input neurons is 1024×256, the size of the weight matrix is 256×2048, and all data are in the 32-bit floating-point format.

AI programming language for AI computing systems

8

The 2017 A.M. Turing Award recipients J.L. Hennessy and D.A. Patterson mentioned in the Turing lecture "A New Golden Age for Computer Architecture" that "domain-specific languages (DSLs) ⋯ is an interesting research challenge for language designers, compiler creators, and DSA architects" [151]. As a bridge between the intelligent programming framework and the intelligent computing hardware, the AI programming language is not only the basis of implementing operators of the programming frameworks, but also the core user interface for efficient programming of intelligent computing hardware. This chapter will introduce the abstract hardware architecture, programming model, basis of programming language, programming interface, functional debugging, performance tuning, and system-level programming of AI computing systems. Specifically, Section 8.1 introduces the limitations of traditional programming languages for AI computing systems, clarifying the core requirements of AI programming languages, namely *high productivity*, *high performance*, and *high portability*. Section 8.2 introduces the abstract hardware architecture of the AI computing system. Section 8.3 introduces the programming model based on the hardware abstraction of the AI computing system. Section 8.4 takes the BANG C Language (BCL) as an example to introduce the basis of AI programming language, including syntax, data types, built-in functions, and programming examples. Section 8.5 introduces the programming interfaces of AI programming language. Section 8.6 introduces the methods, interfaces, tools, and examples for functional debugging of intelligent programs. Section 8.7 introduces the methods, interfaces, tools, and examples for performance tuning of intelligent programs. Section 8.8 introduces system-level programming based on the AI programming language, including how to develop operators of high-performance libraries and programming frameworks and how to perform system-level optimization.

8.1 Necessity of AI programming language

A variety of different programming languages have been developed on the traditional general-purpose computing platform, including platform-specific assembly languages (such as x86 assembly, ARM assembly, and RISC-V assembly languages), user-friendly high-level languages (such as C/C++, JAVA, and Python) convenient for users, and declarative programming languages (such as Prolog) for problem solving.

AI Computing Systems. https://doi.org/10.1016/B978-0-32-395399-3.00014-7

These programming languages encounter many problems in deep learning processor (DLP)-based AI computing systems. As shown in Fig. 8.1, there are three gaps between traditional programming languages and AI computing systems. The first one is the *Semantic Gap*. With traditional programming languages, it is difficult to describe efficiently high-level intelligent computing semantics, resulting in low development productivity of AI applications. The second is the *Hardware Gap*. With traditional programming languages, it is hard to effectively abstract the characteristics of intelligent computing hardware, resulting in low-performance executable binaries. The third is the *Platform Gap*. As the types of intelligent computing hardware platforms are variable and are continuously growing, it is difficult to realize *cross-platform portability*, i.e., that programs optimized for a specific platform can be executed normally on different platforms and achieve high computing efficiency as well.

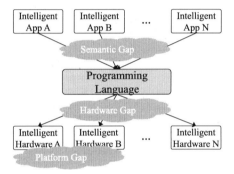

FIGURE 8.1

Three major gaps between traditional programming languages and AI computing systems.

8.1.1 Semantic gap

Traditional programming languages, such as C/C++, are based on scalar operations such as addition, subtraction, multiplication, and division for general-purpose computing. Usually, they do not have high-level semantics related to specific tasks and application scenarios, which leads to inefficient development of new emerging intelligent computing primitives.[1] Considering that the core of many intelligent computing tasks represented by deep learning is vector and matrix computation, programming languages such as Python and MATLAB®, which directly provide a semantic description of vector and matrix computation, can improve programming efficiency to a certain extent. However, the ability of these languages to provide higher-level intelligent computing semantics is still very limited. Taking the convolution operation, the core operation of deep learning, as an example, developmental efficiency has been significantly improved after embedding high-level semantics in the programming lan-

---

[1] In TensorFlow, the number of operators continues to increase.

guage, as shown in Fig. 8.2. Among them, the convolution operation written in C++ with pure scalar calculation contains seven nested loops, while the convolution operation written in Python with vector (namely array) semantics only needs four nested loops to complete. If the programming language with Conv statement and Tensor type is used for implementing the convolution operation, only one statement is necessary, which reduces the amount of code and improves the development efficiency.

To further improve the development productivity, in addition to providing core operations with high-level semantics of intelligent computing directly, the abstraction level of AI programming languages is constantly rising for specialization, e.g., the programming language Kaldi [152] for speech recognition and the programming language SCENIC [153] for automatic driving test scenario generation. Fig. 8.3 provides an example of the SCENIC programming language, which is essentially a *probability programming language* for domain-specific intelligent tasks (e.g., automatic driving test scenario generation). The physical world and agents that satisfy the constraints can be generated by specifying a probability distribution. In this example, a typical test scenario can be generated with only three lines of code: the car is parked 0.5 m to the left of the road edge, and the angle between the front of the car and the road edge is 10–20 degrees. Certainly, the above languages are only suitable for specific application scenarios (e.g., voice and autonomous driving) and cannot meet the universal needs of different kinds of AI application scenarios.

8.1.2 **Hardware gap**

Compared with traditional general-purpose processors, the intelligent computing hardware has its distinct characteristics in *control logic*, *memory hierarchy*, and *computational logic*. Such characteristics make it difficult for traditional (high-level) programming languages to effectively describe the hardware and pass it to the compiler for specific optimizations.

For the *control logic*, traditional general-purpose processors, represented by the multilevel instruction pipelines of RISC and CISC, generate the corresponding control signals after the translation of instructions (or microcodes). The specific control logic is not exposed to users in traditional programming languages such as C/C++. Instead, the parallelism of code (such as instruction-level parallelism, data-level parallelism, etc.) is fully exploited through compilation optimization and hardware architecture optimization to fill the gap between user programs and underlying hardware characteristics. Regarding the intelligent computing hardware, its instructions are mainly vector instructions or macro instructions, which are highly parallel and relatively regular. Therefore, the control flow of traditional programming languages, a large number of scalar operations, and the relatively time-consuming off-chip memory access easily lead to pipeline "bubbles," which affect the computing efficiency of the array of functional units. To address these problems of traditional programming languages, AI programming languages are required to expose users to more underlying hardware features, such as (1) special control flow instructions to reduce the

```
1   // Declare C++ array type
2   T input = new T[ni * ci * (hi + 2 * pad) * (wi + 2 * pad)];
3   T filter = new T[co * ci * hk * wk];
4   T bias = new T[co];
5   int ho = (hi + 2 * pad - hk) / stride + 1;
6   int wo = (wi + 2 * pad - wk) / stride + 1;
7   T output = new T[ni * co * ho * wo];
8   // Compute
9   for (int ni_idx = 0; ni_idx < ni; ni_idx++) {
10    for (int co_idx = 0; co_idx < co; co_idx++) {
11      for (int ho_idx = 0; ho_idx < ho; ho_idx++) {
12        for (int wo_idx = 0; wo_idx < wo; wo_idx++) {
13          T sum = T(0);
14          for (int ci_idx = 0; ci_idx < ci; ci_idx++) {
15            for (int hk_idx = 0; hk_idx < hk; hk_idx++) {
16              for (int wk_idx = 0; wk_idx < wk; wk_idx++) {
17                int hi_idx = ho_idx * stride + hk_idx;
18                int wi_idx = wo_idx * stride + wk_idx;
19                sum += input[((ni_idx * ci + ci_idx) *
20                (hi + 2 * pad) + hi_idx) * (wi + 2 * pad) +
21                wi_idx] *filter[((co_idx * ci + ci_idx) * hk
22                + hk_idx) * wk + wk_idx];
23              } } }
24          output[((ni_idx * co + co_idx) * ho + ho_idx) * wo
25            + wo_idx] = sum + bias[co_idx];
26        } } } }
```

```
1   # Declare numpy array type
2   input = numpy.array(padded_input_data_list).reshape(ni, ci,
3     hi+2*pad, wi+2*pad)
4   filter = numpy.array(filter_data_list).reshape(co, ci, hk, wk)
5   bias = numpy.array(bias_data_list).reshape(1, co, 1, 1);
6   ho = (hi + 2 * pad - hk) / stride + 1
7   wo = (wi + 2 * pad - wk) / stride + 1
8   output = numpy.array([0,]*(ni*co*ho*wo)).reshape(ni, co, ho, wo)
9   # Compute
10  for ni_idx in range(ni):
11    for co_idx in range(co):
12      for ho_idx in range(ho):
13      for wo_idx in range(wo):
14        hi_idx = ho_idx * stride
15        wi_idx = wo_idx * stride
16        output[ni_idx, co_idx, ho_idx, wo_idx] =
17        np.sum(input[ni_idx, :, hi_idx:hi_idx+hk,
18        wi_idx:wi_idx+wk] * filter[co_idx, :, :, :]) +
19        bias[0, co_idx, 0, 0]
```

```
1   // Declare tensors type
2   Tensor input(ni, ci, hi, wi);
3   Tensor filter(co, ci, hk, wk);
4   Tensor bias(1, co, 1, 1);
5   Tensor output(ni, co, (hi+2*pad-hk)/stride+1, (wi+2*pad-wk)/stride+1)
6   // Compute
7   conv(input, filter, bias, output, pad, stride)
```

FIGURE 8.2

Examples of convolution operations implemented in different languages: C++ (top), Python (middle), and a language with Conv semantics (bottom).

```
spot = OrientedPoint on visible curb
// OrientedPoint is a built-in class, including info on location & orientation;
// visible curb is a built-in class, specifies region;
// OrientedPoint should be randomly distributed in this region.
badAngle = Uniform(1.0, -1.0) * (10, 20) deg
// badAngle specifies a random angle between 10-20°.
Car left of spot by 0.5, \
    facing badAngle relative to roadDirection
// Output result: The vehicle is parked at 0.5m to the left edge of the road,
// and the front of the vehicle is distributed at an angle of 10-20°
// to the edge of the road.
```

FIGURE 8.3

Sample code of the SCENIC programming language for generating automated driving test scenarios.

overhead of branch control[2]; (2) programming interfaces of special vector or macro instructions supported by the underlying hardware architecture, instead of a large number of scalar operations, which are parallelized by the compiler with high development burden and low execution efficiency; and (3) high-level language features to make it easier for users to balance the computation and memory access. Fig. 8.4[3] provides performance improvements by using different programming languages and different hardware features, including functions implemented by specific hardware instructions and the balance between computation and memory access. For a simple matrix multiplication (which has a size of 4000×4000), a C-based implementation that is closer to the underlying hardware has a simpler instruction control flow than a higher-level programming language such as Python/JAVA, resulting in 47 times better performance. After considering the parallelism, memory hierarchy, and vector instructions provided by the underlying hardware, the performance of the realized program improves 62,806-fold compared with the original one. As a result, the computation efficiency improves from nearly 0% to 40% [154].

For *memory hierarchy*, especially on-chip memory, conventional general-purpose processors typically contain hardware-managed caches which are transparent to the programmers and programmer-visible registers. As traditional programming languages (especially high-level languages) are not aware of the above memory hierarchy explicitly, the programmers only need to access the data in memory directly. Then, compilers (such as adopting data prefetching and register allocation) and hardware architectures (such as adopting hardware cache management and dynamic pipeline scheduling) make full use of on-chip memory to alleviate the "memory wall".[4] However, this paradigm cannot maximize the computing performance of the intelligent computing hardware represented by the DLP. The main reasons are as follows. First, it brings a great burden to compiler optimization and code generation,

---

[2] For example, TensorFlow introduces specially designed control flow operators.

[3] Data source of Fig. 8.4: Figure 1-1 of [154].

[4] "Memory wall" refers to the growing gap between the processing speed of computing logic and memory, which makes memory access a key bottleneck of the whole processing.

Comparison of 4k x 4k matrix multiplication performance

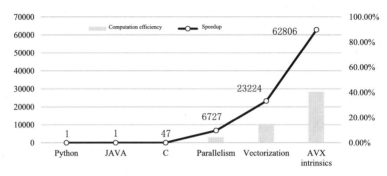

FIGURE 8.4

Comparison of matrix multiplication performance by using different programming languages and considering different hardware features such as parallelism, memory hierarchy, vector instructions, etc.

which requires the compiler to automatically maximize the utilization of on-chip memory. Second, it greatly increases the overhead of hardware control logic and reduces the computing capacity per unit area. Generally speaking, intelligent computing hardware uses scratchpad memory (SPM)[5] to reduce hardware overhead and enhance flexibility. Due to the huge gap in bandwidth and latency between dynamic RAM (DRAM) and on-chip SPM, there is an order of magnitude difference in execution efficiency when using SPM programming.

For *computational logic*, traditional general-purpose processors mainly provide arithmetic logic units (ALUs) and floating-point units (FPUs), but generally do not provide customized computing units with intelligent computing characteristics, such as low-bit-width computing units. Fig. 8.5 shows a comparison of the current common formats of the operational units, including 32-bit IEEE-754 standard single-precision floating point (FP32), 16-bit IEEE-754 standard floating point (FP16), brain floating point (BF16), 16-bit fixed point (INT16), and 8-bit fixed point (INT8). The main reason of using low-bit-width computing units is that intelligent computing applications have a certain tolerance of error. In other words, high-precision computing units are not required in many scenarios. Taking the inference task in visual processing as an example, the precision of 8-bit fixed-point ALUs can well meet the requirements of many scenarios (such as image classification and target detection). As shown in Fig. 8.6, for typical deep learning algorithms, the accuracy loss of 8-bit fixed-point and 16-bit floating point is almost negligible compared with 32-bit floating point arithmetic. Taking the typical classification network, i.e., ResNet50, as an example, the precision (top one accuracy) degradation of INT8 and FP16 is

---

[5] The register files can also be considered as a special SPM accessed by programmers.

only 0.1% and 0.2%, respectively, compared to FP32. In addition, the low-bit-width ALUs have no loss in precision, and also obtain a great reduction in area and power consumption. Taking INT8 as an example, compared with FP32, its area and power consumption are reduced by 85.54% and 85.73%, respectively [155].

Due to the lack of customized computing units for intelligent computing in traditional general-purpose processors, traditional programming languages mainly provide data types such as INT and FP32, which makes it difficult to fully use the abundant and efficient computing units of AI computing systems, such as FP16 and BF16, or even INT4, INT2, and binary computing units.

FP32	s	exp(8 bits)	mantissa(23 bits)
FP16	s	exp(5 bits)	mantissa(10 bits)
BF16	s	exp(8 bits)	mantissa(7 bits)
INT16	s	mantissa(15 bits)
INT8	s	mantissa(7 bits)

FIGURE 8.5

Data format comparison of common computing units.

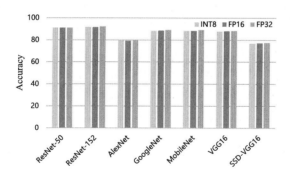

FIGURE 8.6

Accuracy comparison of FP32, FP16, and INT8 data formats used in typical deep neural network algorithms.

Obviously, high-level programming languages have high abstraction of the underlying hardware. In other words, more hardware features are concealed to users. It is expected that an ideal AI programming language should *not only have a high-level abstraction of a particular intelligent task but also provide users with sufficient hardware details.* This requires balancing the abstraction level and hardware details to meet the requirements for both high productivity and high performance.

8.1.3 Platform gap

Due to the rapid development of artificial intelligence (AI) and machine learning, new intelligent computing hardware is constantly emerging. At present, there are many different forms of intelligence computing hardware, e.g., CPU, GPU, FPGA, and ASIC, based on traditional CMOS technology. The emergence of new computing devices (such as digital-analog hybrid computing devices, optoelectronic hybrid computing devices, memristors, and nonvolatile phase-change memory devices) further enriches the underlying intelligent computing hardware. The diversity of hardware platforms makes it challenging to implement programs with functional portability and performance portability, which are well tuned on a particular platform. A lack of *functional portability* means that if a program is written in a platform-specific language (such as calling intrinsic functions of special instructions), it fails to execute on another platform. For example, in Fig. 8.4, the matrix multiplication is optimized on the Intel x86 platform by calling the intrinsic function corresponding to the AVX instruction. Thus, on a platform that does not support AVX, such as an ARM processor, the program cannot be executed, leading to the portability problem. By enhancing the abstraction level of the programming language, such as defining API functions that are closer to the semantics of the algorithm, e.g., the commonly used Basic Linear Algebra Subprograms (BLAS) API, rather than directly using the intrinsic functions of the underlying instructions, the gap between different platforms can be filled to a certain extent. However, this solution brings a challenge to *performance portability*, that is, a program optimized for a particular platform may become dramatically less efficient when executed on a new hardware platform. Taking the BLAS API as an example, if good performance portability is required, expert programmers need to carry out customized optimization on different platforms (such as x86, ARM, GPU, etc.) and only expose well-defined and widely accepted APIs to users at the language level. Clearly, manually specialized optimization on different platforms comes at considerable cost in development. In addition, there exist great differences in the architecture, process, and device aspects of different intelligent computing hardware platforms, which further pose a great challenge for unified cross-platform performance optimization. To alleviate this problem, an ideal programming language should be able to *extract common features of different hardware platforms* and then expose the performance-critical features as language features to users. This requires a lot of effort from programming language designers, compiler designers, and domain-specific architects to obtain an optimal trade-off between the level of hardware abstraction and performance.

8.1.4 Summary

This section analyzes three challenges faced by programming languages, which are originally designed for traditional general-purpose processors, in AI computing systems represented by DLPs: semantic gap, hardware gap, and platform gap. It is difficult to meet the requirements of high productivity, high performance, and high portability at the same time. In Fig. 8.7, we summarize whether a typical program-

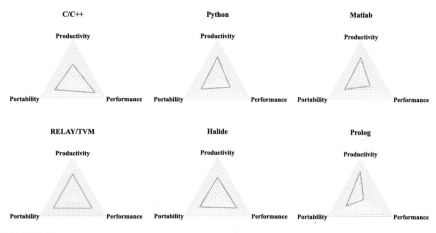

FIGURE 8.7

Comparison of three design principles of high productivity, high performance, and high portability between traditional general-purpose programming languages and domain-specific programming languages.

ming language can meet the above three requirements. Obviously, the higher the abstraction level of the programming language (such as Python), the better the productivity and portability it achieves. However, its performance will face significant challenges. One the other hand, the programming language with lower abstraction level (such as C language and assembly language) can fully exploit the performance of the underlying hardware, but there are problems in productivity and portability. DSLs are an important solution to meet all these three requirements simultaneously. Existing DSLs, such as Prolog for logical reasoning, Halide [156] for image processing, and RELAY/TVM [157] for deep learning, follow the above-mentioned design principles of AI programming languages by abstracting both applications and hardware of a certain domain.

Specifically, based on predicate logic, Prolog has high development efficiency for specific problems such as constraint solving, theorem proving, expert systems, etc. However, because it mainly solves problems by searching and backtracking, operating efficiency is a great challenge. Halide separates computing logic from optimization logic, requiring expert programmers to write complex schedules for different hardware platforms, such as loop transformations, tiling, and thread bindings. To achieve better performance on specific platforms, its development efficiency is still an issue, especially for a wide variety of underlying hardware platforms. The recent RELAY/TVM is essentially a uniform abstraction of the DLP architecture, which identifies some key scheduling primitives, including parallelism, tensorization, and latency hiding. Based on these scheduling primitives, the optimal scheduling policy is automatically searched by machine learning methods instead of manual implementation. This approach raises the level of abstraction and guarantees performance to a certain extent. However, with the rapid evolution of AI algorithms and DLPs, it still requires further exploration whether the abstract granularity/level of AI algorithms and hardware scheduling primitives is the most reasonable and whether the AI programming language has high productivity, high performance, and high portability (especially functional portability).

8.2 Abstraction of AI programming language

Aiming at the challenge of developing AI programming languages, it is necessary to abstract the hardware of an AI computing system to obtain the appropriate abstract hardware architecture. This section begins with a discussion of the hierarchical abstract hardware architecture, where each level includes abstract control, computing, and memory models. Then, we map the typical AI computing system to abstract architecture to demonstrate its effectiveness. Finally, the control, calculation, and memory models are introduced in detail.

8.2.1 Abstract hardware architecture

Because traditional programming languages face challenges in AI computing systems, such as semantics, hardware, and platform, we expect to design AI programming languages that meet the requirements of high development efficiency, high performance, and high portability. In order to meet these objectives, the premise is to build appropriate hardware abstraction for AI computing systems of different scales and forms and provide simple and unified programming interfaces for users upon this basis.

We observe that computing systems of different scales can be abstracted into three parts: memory, control, and computation. A typical multicore processor system, for example, generally consists of a processor chip containing control and computation and off-chip memory such as DRAM. The computing part of the processor chip is composed of computing cores containing control and computing logic and on-chip memory such as cache. Each computing core includes microarchitecture control paths (such as pipeline control), computing units (such as ALUs and FPUs), private caches, and on-chip memory such as registers. Based on these observations, we introduce a hierarchical hardware abstraction for AI computing systems. Each level of an AI computing system contains a memory unit, a control unit, and a number of computing units. Each computing unit is further divided into three parts: a subcontrol unit, a sub-computing unit, and a submemory unit. The whole system is structured recursively in this way, as shown in Fig. 8.8. At the bottom level, each leaf node is a concrete accelerator that performs the most basic computational tasks [42].

8.2.2 Typical AI computing system

DLPs can be used to accelerate various types of deep learning applications. When the DLP is used as an accelerator card of a server, it exchanges data with the host CPU

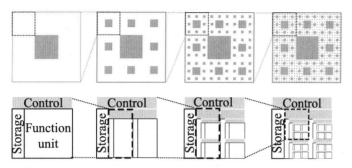

FIGURE 8.8

Abstract hardware architecture of a hierarchical AI computing system.

through the Peripheral Component Interconnect Express (PCIe) bus. An AI computing system built by multiple DLP cards can be abstracted with a hierarchical hardware model. As shown in Fig. 8.9, the multicard DLP server can be abstractly divided into five levels, the server level, the card level, the chip level, the multicore level, and the processor core level. At the top level (i.e., the server level), the whole server system contains several control units composed of CPUs, memory units composed of local DDRs, and several DLP cards interconnected through the PCIe bus as computing units. At the second level (the card level), each DLP card contains the local DRAM (LDRAM) and each processor chip serves as the computing and control units. At the third level (the chip level), each processor chip contains multiple multiprocessors as the computing units. At the fourth level (the cluster level), each multiprocessor contains multiple accelerator cores as the control and computing units and shared RAM (SRAM) as memory units. The fifth level (the core level) is the leaf node. At this level, each accelerator core contains the local memory and the local processing unit array. This architecture can easily increase the computing capacity of the whole system by adding cards, chips, clusters, or cores.

For the five levels of "Server–Card–Chip–Cluster–Core" provided by DLP AI computing systems, the key to user programming is to manage the memory model of each level. The memory that the user can view includes the global memory of the host server, the global memory of the device card, SRAM of the Cluster, neuron RAM (NRAM), weight RAM (WRAM), and Registers of the Core. Users can utilize the computing resources on the Card in the form of *macro instructions* or a *high-performance computing library* at the high level. The data migration and resource partition among different memory levels will be completed by the underlying code; the data migration on the host and device still need to be controlled explicitly. If expert users require better performance, they can explicitly control data movement and access/compute balance between levels below the Card level. In the programming model, both the above two different programming methods should be provided to meet the requirements of different types of users.

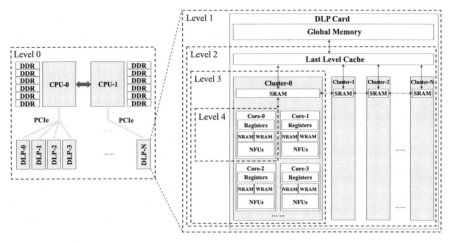

FIGURE 8.9

Hierarchical abstraction of typical AI computing systems.

The different levels of control, computation, and memory models are discussed in detail below.

8.2.3 Control model

Instruction is the key to controlling computation and memory. To design an efficient instruction set, it is necessary to analyze fully the typical computing patterns in the field of AI, extract the most representative operations, and carry out targeted acceleration in the architectural design. These operations can be expressed as macro instructions for users with a higher level of abstraction, thus significantly improving the programming efficiency. For example, in an AI computing system (AICS), a single instruction can be used to perform matrix multiplication of different scales, while the same operation on a general-purpose processor would require dozens or even hundreds of instructions.

Four typical types of operations can be obtained by abstracting the AI algorithm: control, data transfer, and computational and logical operations. The computational operation can be subdivided into scalar operation, vector operation, and matrix operation. Logical operations can be subdivided into scalar and vector operations, as shown in the DLP instruction set in Fig. 6.10. These abstractions allow for both flexibility (implementing more complex operations by programming a combination of fine-grained operations) and efficiency (performing complex computations with a single hardware instruction).

The interaction between computation and memory is also the focus of the control model. Considering the existence of the "memory wall" problem, in order to reduce memory latency, computational operations and memory operations should be parallelized as much as possible. For example, computation instructions and memory access instructions can be sent and executed in different queues separately to improve parallelism. In the hierarchical structure, the control module of the lower nodes is a subset of the upper nodes. Taking Fig. 8.9 as an example, the control and computing module of level 2 is multiple clusters, the control and computing module of level 3 is a single cluster, and the control and computing module of level 4 is the core of the cluster.

8.2.4 Computation model

Here, we focus on customized computing units and parallel computing architectures in terms of the abstraction of the computing model visible to the programmer.

8.2.4.1 Customized computing unit

A typical characteristic of AI application is to have a certain tolerance of error, such as allowing a certain error in the statistical sense. By taking advantage of the error tolerance of AI applications, customized low-bit-width computing units (such as FP16, INT8, BF16, and INT4) are generally adopted in AICSs to improve processing energy efficiency. As described in Section 8.1.2, compared with traditional FPUs (FP32 and FP64), intelligent tasks performed with customized low-bit-width computing units have negligible accuracy degradation, as well as good performance and energy efficiency.

Due to the diversity and complexity of AI applications, there is no unanimous conclusion about which low-bit-width arithmetic unit is most suitable. For example, inference and training, image/video applications, and speech applications have different accuracy requirements. Considering that all kinds of AICS need to be compatible with each other and more compatible with traditional computing systems (for example, deep learning models are generally trained with FP32 data types on GPUs), data types corresponding to various types of customized computing units are needed in AI programming languages. This not only provides flexibility for users, but also ensures the full utilization of hardware resources.

8.2.4.2 Parallel computing architecture

AICSs usually have a parallel computing architecture, as shown in Fig. 8.9. A single Chip contains multiple Clusters, and each Cluster contains multiple Cores. Thus, programmers have to divide tasks and distribute them evenly among a large number of parallel computing units. For computing unit at each level, a corresponding synchronization mechanism is needed to ensure the dependencies between tasks after partition. For example, synchronization mechanisms of different granularities are required among different Cores within the Cluster and among different Clusters within the Chip.

8.2.5 Memory model

AI applications demand massive, data-intensive memory accesses. Thus, reasonable organization of memory hierarchy is equally important as the design of computing units. They should be codesigned to balance computation and memory access to implement highly efficient AI computing. In the hierarchical abstract architecture, memory is uniformly divided into *global memory* and *local memory*. The top level contains large global memory for input and output data, which is visible to the programmer. Each intelligent computing node also has local memory to cache data. This local memory becomes the shared global memory of the children. The entire abstract architecture also manages memory resources hierarchically.

The typical *global memory* is off-chip memory such as DDR. The processor accesses the off-chip memory based on the bus protocol through the on-chip memory control unit (such as the DDR controller). In the whole process, the read and write requests from the internal processor core are converted to external read and write requests according to the bus protocol in order to complete the data exchange. There are two important trends in the development of off-chip memory. The first is the trend towards lower latency and higher bandwidth on the basis of traditional devices. The second is improvement of processing efficiency through new memory devices. This is evidenced by the increasing DDR bandwidth from DDR3 and DDR4 to 3D-stacked high-bandwidth memory. The second trend involves by phase change memory, resistive RAM, and other nonvolatile memory, which is increasingly used as off-chip memory. Certainly, DDR can be regarded as the global memory at the chip level. At lower levels such as the processor core, shared on-chip memory such as shared cache or SPM can be regarded as the global memory per processor core.

The typical *local memory* is the processor's on-chip memory resource. The memory resources of traditional processors, especially on-chip memory such as the Cache, are transparent to the programmer to simplify programming. However, in AI computing systems, programmers are generally required to manage on-chip memory explicitly in order to maximize processing efficiency. Through cooperation of various types of on-chip caches (such as Cache, SPM, and Registers), it can support large-scale and highly concurrent data accesses required for intelligent computing.

On-chip memory is often customized according to the characteristics of AI applications to further improve processing efficiency. Taking the convolution computation as an example, input/output neurons and weights have different data reuse modes, which makes it necessary to consider defining different types of memory units in the abstract memory model, such as the on-chip memory specially designed for neuron and weight data. In addition, considering the large amount of intermediate data during the computation of neural networks, it is necessary to store the intermediate results of each layer of computation in the on-chip cache as much as possible to quickly obtain the corresponding input data when entering the computation of the next layer. Considering that the on-chip cache resources are usually very limited, how to organize and use them properly will be the key of algorithm design and optimization. To efficiently utilize temporal and spatial localities, programmers must organize data in a reasonable manner so that it enters the computing unit in a specific order for computation. For large-scale neural networks, partitioning the network layers is usually required to exploit the on-chip memory's limited capacity.

8.3 Programming models

In the hierarchical abstraction described in Section 8.2, CPU is required in a typical AI computing system. Fig. 8.10 shows four typical heterogeneous AI computing systems, which are DGX-1 with GPU as the computing core, TPU Pod with TPU as the computing core, Brain Wave with FPGA as the computing core, and an AI computing system with DLP as the computing core. In this section, first we introduce the general heterogeneous programming model and then the general AI programming model based on the aforementioned hierarchical abstract architecture.

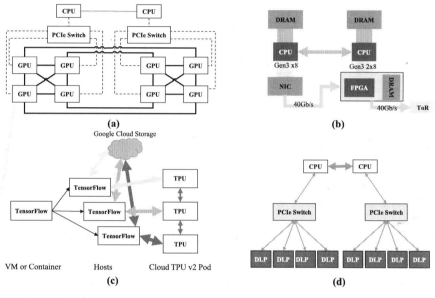

FIGURE 8.10

Current AICSs are mainly based on heterogeneous processing systems. (a) DGX-1 with Nvidia GPU as the computing core. (b) Brain Wave with FPGA as the computing core. (c) A tensor processing system with Google TPU as the computing core. (d) An AI computing system with DLP as the computing core.

8.3.1 Heterogeneous programming model

For the general heterogeneous programming model, we focus on the basic flow of programming and compilation, compiler support, and runtime support.

8.3.1.1 Overview

Heterogeneous computing systems are usually composed of general-purpose processors and multiple domain-specific processors. The general-purpose processor, as the control device (referred to as the host side), is responsible for complex control and scheduling. Domain-specific processors, as slave devices (device side), are responsible for large-scale parallel computing or domain-specific computing tasks. The two processors work together to complete the computing task. For this kind of heterogeneous computing system, the original homogeneous parallel programming model is no longer applicable. Therefore, heterogeneous parallel programming models have gradually become the focus of attention in academia and industry. For example, Nvidia CUDA [28], OpenCL [158], and OpenACC [159] are parallel programming models for heterogeneous systems.

From the user interface's point of view, heterogeneous parallel programming models can be roughly divided into two categories. One is building a new heterogeneous parallel programming language. The other is extending the existing programming language with heterogeneous parallel semantics [160]. Fig. 8.11 shows a comparison of typical heterogeneous parallel programming models. The light and dark colors are used to represent a new heterogeneous parallel programming language and the heterogeneous parallel extension to the existing language, such as in the form of library functions or pragma directives, respectively. The ordinate represents the abstraction level of the programming language, while the abscissa represents the specific content that the programming interface needs to focus on. If a programming language conceals many hardware details, it only needs to focus on task partition; otherwise, it needs to pay attention to data distribution, communication, and synchronization. In particular, Copperhead [161] and Lime [162] are programming languages with a high level of abstraction, similar to Python and Java. Such languages do not require users to specify explicit data layout, communication, and synchronization. Similarly, Intel's Merge (a MapReduce-like heterogeneous parallel programming language) [163] and Microsoft's C++ AMP [164] are both examples of programming interfaces that conceal a lot of hardware details, and both languages are close to the C/C++ syntactic form. The other category requires the user to pay more attention to hardware details. OpenACC is based on C/Fortran and can be extended by adding the pragma directives in the serial program. Nvidia CUDA is a heterogeneous extension of C language, which achieves data parallelism through the single-program multiple-data (SPMD) programming model. Since CUDA requires programmers to explicitly conduct task partition, data layout, communication, task synchronization, etc., programming can be more difficult. To alleviate the burden of CUDA programming, improved heterogeneous parallel programming models such as hiCUDA [165] and OpenStream [166] have been proposed. OpenCL is another widely used programming model; it tries to realize heterogeneous parallel programming across platforms by abstracting all kinds of hardware platforms into a unified platform model.

Next, we introduce the process and characteristics of heterogeneous programming models based on the abstraction of CUDA and OpenCL.

8.3.1.2 Basic process

Heterogeneous programming includes the host side and the device side. The host side mainly includes device acquisition, data/parameter preparation, execution stream cre-

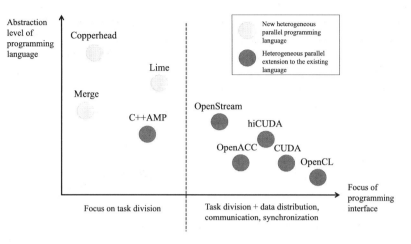

FIGURE 8.11

Comparison of typical heterogeneous parallel programming models.

ation, task description, kernel initialization,[6] and output fetching. Program entry on the device side is performed by the Entry function, which invokes other functions. The device-side program uses the C/C++ language extension in the above heterogeneous programming model and is compiled by a device-specific compiler to generate binary files.

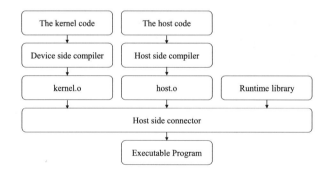

FIGURE 8.12

The compilation and linking process of a heterogeneous programming model.

Fig. 8.12 describes the compilation and linking process of heterogeneous programs. The program adopts a separate programming paradigm, that is, the host-side program and the device-side program are placed in different files (i.e., in the host files

---

[6] The kernel function is the program that runs on the device. Taking the GPU as an example, the kernel is the program run by each thread on the GPU.

and kernel files). The host-side programs and device-side programs of heterogeneous parallel programs need to be compiled with their own compilers. Specifically, the programs on the host side can be ordinary C/C++ programs that users can compile using any C/C++ compiler, such as GCC/CLANG. The device-side program can also be a program based on the C/C++ language extension, where its corresponding compiler is a device-specific compiler. After the host-side and device-side object files are obtained, the host-side linker will be used to combine these object files and runtime library files into an executable program.

8.3.1.3 Compiler support

The compiler is the core tool of the heterogeneous parallel programming model and compiles the heterogeneous code written by the programmer into executable files. The compiler can provide programmers with reasonable abstractions of heterogeneous architecture, so that programmers can make reasonable use of heterogeneous computing resources and ensure a simple programming interface at the same time. Thus, programmers can avoid being trapped in complex hardware details. Therefore, the compiler of heterogeneous parallel programming languages needs to provide low-level support for task partition, data distribution, communication, and synchronization so that programmers can focus more on the processing logic of the applications.

- Task partition

  The programming model needs to provide programmers with parallel programming interfaces to define and partition tasks. The compiler is responsible for the low-level task partition so that the program can be executed efficiently in a parallel manner.

  The device side generally has multiple parallel processing units. Taking CUDA as an example, a thread is the lowest level of abstraction for computation, which is correspondingly executed on a streaming processor. A thread block consists of multiple threads, which are executed on the same multiprocessor (SM), and the threads within a thread block are indexed by 3D coordinates (dim3), which can be reduced to 1D. Threads within a block can communicate with shared memory and synchronize with threads via __syncthreads. There is no thread synchronization between blocks. In addition, the GPU does not guarantee the sequence of execution between blocks. A thread grid is a collection of threads and can be divided into multiple thread blocks. The blocks within a grid are indexed by dim3. All threads in a grid are scheduled to execute on the same GPU. In short, CUDA is a fine-grained parallel programming model which takes fine-grained threads as the basic processing unit and supports massive thread parallelism. For example, in order to complete the addition of 16,384 long vectors, CUDA starts 16,384 threads during runtime, and each thread completes one scalar addition. The program is shown in Fig. 8.13.

  The above process requires a compiler and runtime system to map and schedule instructions on threads, blocks, etc.

```
1   #define N 16384
2   __global__ void add(float* x, float* y, float* z)
3   {
4       int index = threadIdx.x + blockIdx.x * blockDim.x;
5       z[index] = x[index] + y[index];
6   }
```

FIGURE 8.13

A sample example of CUDA's vector addition.

- Data distribution
  In convolutional neural networks, feature maps are usually saved by a 4D array, namely batch size (N), height (H), width (W), and channel (C). Since data can only be stored linearly, each dimension has a corresponding order. Different languages and frameworks store feature maps in different orders. The programming framework Caffe uses NCHW by default, while the default order in TensorFlow is NHWC. NCHW is more suitable for operations that require separate operations for each channel, such as the pooling layer in a neural network. NHWC is more suitable for operations that require some kind of operation on the same pixel of each channel. For the compiler and the underlying runtime system, it is necessary to select the most appropriate data distribution, according to the characteristics of the algorithm and hardware architecture, to guide the subsequent compilation and runtime optimization.

- Data communication
  Since there are often multiple levels of memory on the device side, the compiler needs to support various address space declarations to make it easier for programmers to explicitly control the address space for data storage. On the host side, multiple memory hierarchies such as Cache are usually transparent to the compiler and the programmer, while on the device side, many memory hierarchies are visible to the compiler and the programmer in order to perform computing tasks efficiently. Regarding data communication, it is necessary to support data sharing and add an explicit data migration mechanism to facilitate performance optimization. The compiler also needs to support device-side data migration, such as implicit data migration. The data communication between the device and the host is performed explicitly by calling the related runtime APIs.

- Parallel synchronization
  The device-side programming model is generally aware of the parallel processing of multiple cores, and thus it is required to provide support for a synchronization mechanism. The synchronization interface provided by the programming model can control the synchronization of parallel processor cores on the device side. Only when all cores reach a certain synchronization point can the execution continue. Taking the CUDA programming model as an example, threads within the same thread block on the GPU can be synchronized, but threads in different thread blocks cannot be synchronized. The synchronization primitive for CUDA is __syncthreads ().

8.3.1.4 Runtime support

The main task of heterogeneous runtime is to support task mapping and scheduling, that is, which device or computing unit will the tasks be executed on and in what order. Heterogeneous runtime mechanisms are also divided into host side and device side. Among them, the control part and serial tasks are mostly executed at the host side, while the computation part and parallel tasks are mostly executed at the device side. The runtime provides the host-side API in the above heterogeneous execution process to activate the device. The tasks to be executed are managed by the host-side runtime via the stream. Tasks are continuously put into the stream at runtime and pulled from the stream for execution when hardware resources are available.

Device-side runtime scheduling can be implemented by software or hardware to ensure that hardware resources are fully utilized on processors of different architectures.

8.3.2 General AI programming model

Compared with the typical heterogeneous programming model introduced above, this section focuses on the programming model of general AI computing systems provided by the aforementioned five-level ("Server–Card–Chip–Cluster–Core") DLP.

8.3.2.1 Kernel function

The general AI programming model is based on the heterogeneous programming model. Kernel will be introduced next, including the definition and usage of the Entry function, the Device function, and the Func function.

- Kernel and the Entry function
  Similar to the typical heterogeneous programming model, Kernel is the program that performs tasks on DLPs. DLPs can execute multiple parallel Kernels at the same time if resources are available. Each Kernel has an Entry function, which is specified by __dlp_entry__ in a typical programming language (corresponding to the Entry function). Fig. 8.14 is a specific example.

```
1  __dlp_entry__ void L2LossKernel(half* input, half* output) {
2    ...
3  }
```

FIGURE 8.14

An example of the Kernel Entry function on DLP.

To start Kernel, you need to call the InvokeKernel function of the runtime API. Fig. 8.15 shows the sample code for starting the above L2LossKernel function on the host side.

- Device function
  The Device function is the default function type of the device-side program and has call overhead (inline optimization can be used through compilation options),

```
1   ret = InvokeKernel((void *)(&L2LossKernel), dim,
2                               params, ft, pQueue);
```

FIGURE 8.15

An example of starting the above L2LossKernel function on the host side.

and it is declared by the keyword __dlp_device__. Fig. 8.16 gives a specific example.

```
1   __dlp_device__ void CreateBox(half* box, half* anchor_,
2                               half* delt_, int A, int W,
3                               int H, half im_w, half im_h)
```

FIGURE 8.16

An example of the Device function.

The Device function can be called by the Entry function, and the C/C++ language and the AI programming language extended by C/C++ can be used in the Entry and Device functions, respectively.

- Func function
  The Func function is a Device function with inline attribute by default. Func functions can be used to improve performance when recursive functions are not required. It is declared by the keyword __dlp_func__. Fig. 8.17 gives a specific example.

```
1   __dlp_func__ void CreateBox(half* box, half* anchor_,
2                               half* delt_, int A, int W,
3                               int H, half im_w, half im_h)
```

FIGURE 8.17

An example of the Func function.

The Func function can be called by the Entry function. The Device function and the Func function can call each other.

8.3.2.2 Compiler support

Regarding the aforementioned five-level ("Server–Card–Chip–Cluster–Core") abstract intelligent computing architecture, the compiler needs to provide support in task division, data communication, synchronization support, and built-in computation.

- Task division
  For Clusters and Cores in a single chip, built-in variables clusterDim, clusterId, coreDim, and coreId represent the dimensions and indices of the Cluster and Core,

respectively. The size of the Kernel is described by a Dim3_t type variable. It generally has three dimensions, x, y, and z, and can be specified according to the needs of the application. The example in Fig. 8.18 shows that the task is split into four parts in the x dimension.

```
1   Dim3_t dim;
2   dim.x = 4;
3   dim.y = 1;
4   dim.z = 1;
```

FIGURE 8.18

The task is split into four parts in the x dimension.

The built-in variables that represent the task are taskDim, taskDimX, taskDimY, taskDimZ, taskId, taskIdX, taskIdY, and taskIdZ. Each task is mapped to a computing core, that is, each task is executed by a Core, which is the basic processing unit of DLP. A Kernel can be composed of multiple tasks, and tasks use the Dim3_t data structure for 3D indexing.

The AI programming language corresponds each computing Core to a BLOCK type task. BLOCK is the basic scheduling unit of the programming model layer, which means that tasks in the Kernel will be scheduled for execution on a single Core. Each Cluster corresponds to a UNION1 type task, two clusters for a UNION2 type task, and so on. We call this division the task type. The task type clarifies the number of hardware cores required for a Kernel launch, that is, how many physical cores need to be occupied during the execution of the Kernel. BLOCK type tasks are single-core tasks, while UNION type tasks are multicore parallel tasks.

Take the 16,384-length vector addition as an example, assuming that the task type of the task is UNION4 and dim.x=16. Through 16 tasks, with each task completing a vector addition of N=1024, finally a vector addition of dim.x × N = 16,384 is realized. The source code of the device side is shown in Fig. 8.19. Here, __nram__ represents the neuron cache on the chip and __vec_add is used to complete vector addition.

• Data communication

The compiler also provides data migration. Implicit data transfer is done automatically by the compiler and does not require programmers to be involved. DLPs generally require all scalar calculations to be performed in the general-purpose register (GPR). When the scalar defined on DRAM/NRAM/WRAM is calculated, the compiler will automatically insert load/store instructions to transfer the data to the GPR. After the calculation is completed, the compiler writes the result on the GPR back to DRAM/NRAM/WRAM. Then, the entire data transfer process is automatically completed by the compiler. In order to improve performance, tensor calculation is generally required to be performed in the on-chip NRAM/WRAM as much as possible. The movement of tensor data can be explicitly managed by

```
1   #define N 1024
2   __dlp_entry__ add(float* x, float* y, float* z) {
3   __nram__ float x_tmp[N];
4   __nram__ float y_tmp[N];
5   /* GDRAM2NRAM represents data movement between the global DDR
6   memory and the neuron memory NRAM, which will be described in
7   detail later */
8
9   __memcpy(x_tmp, x + taskId * N, N * sizeof(float), GDRAM2NRAM);
10  __memcpy(y_tmp, y + taskId * N, N * sizeof(float), GDRAM2NRAM);
11  __vec_add(x_tmp, x_tmp, y_tmp, N);
12  __memcpy( z + taskId * N, x_tmp, N * sizeof(float), NRAM2GDRAM);
13  }
```

FIGURE 8.19

An example of vector addition on a deep learning processor.

the programmer: DLP provides the __memcpy interface for data transfer. Data communication can also be achieved through shared memory space. For example, tasks in the Cluster can communicate through internal SRAM.

- Synchronization support

Considering that there is a Cluster level in the abstract hardware architecture, two different types of synchronization operations can be provided:

__sync_all: Use __sync_all to synchronize all cores executed by the task. Only when all cores reach the synchronization point will they continue to execute. The number of cores participating in synchronization is determined by the task type. For example, when the task type is UNION1, only four cores will participate in synchronization (assuming that a cluster contains four cores). When the task type is UNION2, the number of cores participating in synchronization is eight.

__sync_cluster: Use __sync_cluster to synchronize all cores in a Cluster. When all cores in a Cluster reach the synchronization point, the execution can be continued. Compared with CUDA, GPU threads in the same thread block can be synchronized, but threads between thread blocks cannot be synchronized.

- Built-in operations

Taking into account the actual needs of AI applications, the AI programming language provides and implements built-in function interfaces such as __conv and __mlp, which correspond to typical neural network operations such as convolution and fully connected, respectively. These interfaces are extensions to the C/C++ language. These interfaces can be called in the device-side Kernel program translated into the low-level hardware instructions through the compiler. Compared with CUDA, the AI programming model directly realizes the interfaces and instructions of neural network computing, which better supports AI applications.

8.3.2.3 Runtime support

The AI programming model adopts a coarse-grained scheduling strategy. BLOCK or UNIONx is used as the scheduling unit to expand the tasks in the Kernel in time or space dimensions. The scheduling unit needs to be specified by the user during programming. Kernel will be scheduled only when the number of free hardware resources is greater than the number of scheduling units at runtime. Generally speaking, the latency of a single Kernel can be controlled by controlling the number of hardware resources for processing a Kernel, which requires specifying the scheduling unit at runtime. The runtime scheduler allocates resources according to task priority and task size, executes completed tasks, updates task status, and releases resources. During runtime, task mapping and scheduling are performed according to the idle condition of the processor core and the task type.

The general heterogeneous programming model provides the concept of execution flow to manage runtime tasks. In the AI programming model, this concept is generalized and abstracted as an execution queue. Queues manage tasks waiting to be executed. They can work alone or together. The queue operates based on the first-in first-out principle, and the runtime (or hardware) keeps putting tasks into the queue. Once the hardware computing resources are free, a task will be taken out of the queue for execution.

Fig. 8.20 explains the runtime task mapping and scheduling process in detail through three specific examples of Kernel.

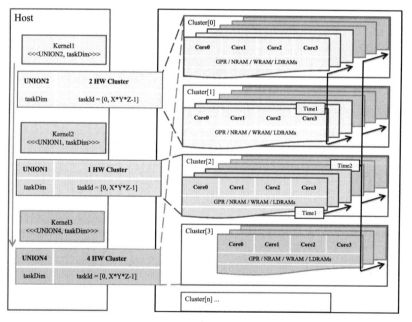

FIGURE 8.20

Examples of DLP task mapping and scheduling.

(1) The host side sends three Kernels to the queue asynchronously. According to the synchronization and communication needs, the user can call the runtime queue synchronization interface SyncQueue anywhere between or after the three transmissions, wait for the tasks in the queue to be completed, and then execute the program behind the host-side SyncQueue.

(2) Kernel 1 enters the queue immediately after Time 1 is sent. When the device finds that all cores are currently idle, Kernel 1 is executed immediately. Because the task type of Kernel 1 is UNION2, it will take up two Clusters to perform calculations starting from Time 1.

(3) Since SyncQueue is not called, the host side will transmit Kernel 2 immediately after Kernel 1. The device-side scheduler finds that the queue has a new Kernel 2 after the execution of Kernel 1. Then it starts to execute Kernel 2 at Time 1. Because the task type of Kernel 2 is UNION1, it will take one Cluster to perform calculations from Time 1.

(4) Assuming that the task size taskDim of Kernel 1 and Kernel 2 exceeds the number of cores indicated by the task type (for example, UNION2 needs to occupy eight cores in Kernel 1), the scheduler will execute the same Kernel program multiple times in time series.

(5) It is assumed that Kernel 1 and Kernel 2 are executed by the scheduler almost simultaneously and both ended at Time 2.

(6) Going back to the execution process on the host side in step 4, when Kernel 2 is launched and no synchronization is performed, Kernel 3 will also be launched immediately. This moment is also Time 1.

(7) If the task type of Kernel 3 is UNION4, four Clusters are required. Since three Clusters out of four are occupied from Time 1 to Time 2 (assuming there are only four Clusters), the device-side scheduler will wait for the four Clusters at Time 2 to be free before actually starting to execute Kernel 3.

The above process illustrates the task mapping and scheduling of a typical DLP. Users can optimize the overall execution performance of the application by controlling the task type, startup timing, and task synchronization.

8.4 **Fundamentals of AI programming language**

Based on the above-mentioned abstract architecture of the AI computing system and the corresponding programming model, taking into account the three design principles of the AI programming language, this section will introduce a specific example of the AI programming language BCL. It further elaborates how to develop AI computing system applications, including serial and parallel applications, based on BCL.

8.4.1 **Syntax overview**

There are different types of mainstream programming languages, such as procedural languages, functional languages, and logical languages. The AI programming language BCL, introduced in this chapter, focuses on procedural languages. There are two main reasons. One is that most of the current languages are procedural, which can reduce the user's learning costs. The other is that the current mainstream AI algorithms can be described as a clear process, suitable for procedural language description.

With reference to the classic procedural language C/C++, the AI programming language we defined also has two basic elements: data and functions. The data is the object to be processed, including numbers, characters, structures, unions, pointers, etc., in traditional programming languages. The syntax description of creating (declaring) data is shown in Fig. 8.21.

```
1    [attribute] dataType dataName [= initialValue]
2         [, dataName2 = initialValue2];
```

FIGURE 8.21

Syntax for creating (declaring) data.

For example, to declare the integer 3, it can be expressed as follows: int a = 3. If no initial value is assigned, the default initial value of the data type or the original value in memory will be used. The declared attribute can add the keyword *const* to mark the data as a constant. The syntax for declared data assignment is shown in Fig. 8.22.

```
1    dataName = value;
```

FIGURE 8.22

Declared data assignment syntax.

The function describes the process of processing data. The declaration of a function consists of the function name, input parameters, return value, etc. The syntax is shown in Fig. 8.23.

```
1    returnDataType functionName([dataType param1, dataType params,
2         ...]);
```

FIGURE 8.23

Function declaration.

For example, the function for declaring an integer addition is as follows:
int add_func(int a, int b);
The definition of a function is the function body, which is used to record the internal behavior of the function. The syntax is to wrap the function declaration with

```
1  int add_func (int a, int b) {
2    int c = a + b;
3    return c;
4  }
```

FIGURE 8.24

Definition of the function body for the add_func function.

curly braces and write the specific processing logic within it. For example, the function body that defines the above add_func function is shown in Fig. 8.24.

The function body can support the basic program control flow such as sequence, loop, branch, etc. For more grammatical details, please refer to the description of C/C++.

8.4.2 Data type

There are two main categories of data types that AI programming languages support: the data type of different precision at the arithmetic level (such as fixed-point and floating-point types), which is more related to hardware details and convenient for users to perform low-level optimization, and a high-level data type with semantic information (such as Tensor, specific type, etc.), which is closer to the expression of high-level applications and allows users to describe and program in an easier manner.

8.4.2.1 Precision type

The data precision supported by the AI programming language includes fixed-point, floating-point, and Boolean.

- *Fixed-point*
  We use a sequence of binary digits to represent decimal numbers in which binary numbers can be represented as unsigned or signed. Binary numbers with different bit-widths have different ranges of decimal numbers. The range of fixed-point numbers typically used for intelligent computation is shown in Table 8.1.

- *Floating-point*
  As shown in Fig. 8.5, by dividing a binary number into a sign bit, an exponent bit, and a mantissa bit, floating-point numbers with different ranges and precision can be presented. Among them, FP32 and FP16 are floating-point representation methods that comply with the IEEE 754 standard, and BF16 (Brain Float) is a special data type proposed for the needs of AI algorithms.

- *Boolean*
  A Boolean can only have values true (1) and false (0). Booleans are mainly used for conditional judgment in traditional programming languages. In AI algorithms, a 1-bit weight for certain application scenarios can still guarantee the accuracy

Table 8.1 Different bit-width fixed-point number types and the corresponding decimal number range.

Fixed-point number type	Minimum representable decimal	Maximum representable decimal
uint4 (unsigned int4)	0	15
int4	−8	7
uint8 (unsigned char)	0	255
int8 (char)	−128	127
uint16 (unsigned short)	0	65,535
int16 (short)	−32,768	32,767
uint32 (unsigned int)	0	4,294,967,295
int32 (int)	−2,147,483,648	2,147,483,647

of computation in a statistical sense, so it can also be used for neural network computation.

Based on the above mentioned basic precision types, more complex composite data types can be defined, e.g., array types.

8.4.2.2 Semantic type

According to the characteristics of AI applications, data types with certain high-level semantics can be defined. Since machine learning is mainly for computation of a large number of tensors, the tensor type can be defined. At the same time, in view of the characteristics of neural network computing, it is possible to further define data types with high-level semantics, such as neuron type and filter type.

- *Tensor*

  The multidimensional tensor can be regarded as the basic type of machine learning, which can meet the requirements of expressing different types of computation. For example, in a high-level deep learning framework such as TensorFlow, tensor is the basic data type. In addition, in deep neural networks, the most computationally intensive operations are convolution and fully connected operations, which involve two kinds of data types: synapses (weights) and neurons. A batch of neurons are used only once, while the weights will be used multiple times and computed with multiple batches of neurons. Therefore, in BCL, these two types of data have different data reuse characteristics, and the on-chip cache can be divided into two categories, neuron cache and weight cache, which facilitates the adoption of different reuse policies. At the same time, to fully exploit the computing capacity of the hardware, it is also necessary to optimize the data layout according to the characteristics of hardware architecture. For example, NCHW and NHWC have different computing efficiencies for GPUs. Therefore, the tensor type in AI algorithms can be further divided into the neuron and filter types.

Table 8.2 Examples of built-in variables.

Built-in variable name	Concrete meaning
coreId	The logical number of the core
clusterId	The logical number of the cluster
taskId	The logical number of the assigned task at runtime

- *Neuron and filter*
  Neuron and filter have three basic attributes: data precision, dimension order, and dimension value for each dimension. (1) Data precision describes the number of digits of the data, such as FP16, INT8, etc. (2) The dimension order specifies the number of dimensions and the storage order of each dimension. For example, RGB images have three dimensions: height (H), width (W), and channel (C). In addition to H, W, and C, other dimensions are also commonly used. N represents the number of batches; D represents multiple consecutive pictures in a time series, often used in 3D convolution; and T represents the time dimension, often used in RNN. (3) Each dimension value corresponds to the size of each dimension of the array.

8.4.3 Macros, constants, and built-in variables

These concepts are all constants; the first two are defined by the user, and the latter is predefined by the language.

- *Macros and constants*
  The macros not only define constant data but also a piece of code and copy the content of the macro definition to the place where the macro is called in the precompilation stage. In DLPs, to meet compatibility requirements, macros are usually defined that are closely related to the architecture. The constants are unmodifiable data and can only be assigned during initialization. Usually, the constant will be prefixed with the *const* keyword before the data precision type when it is defined by programmers, indicating that the data is a constant.
- *Built-in variables*
  Built-in variables are constants and variables provided by the programming language itself. They do not need to be defined by users and can be used directly. To make full use of hardware resources and improve performance of DLPs, we introduce the built-in variables in the programming model based on the hardware architecture of DLPs. According to the content described in Section 8.3.2, Table 8.2 provides examples of some built-in variables.

8.4.4 I/O operation

As introduced in Section 8.2, intelligent processing nodes at different levels have their own local memory, which brings a multilevel memory hierarchy. To facilitate programming and improve processing efficiency, AI programming languages also need to provide data transfer between different levels of memory hierarchy.

Taking the four-level ("Card–Chip–Cluster–Core") memory hierarchy of the DLP as an example, we will detail the programming language, compiler, and I/O operations provided by the runtime system at different levels (Fig. 8.25). In this abstract architecture, the card layer (layer 0) has two physical memories, DDR0 and DDR1. There are two memory controllers on the chip to independently control the above-mentioned memory. This structure is a typical nonuniform memory access (NUMA) architecture, where different processing cores have different latency for accessing different locations of the memory. For core 0, the speed of accessing device memory DDR0 is faster than that of DDR1. DDR0 is local memory (LDRAM) for core 0, while DDR1 is the remote memory, which is part of the entire global memory (global DRAM [GDRAM]). For on-chip memory, in addition to the neuron memory (NRAM) and weight memory (WRAM) in the single core mentioned earlier, there is also a type of shared memory (SRAM), which can be used for multicore sharing within a cluster. Therefore, in the above-mentioned typical architecture, three types of on-chip memory and two types of device memory can have many different types of data transfer operations. The details are shown in Table 8.3.

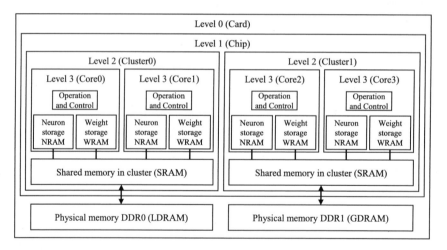

FIGURE 8.25

The abstract four-level DLP architecture.

For the above types of transfer operations, the corresponding built-in function __memcpy can be defined in the AI programming language to facilitate users to move different types of data, as shown in Fig. 8.26.

8.4.5 Scalar computation

Scalar is the computation of a single piece of data. The scalar computation is the basic function of a programming language. The scalar computation statement of the

Table 8.3 Common types of
data movement operations.

NRAM	NRAM <-> GDRAM
	NRAM <-> LDRAM
	NRAM <-> SRAM
WRAM	WRAM <-> GDRAM
	WRAM <-> LDRAM
	WRAM <-> SRAM
SRAM	SRAM <-> GDRAM
	SRAM <-> LDRAM
	SRAM <-> SRAM
NRAM	NRAM <-> NRAM

```
1   void __memcpy(void* dst, void* src, uint32 bytes,
2       Direction_t dir);
```

FIGURE 8.26

Memcpy function.

AI programming language has two forms: arithmetic symbols (such as $+$, $-$, $\times$, etc.) and built-in functions (such as __abs, __max, __min, etc.). The scalar computation statement of the AI programming language will be mapped by the compiler to the scalar computation unit of the processor. Although the throughput is not comparable to tensor computation, it has good versatility and flexibility.

8.4.6 Tensor computation

The tensor computation is the main feature of the AI programming language, which can be directly mapped to the tensor computation unit through a built-in function. Tensor computation can directly operate on data of either precision type or semantic type. The basic syntax format is shown in Fig. 8.27. It includes pointers for input and output data, as well as necessary parameters that define the computation operation, such as the size of the convolution kernel and the sliding step length of the convolution operation. Table 8.4 gives examples of common tensor computation statements.

```
1   returnValue __funcName(DataType1* tensor1, DataType2* tensor2,
2       ..., paraType1 param1, paraType2 param2);
```

FIGURE 8.27

Basic syntax format of tensor computation.

Table 8.4 Examples of common tensor computation statements.

Tensor computation statement	Concrete function
__vec_add(float* out, float* in1, float* in2, int size)	Vector addition
__vec_sub(float* out, float* in1, float* in2, int size)	Vector subtraction
__vec_mul(float* out, float* in1, float* in2, int size)	Vector multiplication
__conv(half* out, int8* in, int8* weight, half* bias, int ci, int hi, int wi, int co, int kh, int kw, int sh, int sw)	Convolution operation
__mlp(half* out, int8* in, int8* weight, half* bias, int ci, int co)	Fully connected operation
__maxpool(half* out, half* in, int ci, int hi, int wi, int kh, int kw, int sh, int sw)	Max pooling operation

8.4.7 Control flow

Like general programming languages, AI programming languages also provide control flow statements such as branches and loops.

8.4.7.1 Branch

The branch statement of the AI programming language is used to process the selection logic of the program, which is composed of judgment conditions and branch code segments, similar to traditional programming languages.

8.4.7.2 Loop

The loop statement in the AI programming language is used to process the program loop logic, which is composed of loop execution conditions and loop code segments, similar to traditional programming languages.

8.4.7.3 Synchronization

Synchronization statements are mainly used in multiple cores to solve the problem of parallel data dependence between different cores, which is a necessary method to ensure that the final computation results are correct. Synchronization statements are mainly divided into two categories: intracluster synchronization and global synchronization (Table 8.5). Among them, intracluster synchronization only ensures that all cores in a cluster are synchronized, while global synchronization guarantees that all cores of all clusters in the chip are synchronized.

8.4.8 Serial program example

According to the stated grammar, data types, design principles, built-in functions, and variables introduced above, Fig. 8.28 illustrates a concrete example of a single-

Table 8.5 Synchronization.

Synchronization type	Programming APIs
Synchronization within the cluster	__sync_cluster
Synchronization within the chip	__sync_all

core program written in the AI programming language. In this example, we square all numbers in a vector. The computation is performed by the vector multiplication operation for 64 numbers each cycle. The two pointers in the function parameter list are referred to the numbers on GDRAM, so you need to move them to NRAM first, then conduct multiplication in place, and then move them back to GDRAM. Taking into account the size of the on-chip memory NRAM, we choose 64 numbers as the basic unit for each data movement and computation. The former for loop is used to process the integer section, and the latter if statement is used to process the remainder section. The application for temporary space on NRAM needs to be prefixed with "__nram__."

```
1    #define BASE_NUM 64
2    void __dlp_entry__ mySquare(float* in, float* out, int size) {
3      int quotient = size / BASE_NUM;
4      int remainder = size % BASE_NUM;
5      __nram__ float tmp[BASE_NUM];
6
7      for (int i = 0; i < quotient; i++) {
8        __memcpy(tmp, (in + i * BASE_NUM),
9          (BASE_NUM * sizeof(float)), GDRAM2NRAM);
10       __vec_mul(tmp, tmp, tmp, BASE_NUM);
11       __memcpy((out + i * BASE_NUM), tmp,
12         (BASE_NUM * sizeof(float)), NRAM2GDRAM);
13     }
14
15     if (remainder != 0) {
16       __memcpy(tmp, (in + quotient * BASE_NUM),
17         (remainder * sizeof(float)), GDRAM2NRAM);
18       __vec_mul(tmp, tmp, tmp, remainder);
19       __memcpy((out + quotient * BASE_NUM), tmp,
20         (remainder * sizeof(float)), NRAM2GDRAM);
21     }
22   }
```

FIGURE 8.28

An example of a single-core program squaring all numbers in a vector.

8.4.9 Parallel program example

By using multicore computing resources on DLP, processing efficiency can be further improved. Here we consider an example of matrix multiplication, which is split into four cores for parallel computation. Fig. 8.29 shows the program executed on each core.

In this program, since the code on each core is identical, we need to partition the task when the host is running. The program at the host side is shown in Fig. 8.30 (detailed runtime APIs will be introduced in subsequent sections). Among them, dim.x is used to specify the scale of the task, that is, how many tasks of matrix multiplication (i.e., the mm function) are generated. Each task corresponds to a taskId. We fill in the parameter UNION1 in InvokeKernel, which means that these tasks will be executed by one Cluster (assuming that it contains four Cores), and each core will be assigned a task to jointly complete the matrix multiplication operation.

```
1   void __dlp_entry__ mm(int* left, int* right, int* out) {
2     if (taskID == 0) {
3       __nram__ int tmp[4][32];
4       __write_zero(tmp, 4*32*sizeof(int));
5       __memcpy(out, tmp, 4*32*sizeof(int), NRAM2GDRAM);
6     }
7
8     __sync_all();
9     for (int j = 0; j < 32; j++) {
10      for (int k = 0; k < 32; k++) {
11        out[taskIdX * 32 + j] +=
12            left[taskIdX * 32 + k] * right[k * 32 + j];
13      }
14    }
15  }
```

FIGURE 8.29

An example of the multicore matrix multiplication.

```
1   Dim_t dim; dim.x = 4; dim.y = 1; dim.z = 1;
2   int left[4][32]; int right[32][32]; int out[4][32];
3
4   // Initialize the calculation matrix
5   void* left_dev, right_dev, out_dev;
6   devMalloc(&left_dev, 4*32*sizeof(int));
7   devMalloc(&right_dev, 32*32*sizeof(int));
8   devMalloc(&out_dev, 4*32*sizeof(int));
9
10  Memcpy(left, left_dev, 4*32*sizeof(int), HOST2DEV);
11  Memcpy(right, right_dev, 32*32*sizeof(int), HOST2DEV);
12
13  KernelParamsBuffer_t params;
14  GetKernelParamsBuffer(&params);
15  KernelParamsBufferAddParam(params, &left_dev, sizeof(void*));
16  KernelParamsBufferAddParam(params, &right_dev, sizeof(void*));
17  KernelParamsBufferAddParam(params, &out_dev, sizeof(void*));
18
19  Queue_t queue;
20  CreateQueue(&queue);
21
22  // Start 4 cores to perform matrix multiplication in parallel
23  InvokeKernel((void*)(&mm), dim, params, UNION1, queue);
24  SyncQueue(queue);
25
26  Memcpy(out_dev, out, 4*32*sizeof(int), DEV2HOST);
27  ... ...
```

FIGURE 8.30

The key code of the host-side runtime program.

8.5 Programming interface of AI applications

Machine learning applications can be developed directly using various programming frameworks (such as TensorFlow and PyTorch), or they can also be developed directly using AI programming languages while operating the intelligent computing hardware through the programming interface of AI applications. The AI application programming interface provides a set of high-level interfaces for intelligent computing devices, which can be divided into two major categories, a Kernel function interface and a runtime interface. The kernel function interface focuses on task partitioning and hardware mapping (i.e., how to divide complex tasks into multiple tasks that are executed concurrently and map them to the underlying hardware architecture). The runtime interface focuses on device management, task queue management, and memory management. Device management provides related interfaces for managing devices, such as device initialization, device settings, and device destruction. Task queue management provides interfaces for queue creation, synchronization, and destruction. Memory management mainly provides interfaces for memory allocation and release.

8.5.1 Kernel function interface

The programmer uses an AI programming language to implement user-defined functions inside the Kernel function. Based on the heterogeneous programming model, in order to effectively utilize resources, programmers need to effectively partition tasks within the Kernel function and then configure and call the corresponding Kernel function interface on the host to start task execution.

8.5.1.1 Overview

This section still takes the typical AI computing system corresponding to the "Server–Card–Chip–Cluster–Core" abstract hardware architecture as an example. First, we will introduce the concepts, built-in variables, and the corresponding API, related to the internal task partition inside the kernel function.

- *Queue*
  User-developed multicore Kernel functions can be bound to the same queue and handed over to the task scheduler for scheduling and execution. Kernel functions inside the queue are executed in the order in which they are bound. Kernel functions that are not in the same queue are launched and executed asynchronously based on the scheduling rules of the runtime system.
- *coreDim*
  This is a built-in variable of the AI programming language. It equals the number of computing cores within a single cluster.
- *coreId*
  This is a built-in variable of the AI programming language. It corresponds to the logical ID of each hardware computing core in the cluster. The value range is [0, coreId-1].
- *clusterDim*
  This is a built-in variable of the AI programming language. It is the number of Clusters called by the UNION type task specified when the Kernel is launched.

- *clusterId*

  This is a built-in variable of the AI programming language. It corresponds to the logical ID of the cluster where the program is running. The value range is [0, clusterId-1].

- *taskDim*

  This is a built-in variable of the AI programming language. It equals the total scale of the task specified by the user, taskDim = taskDimX × taskDimY × taskDimZ.

- *taskDimX*

  This is a built-in variable of the AI programming language. There are three dimensions (X, Y, Z), where the value of taskDimX is equal to the scale in the X direction.

- *taskDimY*

  This is a built-in variable of the AI programming language. There are three dimensions (X, Y, Z), where the value of taskDimY is equal to the scale in the Y direction.

- *taskDimZ*

  This is a built-in variable of the AI programming language. There are three dimensions (X, Y, Z), where the value of taskDimZ is equal to the scale in the Z direction.

- *taskIdX*

  This is a built-in variable of the AI programming language. It corresponds to the logic task ID in the X dimension of the task. The value range is [0, taskDimX-1].

- *taskIdY*

  This is a built-in variable of the AI programming language. It corresponds to the logic task ID in the Y dimension of the task. The value range is [0, taskDimY-1].

- *taskIdZ*

  This is a built-in variable of the AI programming language. It corresponds to the logic task ID in the Z dimension of the task. The value range is [0, taskDimZ-1].

- *taskId*

  This is a built-in variable of the AI programming language. It corresponds to the logic task ID of the task. The value range is [0, taskDim-1]. The value of taskId is equal to the task ID by flattening the logical dimensions. As a result, taskId = taskIdZ × taskDimY × taskDimX + taskIdY × taskDimX + taskIdX.

8.5.1.2 API introduction

The AI application programming interface can load the program written in the AI programming language to the DLPs for execution. The programming interface related to the kernel function mainly focuses on Kernel parameter setting and Kernel invocation.

- *GetKernelParamBuffer(KernelParamsBuffer_t *params);*
  Get the param in the Kernel. Return RET_SUCCESS if successful, otherwise return the corresponding error code.
- *CopyKernelParamsBuffer(KernelParamsBuffer_t dstbuf, KernelParamsBuffer_t srcbuf);*
  Copy parameters from srcbuf to dstbuf. Return RET_SUCCESS if successful, otherwise return the corresponding error code.
- *KernelParamsBufferAddParam(KernelParamsBuffer_t params, void* data, size_t bytes);*
  Add constant parameters to KernelParamsBuffer_t. Return RET_SUCCESS if successful, otherwise return the corresponding error code.
- *DestroyKernelParamsBuffer(KernelParamsBuffer_t params);*
  Destroy the KernelParamsBuffer_t variable. Return RET_SUCCESS if successful, otherwise return the corresponding error code.
- *InvokeKernel(const void * function, Dim3_t dim, KernelParamsBuffer_t params, FunctionType_t funcType, Queue_t queue);*
  Call Kernel through the given function parameters on the device. Return RET_SUCCESS if successful, otherwise return the corresponding error code. As introduced in Section 8.3.2.2, FunctionType_t includes BLOCK and UNIONx (such as UNION1 and UNION2, depending on the scale of the system), representing single-core tasks and multicore parallel tasks, respectively.

There exists a copying process of function parameters from the host to the device when InvokeKernel is called. Therefore, the number of InvokeKernel should be reduced as much as possible to achieve high performance.

8.5.2 Runtime interface

The runtime interface generally includes device management, queue management, and memory management. This section mainly lists commonly used runtime interfaces and function descriptions for host-side programs.

8.5.2.1 Device management

Device operation mainly involves a series of operations such as initialization, device setting, and device destruction.

- *Init(unsigned int flags);*
  This function is used to initialize the runtime environment of the specified device in the current system. The flag indicates different types of devices. For example, when the flag is set to 1, the real device is initialized. When the flag is 0, the fake device can be initialized, which can be used for device simulation.
  This function can be called once at the beginning or in each thread. But the number of calls should match the number of Destroy calls, where this method should be called before using device resources. Specifically, the entire process calls Init once

at the beginning and Destroy once at the end; if calling Init once in each thread, it is required to call Destroy once at the end of each thread. Note that it is required to call this function to initialize the environment before calling any other runtime functions to ensure thread safety.

- *GetDeviceCount(unsigned int* dev_num);*
  This function is used to get the number of devices in the system, where dev_num is the output parameter and its value is the number of devices.
- *GetDeviceHandle(Dev_t* pdev, int ordinal);*
  This function is used to obtain the device handler by the specified device number. Note that the device must be initialized before calling this function and the device number must be in the range of [0, GetDeviceCount()-1].
- *SetCurrentDevice(Dev_t dev);*
  This function is used to set the device used by the current thread context. After being called, all subsequent interfaces of the thread that interact with the device will be executed on the specified device. It is required to call this function before calling other device functions.
- *GetCurrentDevice(Dev_t* pdev);*
  This function is used to get the device handler of the current thread. Before being called, it is necessary to call GetCurrentDevice to obtain the device used by the current thread.
- *Destroy(void);*
  This function is used to release the device memory and shut down the device. Before being called, it is required to call Init to initialize the device. This function can be called once when the process exits or within each thread, but the number of calls must match that of the Init calls. Note that calling this function at the end destroys all resources on the device, including shutting it down.

8.5.2.2 Queue management

A queue is an environment used to perform tasks. Computing tasks can be sent to the queue for execution. The same queue can hold multiple tasks. Specifically, the queue has the following attributes.

(1) Sequential: Tasks sent to the same queue are executed sequentially in the order in which they were issued.
(2) Asynchronous: Tasks are issued to the queue asynchronously. In other words, the program will return immediately when the task is issued and the host program will continue to execute. The runtime environment provides a queue synchronization interface for waiting for the completion of all tasks in the entire queue. Task synchronization needs to be initiated by actively calling the synchronization interface.
(3) Parallel: Tasks in different queues are executed in parallel.

For tasks to be executed in parallel, users can create multiple queues and assign tasks to different queues. Typical queue-related APIs include the following categories.

- CreateQueue(Queue_t *queue);
  CreateQueue is used to create a queue. This method can be called multiple times to create multiple queues and deliver tasks to different queues for parallel execution. This requires the same number of times to create a queue and start the kernel. If the Kernel startup function is called multiple times but passed in the same queue, the execution efficiency cannot be improved because the tasks in the queue are executed serially.
- SyncQueue(Queue_t queue);
  This method synchronizes all tasks in the queue and waits for the tasks to be completed. This method should be called after InvokeKernel. Because InvokeKernel is asynchronous, a synchronous mechanism is needed to wait for the completion of all tasks in the queue.
- DestroyQueue(Queue_t queue);
  This method destroys the created queue and generally executes this method when the process or thread exits. Before calling this method, it is necessary to create a queue and pair it with CreateQueue.

8.5.2.3 Memory management

Memory management is mainly divided into three types: host-side memory management, device-side memory management, and the memory copy between host and device. The typical memory management interface and its functions are shown below.

- hostMalloc(void **ptr, size_t bytes, ...);
  Allocate a given size of host memory. Return RET_SUCCESS if the allocation is successful, otherwise return the corresponding error code.
- hostFree(void *ptr);
  Release host memory. Return RET_SUCCESS if the release is successful, otherwise return the corresponding error code.
- devMalloc(void **ptr, size_t bytes);
  Allocate a given size of device memory. Return RET_SUCCESS if the allocation is successful, otherwise return the corresponding error code.
- devFree(void *ptr);
  Release the device memory space pointed to by ptr. Return RET_SUCCESS, otherwise return the corresponding error code.
- Memcpy(void *dst, void *src, size_t bytes, MemTransDir_t dir);
  Copy the given bytes of data from address src to address dst, where dir specifies the direction of data copy (such as copy from the host side to the device side, copy from the device side to the host side, etc.).

8.5.3 Usage example

The application program of the AI computing system includes two parts. One is the C/C++ program on the host side, which runs on general-purpose processors such as x86 and ARM. The other is the Kernel program, written in the AI programming language on the device side. We use the single-core summation algorithm as an example to illustrate the use of the complete AI application programming interface. As mentioned before, a complete AI application includes a host-side program and a device-side program. The development of AI applications is mainly divided into the following steps: Kernel function writing, device initialization, host- and device-side data preparation, device-side memory space allocation, data copy to the device side, invoking the Kernel to start the device, obtaining the result, and resource release, etc.

8.5.3.1 Writing kernel function

The program on the device side is used to realize the core computing functions of AI applications. The device code in this example is shown in Fig. 8.31.

```
1   __dlp_entry__  void  kernel(int  *input,  int  len,  int  *output)  {
2     int  sum = 0;
3     for  (int  i = 0;  i < len;  i++)  {
4       sum += input[i];
5     }
6     *output = sum;
7   }
```

FIGURE 8.31

Single-core accumulation algorithm example.

For each program written in an AI programming language, as described in Section 8.3.2.1, there is only one kernel function marked as __dlp_entry__, which represents the entrance of the entire kernel function. Its return value type must be void.

8.5.3.2 Device initialization

The device needs to be initialized before use. The main tasks include querying available device, selecting a certain device to execute, and setting the task scale. The sample code is shown in Fig. 8.32. In this example, a single-core program is running, so $dim.x$, $dim.y$, and $dim.z$ are all set to 1.

```
1    Init(0);
2    Dev_t dev;
3    GetDeviceHandle(&dev,  0);
4    SetCurrentDevice(dev);
5    Queue_t pQueue;
6    CreateQueue(&pQueue);
7    Dim3_t dim;
8    dim.x = 1;
9    dim.y = 1;
10   dim.z = 1;
```

FIGURE 8.32

Device initialization example.

8.5.3.3 Host/device-side data preparation

Before performing specific calculations, input data needs to be prepared and preprocessed on the host side. Take the FP32 data on the CPU as an example. If the FP32 data type is not supported, the data type needs to be converted on the host side first, such as FP16 or INT8 data type. The above process is generally performed on the host side.

8.5.3.4 Device-side memory space allocation

The input and output space on the device side is allocated on the host side through the runtime interface and then passed to the Kernel function. An example of memory space allocation is shown in Fig. 8.33, where the half type corresponds to the FP16 type.

```
1   half *d_input;
2   half *d_output;
3   half *dlp_result;
4   hostMalloc(dlp_result, data_num * sizeof(half));
5   devMalloc((void **)&d_input, data_num * sizeof(half));
6   devMalloc((void **)&d_output, data_num * sizeof(half));
```

FIGURE 8.33

Device-side memory space allocation.

8.5.3.5 Copy data to the device

Data copy is mainly performed to copy the input data prepared on the host side to the device side. The specific code is shown in Fig. 8.34.

```
1   Memcpy(d_input, h_a_half, sizeof(half)*data_num, HOST2DEV);
```

FIGURE 8.34

Copy data to the device.

HOST2DEV indicates that the data is copied from the host side to the device side.

8.5.3.6 Invoking kernel to start the device

The core data structure of the Kernel function for passing parameters is KernelParamBuffer, where the order of setting parameters must be consistent with the order of declaration of kernel function parameters. Fig. 8.35 provides specific sample codes.

8.5.3.7 Obtaining the result

SyncQueue needs to be called before obtaining the running result to ensure that calculation on the device side has been completed. At this time, the correct calculation

```
1  KernelParamsBuffer_t  params;
2  GetKernelParamsBuffer(&params);
3  KernelParamsBufferAddParam(params, &d_input, sizeof(half *));
4  KernelParamsBufferAddParam(params, &size, sizeof(uint32_t));
5  KernelParamsBufferAddParam(params, &d_output, sizeof(half *));
6  /* After setting the kernel function parameters, you can call
7  the InvokeKernel interface to start the calculation task*/
8  InvokeKernel((void *)&kernel, dim, params, func_type, pQueue);
9  SyncQueue(pQueue);
```

FIGURE 8.35

Invoke Kernel to start the Device.

result will be stored on the device DDR. The calculation result can be copied from the device side to the host side by calling the Memcpy interface. The specific code is shown in Fig. 8.36.

```
1  Memcpy(dlp_result, d_output, data_num * sizeof(half), DEV2HOST);
```

FIGURE 8.36

Obtain the result.

DEV2HOST indicates that the data is copied from the device side to the host side.

8.5.3.8 Resource release

After the program is executed, various resources on the host side and the device side need to be released. The specific code is shown in Fig. 8.37.

```
1  devFree(d_input);
2  devFree(d_output);
3  hostFree(dlp_result);
4  DestroyQueue(pQueue);
5  DestroyKernelParamsBuffer(params);
```

FIGURE 8.37

Resource release.

8.6 Debugging AI applications

From the perspective of debugging AI application functions, this chapter first introduces the basic methods of functional debugging and then introduces the functional debugging interfaces and tools. Considering the important role of precision in AI applications, the precision debugging method is introduced afterward. Finally, the debugging practice based on BCL is introduced.

8.6.1 Functional debugging method

8.6.1.1 Overview

The mainstream AI application programming method has two levels, the low-level programming language layer and the high-level programming framework layer. Therefore, the debugging objects of AI applications are mainly *machine code* generated by the compiler, based on the AI programming language, and a *computation graph* framework-level compiler, based on the programming framework. The corresponding debugging methods are also divided into *programming language-level debugging methods* and *programming framework-level debugging methods*.

Programming languages generally have corresponding compiling and debugging toolchains and runtime environments to assist in observing runtime status information. At the same time, there are debugging-related printing interfaces in the language specification. In addition, we can locate the problem with the assistance of mechanisms of the operating system such as exception handling and core dumping.

The programming framework is an important bridge connecting the application and the underlying software, involving different language levels: (1) The user API layer mainly uses high-level languages such as Python or JavaScript to facilitate the writing of specific applications. (2) The core layer of the framework mainly uses the C++ language to implement the internal architecture. (3) The bottom layer of the framework calls the target architecture programming language or high-performance library to fully tap the performance of the underlying hardware. The debugging methods of each level will be introduced in detail according to different debugging object levels in the following sections.

8.6.1.2 Programming language debugging

In addition to directly calling the print interface in the application code, debugging through a source-level debugger is a more intuitive and reasonable way. Through the source-level debugger, you can execute the program source code, set breakpoints, print variable values, etc., in a single-step manner. To realize the function of the debugger, it is necessary to add debugging information in the compilation phase to coordinate the functions of the compiler and the debugger.

• Source code compilation generates debugging information

To support efficient debugging, it is necessary to save the mapping relationship between the program source code and the generated machine instructions during the compilation phase and establish a corresponding symbol mapping mechanism for the debugger to analyze and use. The mapping relationship collected in the compilation stage needs to solve two key problems. One is how to associate the binary instructions deeply optimized by the compiler with the original program source code. Using common peephole optimization (Peephole) as an example, the instruction sequence may be adjusted, making it difficult to associate it with the original code. The second problem is describing the relationship between the binary program and the source code in detail with lower time and storage overhead. To solve this problem, a reasonable debugging information format needs to be defined. We will use DWARF, the most widely used debugging format, as an example to introduce the debugging format information.

- Debug information format: DWARF [167]

The acronym DWARF stands for Debugging With Attributed Record Formats. It is a debugging method that uses attributed record format. The debugging information format is developed together with the ELF object file format. DWARF is organized into a tree structure as a whole, where each node can have children or siblings. These nodes can represent types, variables, or functions.

Specifically, the basic description debugging information entry (DIE) in DWARF is organized into a tree structure. Each DIE has its parent DIE (except for the topmost layer) and may have a brother DIE or a child DIE. Each DIE has a clearly defined specific description object and the corresponding attribute list. The attributes may contain various values, such as constants (function names), variables (function start addresses), references to other DIEs (such as function return value types), etc. Fig. 8.38 simplifies the description of the DIE items of Compilation Unit, Subprogram, and Base Type. For the classic Hello World program, the top DIE represents the compilation unit. It has two children, which are the subroutine DIE describing the main function and the basic type DIE referenced by it, corresponding to the int type return value of the main function. The following is a detailed introduction to the DIE content of the compilation unit, subroutines, and basic types.

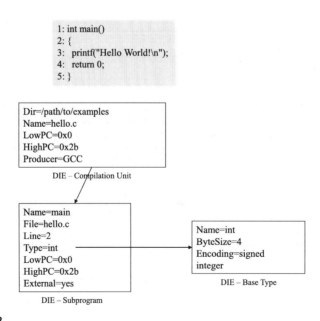

FIGURE 8.38

An example of DWARF DIE.

Compilation unit. A program usually contains multiple source files, where each source file is compiled separately. In DWARF, each separately compiled source file is called a compilation unit. The general information of the compilation unit is placed in the corresponding DIE, including the directory, the source file name (such as hello.c), the programming language, the string identifying the source of the DWARF data (such as GCC), and the offset value of the DWARF data section, used for positioning line numbers, macro information, etc.

Subroutine. DWARF uses subprogram DIE to process function for both the function with return values and without return values. The DIE consists of the name (DW_AT_name) and the source location ternary (DW_AT_decl_file, DW_AT_decl_line, DW_AT_prototyped), and indicates whether the subroutine is an external attribute (DW_AT_external) and other information. In addition, there are expressions such as DW_AT_ frame_base to calculate the stack frame address of this function, as shown in Fig. 8.39.

```
1   <1><2a>: Abbreviation number:2 (DW_TAG_subprogram)
2       <2b> DW_AT_low_pc : 0x0
3       <33> DW_AT_high_pc : 0x3f
4       <37> DW_AT_frame_base : 1 byte block: 56 (DW_OP_reg6 (rbp))
5       <39> DW_AT_name : (indirect string, offset: 0x5a): main
6       <3d> DW_AT_decl_file : 1
7       <3e> DW_AT_decl_line : 5
8       <3f> DW_AT_prototyped : 1
9       <3f> DW_AT_type : <0x6e>
10      <43> DW_AT_external : 1
11      ...
```

FIGURE 8.39

An example of subroutine DIE.

Basic type. Programming languages usually define basic scalar data types. These data types will eventually be mapped to the registers and arithmetic units of the target machine. Therefore, the debugging information must provide the lowest mapping relationship for the basic types, which is DW_TAG in DWARF _base_type. For AI applications, as mentioned above, due to the customized arithmetic unit and data type (such as FP16, etc.), it is also necessary to add special debugging information mapping.

In addition to the above DIE items, there are corresponding DIE descriptions for arrays, structures, variables, and macros. For more detailed information, refer to DWARF's design manual [168].

DWARF information usually needs to be used together with the ELF format, where different types of DWARF are stored in the corresponding segment of the ELF. The names of all these DWARF sections start with ".debug_," as shown in Table 8.6.

8.6.1.3 *Programming framework debugging*

The programming framework focuses on deep learning or machine learning models, in which the computing nodes are defined as operators. The operators are differ-

Table 8.6 The name and meaning of the debugging information segment in ELF.

Debug section name	Specific meaning
.debug_abbrev	Used for abbreviations in the .debug_info section
.debug_arranges	Mapping between memory address and compilation unit
.debug_frame	Call stack information
.debug_info	DWARF data containing DIE
.debug_line	Line number program
.debug_loc	Positioning description
.debug_macinfo	Macro description
.debug_pubnames	Global object and function lookup table
.debug_pubtypes	Lookup table of global type
.debug_ranges	The range of address referenced by DIE
.debug_str	The string table used by .debug_info
.debug_types	Type description

ent in the functionality, amount of calculation, and complexity, but if the operators are abstracted, the programming of the entire network model can also be abstracted as programming in a high-level language. Framework-level programming languages usually have control flow and data flow. The objects operated by operators can also be analogized to data structures in programming languages. Therefore, the debugging method of the programming framework is similar to the programming language introduced above. It is necessary to use the framework-level debugging interface or debugger to help quickly view the core data structure and other content in the model network development. In addition, some data analysis and transformation methods are needed to assist network-level programming from other dimensions.

As a systematic software stack, a programming framework involves many levels and modules. For different debugging levels, target users and specific debugging objects are also very different. Table 8.7 details different levels of debugging objects and information of interest, including framework application layer, framework core layer, and framework adaptation layer.

- *Framework application layer debugging*. Framework application layer debugging mainly takes algorithm or model correctness as the primary goal. The programming framework represented by TensorFlow provides methods such as *visualization* to help users check whether the internal control flow and data flow of the network meet expectations. Typical visualization methods include computational graph visualization, embedded visualization, training visualization, and histogram visualization.

The visualization of the computational graph mainly uses TensorBoard to display the computational graph information of TensorFlow to the developer in a foldable and draggable manner, which not only ensures flexibility but also reduces the difficulty of debugging. Embedding visualization mainly focuses on data visualization from high-dimensional data to low-dimensional space by dimensionality reduction. Commonly

Table 8.7 Different levels of programming framework debugging.

Software level	Role of debugger	Target of debugging	Information of concern
Application layer	Framework users	Python/C++ API	Visualization of computation graph structure, input and output of compute node, inference speed and accuracy, training convergence, etc.
Core layer	Framework developers	Host-side programs written in C++	Framework core class objects (such as runtime management, distributed, cross-platform, computation graph optimization, etc.)
Adaptation layer	Framework developers and hardware manufacturers	Operators implemented by target platform language hardware, manufacturers' own engine adaptation	Target platform adaptation-related logic (such as target platform library API, target architecture code compile and run, frame diagram compilation and operator registration, etc.)

used dimensionality reduction visualization methods include linear principal component analysis (PCA), nonlinear T-distributed random neighborhood embedding, etc. Training visualization can help developers better adjust models and parameters, such as the learning rate, the total loss of the model, and other indicators that change with the number of training iterations. A typical training visualization example is shown in Fig. 8.40. Histogram visualization is an estimate of the probability distribution of continuous variables, which can help developers observe the distribution of numerical data. For example, TensorFlow developers can observe the distribution changes of tensors in the time dimension through histograms.

- *Framework core layer debugging.* The main functions of the core layer of the framework are processing the algorithm logic input by the user API; constructing computational graphs; optimizing execution, runtime environment, and distributed control; and providing debugging interfaces. Therefore, log methods based on their own code style or functional characteristics are generally provided. The core idea of debugging as a framework developer is to insert the printing of key information into the core logic code of the framework and then configure environment variables to analyze the log after execution or debug the internal logic of the framework with tools such as traditional the GNU Project Debugger (GDB).

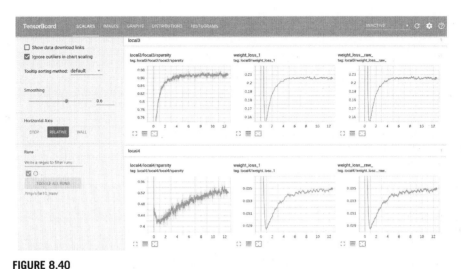

FIGURE 8.40

TensorFlow's training visualization example.

- *Framework adaptation layer debugging.* The framework adaptation layer and the core layer are highly coupled with functions such as optimized execution, runtime environment, and distributed control. Generally, the abstract class of the core layer can describe multiplatform and multiarchitecture. The target platform uses the mechanism or method registration provided by the core layer. Therefore, the debugging method of the adaptation layer is similar to that of the core layer. The main difference is that except for the adaptation interface in the debugging framework Correctness, it is also necessary to consider the correctness of generating the target architecture binary at compiletime or executing the target architecture binary library at runtime. In this case, the debugging methods, interfaces, and tools provided by the target architecture need to be used.

8.6.2 Function debugging interface
8.6.2.1 Functional debugging interface of programming language
- *Print function interface*

On the traditional general-purpose CPU, abundant formatting printing interfaces are provided for different programming languages, for example, the most commonly used C language printf function and fprintf, dprintf, sprintf, etc., the std::cout interface of the iostream class of C++ language, and the print function of Python or Swift.

In order to achieve compatibility with the general-purpose CPU printing interface and reduce user learning costs, the AI programming language needs to provide corresponding formatting and printing functions. Because the basic programming model is heterogeneous, the underlying runtime system has the characteristics of heteroge-

Table 8.8 Key problems and solutions of parallel printing with intelligent language.

Key issues	Solutions
Variable scope and life cycle issues	Variables have strict scope and life cycle constraints; parallel printing must comply with the language execution model to avoid cross-border access between cores.
Timing and readability issues	The address space of the off-chip memory needs to be allocated when the timing and language are running. Computing core needs to clearly print the destination address to avoid out-of-bounds access. After printing, the host side needs to analyze and distinguish multicore data according to the timestamp.
Read and write consistency issues	When the task is executed in parallel, the sequence of read and write access to the shared memory requires support of the multicore synchronization mechanism to ensure the atomicity of read and write operations.

neous communication and storage, which brings challenges to the realization of a printing interface compatible with general-purpose CPUs. (1) Heterogeneous printing is not instantaneous and the computing on the device side for the pursuit of high efficiency is such that it cannot be interrupted frequently by the host under most circumstances. For example, the Kernel task with __printf printing running on DLP must call the synchronization interface after it is launched and executed to obtain the printing result. (2) The cost of heterogeneous printing copy is high, mainly because both the host side and the device side have independent off-chip memory. (3) DLP is generally a parallel architecture, which poses a challenge to multicore or multithreaded parallel printing within the chip. Specifically, as shown in Table 8.8, the key problems and solutions of parallel printing in the AI programming language are mainly concentrated in three aspects.

• *Exception reporting*

There are two main exception reporting mechanisms, namely the Assert mechanism in debug mode and the Core Dump function provided by the system.

The main goal of the Assert mechanism is to provide programmers with a proactively triggered check mechanism. Its main function is to allow developers to predict code with potential problems in advance. Checking the validity of input parameters at the entry of the function and checking the return value at the return of the function can save a lot of time and effort. Generally, the assertion information mainly includes file name, line number, and function name. The assertion example of the AI programming language BCL is shown in Fig. 8.41.

Compared with the assertion mechanism usually used in the development and debugging phase (which will bring additional execution overhead), the Core Dump mechanism can trigger hardware exceptions to illegal software and hardware behav-

```
1   __dlp_device__ void __assert_fail(const char *__message,
2                                     const char *__file,
3                                     unsigned __line,
4                                     const char *__function) {
5       __printf("%s:%d_%s:_Assertion_\'%s\'_failed.\n",
6               __file, __line, __function, __message);
7               __abort();
8   }
9
10  __dlp_device__ void __assert(const char *__assertion,
11                                const char *__file,
12                                int __line) {
13      __printf("%s:%d:_Assertion_\'%s\'.\n",
14              __file, __line, __assertion);
15  }
```

FIGURE 8.41

The assertion example of AI programming language.

iors when the program is running and generate a core dump file in a specific format, assisting in locating the problem after an error occurs in nondebug mode.

Using the Linux system as an example, when a program executes abnormally or crashes, the kernel saves memory snapshots and key program states as files in the directory where the executable file is located. For AI programming languages, because the programming objects are usually heterogeneous, it is necessary to initiate an interrupt to the host through the heterogeneous bus interface or directly send the processed core dump information to the host when the computing core of the device falls into a hardware exception.

8.6.2.2 Functional debugging interface of programming framework

- *Assertions and printer mechanism at the application layer of the framework*

In the TensorFlow application layer, the tf.Assert check interface and the tf.Print print interface are provided. Fig. 8.42 shows an example of using Assert.

- *Log printing macro of the core layer of the framework*

The log in TensorFlow is different in different log levels. You can get the user's environment variable TF_CPP_MIN_LOG_LEVEL through getenv. The value and meaning of the log level it refers to are shown in Table 8.9. In addition, TensorFlow also provides more detailed log printing, which can be set through TF_CPP_MIN_VLOG_LEVEL. The higher the level, the more content will be printed. Since TF_CPP_MIN_VLOG_LEVEL performs log output at the INFO level, when TF_CPP_MIN_LOG_LEVEL is not at the INFO level, the output content of TF_CPP_MIN_VLOG_LEVEL will be blocked.

```
1   import tensorflow as tf
2
3   x = [1, 2, 3]
4   y = [1, 2, 3, 4]
5   assert_x = tf.Assert(tf.less_equal(tf.reduce_max(x), 3), x)
6   assert_y = tf.Assert(tf.less_equal(tf.reduce_max(y), 3), y)
7   sess = tf.Session()
8
9   with tf.control_dependencies([assert_x]):
10    print(sess.run(tf.identity("PASSED")))
11
12  with tf.control_dependencies([assert_y]):
13    print(sess.run(tf.identity("PASSED")))
```

FIGURE 8.42

Typical Assert example.

Table 8.9 Value and meaning of log level.

Corresponding LOG level	Output information
INFO	INFO + WARNING + ERROR + FATAL
WARNING	WARNING + ERROR + FATAL
ERROR	ERROR + FATAL
FATAL	FATAL

- *Target architecture debugging of framework adaptation layer*

When the framework adapts to a new target platform, the VLOG and LOG are reused because it is tightly coupled with the core layer. In practice, a more effective debugging idea is to refer to the adaptation and registration mechanism of the existing architecture (such as x86, GPU, ARM, etc.) of the framework adaptation layer. If there is a problem, the debugging interface provided by the target architecture (such as printing interface, core dump, etc.) will be used for debugging.

8.6.3 Function debugging tool

8.6.3.1 Debugger for programming languages

Programming language-oriented debuggers should have the same functions as traditional programming language debuggers, such as breakpoint mapping relationship analysis, breakpoint setting, and recovery/hardware exception reporting. They should also have the ability to print or modify tensor data at the interruption. Dumping/reloading intermediate tensors, state management, and switching of multicore debugging are unique functions of intelligent language. We use the BCL-GDB debugging tool of the AI programming language BCL as an example to introduce in detail the use process: preparation before debugging, debugger hosting, status viewing, error analysis, etc.

- *Preparation before debugging*

The predebugging preparations generally include the process of configuring the debugging target device number, adding debugging information, and configuring core dumps. For example, if the device number to be debugged is 1, use the command shown in Fig. 8.43 to configure.

```
1   export DLP_VISIBLE_DEVICES = 1
```

FIGURE 8.43

Configuration command used when debugging device number 1.

In order to add debugging information during compilation, add the corresponding compilation option -g in the compilation phase (using the BCL Compiler [BCLC]), and then increase the debugging information level. A typical example is shown in Fig. 8.44.

```
1   bclc −g foo.dlp −o foo
2   bclc −g1 foo.dlp −o foo
3   bclc −g2 foo.dlp −o foo
4   bclc −g3 foo.dlp −o foo
```

FIGURE 8.44

Add debugging options when compiling.

- *Debugger hosting*

The user program of heterogeneous programming must be started by the host-side program. The debugging method of the host side can be consistent with GDB, and it will automatically enter the device-side program execution when it continues to execute from the host side. If you need to stop at the entrance of the Kernel on the device side, you can use the command shown in Fig. 8.45.

```
1   (bcl−gdb) bcl−gdb breakpoint on
2   # Use the breakpoint function on the device−side
3   (bcl−gdb) break *0x1
4   # Set a breakpoint on the first instruction of the Kernel
5   # function
6   (bcl−gdb) run # Execute program
```

FIGURE 8.45

Command stopped at the entrance of the Kernel.

In multithreaded debugging, it is usually necessary to switch the debugging thread, using the info command to view the current thread and the focus command to switch. Fig. 8.46 illustrates the use of the focus command to switch the monitoring state from $(0, 0, 0)$ core to $(0, 2, 1)$ core (the triples correspond to Device, Cluster, and Core, respectively).

```
1   (bcl-gdb) bcl-gdb info
2   device cluster core pc core state         focus
3      0      0     0  1  KERNEL_BREAKPOINT    *
4      0      0     1  0  KERNEL_BREAKPOINT
5      0      0     2  0  KERNEL_BREAKPOINT
6   ... ...
7      0      3     2  0  KERNEL_BREAKPOINT
8
9   (bcl-gdb) bcl-gdb focus cluster 2 core 1
10  [Switch from logical device 0 cluster 0 core 0 to logical
11  device 0 cluster 2 core 1.]
12  device cluster core pc core state         focus
13  ... ...
14     0      2     0  0  KERNEL_BREAKPOINT
15     0      2     1  0  KERNEL_BREAKPOINT *
16     0      2     2  0  KERNEL_BREAKPOINT
17  ... ...
```

FIGURE 8.46

Debug thread switching.

Use the break command to add breakpoints based on the function name, code line number, instruction address, and Kernel entry. In the break command, use the if statement to configure conditional breakpoints. Viewing and deleting breakpoints can be done by using the info and delete commands, respectively. A typical example of breakpoints is shown in Fig. 8.47.

```
1   (bcl-gdb) break my_function
2   (bcl-gdb) break my_class::my_method
3   (bcl-gdb) break int my_templatized_function<int>(int)
4   (bcl-gdb) break foo.dlp:185
5   (bcl-gdb) bcl-gdb breakpoint on
6   (bcl-gdb) break *0x1
7
8   (bcl-gdb) break foo.dlp:23 if taskIdx == 1 && i < 5
9
10  (bcl-gdb) info break
11  (bcl-gdb) i b
12
13  (bcl-gdb) delete break 1
14  (bcl-gdb) d b 2 3 4
```

FIGURE 8.47

Breakpoint command usage example.

- *Status view*

When the -g option is added during compilation, the print command can be used to print the relevant content directly according to the variable name during debugging. The contents of the registers can be viewed using the info registers command.

The data content in the specified address can be viewed through the examine command. For more detailed methods, check the manual of the corresponding hardware programming language.

8.6.3.2 Debugger for programming framework

This section takes the built-in TensorFlow Debugger (tfdbg) as an example to introduce the debugger for the programming framework. Unlike traditional programming language-level debuggers that directly debug compiled programs, tfdbg provides a set of Python API interfaces, which users can insert in the code before use and then enter the debugging commands through the session (Session) package when re-executed OK. Its main API is shown in Fig. 8.48.

```
1   # Used to add debugging information, modify the runtime
2   # parameter RunOptions to specify the data to be monitored
3   tfdbg.add_debug_tensor_watch
4   tfdbg.watch_graph
5   tfdbg.watch_graph_with_blacklists
6
7   # Used to specify debug dump data and directory
8   tfdbg.DebugTensorDatum
9   tfdbg.DebugDumpDir
10
11  # Used to load debug dump data
12  tfdbg.load_tensor_from_event_file
13
14  # Used to determine whether there are nan or inf values in the
15  # intermediate tensor (the tensor in the Session.run path from
16  # input to output)
17  tfdbg.has_inf_or_nan
18
19  # Used to debug ordinary TensorFlow models and
20  # tf.contrib.learn models
21  tfdbg.DumpingDebugHook
22  tfdbg.DumpingDebugWrapperSession
23  tfdbg.LocalCLIDebugHook
24  tfdbg.LocalCLIWrapperSession
```

FIGURE 8.48

API to add debug table.

Fig. 8.49 provides a specific example of how to use the tfdbg API to debug TensorFlow models. Insert LocalCLIDebugWrapperSession into the source code to encapsulate the session sess to be debugged with tfdbg and specify ui_type="readline," then enter the debug command-line interface of tfdbg when running the Python program.

8.6.4 Precision debugging method

Since DLP usually uses customized computing units, such as FP16, BF16, and INT8, there is a difference in accuracy and range of expression from the standard FP32/FP64 arithmetic unit on the CPU, and there is an inevitable need to debug the program

```
1   import numpy as np
2   import tensorflow as tf
3   from tensorflow.python import debug as tf_debug
4   xs = np.linspace(-0.5, 0.49, 100)
5   x = tf.placeholder(tf.float32, shape=[None], name="x")
6   y = tf.placeholder(tf.float32, shape=[None], name="y")
7   k = tf.Variable([0.0], name="k")
8   y_hat = tf.multiply(k, x, name="y_hat")
9   sse = tf.reduce_sum((y - y_hat) * (y - y_hat), name="sse")
10  train_op =
11  tf.train.GradientDescentOptimizer
12              (learning_rate=0.02).minimize(sse)
13
14  sess = tf.Session()
15  sess.run(tf.global_variables_initializer())
16  # Encapsulate session sess with tfdbg
17  sess =
18  tf_debug.LocalCLIDebugWrapperSession(sess, ui_type="readline")
19
20  for _ in range(10):
21      sess.run(y_hat, feed_dict={x:xs,y:10*xs})
22      sess.run(train_op, feed_dict={x: xs, y: 42 * xs})
```

FIGURE 8.49

Specific examples of debugging using tfdbg API.

accuracy. Generally speaking, precision debugging on DLP is achieved by comparing the calculation results of FP32 on the CPU. Similar to traditional function debugging, the comparison result can be obtained by printing data in different formats (floating-point or fixed-point data) through the AI programming language debugger.

8.6.5 Function debugging practice

This section takes the AI programming language BCL and the corresponding debugger BCL-GDB as examples to explain the functional debugging and precision debugging examples of serial and parallel programs.

8.6.5.1 Serial program debugging

The quick sort program (the corresponding file name is kernel.dlp) implemented by the aforementioned AI programming language is shown in Fig. 8.50.

First, use the device-side compiler to compile the device-side binary kernel.o with debugging information, and use GCC to compile and link the host-side executable program. Use the debugger command to insert a breakpoint directly in the source code according to the function name SplitMiddle, as shown in Fig. 8.51.

Use the backtrace (bt) command to view the call stack of the current function, as shown in Fig. 8.52.

Use the layout src command to view the source code and current breakpoints, as shown in Fig. 8.53.

Use the display command and single-step execution to observe the variable status, as shown in Fig. 8.54.

```
1   #define DATA_SIZE 64
2   __dlp_func__ int32_t QuickSort(int left,
3                                  __nram__ int32_t *m,
4                                  int32_t right) {
5     int32_t tag = m[left];
6     int32_t temp;
7     for (;;) {
8       if (left < right) {
9         while (m[right] > tag)
10          right --;
11        if (left >= right)
12          break;
13    ... ...
14    return right;
15  }
16
17  __dlp_device__ void SplitMiddle(int32_t left,
18                                  __nram__ int32_t *m,
19                                  int32_t right) {
20    int middle;
21    if (left < right) {
22      middle = QuickSort(left, m, right);
23      SplitMiddle(left, m, middle - 1);
24      SplitMiddle(middle + 1, m, right);
25    }
26  }
27
28  __dlp_entry__ void kernel(int32_t *pData,
29                            int32_t num,
30                            int32_t left) {
31    __nram__ int32_t nBuff[DATA_SIZE];
32    __memcpy(nBuff, pData, num * sizeof(int32_t), GDRAM2NRAM);
33    SplitMiddle(left, nBuff, num - 1);
34    __memcpy(pData, nBuff, num * sizeof(int32_t), NRAM2GDRAM);
35  }
```

FIGURE 8.50

Kernel code for quick sort.

```
1   (bcl-gdb) b kernel.dlp:SplitMiddle
2   Breakpoint 1 at 0x554: file kernel.dlp, line 48.
3   (bcl-gdb) r
4   Starting program: /xxx/demo/a.out
5   [Thread debugging using libthread_db enabled]
6   Using host libthread_db library
7       "/lib/x86_64-linux-gnu/libthread_db.so.1".
8
9   Breakpoint 1, SplitMiddle (left=0, m=0x200440, right=63)
10      at kernel.dlp:48
11  48 if (left < right) {
12  (bcl-gdb)
```

FIGURE 8.51

An example of breakpoint command.

Use the up command to return to the previous call stack, and then print the data in the NRAM address space variable nBuff, as shown in Fig. 8.55.

```
1  (bcl-gdb) bt
2  #0  SplitMiddle  (left=0,  m=0x200440,  right=63)  at  kernel.dlp:48
3  #1  0x00000000000002c4  in  kernel  (pData=0xfffff9c000 ,  num=64,
4  #left=0)  at
5  kernel.dlp:61
6  (bcl-gdb)
```

FIGURE 8.52

Use the backtrace (bt) command to view the call stack of the current function.

```
1  (bcl-gdb) layout src
2  +--kernel.dlp----------------------------------------+
3  |29  }
4  |
5  |30  if  (left  >=  right)  {
6  ...  ...
7  |
8  |69
9  +--------------------------------------------------+
10 multi-thre  Thread  0x7ffff7fcf8  In:  SplitMiddle  L48  PC:
11 0x554
```

FIGURE 8.53

Use the layout src command to view the source code and current breakpoints.

```
1  (bcl-gdb) display *m
2  1: *m = 869
3  (bcl-gdb) n
4  1: *m = 869
5  1: *m = 128
6  (bcl-gdb) n
7
8  Breakpoint 1, SplitMiddle (left=0, m=0x200440, right=54) at
9  kernel.dlp:48
10 1: *m = 128
11 1: *m = 128
12 1: *m = 112
13
14 Breakpoint 1, SplitMiddle (left=0, m=0x200440, right=6) at
15 kernel.dlp:48
16 1: *m = 112
17 (bcl-gdb)
```

FIGURE 8.54

Use the display command and single-step execution to observe the state of variables.

8.6.5.2 Parallel program debugging

We introduce parallel program debugging examples with the parallel program (file name kernel.dlp) shown in Fig. 8.56.

Since the above Kernel program is a parallel program for four DLP cores, the task of UNION1 type is configured on the host side to start execution (as described in

```
1    (bcl−gdb) up
2    #1 0x000000000000069a in SplitMiddle
3    #(left=0, m=0x200440, right=54) at
4    kernel.dlp:50
5    50 SplitMiddle(left, m, middle − 1);
6    (bcl−gdb) up
7    #2 0x000000000000069a in SplitMiddle
8    #(left=0, m=0x200440, right=63) at
9    kernel.dlp:50
10   50 SplitMiddle(left, m, middle − 1);
11   (bcl−gdb) up
12   #3 0x00000000000002c4 in kernel
13   #(pData=0xfffff9c000, num=64, left=0) at
14   kernel.dlp:61
15   61 SplitMiddle(left, nBuff, num − 1);
16   (bcl−gdb)
17   (bcl−gdb) x /64w nBuff
18   0x600000000000440: 112 80 125 39
19   0x600000000000450: 91 43 23 128
20   ... ...
21   0x600000000000520: 973 929 912 978
22   0x600000000000530: 918 963 986 924
23   (bcl−gdb)
```

FIGURE 8.55

An example of the up command.

```
1    //Examples of parallel programs
2
3    ... ...
4
5    __nram__ int local[4][8];
6    __dlp_device__ int go_deeper(int i) {
7      if (i == 0) {
8      return 1;
9      } else {
10       return 1 + go_deeper(i − 1);
11     }
12   }
13
14   __dlp_entry__ void kernel(int* input, int len) {
15     int line_size = sizeof(int[8]);
16     __memcpy(local, input, len * line_size, GDRAM2NRAM);
17     local[taskId][0] = go_deeper(taskId + 1);
18     __sync_all();
19     __memcpy(input + taskId * 8, local + taskId * 8, line_size,
20   NRAM2GDRAM);
```

FIGURE 8.56

An example of a parallel program.

Section 8.3.2). The example steps in Fig. 8.57 show in detail how to use break, print, display, info, continue, and other commands to observe how multicore calculations are performed and automatically switch the core to be debugged.

```
1   __nram__ int local[4][8];
2   (bcl-gdb) b kernel.dlp:17
3   Breakpoint 1 at 0x32e: file kernel.dlp, line 17.
4   (bcl-gdb) r
5   Starting program: /xxx/xxx/a.out
6   [Thread debugging using libthread_db enabled]
7   Using host libthread_db library
8       "/lib/x86_64-linux-gnu/libthread_db.so.1".
9
10  Breakpoint 1, ?? () at kernel.dlp:17
11  17 local[taskId][0] = go_deeper(taskId + 1);
12  (bcl-gdb) bcl-gdb info
13  device cluster core pc  core state         focus
14     0       0     0  814 KERNEL_BREAKPOINT *
15     0       0     1   0  KERNEL_BREAKPOINT
16     0       0     2   0  KERNEL_BREAKPOINT
17     0       0     3   0  KERNEL_BREAKPOINT
18     0       0     4   0  KERNEL_BREAKPOINT
19
20  (bcl-gdb) display local[taskId][0]
21  1: local[taskId][0] = 2
22
23  (bcl-gdb) n
24  [Switch from logical device 0 cluster 0 core 0 to logical
25      device 0 cluster 0 core 1.]
26  ?? () at kernel.dlp:14
27  14 int line_size = sizeof(int[8]);
28  1: local[taskId][0] = 0
29
30  (bcl-gdb) n
31  15
32  1: local[taskId][0] = 0
33
34  (bcl-gdb)
35  16 __memcpy(local, input, len * line_size, GDRAM2NRAM);
36  1: local[taskId][0] = 269
37
38  (bcl-gdb) bcl-gdb info
39  device cluster core pc  core state         focus
40     0       0     0  842 KERNEL_SYNC
41     0       0     1  782 KERNEL_BREAKPOINT *
42     0       0     2   0  KERNEL_BREAKPOINT
43     0       0     3   0  KERNEL_BREAKPOINT
44     0       0     4   0  KERNEL_BREAKPOINT
45
46  (bcl-gdb) c
47  Continuing.
48  Breakpoint 1, ?? () at kernel.dlp:17
49  17 local[taskId][0] = go_deeper(taskId + 1);
50  1: local[taskId][0] = 269
51
52  (bcl-gdb) bcl-gdb info
```

FIGURE 8.57

An example of parallel program debugging.

8.6.5.3 Precision debugging

Fig. 8.58 shows a specific example of precision debugging of AI applications. The vector floating-point type conversion functions

```
53   device cluster core pc   core state          focus
54      0       0    0  842 KERNEL_SYNC
55      0       0    1  814 KERNEL_BREAKPOINT *
56      0       0    2  0   KERNEL_BREAKPOINT
57      0       0    3  0   KERNEL_BREAKPOINT
58      0       0    4  0   KERNEL_BREAKPOINT
59
60   (bcl-gdb) c
61   Continuing.
62   [Switch from logical device 0 cluster 0 core 1 to logical
63   device 0 cluster 0 core 2.]
64   Breakpoint 1, ?? () at kernel.dlp:17
65   17 local[taskId][0] = go_deeper(taskId + 1);
66   1: local[taskId][0] = 843
67
68   (bcl-gdb) bcl-gdb info
69   device cluster core pc   core state          focus
70      0       0    0  842 KERNEL_SYNC
71      0       0    1  842 KERNEL_SYNC
72      0       0    2  814 KERNEL_BREAKPOINT *
73      0       0    3  0   KERNEL_BREAKPOINT
74      0       0    4  0   KERNEL_BREAKPOINT
75
76   (bcl-gdb) bcl-gdb focus cluster 0 core 3
77   [Switch from logical device 0 cluster 0 core 2 to logical
78   device 0 cluster 0 core 3.]
79
80   (bcl-gdb) bcl-gdb info
81   device cluster core pc   core state          focus
82      0       0    0  842 KERNEL_SYNC
83      0       0    1  842 KERNEL_SYNC
84      0       0    2  814 KERNEL_BREAKPOINT
85      0       0    3  0   KERNEL_BREAKPOINT *
86      0       0    4  0   KERNEL_BREAKPOINT
87
88   (bcl-gdb) list
89   12
90   13 __dlp_entry__ void kernel(int* input, int len) {
91   14 int line_size = sizeof(int[8]);
92   15
93   16 __memcpy(local, input, len * line_size, GDRAM2NRAM);
94   17 local[taskId][0] = go_deeper(taskId + 1);
95   18 __sync_all();
96   19 __memcpy(input + taskId * 8, local + taskId * 8, line_size,
97   NRAM2GDRAM);
98   20 }
99
100  (bcl-gdb) i b
101  Num Type Disp Enb Address What
102  1 breakpoint keep y 0x000000000000032e kernel.dlp:17
103  breakpoint already hit 3 times
```

FIGURE 8.57

(*continued*)

__vec_float2half_tz and __vec_half2float are called. The result obtained after this program is executed is shown in Fig. 8.59.

You can see that using the vector data type conversion function __vec_float2half_tz to convert FP32 to FP16 and then call __vec_half2float to con-

```
1   __dlp_entry__ void kernel(float* input, int len) {
2     __nram__ float dataF32[1024];
3     __nram__ half dataF16[1024];
4     __memcpy(dataF32, input, len * sizeof(float), GDRAM2NRAM);
5     __printf("\n—— before ———\n");
6     for (int i = 0; i < len; ++i) {
7       __printf("dataF32[%d] = %.4f\t", i, dataF32[i]);
8       if ((i + 1) % 4 == 0) { printf("\n"); }
9     }
10    __vec_float2half_tz(dataF16, dataF32, len);
11    __vec_half2float(dataF32, dataF16, len);
12    printf("\n—— after ———\n");
13    for (int i = 0; i < len; ++i) {
14      __printf("dataF32[%d] = %.4f\t", i, dataF32[i]);
15      if ((i + 1) % 4 == 0) { printf("\n"); }
16    }
17  }
```

FIGURE 8.58

Precision debugging for applications.

```
1   —— before ——
2   dataF32[0] = 0.6000  dataF32[1] = 8.5500  dataF32[2] = 8.1300
3        dataF32[3] = 9.9900
4   ... ...
5   —— after ——
6   dataF32[0] = 0.5996  dataF32[1] = 8.5469  dataF32[2] = 8.1250
7        dataF32[3] = 9.9844
```

FIGURE 8.59

The result of precision debugging for application.

vert back to FP32 leads to a large loss of accuracy. We use the debugger to debug, as shown in Fig. 8.60.

The debugging command x used above is the abbreviation of examine, and its format is x/<count/format/unit> <addr>, where count, format, and unit are optional. For example, the x/64f command used in the above example means to print 64 units of data in float format with an immediate or pointer of an address as the starting address. The default value of 4 bytes is used if the unit is not specified. For a more detailed format description, please refer to the GDB manual [169].

It can be seen from this example that by specifying different print formats through the debugger, you can view the memory layout and specific values of the data in detail and facilitate the comparison of results.

8.7 Optimizing AI applications

This chapter focuses on how to optimize the performance of AI applications. First, we will introduce the commonly used performance optimization methods, including

```
1   (bcl-gdb) b kernel.dlp :15
2   Breakpoint 1 at 0x3e5: file kernel.dlp, line 15.
3   ... ...
4   (bcl-gdb) x /64f dataF16
5   0x600000000000440: 0 0 0 0
6   0x600000000000450: 0 0 0 0
7   ... ...
8   (bcl-gdb) x /64f dataF32
9   0x600000000000c40: 6.63000011  2.5  3.6400001  2.0999999
10  0x600000000000c50: 8.88000011  7.98000002  4.15999985  4.13999987
11  ... ...
12  (bcl-gdb) n
13  16 __vec_half2float(dataF32, dataF16, len);
14  (bcl-gdb) x /64f dataF16
15  0x600000000000440: 8.01724339  2.80098128  128144.875  653.064941
16  0x600000000000450:
17         8.32812977  2.95752239  4.51240485e-05  28195.9199
18  ... ...
19  (bcl-gdb) n
20  18 printf("\n——_after_---\n");
21  (bcl-gdb) x /64f dataF32
22  0x600000000000c40: 6.62890625  2.5  3.63867188  2.09960938
23  0x600000000000c50: 8.875  7.9765625  4.15625  4.13671875
24  0x600000000000c60: 2.00976562  2.50976562  8.09375  2.11914062
25  ... ...
```

FIGURE 8.60

Debug with a debugger.

how to use on-chip memory, tensorization, and multicore parallelism. After that, the performance tuning interface and tools are introduced in detail to analyze the performance of the program, as well as to find the potential performance optimization points and to use the most suitable optimization method. Finally, we use the discrete Fourier transformation (DFT) as an example to introduce how to exploit performance optimization on the basis of above methods and tools.

8.7.1 Performance tuning method

8.7.1.1 Overview

Compared with traditional programming languages, the performance tuning of AI programming languages pays more attention to making full use of abundant parallel computing units in intelligent processors, because the most significant advantage of intelligent processors over general-purpose processors is that they have a large number of parallel computing units that can process large-scale data. For example, using a tensor computing unit to calculate vector multiplication is faster than using a scalar computing unit. The commonly used performance optimization methods for AI applications are introduced as follows.

8.7.1.2 Use on-chip memory

The on-chip memories (such as the intracore NRAM, WRAM, and the intercore SMEM described above) are the closest storages to computing units, and these storages have the highest read and write efficiency. Therefore, for AI applications, NRAM and WRAM are given priority to replace LDRAM and GDRAM to improve program running speed. Fig. 8.61 shows an example of vector_mult, which performs an elementwise multiplication of two vectors. The original two inputs and outputs are on the global memory GDRAM.

```
1   #define LEN 16384;
2   __dlp_entry__ void vector_mult(float* in1, float* in2,
3       float* out) {
4     for (int i = 0; i < LEN; i++) {
5       out[i] = in1[i] * in2[i];
6     }
7   }
```

FIGURE 8.61

An example of vector multiplication.

After using NRAM, the program can be rewritten as shown in Fig. 8.62.

```
1    #define LEN 16384;
2    __dlp_entry__ void vector_mult(float* in1, float* in2,
3        float* out) {
4      __nram__ float tmp1[LEN];
5      __nram__ float tmp2[LEN];
6      __memcpy(tmp1, in1, LEN * sizeof(float), GDRAM2NRAM);
7      __memcpy(tmp2, in2, LEN * sizeof(float), GDRAM2NRAM);
8      for (int i = 0; i < LEN; i++) {
9        tmp2[i] = tmp1[i] * tmp2[i];
10     }
11     __memcpy(out, tmp2, LEN * sizeof(float), NRAM2GDRAM);
12   }
```

FIGURE 8.62

Use NRAM to improve the efficiency of vector multiplication.

The main ideas are as follows. (1) First, we allocate a block of memory on NRAM for loading input operators. (2) Then, computing units fetch operators directly from NRAM and write results back to NRAM after calculation. (3) After that, calculation results are sent to GDRAM. If the data to be processed on the GDRAM is too large to fit on the NRAM space, it needs to be moved and calculated in different batches. Further, if the parallelism of memory access and computing is supported, data transfer and arithmetic computing can be pipelined in parallel to improve overall performance.

8.7.1.3 Tensor computation

The basic principle of tensorization is to merge a large number of scalar computations into tensor computations, rewrite the code by using tensor computation statements of the AI programming language, and make full use of the tensor computation unit of the hardware to improve the running speed of the program. Take the NRAM-optimized program in Fig. 8.62 as an example. You can continue to use tensor computation statements to rewrite the for-loop statement in it.

```
1   #define LEN 16384;
2   __dlp_entry__  void vector_mult(float* in1, float* in2,
3           float* out) {
4     __nram__ float tmp1[LEN];
5     __nram__ float tmp2[LEN];
6     __memcpy(tmp1, in1, LEN * sizeof(float), GDRAM2NRAM);
7     __memcpy(tmp2, in2, LEN * sizeof(float), GDRAM2NRAM);
8     __vec_mul(tmp2, tmp1, tmp2, LEN);
9     __memcpy(out, tmp2, LEN * sizeof(float), NRAM2GDRAM);
10  }
```

FIGURE 8.63

Use the vector computation unit to improve vector multiplication efficiency.

In Fig. 8.63, the original for-loop statement uses the hardware scalar computation unit, and the new __vec_mul tensor computation statement uses the hardware vector computation unit for accelerating.

8.7.1.4 Multicore parallel

For multiple cores (which are visible to the programmer), a task can be divided into multiple cores and be processed in parallel to further improve program performance. Take the program in Fig. 8.63 that uses vector units for optimization as an example. You can further use built-in variables to make the program run on four cores in parallel. The sample code is shown in Fig. 8.64.

```
1   #define LEN 16384;
2   #define CORE_NUM 4;
3   #define PER_CORE_LEN (LEN / CORE_NUM);
4   __dlp_entry__  void vector_mult(float* in1, float* in2,
5           float* out) {
6     __nram__ float tmp1[PER_CORE_LEN];
7     __nram__ float tmp2[PER_CORE_LEN];
8     __memcpy(tmp1, in1 + taskId * PER_CORE_LEN, PER_CORE_LEN *
9         sizeof(float), GDRAM2NRAM);
10    __memcpy(tmp2, in2 + taskId * PER_CORE_LEN, PER_CORE_LEN *
11        sizeof(float), GDRAM2NRAM);
12    __vec_mul(tmp2, tmp1, tmp2, PER_CORE_LEN);
13    __memcpy(out + taskId * PER_CORE_LEN, tmp2, PER_CORE_LEN *
14        sizeof(float), NRAM2GDRAM);
15  }
```

FIGURE 8.64

Use multicore to improve the efficiency of vector multiplication.

In the code, the vector with the original length of 16,384 is equally divided into four pieces, and each piece is calculated by one core. Each core uses taskId to identify the data to be calculated.

8.7.2 Performance tuning interface

To facilitate program performance tuning and obtain hardware execution time and status information, AI programming languages need to provide the interface for the hardware running time and performance counters. Among them, the timing interface can be implemented through the "Notifier" mechanism at the software level, and the hardware performance counter interface relies on the hardware support. First, use the "Notifier" mechanism to analyze the approximate execution of the program, then use the hardware counter for the bottleneck to further analyze in detail.

8.7.2.1 Notifier interface

Notifier is a lightweight task and does not occupy computing resources like computing tasks but reads some operating parameters from the hardware through the driver. By placing notifiers before and after the computing task, you can obtain the hardware execution status or control the hardware operation. For example, performance notifiers can obtain the start and end timestamps of computing tasks, or synchronization notifiers can enable multiple computing tasks among multiple cores to wait for each other. The user can use the corresponding notifier in the program as needed.

For the performance notifier, the driver obtains the timestamp from the hardware, so it can also be called the timestamp notifier. The interface provided to users is mainly embodied in the runtime program on the host side. Typical performance notifiers are shown in Table 8.10.

Table 8.10 Typical performance notifier interface example.

Interface example	Specific function
CreateNotifier(Notifier_t *notifier)	Create notifier
DestroyNotifier(Notifier_t *notifier)	Destruction notifier
PlaceNotifier(Notifier_t notifier, Queue_t queue)	Place the notifier task in the task queue
NotifierDuration(Notifier_t start, Notifier_t end, float *us)	Get the time duration between two notifier tasks, The return value is microseconds (us)

For the vector_mult function example mentioned earlier, you can add a performance event interface to its supporting host-side runtime program, as shown in Fig. 8.65. The variable time is the execution time of vector_mult.

8.7.2.2 Hardware performance counter interface

A hardware performance counter is usually designed to count fine-grained hardware behaviors, such as the number of on-chip memory accesses, the number of operations in arithmetic units, etc. The AI programming language can provide an interface to acquire the performance counter, which is convenient for developers to analyze and optimize the behavior of the program in a fine-grained manner. Table 8.11 gives examples of typical hardware performance counters in DLP, which are divided into two main categories, the built-in function of the AI programming language (indicated by __) and the external acquisition interface on the host side. The built-in functions

```
 1   Notifier_t start;
 2   CreateNotifier(&start);
 3   Notifier_t end;
 4   CreateNotifier(&end);
 5
 6   Queue_t queue;
 7   CreateQueue(&queue);
 8   PlaceNotifier(start, queue);
 9   InvokeKernel((void*)(&vector_mult), dim, params, UNION1, queue);
10   PlaceNotifier(end, queue);
11   SyncQueue(queue);
12
13   float time;
14   NotifierDuration(start, end, &time);
```

FIGURE 8.65

An example of using a notifier interface to obtain execution time.

are used mostly to obtain relevant information in the DLP core, and the external acquisition interface on the host side can obtain relevant information about the processor cores, such as the amount of reading and writing access on the PCIe bus.

Table 8.11 Typical performance counter interface example.

Interface example	Specific function
__perf_start	Enable hardware performance counter to start counting
__perf_stop	Enable hardware performance counter to stop counting
__perf_get_clock	Get current hardware timestamp
__perf_get_executed_inst	Get the number of executed instructions
__perf_get_cache_miss	Get the number of instruction cache misses
__perf_get_compute_alu	Get the calculation amount of the scalar operation unit
__perf_get_compute_nfu	Obtain the calculation amount of the NRAM-based tensor computation component
__perf_get_compute_wfu	Obtain the calculation amount of WRAM-based tensor computation component
__perf_get_memory_dram_read	Get the amount of data read from DRAM
__perf_get_memory_dram_write	Get the amount of data written to DRAM
__perf_get_memory_sram_read	Get the amount of data read from the on-chip shared SRAM
__perf_get_memory_sram_write	Get the amount of data written to the on-chip shared SRAM

For the previous vector_mult function example, you can insert the corresponding hardware counter interface into the source program, as shown in Fig. 8.66(a). After the program runs, the printed result is shown in Fig. 8.66(b).

It can be seen that the program uses the tensor computation unit to access the neuron buffer NRAM.

```
1    #define LEN 64;
2    __dlp_entry__ void vector_mult(float* in1, float* in2,
3          float* out) {
4      __nram__ float tmp1[LEN];
5      __nram__ float tmp2[LEN];
6
7      __perf_start();
8
9      __memcpy(tmp1, in1, LEN * sizeof(float), GDRAM2NRAM);
10     __memcpy(tmp2, in2, LEN * sizeof(float), GDRAM2NRAM);
11     __vec_mul(tmp2, tmp1, tmp2, LEN);
12     __memcpy(out, tmp2, LEN * sizeof(float), NRAM2GDRAM);
13
14     __perf_stop();
15
16     int nComputeNram = __perf_get_compute_nfu();
17     int nReadDram = __perf_get_memory_dram_read();
18     int nWriteDram = __perf_get_memory_dram_write();
19
20     printf("nComputeNram_=_%d_Byte,_nReadDram_=_%d_Byte,
21   ____nWriteDram_=_%d_Byte\n", nComputeNram, nReadDram,
22        nWriteDram);
23   }
```

```
1    nComputeNram = 256 Byte, nReadDram = 512 Byte,
2    nWriteDram = 256 Byte
```

FIGURE 8.66

(a) Use a hardware performance counter interface (top). (b) Print the result after running (bottom).

We can also insert a hardware performance counter interface into the host-side source program to observe the hardware behavior of processor cores and peripheral interfaces. For example, the code for observing the device PCIe bus read data amount on the host side is shown in Fig. 8.67(a), and the output result after execution is shown in Fig. 8.67(b). The RawGetCounter function is used to obtain the information of the performance counter.

8.7.3 Performance tuning tools

In addition to monitoring the program by exploiting the performance tuning interface, developers sometimes want to monitor the running status of the program without affecting the execution flow, which requires the provision of corresponding performance tuning tools. This section introduces two types of performance tuning tools. The performance analysis tool of *application level*, and the performance monitoring tool of *system level*, which can be used for multitask resource monitoring to facilitate task scheduling and resource allocation to improve the concurrent performance of multiple programs.

```
1   uint64_t in, out;
2   ... ...
3   RawGetCounter(0, monitor, PCIE_READ_BANDWIDTH, &in)
4   InvokeKernel((void*)(&vector_mult), dim, params, UNION1, queue);
5   SyncQueue(queue);
6   RawGetCounter(0, monitor, PCIE_READ_BANDWIDTH, &out)
7   ... ...
8   printf("nReadCon_=_%d_\n", out-in);
```

```
1   nReadCon = 65536
```

FIGURE 8.67

An example of observing PCIe access statistics and printing the output result.

Table 8.12 Examples of application-level profiling commands.

Command example	Specific function
record	Run the program and save the generated performance data to the output folder
report	Display the function running time, I/O throughput, and calculation efficiency of the target program in the terminal
replay	Display the function call relationship, execution time, and other information in the terminal

8.7.3.1 Application-level profiling tools

The application-level performance analysis tool is based on performance events. It is convenient for users to perform statistics on the execution details of each program segment through a series of encapsulated command lines or graphical interfaces and provides targeted information for Kernel functions, such as providing tuning suggestions to users by analyzing user functions and analyzing user functions through hardware counters. In addition, it generally provides functions such as host memory, device memory usage query, and function call stack information acquisition. The typical commands of the profile tool are shown in Table 8.12.

There are two stages of the specific process. (1) Use the record command to run the executable program and generate the corresponding performance analysis report. (2) Use the report or replay command to view the performance analysis report and obtain the execution time, call relationship, performance counters information, etc. We can use the executable program vecMult compiled by the aforementioned vector_mult as an example to illustrate how to use the above commands. First, run record vecMult ./info_dir and put the performance analysis report into info_dir. Then run the report command to get the information shown in Fig. 8.68.

For the Kernel function, in addition to displaying its execution time, the corresponding hardware performance counter information will also be displayed, such as memory access bandwidth and MAC efficiency. Besides, as shown in Fig. 8.69, users

```
1    report info_dir/  # The terminal displays the following
2    information
3    # PID    Total time   Calls   Function
4    # ===    ===========  =====   ========================
5    # 2510   918.00 us    1       SetCurrentDevice
6    #        698.00 us    3       devMalloc
7    #         66.00 us    1       InvokeKernel
8    # ......
9    # ——     ————         ——      ———————————————————————
10   # Kernels Info:
11   # PID    Duration   ComputeSpeed   IOSpeed    IOCount   Function
12   # ===    ========   ============   =======    =======   ==========
13   # 2510   15.00us    7721GOPs       4.973GiB/s  196608   vector_mult
14   # ——     ————       ————————       ———————    ———————   ——————————
15   # DEVICE_TO_HOST size: 64kB   speed: 0.3 GB/s
16   # HOST_TO_DEVICE size: 192kB  speed: 0.5 GB/s
```

FIGURE 8.68

Use report to display running information.

can also use the replay function to understand the execution time of the function in a timeline format.

```
1    replay info_dir/  # The terminal displays the following
2    information
3    # PID         TIMESTAMP         TIME           Function
4    # =====       =============     ============   ============
5    # ......
6    # 2510        [386ms,410us]                    InvokeKernel {
7    # 2510        [386ms,410us]                       vector_mult {
8    # 2510        [386ms,425us]     [ 15.000 us]      } /*vector_mult*/
9    # 2510        [386ms,476us]     [ 66.000 us]    } /*InvokeKernel*/
10   # ......
```

FIGURE 8.69

Use replay to display function execution time in a timeline format.

8.7.3.2 System-level monitoring tools

System-level performance monitoring tools mainly use drivers to collect static and dynamic information of hardware by accessing registers. The tool encapsulates user-mode commands and graphical interfaces for users. Typically, the available information includes board model, driver version, computing core utilization, device memory usage, power consumption, and temperature. The typical command examples are shown in Table 8.13.

For the program to be monitored (e.g., the program vecMult corresponding to the aforementioned vector_mult function), you should start a new terminal and enter the above command to view the information of interest. Through real-time monitoring of hardware memory usage, hardware computing unit utilization, and other dynamic information, users can rationally allocate hardware resources and multitask scheduling to improve resource utilization and multitask concurrency.

Table 8.13 The example of system-level monitoring commands.

Command examples	Specific functions
monitor-info	displays all the following information
monitor-type	display board model
monitor-driver	display driver version
monitor-fan	display fan speed ratio
monitor-power	display operating power consumption
monitor-temp	display chip temperature
monitor-memory	display physical memory usage
monitor-bandwidth	display the maximum access bandwidth of the computing core to the device memory
monitor-core	display the utilization rate of each computing core

8.7.4 Performance tuning practice

This section takes the DFT algorithm as an example to introduce the performance tuning process.

8.7.4.1 Overall process

DFT is an algorithm that transforms a signal from the time domain to the frequency domain, and both the time domain and the frequency domain are discrete. DFT can find out which sine waves are superimposed on a signal, and the result is the amplitude and phase of these sine waves. The transformation formula is

$$X(k) = \sum_{n=0}^{N-1} x(n)e^{-j\frac{2\pi}{N}kn}.$$

In the formula, $X(k)$ is the frequency-domain sequence after transformation and $x(n)$ is the time-domain sequence before transformation (the sampled signals are all real numbers without imaginary parts). If we replace $e^{-j\frac{2\pi}{N}kn}$ in the above formula with Euler's formula $e^{jx} = \cos(x) + j\sin(x)$, we get the following formula:

$$X(k) = \sum_{n=0}^{N-1} x(n)[\cos(-\frac{2\pi}{N}kn) + j\sin(-\frac{2\pi}{N}kn)]$$

$$= \sum_{n=0}^{N-1} [x(n)\cos(\frac{2\pi}{N}kn) - jx(n)\sin(\frac{2\pi}{N}kn)].$$

The real and imaginary parts of $X(k)$ are

$$real(k) = \sum_{n=0}^{N-1} x(n)\cos(\frac{2\pi}{N}kn),$$

$$imag(k) = \sum_{n=0}^{N-1} -x(n)\sin\left(\frac{2\pi}{N}kn\right).$$

From this, the magnitude of $X(k)$ is

$$Amp(k) = \sqrt{real(k)^2 + imag(k)^2}.$$

We first use the scalar statement of the AI programming language to implement this calculation logic to facilitate understanding. The specific code is shown in Fig. 8.70.

```
1   #define PI 3.14159265
2   #define N 128
3   __dlp_entry__ void DFT (float* x, float* Amp) {
4     for (int k = 0; k < N; k++) {
5       float real = 0.0;
6       float imag = 0.0;
7       for (int n = 0; n < N; n++) {
8         real += x[n] * cos(2 * PI / N * k * n);
9         imag += -x[n] * sin(2 * PI / N * k * n);
10      }
11      Amp[k] = sqrt(real * real + imag * imag);
12    }
13  }
```

FIGURE 8.70

The basic DFT algorithm implemented by scalar.

The main body of the program is a two-level for loop statement. Each level of the for loop is N steps, and the time complexity of the program is $O(n^2)$. The input and output of the program both occupy an array of N elements. In addition, there are only a few temporary variables such as "real" and "imag," so the space complexity of the program is $O(n)$. The main multiplication and addition calculations of this program are embodied in "k * n," "x[n] * sin()," "x[n] * cos()," "real * real," "imag * imag," "Real +=," "imag +=," and "real * real + imag * imag," so our optimization mainly focuses on these operations. The program will be optimized later, based on the aforementioned performance optimization method.

8.7.4.2 Use on-chip cache

The original program uses the device memory GDRAM. Now we move the input and output data to the NRAM and then perform calculations. The modification code is shown in Fig. 8.71. We apply for a piece of NRAM space, move the input data from GDRAM to NRAM, and move the output data from NRAM back to GDRAM after calculation.

8.7.4.3 Tensorization

The original program uses scalar calculation statements. We first optimize the statement "out[k] = sqrt(real * real + imag * imag)" into a tensor calculation statement in

```
1   #define PI 3.14159265
2   #define N 128
3   __dlp_entry__ void DFT (float* x, float* Amp) {
4     __nram__ float in[N];
5     __nram__ float out[N];
6     __memcpy(in, x, N * sizeof(float), GDRAM2NRAM);
7
8     for (int k = 0; k < N; k++) {
9       float real = 0.0;
10      float imag = 0.0;
11      for (int n = 0; n < N; n++) {
12        real += in[n] * cos(2 * PI / N * k * n);
13        imag += -in[n] * sin(2 * PI / N * k * n);
14      }
15      out[k] = sqrt(real * real + imag * imag);
16    }
17    __memcpy(Amp, out, N * sizeof(float), NRAM2GDRAM);
18  }
```

FIGURE 8.71

Use on-chip cache to optimize DFT algorithm.

the AI programming language BCL. As for the inner loop, we will do more in-depth algorithm optimization in the next step. The modification code is shown in Fig. 8.72, with direct usage of the built-in tensorization function sqrt.

```
1   #define PI 3.14159265
2   #define N 128
3   __dlp_entry__ void DFT (float* x, float* Amp) {
4     __nram__ float in[N];
5     __nram__ float out[N];
6     __nram__ float real[N];
7     __nram__ float imag[N];
8     __memcpy(in, x, N * sizeof(float), GDRAM2NRAM);
9
10    for (int k = 0; k < N; k++) {
11      real[k] = 0.0;
12      imag[k] = 0.0;
13      for (int n = 0; n < N; n++) {
14        real[k] += in[n] * cos(2 * PI / N * k * n);
15        imag[k] += -in[n] * sin(2 * PI / N * k * n);
16      }
17    }
18
19    __vec_mul(real, real, real, N);
20    __vec_mul(imag, imag, imag, N);
21    __vec_add(out, real, imag, N);
22    __vec_active_sqrt(out, out, N);
23    __memcpy(Amp, out, N * sizeof(float), NRAM2GDRAM);
24  }
```

FIGURE 8.72

The vector optimization for DFT algorithm.

8.7.4.4 Algorithm optimization

The optimizations that can be performed at the algorithm logic level are as follows. (1) In the original algorithm, sinf and cosf have the same value in parentheses, so the calculation can be done once. (2) The first three of the five numbers "2 * PI / N * k * n" are constants, so there is no need for repeating calculation, and we just calculate it once outside the loop. (3) Imag needs to be squared later, so you do not need to use a negative number when accumulating. The corresponding optimized code is shown in Fig. 8.73.

```
1   #define PI 3.14159265
2   #define N 128
3   __dlp_entry__ void DFT (float* x, float* Amp) {
4       __nram__ float in[N];
5       __nram__ float out[N];
6       __nram__ float real[N];
7       __nram__ float imag[N];
8       __memcpy(in, x, N * sizeof(float), GDRAM2NRAM);
9
10      float con = 2 * PI / N;
11      for (int k = 0; k < N; k++) {
12          real[k] = 0.0;
13          imag[k] = 0.0;
14          for (int n = 0; n < N; n++) {
15              float tmp = con * k * n;
16              real[k] += in[n] * cos(tmp);
17              imag[k] += -in[n] * sin(tmp);
18          }
19      }
20
21      __vec_mul(real, real, real, N);
22      __vec_mul(imag, imag, imag, N);
23      __vec_add(out, real, imag, N);
24      __vec_active_sqrt(out, out, N);
25      __memcpy(Amp, out, N * sizeof(float), NRAM2GDRAM);
26  }
```

FIGURE 8.73

The algorithm optimization for the DFT algorithm.

At this time, the "real" and "imag" calculations left by the program are not optimized yet. There are two main calculations in the inner loop. One is k*n, the other is "real[k] += in[n] * cos()" and "imag[k] += in[n] * sin()." We consider using matrix multiplication to transform the above operations separately.

For k*n in the two-level for loop statement, a total of N^2 results will be produced, and the result of Fig. 8.74(a) is obtained by matrix multiplication.

In this way, the results of k*n are stored in the matrix, and the subsequent process of multiplying by 2*PI/N can be completed with __cycle_mul (the principle is shown in Fig. 8.74(b)). This function mainly multiplies the short vector by the long vector in a circular fashion which is equivalent to making multiple copies of the short vector and then doing the elementwise multiplication with the long vector. In the DFT optimization example, it is multiplied by a scalar number.

(a) k*n by matrix multiplication   (b) Cyclic multiplication of long and short vectors

FIGURE 8.74

Examples of matrix multiplication and cyclic multiplication.

The subsequent sinf and cosf can be replaced with vector calculations. The real and imag in the remaining inner loop can also be converted into matrix multiplication operations, as shown in Fig. 8.75.

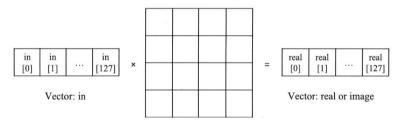

FIGURE 8.75

Convert the original calculation of real and imag to matrix multiplication.

The final code is shown in Fig. 8.76. The original two-level nested loop has been completely replaced by a series of vector and matrix operations.

8.7.4.5 Constant preprocessing

The value in the "k*n" matrix in the above program is fixed, which means that the value of sin and cos after the calculation is also fixed. Thus, there is no need of duplicate calculations. We calculate these constants in advance and pass them directly as parameters. The code is changed as shown in Fig. 8.77.

Among them, the calculation of cos_mat and sin_mat is completed in the runtime program on the host side, and it is prepared before copying the data from the host memory to the device memory (GDRAM).

8.7.4.6 Analysis of optimization results

Based on the above optimization, the calculation of DFT has changed from the original pure scalar calculation with 11 lines of code of accessing GDRAM to nearly 30 lines of code after optimization. Except for a small piece of code that assigns initial values to the arrays, which can only hold scalar statements, the rest have been re-

```
1    #define PI 3.14159265
2    #define N 128
3    __dlp_entry__ void DFT (float* x, float* Amp) {
4      __nram__ float in[N];
5      __nram__ float real[N];
6      __nram__ float imag[N];
7      __nram__ float con[1];
8      __nram__ float sequence[N];
9      __nram__ float kn[N * N];
10     __nram__ float cos_res[N * N];
11     __memcpy(in, x, N * sizeof(float), GDRAM2NRAM);
12     con[0] = 2 * PI / N;
13     for (int k = 0; k < N; k++) {
14       sequence[k] = k;
15     }
16
17     __mlp(kn, sequence, sequence, N, 1, N);
18     // Construct "k*n" matrix
19     __cycle_mul(kn, kn, con, N * N, 1);
20     // Multiply the "k*n" matrix by the constant 2 * PI / N
21     __vec_active_cos(cos_res, kn, N * N);
22     // Calculate cos(kn)
23     __vec_active_sin(kn, kn, N * N);
24     // Calculate sin(kn) and save the result in kn
25     __mlp(real, in, cos_res, 1, N, N);
26     // Calculate the real vector
27     __mlp(imag, in, kn, 1, N, N);
28     // Calculate the imaginary part imag vector
29
30     __vec_mul(real, real, real, N);
31     __vec_mul(imag, imag, imag, N);
32     __vec_add(imag, real, imag, N);
33     // The sum result of real and imag is still stored in imag
34     __vec_active_sqrt(imag, imag, N);
35     __memcpy(Amp, imag, N * sizeof(float), NRAM2GDRAM);
36   }
```

FIGURE 8.76

Optimizing the DFT algorithm with matrix multiplication.

placed with tensor calculation statements with the usage of NRAM.[7] Although the number of lines of code has increased, the overall performance has greatly improved, with the final performance increasing by nearly 1800 times. The performance improvement brought about by different optimization methods is shown in Table 8.14.

From the above optimization example, it can be seen that the entire performance tuning process brings data closer to the arithmetic unit. At the same time, it also gradually eliminates the for loop and gradually replaces the scalar calculation statements with tensor calculation statements. If you add multicore parallelism, it also involves splitting the calculation. In summary, the main task of performance tuning is to make full use of hardware resources, including at least four aspects: (1) Making full use of near-end memory (using on-chip buffers); (2) Making full use of the tensor computa-

---

[7] Currently, only single-core optimization is performed. If multicore optimization is performed, the performance can be improved further.

```
1   #define PI 3.14159265
2   #define N 128
3   __dlp_entry__ void DFT (float* x, float* cos_mat,
4   float* sin_mat, float* Amp) {
5       __nram__ float in[N];
6       __nram__ float real[N];
7       __nram__ float imag[N];
8       __nram__ float cos_res[N * N];
9       __nram__ float sin_res[N * N];
10
11      __memcpy(in, x, N * sizeof(float), GDRAM2NRAM);
12      __memcpy(cos_res, cos_mat, N * N * sizeof(float), GDRAM2NRAM);
13      __memcpy(sin_res, sin_mat, N * N * sizeof(float), GDRAM2NRAM);
14
15      __mlp(real, in, cos_res, 1, N, N);
16      // Calculate the real vector
17      __mlp(imag, in, sin_res, 1, N, N);
18      // Calculate the imaginary part imag vector
19
20      __vec_mul(real, real, real, N);
21      __vec_mul(imag, imag, imag, N);
22      __vec_active_add(imag, real, imag, N);
23      // The sum result of real and imag is still stored in imag
24      __vec_active_sqrt(imag, imag, N);
25      // tensor formula statement
26      __memcpy(Amp, imag, N * sizeof(float), NRAM2GDRAM);
27  }
```

FIGURE 8.77

The optimization of constant preprocessing.

Table 8.14 Performance improvement of different optimization methods.

Optimization method	Multiples of performance improvement
Original scalar program	1 (benchmark performance)
Use on-chip cache	1.49
Tensorization	10.65
Algorithm optimization	29.27
Constant preprocessing	1794

tion units (tensorization); (3) Reducing the amount of calculation and save memory space, including algorithm optimization and constant preprocessing; (4) Making full use of multicore parallel (computing task split), etc.

8.8 System development on AI programming language

For different scenarios, different levels of APIs, such as programming frameworks, high-performance libraries, or runtime system interfaces, can be used to develop applications. Specifically, for scenarios with requirements of low performance but high flexibility (for example, rapid deployment where the algorithm may change frequently), programming framework APIs are generally used directly for application development, and applications developed with programming framework APIs can be migrated quickly and with good portability to different platforms. For scenarios with higher performance requirements and relatively fixed algorithms, users can use high-performance libraries to call underlying operators directly (such as Conv, MLP, and Pooling operators in the high-performance library) for development. Furthermore, for scenarios with extreme performance requirements and resource constraints (such as terminal devices), users can generate binary instructions in advance and use runtime system APIs to directly parse, load, and execute the instructions. No matter which level of API is used for system-level application development, its core goal is to enable AI algorithms to be executed efficiently on DLP, which involves the support of various operators in the algorithm on DLP. This section focuses on how to support user-defined operators in high-performance libraries and programming frameworks, as well as system-level development and optimization practices.

8.8.1 High-performance library operator development

High-performance libraries (such as OpenBLAS [170], MKL [171] on the CPU and cuDNN [172] on the GPU) provide high-performance implementations of common operators in AI applications on specific platforms, and users can directly call the corresponding APIs. For example, on DLP, common operators (such as convolution and pooling) used in the aforementioned VGG19 network for image style transfer have been implemented efficiently in high-performance libraries and provided to users in the form of APIs. This section describes how to develop high-performance library operators to extend the high-performance library.

8.8.1.1 Principle and process

The process of developing customized operators in high-performance libraries and realizing AI applications can be divided into the following activities. (1) Develop the customized operator through the AI programming language and obtains the corresponding Kernel source code. (2) Get the Kernel binary machine code by compiling the Kernel source code through the compilation tool chain. (3) Integrate into a high-performance library operator through the *customized operator interface* of the high-performance library. (4) Use the host-side compiler to integrate the Kernel binary machine code and application program and link the original runtime library, and become an executable program. (5) Run the program on the host side. The specific process is shown in Fig. 8.78.

    The key to the development of high-performance library operators lies in the development and optimization of Kernel code and the use of high-performance library operator interface APIs. The previous sections introduced the development and optimization of Kernel code, and the following sections will focus on how to use the high-performance library operator interface API to customize operators through integration.

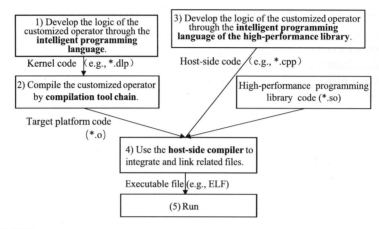

FIGURE 8.78

The process of developing customized operators.

8.8.1.2 Customized operator integration

Fig. 8.79 shows the main APIs for customized operator integration in a typical high-performance library, including the creation of customized operators (CreateCustomizedOp), (forward) calculation (ComputeCustomizedOp), destruction (Destroy-BaseOp), and other interfaces.

```
1   // Create a new customized operator descriptor
2   CreateCustomizedOp ();
3
4   // Perform CustomizedOp operation on the specified
5   // device
6   ComputeCustomizedOp ();
7
8   // Destroy the customized operator descriptor
9   DestroyBaseOp ();
```

FIGURE 8.79

The main API of high-performance library customized operators.

Customized operators are mainly divided into two categories, basic operators and fusion operators. The basic operator refers to a single layer (or operation) in the network, such as convolution, fully connected, activation, etc. The fusion operator refers to the combination of basic operators, such as convolution (Conv) + scaling (Scale), etc. The integration process of the two types of operators is introduced below.

- *Basic operator integration*

Fig. 8.80 describes the main process of integrating basic operators into the framework, which can be divided roughly into two stages. The first is the data preparation and compilation stage. The host prepares the input data and then creates the tensor required for the customized operation. After specifying the corresponding parameter space, create a customized operation and compile it (CompileBaseOp) to get the corresponding instruction,[8] and allocate corresponding space for input and output data. The second stage is the running stage, the core of which is to create an execution queue in which the calculation of the corresponding operator is completed and the result is returned.

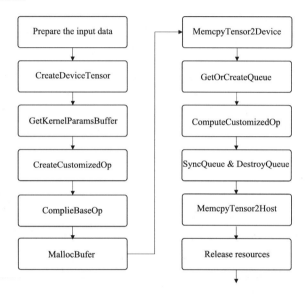

FIGURE 8.80

Basic operator integration process.

- *Fusion operator integration*

It can be seen from the basic operator integration process that each operator has to interact with the host-side data. Considering that deep learning is usually a combination of multiple operators, frequent data interaction uses a lot of overhead. Therefore, we try combining multiple operators to reduce interaction overhead. In addition, the fusion of multiple operators can also make full use of on-chip memory, greatly improving execution efficiency through data multiplexing between layers. Fig. 8.81 describes the main process of integrating the fusion operator into the framework. Compared with basic operators, it mainly increases the creation and configuration of fusion operations (CreateFusionOp), including adding customized operators to fusion operators (AddFusionOp), configuring the input, output, and number of fusion operations (SetFusion), compiling (CompileFusionOp), etc.

---

[8] Assuming that the high-performance library is an imperative programming method that is compiled and then executed.

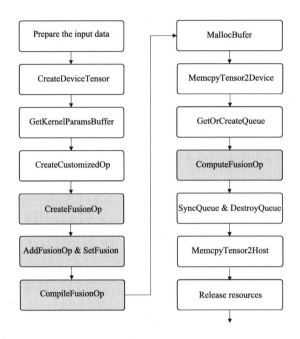

FIGURE 8.81

Fusion operator integration process.

8.8.1.3 High-performance library operator development example

We use the Power operator in the real-time style transfer algorithm [112] as an example to introduce the development process of customized operators, including Power as a basic operator integration and integrating it with existing operators in the high-performance library.

- *Basic operator*

Following the aforementioned development process, first, use the AI programming language BCL to implement the code logic of the customized operator Power. Its calculation formula is $y = x^c$ $(x > 0)$. In order to use the BCL tensor calculation statement as much as possible, the formula is transformed as follows:

$$y = x^c = e^{lnx^c} = e^{clnx} \ (x > 0).$$

Therefore, the three tensor statements of __vec_log, __cycle_mul, and __vec_exp in BCL can be used to combine the above calculation process. The code written in BCL is shown in Fig. 8.82 (power.dlp file).

The second step is using the BCL compiler to compile the customized operator and generate the corresponding object code (power.o file).

```
1   #define N 1024
2   __dlp_entry__  void myPower(float* x, float* c, float* y) {
3       __nram__ float in[N];
4       __nram__ float cc[1];
5       __memcpy(in, x, N * sizeof(float), GDRAM2NRAM);
6       __memcpy(cc, c, sizeof(float), GDRAM2NRAM);
7
8       __vec_log(in, in, N);   // Tensor ln statement
9       __cycle_mul(in, cc, in, N, 1);
10      // Long and short vector cycle multiplication
11      __vec_exp(in, in, N);   // Tensor exp statement
12
13      __memcpy(y, in, N * sizeof(float), NRAM2GDRAM);
14  }
```

FIGURE 8.82

Function written in AI programming language BCL.

The third step is using the high-performance library interface to integrate the kernel function in power.dlp as a customized operator of the high-performance library. The specific code written in C++ is shown in Fig. 8.83 (power.cpp file).

Finally, use a host-side compiler (such as GCC, etc.) to compile and link three files (power.o, power.cpp, and dynamic lib.so file of the high-performance library) to obtain an executable program that can be directly executed on the host side.

- *Fusion operator*

Further, we consider how to integrate the Power operator and the existing operators in the high-performance library to obtain a more complete network model. For example, we hope to fuse Power with the existing convolution and ReLU operators in the high-performance library to obtain the Conv-Power-ReLU fusion operator. The overall development process is similar to the above-mentioned Power basic operator development; the difference lies in the third step. It is necessary to call the existing convolution and ReLU operators in the high-performance library as well as the related interfaces of the fusion operator. The obtained code is shown in Fig. 8.84 (fusionop.cpp).

Similarly, use a host-side compiler (such as GCC, etc.) to compile and link three files (power.o, fusionop.cpp, and dynamic lib.so file of high-performance library) to obtain an executable program that can be executed directly on the host side.

8.8.2 Programming framework operator development

For operators that are not supported in the programming framework, they can be developed directly through the AI programming language so that the complete algorithm (network) can be executed on the DLP and the overall execution efficiency is

```
1   int main() {
2       // Create Tensor
3       Tensor_t input;
4       CreateTensor(&input,FLOAT32,DIM_NCHW,1,1,1,1024);
5       Tensor_t powerC;
6       CreateTensor(&powerC,FLOAT32,DIM_NCHW,1,1,1,1);
7       Tensor_t output;
8       CreateTensor(&output,FLOAT32,DIM_NCHW,1,1,1,1024);
9
10      ... ...
11      // Create customized operator
12      BaseOp_t powerOp;
13      CreateCustomizedOp(&powerOp, "kernel",
14      reinterpret_cast<void*>(&Power), {input, powerC}, 2,
15      {output}, 1, nullptr, 0);
16
17      // Compile customized operator
18      CompileBaseOp(powerOp);
19
20      // Allocate memory space on the device side
21      void* input_d = devMalloc(1024 * sizeof(float));
22      void* c_d = devMalloc(sizeof(float));
23      void* output_d = devMalloc(1024 * sizeof(float));
24
25      // Allocate memory space on the host side
26      void* input_h = hostMalloc(1024 * sizeof(float));
27      void* c_h = hostMalloc(sizeof(float));
28      void* output_h = hostMalloc(1024 * sizeof(float));
29      ... ...
30
31      /* Copy the input data from the memory on the host
32      side to the memory on the device side */
33      Memcpy(input_d, input_h, 64 * 64 * sizeof(float),
34      HOST2DEV);
35      Memcpy(c_d, c_h, sizeof(float), HOST2DEV);
36
37      // Device computation
38      Queue_t queue;
39      CreateQueue(&queue);
40      InvokeKernel((void*)(&Power), params, dim, BLOCK, queue);
41      SyncQueue(queue);
42      DestroyQueue(queue);
43
44      // Copy output data from device memory to host memory
45      Memcpy(output_h, output_d, 32 * 32 * sizeof(float),
46      DEV2HOST);
47
48      // Free up memory space
49      ... ...
50  }
```

FIGURE 8.83

Basic operator.

improved. This section introduces how to implement new user-customized operators in the programming framework so that users can call the corresponding interfaces directly through the deep learning programming framework to implement AI applications.

```
1    int main() {
2      // Create Tensor
3      Tensor_t input = CreateTensor(&input, FLOAT32, DIM_NCHW, 1, 1, 128, 128);
4      Tensor_t filter = CreateTensor(&filter, FLOAT32, DIM_NCHW, 1, 1, 2, 2);
5      Tensor_t convOut = CreateTensor(&convOut, FLOAT32, DIM_NCHW, 1, 1, 64, 64);
6      Tensor_t powerC = CreateTensor(&powerC, FLOAT32, DIM_NCHW, 1, 1, 1, 1);
7      Tensor_t powerOut = CreateTensor(&powerOut, FLOAT32, DIM_NCHW, 1, 1, 64, 64);
8      Tensor_t reluOut = CreateTensor(&reluOut, FLOAT32, DIM_NCHW, 1, 1, 64, 64);
9      ... ...
10
11     // Create Conv operator, customized operator Power and ReLU operator
12     BaseOp_t conv;
13     CreateConvOp(&conv, conv_param, input, convOut, filter, NULL);
14     BaseOp_t power;
15     CreateCustomizedOp(&power, "kernel", reinterpret_cast
16       <void*>(&Power), params, {convOut, powerC}, 2, {powerOut}, 1, NULL, 0);
17     BaseOp_t relu;
18     CreateActiveOp(&relu, ACTIVE_RELU, powerOut, reluOut);
19
20     // Create fusion operator and compile
21     FusionOp_t net;
22     CreateFusionOp(&net);
23     AddFusionOp(conv, net);
24     AddFusionOp(power, net);
25     AddFusionOp(relu, net);
26     SetFusionIO(net, {input, filter, powerC}, 3, {reluOut}, 1);
27     CompileFusionOp(net);
28
29     // Apply for device side space: input_d, filter_d, reluOut_d
30     ... ...
31
32     // Apply for host-side space in host memory: input_h, filter_h, reluOut_h
33     ... ...
34
35     // Copy input data from host memory to device memory
36     Memcpy(input_d, input_h, 128 * 128 * sizeof(float), HOST2DEV);
37     Memcpy(filter_d, filter_h, 2 * 2 * sizeof(float), HOST2DEV);
38     Memcpy(powerC_d, powerC_h, sizeof(float), HOST2DEV);
39
40     // Computing network
41     Queue_t queue;
42     CreateQueue(&queue);
43     ComputeFusionOp(net, {input_d, filter_d, powerC_d}, {reluOut_d}, queue);
44     SyncQueue(queue);
45     DestroyQueue(queue);
46
47     // Copy output data from device memory to host memory
48     Memcpy(reluOut_h, reluOut_d, 32 * 32 * sizeof(float), DEV2HOST);
49
50     // Release the memory space on the device side and the host side
51     ... ...
52   }
```

FIGURE 8.84

Fusion operator.

8.8.2.1 Principle and process

As shown in Fig. 8.85, the basic principle of programming framework operator development is based on the operators provided by the high-performance library, combining codes developed by the user with some existing programming framework codes to realize the decoupling of operator logic development and programming framework operator extensions. Therefore, the development of high-performance library operators is the foundation. After customized operators are integrated in the high-performance library, the programming framework further calls and integrates the corresponding operators to realize the expansion of the programming framework operators. The previous sections introduced in detail how to extend the high-performance library operator; the following section focuses on how to integrate it into the programming framework.

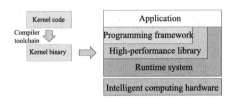

FIGURE 8.85

Use AI programming language to develop operators.

8.8.2.2 TensorFlow integrates customized operators

Through the customized operator of the high-performance library, the operator developed by the user with the AI programming language can be integrated into the programming framework such as TensorFlow. We use TensorFlow as an example to illustrate how to integrate customized operators in a deep learning framework. The main process includes: (1) Registering for a new customized operator; (2) Writing forward inference interface functions for the new customized operator; (3) Writing the low-level implementation of the customized operator according to the new customized operator interface; and (4) Improving the Bazel Build and header files and recompiling the TensorFlow source code.

Use integrating the customized operator named anchor_generator[9] [84] to TensorFlow as an example. The TensorFlow directory tree involved in the modification is shown in Fig. 8.86. The modification under tensorflow/core is mainly to complete the C++ interface declaration and registration of the customized operator and the wrapper implementation of the forward inference function. The modification in the tensorflow/python directory is made mainly to complete the Python interface registration of the customized operator. The modification in the tensorflow/stream_executor/dlp directory is made mainly to add a new DLP customized operator implementation.

To register a customized operator in tensorflow/core/ops/anchor_generator_ops. cc, the users need to specify the name of the registered operator, the name and number of input and output tensors, and other parameters' name, type, and default value of the

[9] GitHub address: http://github.com/rbgirshick/py-faster-rcnn/tree/master/lib/rpn.

customized operator. Fig. 8.87 shows a sample code for specific operator registration. The registered customized operator is called AnchorGenerator. There is an input and an output tensor, which are input feature_map_shape of type int32 and output anchors of type float. In addition, there are five attribute values (including their type and default value).

In tensorflow/core/kernels/anchor_generator_dlp_op.cc, you need to implement the outermost wrapper function of the forward inference of the customized operator, which is the entry point for the customized operator to run on DLP. As shown in Fig. 8.88, it contains a class named DLPAnchorGeneratorOp. The Compute function in this class is the entry point for forward inference by a customized operator. This function creates the output tensor by obtaining the input tensor and attributes of the customized operator, allocating memory for it, and finally calling the high-performance library interface that performs the operation in the executor.

The C++ code under ops and lib_ops in tensorflow/stream_executor/dlp is where the forward operation of the operator is actually implemented using the high-performance library customized operator interface. Follow the programming process in Section 8.8.1 to allocate memory for input and output tensors in turn, copy the input tensor to DLP, create descriptors for customized operators, and finally perform

```
 1    tensorflow/
 2    ├ core
 3    │    ├ BUILD
 4    │    ├ kernels
 5    │    │    ├ anchor_generator_dlp_op.cc
 6    │    │    └ BUILD
 7    │    └ ops
 8    │         └ anchor_generator_ops.cc
 9    ├ python
10    │    ├ BUILD
11    │    └ ops
12    │         ├ anchor_generator_ops.py
13    │         └ standard_ops.py
14    └ stream_executor
15         ├ BUILD
16         └ dlp
17              ├ lib_ops
18              │    ├ dlp_anchor_generate_op.cc
19              ├ macro.h
20              ├ dlp_anchor_generator_kernel.dlp
21              ├ dlp_anchor_generator_kernel.o
22              ├ dlp.h
23              ├ dlp_lib_common.cc
24              ├ dlp_lib_math_ops.h
25              ├ dlp_lib_nn_ops.h
26              ├ dlp_stream.cc
27              ├ dlp_stream.h
28              └ ops
29                   └ anchor_generator_op.cc
```

FIGURE 8.86

Directory tree that needs to be modified when integrating customized operators into Tensor-Flow.

```
1   namespace tensorflow {
2
3   REGISTER_OP("AnchorGenerator")
4       .Input("feature_map_shape:_int32")
5       .Output("anchors:_float")
6       .Attr("scales:_list(float)_=_[0.5,_1,_2]")
7       .Attr("aspect_ratios:_list(float)_=_[0.5,_1,_2]")
8       .Attr("base_anchor_sizes:_list(float)_=_[256,_256]")
9       .Attr("anchor_strides:_list(float)_=_[16,_16]")
10      .Attr("anchor_offsets:_list(float)_=_[8,_8]")
11      // others attrs
12
13      .SetShapeFn(AnchorGeneratorShapeFn);
14
15  }   // namespace tensorflow
```

FIGURE 8.87

AnchorGenerator operator registration.

```
1   namespace tensorflow {
2
3   class DLPAnchorGeneratorOp : public OpKernel {
4     public:
5       explicit DLPAnchorGeneratorOp(OpKernelConstruction*context):
6         OpKernel(context) {
7       }
8
9       void Compute(OpKernelContext* context) override {
10  // Get the input tensor and attributes of the customized operator
11        Tensor input_tensor = GetInputTensor();
12  // Create output tensor
13        Tensor output_tensor = CreateAndMallocOutputTensor();
14  // Call the interface for performing calculations in the executor
15        context->Compute();
16      }
17  };
18
19  REGISTER_KERNEL_BUILDER(Name("AnchorGenerator").Device(DEVICE_DLP),
20  DLPAnchorGeneratorOp);
21
22  }   // namespace tensorflow
```

FIGURE 8.88

Class definition of DLPAnchorGeneratorOp.

corresponding forward inference operations. As shown in Fig. 8.89, the interfaces that need to be called are CreateCustomizedOp and ComputeCustomizedOp, where CreateCustomizedOp is based on the number of inputs and outputs in the current customized operator, the name of the Kernel function, and other attributes, to create a new operator and map it to the operator logic developed by the AI programming language. ComputeCustomizedOp is the real calculation of the customized operator, and the program enters the internal logic of the customized operator Kernel and starts to execute the corresponding instructions on the DLP.

```
1   namespace stream_executor {
2   namespace dlp {
3
4   DLPStatus DLPStream :: AnchorGenerate ( std :: vector <Tensor*> inputs ,
5                                  std :: vector <Tensor*> outputs ,
6                                  half *feature_map_shape_dlp ,
7                                  /* other params */
8                                  ... ...) {
9       ... ...
10
11      // Create parameter cache
12      KernelParamsBuffer_t params ;
13      GetKernelParamsBuffer(&params );
14      KernelParamsBufferAddParam ( params ,
15      &feature_map_shape_dlp , sizeof ( half *));
16
17      // Create a customized operator
18      BaseOp_t op ;
19      CreateCustomizedOp(&op , "anchorgenerator" ,
20              reinterpret_cast <void *>(AnchorGeneratorKernel ),
21              params ,
22              inputs . data () , inputs . size () ,
23              outputs . data () , outputs . size () ,
24              nullptr , 0);
25
26      // Compile the basic operator
27      CompileBaseOp ( op );
28
29      // Data assignment and preparation
30      ... ...
31      // Customized operator calculation
32      ComputeCustomizedOp ( op ,
33                          inputs . data () ,
34                          inputs . size () ,
35                          outputs . data () ,
36                          outputs . size () ,
37                          queue );
38      ... ...
39      return DLP_STATUS_SUCCESS ;
40  }
41  } // namespace dlp
42  } // namespace stream_executor
```

FIGURE 8.89

Calling a high-performance library interface in customized operator implementation.

8.8.3 System development and optimization practice

This section uses the typical detection network Faster R-CNN introduced in Section 3.3.2.3 as an example to illustrate the system-level development and optimization methods. The core goal is to improve the overall performance of the network as much as possible while meeting accuracy requirements.

Faster R-CNN is a typical two-stage detection network in which the region proposal network (RPN) layer is proposed to solve the time-consuming problem of traditional detection networks generating bounding boxes. The bounding boxes are directly generated through the RPN layer, which greatly improves the performance of the detection network. The Faster R-CNN network structure is shown in Fig. 8.90, which can be divided into four parts:

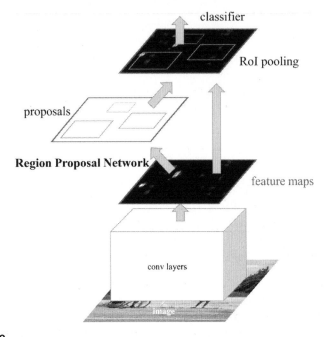

FIGURE 8.90

Faster R-CNN execution process.[10]

(1) *Backbone*, a set of deep convolutional networks based on Conv+ReLU+ Pooling as the backbone network for feature extraction. VGG, ResNet series, or Inception series networks can be used as the backbone network. The extracted network features are shared by the subsequent RPN layer and classification network.

(2) *Region Proposal Network* (RPN), used to generate the detection candidate frame Region Proposals, combined with the Anchors preset at each feature point. This layer first determines whether each Anchor belongs to a positive sample or a negative sample through softmax and then uses position regression to obtain more accurate Region Proposals. This is the first stage of the network.

(3) *Region of interest (ROI) pooling* takes the feature map and Region Proposals as input, maps each Proposal to the corresponding feature map, takes out the Feature to perform Resize to get the same size, and sends it to the subsequent classification layer.

(4) The *classification layer* performs category judgment and position regression correction on the feature map processed by ROI pooling to obtain the final category and location. This is the second stage of the network.

In order to obtain better performance, the Faster R-CNN network has become more complicated. In addition to the above-mentioned RPN layer, Anchor generation, and ROI pooling layer, there are corresponding first-stage and second-stage postprocessing networks. These not only present challenges for the implementation of the entire network, but also provide opportunities for network optimization. The following content will elaborate on the network development and optimization of Faster R-CNN.

8.8.3.1 Overall performance analysis

The Faster R-CNN officially provided by TensorFlow is based on ResNet101 as the backbone network and a fully trained network model on the Microsoft COCO [173] dataset. The inference structure and weights of the network are stored in frozen_inference_graph.pb. Without any optimization, if you run the official model file directly on the specific version of the software stack and perform forward inference on the pictures in the COCO dataset, there will be operators that are not currently supported by the current DLP software stack.

Fig. 8.91 shows part of the Faster R-CNN computational graph structure. In the initial state, the dark nodes are already executed on DLP, while the light nodes are temporarily not supported by the current DLP software stack (including programming frameworks and high-performance libraries, etc.) and will be executed on the CPU. It can be found that there are a large number of nodes executing on the CPU in the network. At the same time, the nodes on the CPU and the DLP are often alternately performed, making it difficult to optimize the fusion operator, which is the main reason for the poor performance of the entire network. Table 8.15 further gives a breakdown of the execution time, of which nearly half is spent on the CPU and the data interaction between CPU/DLP. In particular:

Table 8.15 The original Faster R-CNN execution time ratio.

Network name	CPU execution time	Data copy time	DLP execution time
Faster R-CNN	26.23%	17.04%	55.40%

(1) Nodes not supported by DLP will be placed on the CPU for calculation, which will increase the copy of the data: the data needs to be copied from the DLP to the CPU and then copied back to the DLP after running on the CPU.
(2) The performance of the operation running on the CPU is not optimal.
(3) The occurrence of CPU operations in the middle of the network will interrupt the network fusion strategy, resulting in a large number of segments in the fusion of the entire network. Since the fusion strategy is not optimal, the copy between the CPU and the device also increases accordingly.

Based on the above analysis, a reasonable network optimization idea is: *Reduce CPU operations in the network so that more operations are run on DLP, thereby reducing data copying costs and obtaining fewer fusion segments and better fusion strategies.* By analyzing the position and function of the operation running on the CPU in the network, we can regard operations that have close positions and can realize a complete summary of functional operations as a customized operator, defining and optimizing the customized operator by AI programming language, and replacing the original discrete operations that are not currently supported by the DLP software stack to achieve performance optimization. Specifically, the main process of using AI programming language to develop and optimize customized operators is:

(1) Analyze the locations and functions of operations that are not currently supported in the network and specify the scope of customized operators to be developed.
(2) Use AI programming language to realize and optimize the customized operator analyzed.
(3) Use the graph optimization tool (described in detail in Section 8.8.3.3) to modify and replace the original network.
(4) Use the customized operator interface to integrate the newly developed customized operator into the TensorFlow framework and recompile.
(5) Use TensorFlow integrated with customized operators to verify the performance and accuracy of the replaced network model.

8.8.3.2 Fusion operator development

We observe that the two-stage postprocessing in the original version of Faster R-CNN is mainly executed on the CPU and the overhead is relatively high. We plan to develop corresponding customized operators for the two-stage postprocessing.

- *First-stage postprocessing fusion operator*

The first stage of postprocessing is behind the RPN network in the network. The main functions are: (1) Decoding the offset of boxes output by RPN and the predefined anchor boxes to obtain the offset detection bounding boxes and crop all the bounding boxes so that they do not exceed the original picture boundary. (2) The two classification (whether there is a target) scores output by RPN are operated on softmax and TopK to obtain K scores with high target probability and their corresponding bounding boxes. (3) Performing nonmaximum suppression (NMS) according to the sorted scores and bounding boxes to filter out potentially redundant bounding boxes, get the final bounding boxes, and send them to the next stage.

Fig. 8.92 provides the operation logic of the first-stage postprocessing fusion operator (the dark part). As mentioned earlier, the fusion operator has a total of four inputs and one output. The inputs are Predict Box, representing the bounding box offset output by RPN; Anchor Box, representing the predefined bounding box output

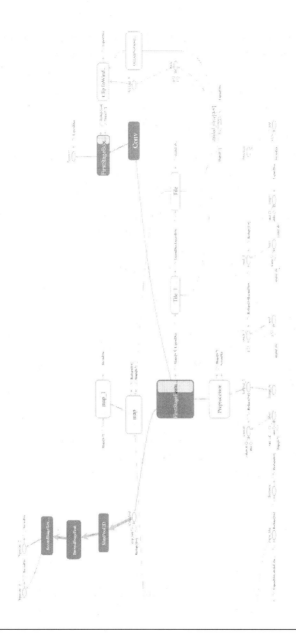

FIGURE 8.91

Part of the Faster R-CNN computation graph viewed from TensorBoard.[11]

by Anchor; Img Shape, representing the image size; and Predict Score, representing the score output by RPN. The output is the Proposal Box for the next stage.

---

[11] Fig. 8.91 and Fig. 8.102 were generated by TensorBoard.

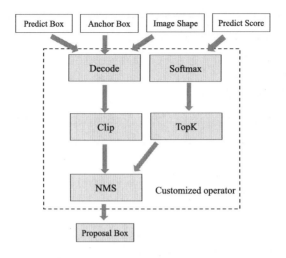

FIGURE 8.92

Faster R-CNN first-stage postprocessing customized operator.

For each part of the operation that needs to be implemented using an AI programming language, the detailed introduction is as follows:

(1) Decode and Clip operation

Decode and Clip operations for Predict Box, Anchor Box, and Img Shape are actually calculating the coordinates (cy, cx) of the center of the Anchor and the width and height (w, h). x0, y0, x1, and y1 are the coordinates of the upper left corner and the lower right corner of each anchor, respectively, and are calculated as follows:

$$cy = (y_0 + y_1)/2,$$
$$cx = (x_0 + x_1)/2,$$
$$h = y_1 - y_0,$$
$$w = x_1 - x_0.$$

The above process uses the tensorizing operation in the AI programming language to accelerate the program (where ANCHOR_NUM is the number of anchors), as shown in Fig. 8.93.

Calculate the center coordinates and width and height of the corrected frame in Decode. dx, dy, dw, and dh are the offsets of the four bounding boxes in each Predict Box, respectively corresponding to the offset of the center coordinates cx, cy and the offset of width and height of the bounding boxes. We have

$$ncy = cy + dy \times h,$$
$$ncx = cx + dx \times w,$$

```
1   __vec_add(cy, anchor_y0, anchor_y1, ANCHOR_NUM);
2   __vec_mul_const(cy, cy, 0.5, ANCHOR_NUM);
3
4   __vec_add(cx, anchor_x0, anchor_yx, ANCHOR_NUM);
5   __vec_mul_const(cx, cx, 0.5, ANCHOR_NUM);
6
7   __vec_sub(h, anchor_y1, anchor_y0, ANCHOR_NUM);
8   __vec_sub(w, anchor_x1, anchor_x0, ANCHOR_NUM);
```

FIGURE 8.93

Anchor coordinate calculation.

$$nh = exp(dh) \times h,$$
$$nw = exp(dw) \times w.$$

The above process is accelerated by the tensorizing operation in the AI programming language, as shown in Fig. 8.94.

```
1    __vec_mul(tmp1, dy, h, ANCHOR_NUM);
2    __vec_add(ncy, tmp1, cy, ANCHOR_NUM);
3
4    __vec_mul(tmp2, dx, w, ANCHOR_NUM);
5    __vec_add(ncx, tmp2, cx, ANCHOR_NUM);
6
7    __vec_exp(tmp3, dh, ANCHOR_NUM);
8    __vec_exp(tmp4, dW, ANCHOR_NUM);
9
10   __vec_mul(nh, tmp3, h, ANCHOR_NUM);
11   __vec_mul(nw, tmp4, w, ANCHOR_NUM)
```

FIGURE 8.94

Correct the center coordinates and width and height of the frame.

Calculate the minimum and maximum x, y coordinates of the corrected frame; that is, perform a clip operation on the decoded bounding boxes. Now we have

$$y_{min} = max(ncy - nh/2, 0.0),$$
$$x_{min} = max(ncx - nw/2, 0.0),$$
$$y_{max} = min(ncy + nh/2, img\_h),$$
$$x_{max} = min(ncx + nw/2, img\_w).$$

The above process is accelerated by the tensorizing operation in the AI programming language, as shown in Fig. 8.95. Among them, __vec_maximum compares all elements in the vector with the specified scalar and takes the maximum value; __vec_minimum compares all the elements in the vector with the specified scalar and takes the minimum value.

```
1   __vec_mul_const(nh, nh, 0.5, ANCHOR_NUM);
2   __vec_sub(tmp1, ncy, nh, ANCHOR_NUM);
3   __vec_maximum(y_min, tmp1, 0, ANCHOR_NUM);
4
5   __vec_mul_const(nw, nw, 0.5, ANCHOR_NUM);
6   __vec_sub(tmp2, ncx, nw, ANCHOR_NUM);
7   __vec_maximum(x_min, tmp2, 0, ANCHOR_NUM);
8
9   __vec_add(tmp3, ncy, nh, ANCHOR_NUM);
10  __vec_minimum(y_max, tmp3, img_h, ANCHOR_NUM);
11
12  __vec_add(tmp4, ncx, nw, ANCHOR_NUM);
13  __vec_minimum(x_max, tmp4, img_w, ANCHOR_NUM);
```

FIGURE 8.95

Clip operation on the bounding box.

(2) Softmax and TopK operations

We perform softmax and TopK operations on the Predict Score output by RPN to obtain K bounding boxes that may be the target with higher probability. The key code for accelerating softmax and TopK operations using AI programming language is shown in Fig. 8.96.

```
1   //do softmax:
2   //exp(score_ + ANCHOR_NUM)/(exp(score_)+exp(score_+ANHOR_NUM)
3   __vec_exp(tmp1, score_ + ANCHOR_NUM, ANCHOR_NUM);
4   __vec_exp(tmp2, score_, ANCHOR_NUM);
5   __vec_add(tmp2, tmp1, tmp2, ANCHOR_NUM);
6   __vec_recip(tmp2, tmp2, ANCHOR_NUM);
7   __vec_mul(score_, tmp1, tmp2, ANCHOR_NUM);
8
9   //find top score
10  __vec_max(result, score_, ANCHOR_NUM);
11  local_max_idx = (int16_t)(*(uint16_t *)(result + 1));
12  local_max_score = result[0];
```

FIGURE 8.96

Softmax and TopK calculation acceleration.

(3) NMS operation

According to the ranking score and the bounding boxes, NMS is performed to filter out the bounding boxes that may be redundant, to obtain the final bounding boxes and send them to the next stage. The main calculation steps of NMS are: (1) Calculating the area of all candidate boxes (BOX_COUNT); (2) Taking out the box with the highest probability in the current candidate box and set its probability score as NE_INF; (3) Selecting the candidate boxes and the remaining boxes, then calculate their intersection ratio (IoU) in turn; (4) For boxes with IoU greater than the threshold, set the probability score to NE_INF; (5) Looping back to step 2 to continue until NMS_NUM candidate boxes are found. The corresponding key AI programming language code is shown in Fig. 8.97.

```
1    //calc box_area
2    __vec_sub(box_h, box_y2, box_y1, BOX_COUNT);
3    __vec_sub(box_w, box_x2, box_x1, BOX_COUNT);
4    __vec_mul(area, box_h, box_w, BOX_COUNT);
5    //find_top_score
6    __vec_max(result, score, BOX_COUNT);
7    max_score = result[0];
8    idx = (int16_t)(*(uint16_t *)(result + 1));
9    box_target_0 = box_x1[idx];
10   box_target_1 = box_x2[idx];
11   box_target_2 = box_y1[idx];
12   box_target_3 = box_y2[idx];
13   area_idx = area[idx];
14   __memset(tmp_area, area_idx, BOX_COUNT);
15   //calc IOU
16   __vec_maximum(inter_x1, box_x1, box_target_0, BOX_COUNT);
17   __vec_minimum(inter_x2, box_x2, box_target_1, BOX_COUNT);
18   __vec_maximum(inter_y1, box_y1, box_target_2, BOX_COUNT);
19   __vec_minimum(inter_y2, box_y2, box_target_3, BOX_COUNT);
20
21   //max(0, inter_x2 - inter_x1);
22   __vec_sub(tmp1, inter_x2, inter_x1, BOX_COUNT);
23   __vec_relu(inter_x, tmp1, BOX_COUNT);
24
25   //max(0, inter_y2 - inter_1);
26   __vec_sub(tmp2, inter_y2, inter_y1, BOX_COUNT);
27   __vec_relu(inter_y, tmp2, BOX_COUNT);
28
29   /*inter area = max(0, inter_x2 - inter_x1) *
30   max(0, inter_y2 - inter_y1);*/
31   __vec_mul(inter_area, inter_x, inter_y, BOX_COUNT);
32
33   //over = area[idx] + area[k] - inter_area
34   __vec_add(over_area, tmp_area, area, BOX_COUNT);
35   __vec_sub(over_area, over_area, inter_area, BOX_COUNT);
36   //iou
37   __vec_mul_const(tmp_iou, over_area, NMS_THRESH, BOX_COUNT);
38   __vec_le(iou, inter_area, tmp_iou, BOX_COUNT);
39   __vec_not(final, iou, BOX_COUNT);
40   __vec_mul_const(final, final, NE_INF, BOX_COUNT);
41   __vec_mul(score, score, iou, BOX_COUNT);
42   __vec_add(score, score, final, BOX_COUNT);
```

FIGURE 8.97

NMS computing acceleration.

- *Second-stage postprocessing fusion operator*

The second-stage postprocessing fusion operator is at the end of the entire network, and its main functions are as follows: (1) Performing the Decode operation on the bounding box offsets (i.e., Box Encoding) output by the second-stage and the bounding boxes (i.e., Proposal Box) output by the first-stage postprocessing to obtain the offset bounding boxes and perform cropping operations on all the bounding boxes so that they do not exceed the boundary of the original picture. (2) Performing the softmax operation on multiclassification of the second-stage output (the COCO dataset has 90 categories) score to obtain the probability score to which category each bounding box belongs. (3) Performing NMS according to the multiclassification result after softmax and the bounding boxes after Decode to filter out the bounding boxes that may be redundant in the same category, and get the final bounding box coordinates, category, and score.

Fig. 8.98 provides the operation logic of the second stage postprocessing fusion operator (the dark part). As mentioned earlier, the fusion operator has a total of four inputs and one output. The inputs are the bounding box offset (Box Encoding), representing the output of the second stage; the target bounding box (Proposal Box), representing the output of the first-stage postprocessing; the image shape (Image Shape), representing the size of the picture; and the predict score (Predict Score), representing the score output of the second stage. The output is the output of the entire network, including the coordinates, scores, and categories of the bounding boxes.

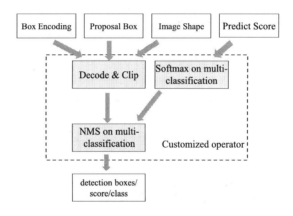

FIGURE 8.98

Faster R-CNN second-stage postprocessing customized operator.

It can be seen that the logic of the second-stage postprocessing fusion operator has something in common with the first-stage postprocessing fusion operator, and both need to perform Decode and Clip operations with offsets on the input bounding box. The logic of the AI programming language code here is similar to the first-stage postprocessing. At the same time, the second-stage postprocessing fusion operator also needs to perform softmax and NMS operations, but here is a process for multiclassification, so both softmax and NMS need to add a "for" loop to process multiclassification.

8.8.3.3 Fusion operator substitution

After the fusion operator logic is realized through the AI programming language, the graph node replacement must be carried out. As shown on the left side of Fig. 8.99, the dark color indicates that the current programming framework has supported operators running on DLP, and the light color indicates that the software stack does not support operators (need to be executed on the CPU). There are three operators in this network that are not currently supported. We have implemented ReplacedOp through

AI programming language to get the network on the right. Specifically, the optimization of the network mainly includes two steps. One is to generate a configuration file, which describes the original operator to be replaced, the replaced operator, and input and output nodes. The other is to optimize the original graph based on the generated configuration file.

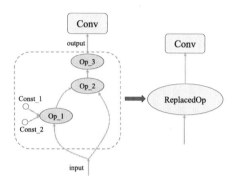

FIGURE 8.99

Fusion operator replacement example.

- *Generate configuration file*

For the network to be optimized, first use TensorBoard to see which operators can be merged into a large operator for replacement. Find out the input and output of these operators, use breadth first search according to the input and output to find out the name of the operator that needs to be replaced, and finally generate the replacement configuration file. As shown in Fig. 8.99, the three operators Op_1, Op_2, and Op_3 can be replaced. The input node names are input, Const_1, and Const_2, and the output node name is output.

Use Faster R-CNN as an example. There are three main operators in the network that need to be replaced. They are the postprocessing in the first stage (following the RPN), Anchor generation, and the postprocessing in the second stage. Get its input and output through TensorBoard, get the name of the operator that needs to be replaced, and replace it with the three operators PostprocessRPN, AnchorGenerator, and SecondStagePostprocess. Furthermore, the corresponding configuration file is automatically generated through the faster_rcnn_node_definition.py script. Fig. 8.100 shows the specific implementation of searching for operators related to Anchor generation in the script.

In the program, match_start_list and match_end_list indicate the input and output names of the operators that need to be replaced, and the bfs_for_reachable_nodes function is used to find the corresponding nodes. The returned node list includes not only unsupported operators, but also other operators under the same name_scope. All operators in the returned list will be replaced at the same time. The final configuration file is shown in Fig. 8.101. Model represents the network name, Replace_Node_Name represents the name of the node to be replaced, Replace_Node

```
1  def anchor_check(op_name):
2      match_start_list=
3          ['Shape_1','strided_slice_2','strided_slice_3']
4      match_end_list = ['ClipToWindow/Gather/Gather']
5      match_name_list = bfs_for_reachable_nodes(match_end_list,
6          tf_graphdef.map_name_to_input_name, match_start_list)
7      match_name_list = set([name.split('/')[0]
8          for name in match_name_list])
9      return match_name_list
```

FIGURE 8.100

Search for operators related to Anchor generation.

represents the operator name and related attribute information after replacement, and Input_Node and Output_Node represent the input and output node names of the converted network, respectively.

- *Generate replacement pb file*

Write a Python script according to the configuration file to convert the original pb. First traverse the entire graph to obtain all computing nodes, then replace the nodes in the network according to the information of the replacement node in the configuration file, and finally generate the converted pb file. The generated network structure is shown in Fig. 8.102, where the two arrows point to the replaced operator, which are the first-stage postprocessing operator PostprocessRPN and the second-stage postprocessing operator SecondStagePostprocess. Among them, AnchorGenerator can save the generated coordinate frame as a constant in pb when replacing the operator.

8.8.3.4 Fusion operator integration

The first-stage and second-stage postprocessing fusion operators developed earlier need to be further integrated into the TensorFlow framework, that is, adding the related calls of PostprocessPRN and SecondStagePostprocess to TensorFlow to enable it to be executed on DLP.

Specifically, the TensorFlow directory tree that needs to be modified is shown in Fig. 8.103. The modification under tensorflow/core is mainly to complete the C++ interface registration of the customized operator and the wrapper implementation of the forward inference function; the modification in the tensorflow/python directory is mainly to complete the Python interface registration of the customized operator; the modification in the tensorflow/stream_executor/dlp directory is mainly to add a customized operator call Implementation of the interface. In the tensorflow/stream_executor/dlp directory, you also need to place the *.o file obtained by compiling the customized operator *.dlp file.

As shown in Fig. 8.104, use the first-stage postprocessing fusion operator as an example. The registration of customized operation in tensorflow/core/ops/ postprocess_rpn_ops.cc requires the user to specify the name of the registered oper-

```
 1   [ Model ]
 2   Faster R–CNN
 3
 4   [ Replace_Node_Name ]
 5   second_stage_postprocess = [ 'detection_boxes ',
 6       u'SecondStagePostprocessor ', 'detection_classes ', u'add ',
 7       'detection_scores ', 'num_detections ', u'Squeeze_2 ',
 8       u'Squeeze_3 ',u'map_1 ']
 9   image_tensor = [ 'image_tensor ']
10   postprocess_rpn = [u'Slice ', u'strided_slice_10 ', u'ExpandDims ',
11       u'Reshape ', u'ExpandDims_4 ', u'ExpandDims_5 ',
12       u'ExpandDims_1 ', u'ExpandDims_2 ',u'ExpandDims_3 ', u'Tile ',
13       u'strided_slice_6 ', u'Reshape_4 ', u'Reshape_2 ',
14       u'BatchMultiClassNonMaxSuppression ', u'Reshape_1 ',
15       u'Squeeze_1 ', u'Squeeze ', u'map ', u'zeros_like ',
16       u'zeros_like_1 ', u'strided_slice_8 ', u'strided_slice_9 ',
17       u'Tile_1 ', u'strided_slice_11 ', u'strided_slice_4 ',
18       u'strided_slice_5 ', u'Shape_3 ', u'Shape_2 ', u'Shape_5 ',
19       u'Shape_4 ', u'concat ', u'Reshape_3 ', u'Decode ',
20       u'ToFloat_5 ', u'Softmax ', u'stack_2 ', u'stack_1 ',
21       u'strided_slice_12 ', u'Tile_2 ']
22   tofloat = [ 'ToFloat_3 ']
23   preprocessor = [ 'Preprocessor/map ']
24   anchor_const = [u'GridAnchorGenerator ', u'ToFloat_4 ',
25       u'strided_slice ', u'ClipToWindow ', u'Shape_1 ',
26       u'strided_slice_1 ', u'stack ', u'strided_slice_2 ',
27       u'strided_slice_3 ']
28   true_image_shape = [ '/Preprocessor/map/TensorArrayStack_1 ']
29
30   [ Replace_Node ]
31   second_stage_postprocess = { 'max_size_per_class ': 20,
32       'max_total_size ': 100, 'iou_thresh ': 0.6,
33       'num_classes ': 90, 'name ': 'postprocess ',
34       'max_num_proposal ': 100, 'int8mode ': 0,
35       'score_thresh ': 0.4, 'scale_x ': 0.1, 'scale_y ': 0.2, 'op ':
36       'SecondStagePostprocess '}
37   image_tensor = { 'dtype ': tf.float32, 'shape ': [1, 600, 800, 3],
38       'name ': 'Input ', 'op ': 'Placeholder '}
39   postprocess_rpn = { 'name ': 'postprocess_rpn ',
40       'max_size_per_class ': 100,
41       'max_total_size ': 100, 'score_thresh ': 0.0,
42       'iou_thresh ': 0.7, 'op ': 'PostprocessRpn '}
43   tofloat = { 'dtype ': tf.float32, 'shape ': [1, 600, 800, 3],
44       'name ': 'Input ', 'op ': 'Placeholder '}
45   preprocessor = { 'dtype ': tf.float32, 'shape ': [1, 600, 800, 3],
46       'name ': 'Input ', 'op ': 'Placeholder '}
```

FIGURE 8.101

Faster R-CNN operator replacement configuration file.

ator, the names and numbers of input and output tensors, and other parameter names, types, and default values of the customized operator. The registered customized operator is named PostprocessRPN, and there are four inputs and one output. In addition, there are seven attribute values, and their types and default values are given.

As shown in Fig. 8.105, in tensorflow/core/kernels/postprocess_rpn_dlp_op.cc, it is necessary to implement the outermost wrapper for forward inference of the customized operator function. As shown in Fig. 8.105, it contains the dlpPostrpcessRpnOp class. The Compute function in this class is the entry point

```
47   anchor_const
48         = {'anchor_offsets': [0.0, 0.0],
49          'shape': [1, 38, 50, 48],
50          'base_anchor_sizes': [256.0, 256.0],
51        'batch_image_shape': [1, 600, 800, 3],
52        'name': 'AnchorGenerator', 'scales': [0.25, 0.5, 1, 2],
53        'dtype': tf.float32, 'anchor_strides': [16.0, 16.0],
54        'feature_map_shape_list': [(38, 50)],
55        'aspect_ratios': [0.5, 1, 2]}
56   true_image_shape = {'dtype': tf.int32, 'shape': [1, 3], 'name':
57        'Batch_image_shape', 'op': 'Placeholder'}
58
59   [Input_Node]
60   node_name1 = [Input]
61   node_name2 = [Batch_image_shape]
62
63   [Output_Node]
64   node_name1 = [postprocess]
```

FIGURE 8.101

(*continued*)

for the forward inference of the customized operator. This function gets the input tensor and attributes of the customized operator, then creates the output tensor and allocates memory for it, and finally calls the PostprocessRpn function that actually performs the operation in the executor.

The C++ code under ops and lib_ops in tensorflow/stream_executor/dlp is where the forward operation of the customized operator is actually implemented. Follow the programming process in Section 8.8.1.2 to open up space for input and output tensors in turn, copy the input tensor to dlp, create a CustomizedOp for the customized operator, and finally perform the corresponding forward inference operation. Among them, the customized operator interfaces that need to be called are CreateCustomizedOp and ComputeCustomizedOp. CreateCustomizedOp creates a customized operator based on the number of inputs and outputs in the current customized operator, the name of the Kernel function, and other attributes, and maps it to the code developed by the AI programming language. ComputeCustomizedOp actually performs forward inference of the customized operator, enters the Kernel function of the customized operator, and starts executing the corresponding instructions on dlp.

Fig. 8.106 shows the definition and execution of the first-stage postprocessing fusion operator. First, four input tensors and one output tensor are defined. After that, specify the corresponding parameter buffer and call the CreateCustomizedOp interface to define a customized operation. The following code shows how to call ComputeCustomizedOp to complete the forward operation, which needs the addresses of the input and output tensors.

The processing of the second-stage postprocessing fusion operator is similar to the above process, including the registration of the operator, the implementation of the wrapper function, and the realization of the forward operation.

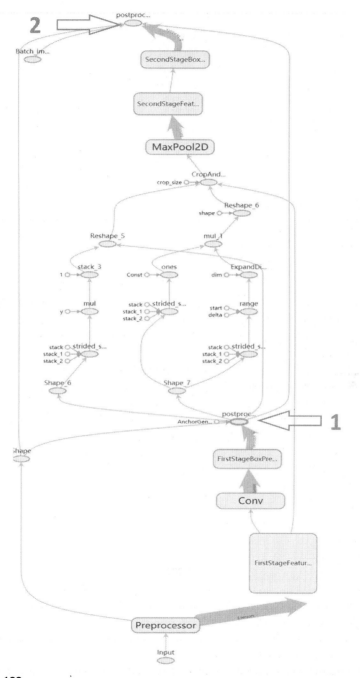

FIGURE 8.102

Faster R-CNN network structure after postprocessing operator replacement.

```
1   tensorflow/
2   ├ core
3   │   ├ BUILD
4   │   ├ kernels
5   │   │   ├ BUILD
6   │   │   ├ postprocess_rpn_op.cc
7   │   │   ├ postprocess_rpn_op.h
8   │   │   ├ postprocess_rpn_op_dlp.h
9   │   │   ├ second_stage_postprocess_op.cc
10  │   │   ├ second_stage_postprocess_op.h
11  │   │   └ second_stage_postprocess_op_dlp.h
12  │   └ ops
13  │       ├ postprocess_rpn_ops.cc
14  │       └ second_stage_postprocess_ops.cc
15  ├ python
16  │   ├ BUILD
17  │   └ ops
18  │       ├ postprocess_rpn_ops.py
19  │       └ second_stage_postprocess_ops.py
20  └ stream_executor
21      ├ BUILD
22      └ dlp
23          ├ lib_ops
24          │   ├ dlp_postprocess_rpn_op.cc
25          │   └ dlp_second_stage_postprocess_op.cc
26          ├ dlp.h
27          ├ dlp_lib_common.cc
28          ├ dlp_lib_math_ops.h
29          ├ dlp_lib_nn_ops.h
30          ├ dlp_stream.cc
31          ├ dlp_stream.h
32          ├ ops
33          │   ├ postprocess_rpn_op.cc
34          │   └ second_stage_postprocess_op.cc
35          ├ postprocess_rpn_kernel.h
36          ├ postprocess_rpn_kernel.dlp
37          ├ postprocess_rpn_kernel.o
38          ├ postprocess_rpn_kernel_singlecore.dlp
39          ├ second_stage_postprocess_kernel.h
40          ├ second_stage_postprocess_kernel.dlp
41          └ second_stage_postprocess_kernel.o
```

FIGURE 8.103

Modify the TensorFlow catalog file to integrate the fusion operator.

8.8.3.5 Analysis of optimization results

Previously, we used Faster R-CNN as an example to perform system-level analysis and optimization. According to the results of the analysis, it is clear that the performance bottleneck is caused by a large number of operators not supported by the DLP software stack. Because these operators run on the CPU, it is impossible to use fusion optimization, and it also leads to an increase in cross-device data communication. By customizing operations with similar locations and the same function as a large fusion operator, using AI programming language, and implementing the replacement of the original node by the customized operator through the graph optimization tool, then finally integrating it through the relevant interface in the framework, the processing performance is improved.

```
1   namespace tensorflow {
2   REGISTER_OP("PostprocessRPN")
3     //input
4     .Input("rpn_box_encodings_batch:_float32")
5     .Input("rpn_objectness_predictions_with_background_batch:
6     _____float32")
7     .Input("image_shapes:_int32")
8     .Input("anchors:_float32")
9     //output
10    .Output("proposal_boxes:_float32")
11
12    //attr
13    .Attr("score_thresh:_float_=_0.0")
14    .Attr("iou_thresh:_float_=_0.7")
15    .Attr("max_size_per_class:_int_=_300")
16    .Attr("max_total_size:_int_=_300")
17    .Attr("scale_xy:_float_=_0.1")
18    .Attr("scale_wh:_float_=_0.2")
19    .Attr("min_nms_score:_float_=_0.01")
20
21    //shape
22    .SetShapeFn([](::tensorflow::shape_inference::
23                InferenceContext* c) {
24    });
25  } //namespace tensorflow
```

FIGURE 8.104

Registration of the first-stage postprocessing fusion operator.

Table 8.16 Data flow diagram before and after Faster R-CNN optimization.

Calculator type	Original Faster R-CNN	Optimized Faster R-CNN
Total number of nodes	11,171	679
Number of DLP processing nodes	3590	370
Number of CPU processing nodes	7581	309
The total number of fusion stages	295	6

Table 8.16 gives the computation graph before and after optimization. The following observations can be made: (1) Due to the use of AI programming languages to implement customized operators, the total number of calculation nodes in the network has dropped significantly, a large number of finely divided nodes originally running on the CPU are integrated into regular customized operators and run on DLP, and the proportion of calculations running on DLP has increased significantly, making full use of the computing resources of DLP. (2) The number of fusion segments has been greatly reduced, from 295 segments to only 6 segments, allowing DLP to perform better fusion strategies and also reducing the cost of data copy between DLP and CPU.

Fig. 8.107 further gives a comparison of the performance. Since the number of nodes running on the CPU has decreased, the data copying time and CPU runtime

```
1   namespace tensorflow {
2
3   class dlpPostprocessRpnOp : public OpKernel {
4   public:
5     /// \brief Constructor.
6     /// \param context
7     explicit dlpPostprocessRpnOp(OpKernelConstruction* context):
8     OpKernel(context) {
9     }
10
11    void Compute(OpKernelContext* context) override {
12      // Get input tensor
13      const Tensor& rpn_box_encodings_batch = context->input(0);
14      const Tensor&
15          rpn_objectness_predictions_with_background_batch =
16          context->input(1);
17      const Tensor& image_shapes = context->input(2);
18      const Tensor& anchors = context->input(3);
19
20      // Create output tensor
21      Tensor* proposal_box = NULL;
22      OP_REQUIRES_OK(context, context->allocate_output(0,
23      proposal_box_shape, &proposal_box));
24
25      auto* stream = context->op_device_context()->dlp_stream();
26      stream->PostprocessRpn(context,
27      const_cast<Tensor*>(&rpn_box_encodings_batch),
28          const_cast<Tensor*>
29          (&rpn_objectness_predictions_with_background_batch),
30          const_cast<Tensor *>(&anchors), &tmp_tensor,
31          batch_size, num_anchors, max_nms_out, iou_thresh_,
32          im_height, im_width,
33          feature_h, feature_w, anchor_per_feature,
34          scale_xy_, scale_wh_, min_nms_score_,
35          proposal_box);
36    }
37  };
38  } //namespace tensorflow
```

FIGURE 8.105

The first-stage postprocessing fusion operator encapsulation.

have dropped significantly, among which the copying time has dropped 6-fold and the total CPU runtime has dropped 12-fold. At the same time, due to the use of optimized customized operators, the runtime on DLP is also greatly reduced, and the overall performance is improved nearly 8-fold.

8.9 Exercises

8.1 Use C++ and Python to write a program to calculate the variance of 4096 random numbers, and then run it on the same hardware platform. Obtain the execution time of both and conduct a brief analysis of their performance and development efficiency.

```
1    Tensor_t input_ptr [4];
2    input_ptr[0] = rpn_box_encodings_batch->dlp_tensor();
3    input_ptr[1] =
4    rpn_objectness_predictions_with_background_batch->dlp_tensor();
5    input_ptr[2] = anchors->dlp_tensor();
6    input_ptr[3] = tmp_tensor->dlp_tensor();
7
8    Tensor_t output_ptr[1];
9    output_ptr[0] = proposal_box->dlp_tensor();
10
11
12   GetKernelParamsBuffer(&params);
13
14   ... ...
15
16   CreateCustomizedOp(&postprocess_rpn_op,
17                  "POSTPROCESSRPN",
18                  reinterpret_cast <void *>(&PostprocessRpnKernel),
19                  params,
20                  input_ptr,
21                  input_num,
22                  output_ptr,
23                  output_num,
24                  nullptr,
25                  0);
26
27   ... ...
28
29   void *in_addr[]   = {inputs[0]->dlp_addr(),
30   inputs[1]->dlp_addr(), inputs[2]->dlp_addr(),
31   inputs[3]->dlp_addr()};
32   void *out_addr[]  = {outputs[0]->dlp_addr()};
33
34   ComputeCustomizedOp(postprocess_rpn_op,
35                     in_addr, inputs.size(),
36                     out_addr, outputs.size(),
37                     queue);
```

FIGURE 8.106

Definition and execution of the first-stage postprocessing fusion operator.

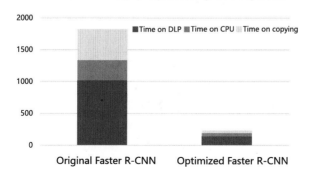

FIGURE 8.107

Performance comparison before and after Faster R-CNN optimization.

```
1   #define N 1024
2   void (int* a, int*b) {
3           for (int i = 0; i < N; i++) {
4                   b[0] += a[i];
5           }
6   }
```

```
1   #define N 1024
2   void (int* a, int*b) {
3           for (int i = 0; i < N / 64; i++) {
4                   sum_pooling(a, b, 64);
5           }
6   }
```

FIGURE 8.108

Scalar statement code (top) and Tensor statement code (bottom).

8.2 Assume that the memory unit of a processor includes an on-chip cache and an off-chip DDR, and the access time is 4 clock cycles and 150 clock cycles, respectively. The workload has a hit rate of 90% on the on-chip cache and the processor will only access the off-chip DDR when the on-chip cache is missed. How many clock cycles is the average access latency of the entire storage hierarchy?

8.3 According to the content of Section 8.3.2, suppose that on a multicore, each task can complete the vector bitwise addition of N=256 at one time. Now we need to complete the vector bitwise addition of two lengths of 2048. (1) Does the task type need to be divided into BLOCK or UNIONx? (2) If UNIONx is selected, what is x?

8.4 In the general processor-side process of the heterogeneous programming model, what are the two process steps between creating STREAM and starting the kernel?

8.5 Suppose an 8-bit binary number is 10011001. (1) If it represents an unsigned integer uint8, what is the number of it if converted to a decimal number? (2) If it represents a signed integer int8, what is the number of it if converted to a decimal number?

8.6 (1) Suppose there is a 32-bit floating-point number whose binary form is 1100 0010 1111 1111 0000 0000 0000 0000. According to the IEEE 754 standard, what is its number if converted to a decimal? (2) If the binary number is 1000 0000 0100 0000 0000 0000 0000 0000, what is its number if converted to a decimal?

8.7 Fig. 8.108 shows two pieces of code with the same function; one is written with scalar statements, and the other is written with tensor statements. Both sum all the data in a vector. Assuming that the hardware requires one clock cycle to complete a scalar addition instruction, it takes eight clock cycles to complete a 64-element vector sum instruction (sum_pooling). Assuming that the time for other operations and memory access in the program is negligible, how many times the performance of the tensor program is that of the scalar program?

8.8 Proof: Why is the maximum representable value of float16 65,504?

*8.9 Programming practice: based on the DLP-BCL AI programming language, use scalar calculation statements to write a program of the L^2 pooling algorithm, including the runtime code on the host side. Find the algorithm yourself. Refer to the BCL user manual.

*8.10 Use the notification interface provided by the DLP runtime library to calculate the runtime of the program written in Exercise 8.9.

*8.11 Optimize the programs written in Exercise 8.9 for "using on-chip cache" and "tensorization," respectively, and use the notification interface to calculate the time.

*8.12 Apply four-core parallel optimization to the program written in Exercise 8.11, and use the notification interface to calculate the time.

Practice: AI computing systems

9

Previous chapters have introduced the basic theories behind artificial intelligent computing systems, including deep learning algorithms, the use and principles of programming frameworks, the principles and architecture of deep learning processors (DLPs), and AI programming languages. This chapter connects the previously introduced content through experiments so that readers can truly understand how to make full use of the DLP hardware features to develop high-performance operators, and how the software stack calls operators to complete deep learning algorithms on hardware, which could enhance systematic understanding of artificial intelligent computing systems. In this chapter, a real-time image style transfer algorithm is implemented on DLP. For the algorithm flow, refer to Section 3.6.2. In the experiment, two key operators of the style transfer process, the difference square operator and the fractionally strided convolution operator, are implemented based on the AI programming language. These operators are integrated into the TensorFlow framework. Finally, the image style transfer algorithm is achieved by calling the TensorFlow API and the runtime system. The environment of the experiment adopts a system with a cloud platform combined with a development board. For detailed introduction and instructions, refer to Appendix B.

9.1 Basic practice: image style transfer
9.1.1 Operator implementation based on AI programming language
This section takes the difference square operator and fractionally strided convolution operator involved in the image style transfer algorithm as an example. This section uses the AI programming language to realize these two operators and analyzes the precision of the implemented operators.

9.1.1.1 Difference square operator
The difference square operator calculates the Hadamard product of two identical tensors of $X-Y$, i.e., the elementwise square of tensor $X-Y$. The implementation definition is

$$Hadamard(X - Y) = (X - Y) \circ (X - Y). \qquad (9.1)$$

The code example that uses the AI programming language to realize the difference square operator is shown in Fig. 9.1.

```
1    #define ONELINE 256
2
3    __dlp_entry__ void SquaredDiffKernel(half* input1,
4        half* input2, half* output, int32_t len)
5    {
6        __nram__ int32_t quotient = len / ONELINE;
7        __nram__ int32_t rem = len % ONELINE;
8        __nram__ half input1_nram[ONELINE];
9        __nram__ half input2_nram[ONELINE];
10
11       for (int32_t i = 0; i < quotient; i++)
12       {
13           __memcpy(input1_nram, input1 + i * ONELINE,
14           ONELINE * sizeof(half), GDRAM2NRAM);
15           __memcpy(input2_nram, input2 + i * ONELINE,
16           ONELINE * sizeof(half), GDRAM2NRAM);
17           __vec_sub(input1_nram, input1_nram, input2_nram, ONELINE);
18           __vec_mul(input1_nram, input1_nram, input1_nram, ONELINE);
19           __memcpy(output +i * ONELINE, input1_nram,
20           ONELINE * sizeof(half), NRAM2GDRAM);
21       }
22
23       if ( rem != 0)
24       {
25           __memcpy(input1_nram, input1 + quotient * ONELINE,
26           rem * sizeof(half), GDRAM2NRAM);
27           __memcpy(input2_nram, input2 + quotient * ONELINE,
28           rem * sizeof(half), GDRAM2NRAM);
29           __vec_sub(input1_nram, input1_nram, input2_nram, rem);
30           __vec_mul(input1_nram, input1_nram, input1_nram, rem);
31           __memcpy(output + quotient * ONELINE, input1_nram,
32           rem * sizeof(half), NRAM2GDRAM);
33       }
34
35   }
```

FIGURE 9.1

Implementation of difference square operator.

9.1.1.2 Fractionally strided convolution operator

Fractionally strided convolution is sometimes called deconvolution. The experimental content of this section uses the AI programming language to implement the fractionally strided convolution operator. Fig. 9.2 shows an example of fractionally strided convolution. The input matrix InputData is a matrix of 2×2, the size of the convolution kernel is 3×3, the convolution stride is 1, and the output matrix OutputData is a matrix of 4×4.

Matrix multiplication can be used to achieve fractionally strided convolution. The specific steps are as follows:

(1) Expand the input matrix InputData into a 4×1 column vector x.
(2) Convert the 3×3 convolution kernel into a 4×16 sparse convolution matrix W,

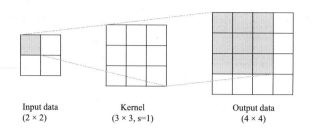

FIGURE 9.2

Fractionally strided convolution.

$$
W = \begin{bmatrix}
w_{0,0} & w_{0,1} & w_{0,2} & 0 & w_{1,0} & w_{1,1} & w_{1,2} & 0 & w_{2,0} & w_{2,1} & w_{2,2} & 0 & 0 & 0 & 0 & 0 \\
0 & w_{0,0} & w_{0,1} & w_{0,2} & 0 & w_{1,0} & w_{1,1} & w_{1,2} & 0 & w_{2,0} & w_{2,1} & w_{2,2} & 0 & 0 & 0 & 0 \\
0 & 0 & 0 & 0 & w_{0,0} & w_{0,1} & w_{0,2} & 0 & w_{1,0} & w_{1,1} & w_{1,2} & 0 & w_{2,0} & w_{2,1} & w_{2,2} & 0 \\
0 & 0 & 0 & 0 & 0 & w_{0,0} & w_{0,1} & w_{0,2} & 0 & w_{1,0} & w_{1,1} & w_{1,2} & 0 & w_{2,0} & w_{2,1} & w_{2,2}
\end{bmatrix}.
$$

where $w_{i,j}$ represents the element in row i and column j of the convolution kernel W.

(3) Compute the matrix transpose of W, that is, $W^\top$:

$$
W^\top = \begin{bmatrix}
w_{0,0} & 0 & 0 & 0 \\
w_{0,1} & w_{0,0} & 0 & 0 \\
w_{0,2} & w_{0,1} & 0 & 0 \\
0 & w_{0,2} & 0 & 0 \\
w_{1,0} & 0 & w_{0,0} & 0 \\
w_{1,1} & w_{1,0} & w_{0,1} & w_{0,0} \\
w_{1,2} & w_{1,1} & w_{0,2} & w_{0,1} \\
0 & w_{1,2} & 0 & w_{0,2} \\
w_{2,0} & 0 & w_{1,0} & 0 \\
w_{2,1} & w_{2,0} & w_{1,1} & w_{1,0} \\
w_{2,2} & w_{2,1} & w_{1,2} & w_{1,1} \\
0 & w_{2,2} & 0 & w_{1,2} \\
0 & 0 & w_{2,0} & 0 \\
0 & 0 & w_{2,1} & w_{2,0} \\
0 & 0 & w_{2,2} & w_{2,1} \\
0 & 0 & 0 & w_{2,2}
\end{bmatrix}.
$$

(4) The fractionally strided convolution operator is equivalent to the product of matrix $W^\top$ and vector x: $y = W^\top \times x$.

(5) The y obtained in the previous step is a vector of 16×1. Modify its shape to a matrix of 4×4 to get the final output data.

The matrix transpose operation in the above procedure can be implemented by calling the __transpose function of the BCL language. The matrix and vector multiplication can be implemented by calling the __mlp function. Refer to the implementation of the difference square operator and use the AI programming language to implement the fractionally strided convolution operator.

9.1.1.3 Precision metrics

To evaluate the precision of the implemented operator on DLP, a common approach is to compare it with the result produced on CPU. The common precision metrics include mean absolute error (MAE) and average relative error (ARE), defined as follows:

$$MAE = \frac{\sum_{i=1}^{n} |CPU_{result} - DLP_{result}|}{n} = \frac{\sum_{i=1}^{n} |e_i|}{n}, \tag{9.2}$$

$$ARE = \frac{\sum |CPU_{result} - DLP_{result}|}{\sum |CPU_{result}|}. \tag{9.3}$$

9.1.1.4 Customized operators integrated into the TensorFlow framework

As introduced in Section 8.8.1, the high-performance library provides a high-performance implementation of common operators on specific platforms. It is convenient for users to directly call them in the form of API. However, for operators that are not defined in the high-performance library, programmers first need to define the operators using the AI programming language, then use the CreateCustomizedOp, ComputeCustomizedOp, and DestroyBaseOp interfaces to implement these customized operators, and finally integrate them into the high-performance library. Next, the programming framework calls and integrates the corresponding operators to expand the supported operators of the programming framework. In this section, the difference square operator and the fractionally strided convolution operator are integrated into the TensorFlow framework. The basic integration process and reference code are given in Section 8.8.1.2 and 8.8.2.2.

9.1.2 Implementation of image style transfer

This section takes the real-time image style transfer algorithm introduced in Section 3.6.2 as an example to introduce implementation of image style transfer prediction on DLP. Refer to the code and data in GitHub.[1] The code can help programmers to complete the image style transfer network training in the TensorFlow framework. In this section, the model parameters are converted into low-bit-width representations. Then, the programming tools are used efficiently to develop the image style transfer based on TensorFlow API and the runtime API.

9.1.2.1 Low-bit-width representation of the model

Deep learning model training usually uses the floating-point format, and the model parameters after training are also in floating-point format. If the size of the deep

---

[1] https://github.com/lengstrom/fast-style-transfer.

learning model is large, the model data in floating-point format, such as the single-precision floating-point format, i.e., float32, may occupy much storage space and memory bandwidth. But if the model file is saved in a low-bit-width data type introduced in Section 6.4.3, such as the 8-bit fixed-point format, the storage space and memory bandwidth can be reduced by three-fourths. The principle of converting a 32-bit floating-point number model into an 8-bit fixed-point number model is briefly described below.

The 32-bit floating point number *value* represented by the int8 type value i is

$$value = \frac{i \times 2^{position}}{scale}, \quad i \in [-128, 127], \tag{9.4}$$

where *position* is the exponential factor and *scale* is the scaling factor, both of which can be obtained through the statistics on the dataset. Deducing the above formula backwards, the int8 type value can be calculated as follows:

$$i = \frac{value \times scale}{2^{position}}. \tag{9.5}$$

Based on Eq. (9.5), a 32-bit floating-point number is converted into an 8-bit fixed-point number. In the experimental setup, a tool called fp32pb_to_quantized_pb.py is provided, which can convert a 32-bit floating-point number model to a fixed-point number model. For the function description, refer to Section 9.1.3.2. The converted model can be directly applied in deep learning inference.

9.1.2.2 Deep learning inference

In the experiment, there are two ways to implement deep learning inference on DLP. The first is to call the high-performance library API from TensorFlow. The API compiles the model files online to generate fused DLP instructions and calls the DLP runtime system API[2] to execute the flow. This process is shown in Fig. 9.3.

The second is to compile the network model file generated by the programming framework and obtain the compiled model file, which has DLP instructions. The model can be directly loaded with the runtime system API to perform inference. This process is shown in Fig. 9.4.

The main difference between the above two approaches is that the former requires online compilation with the overhead of calling the upper framework. The latter does not require online compilation and there is no such overhead; thus the latter executes faster than the former. It is suitable for scenarios with high performance requirements and limited resources, or fixed application scenarios.

1. Programming through the TensorFlow API

The experiment in this section involves implementing image style transfer by calling the high-performance library API using TensorFlow. Specifically, programmers

---

[2] For the runtime system API, please refer to Section 8.5.2.

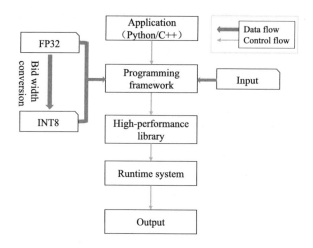

FIGURE 9.3

Programming through the TensorFlow API.

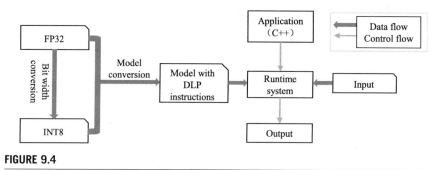

FIGURE 9.4

Programming through the runtime system API.

use TensorFlow API to write code and then load the pb model file to implement the image style transfer. The experiment process is as follows:

(1) Load the model into the computational graph.
(2) Read content image.
(3) Create a session.
(4) Get the input and output tensors in the computational graph through the node names.
(5) Execute the session, read the content image data, and compute the output after the style transfer.
(6) Write output data to image file.

Part of the program code is shown in Fig. 9.5. Fill in the code to complete the program and run the program based on the comments.

```
1   import os
2   import tensorflow as tf
3   from tensorflow.python.platform import gfile
4   import argparse
5   import numpy as np
6   import cv2 as cv
7
8   def parse_arg():
9       parser = argparse.ArgumentParser()
10      parser.add_argument('pb', default='transform.pb')
11      args = parser.parse_args()
12      return args
13
14  def run_pb():
15      args = parse_arg()
16      config = tf.ConfigProto()
17
18      with tf.gfile.FastGFile(args.pb,'rb') as f:
19          graph_def = tf.GraphDef()
20          #todo: 1. parse pb file
21
22          #todo: 2. import graph define
23
24          #todo: 3. read image
25
26          #todo: 4. resize image to 256 x 256
27
28
29      with tf.Session(config=config) as sess:
30          sess.graph.as_default()
31          sess.run(tf.global_variables_initializer())
32
33          #todo: 5. get input tensor by name
34
35          #todo: 6. get out tensor by name
36
37          #todo: 7. run session
38
39          #todo: 8. reshape tensor to [256, 256, 3]
40
41          #todo: 9. convert to numpy tensor
42
43          #todo: 10. write image to jpg file
44
45  def main():
46      run_pb()
47
48  if __name__ == '__main__':
49      main()
```

FIGURE 9.5

Part of the program to realize image style transfer through TensorFlow API programming.

2. Programming through the runtime system API

The experiment in this section uses the runtime system API to implement image style transfer. During the experiment, the programmers first compile the network model pb file generated by TensorFlow and obtain a model file containing DLP instructions. Then, the programmers call the runtime system API to load the pretrained model file and perform prediction. For the runtime system API, refer to Section 8.5.2.

The process of programming using the runtime API is as follows:

(1) Read the image and perform preprocessing.
(2) Initialize the runtime system.
(3) Load model.
(4) Allocate memory on CPU and DLP.
(5) Copy input data from CPU to DLP.
(6) Perform computation on DLP.
(7) Copy output data from DLP to CPU.
(8) Postprocess the output data and write to image file.

9.1.3 Image style transfer practice

9.1.3.1 Implementation of image style transfer based on a cloud platform

1. Programming through TensorFlow API

In the cloud platform experimental environment, the code directory is ~/DLP-Test/style_transfer/style_transfer_online. Edit the load_transform.py file in this directory, complete the code based on the comments, and run. The input content image file is ./images/content.jpg, the network model file is style_transfer.pb, and the image generated after the style transfer is ./result.jpg. The execution of the program is shown in Fig. 9.6.

```
1   cd ~/DLP-Test/style_transfer/style_transfer_online
2   python load_transform.py style_transfer.pb
```

FIGURE 9.6

TensorFlow image style transfer program execution.

After running, a model file style_transfer.DLP with DLP instructions is generated. At the same time, the model file is copied to the program directory ~/DLP-Test/style_transfer/style_transfer_offline to load the program, as shown in Fig. 9.7.

```
1   cp style_transfer.DLP ../style_transfer_offline/offline_model/
```

FIGURE 9.7

Copy model files.

2. Programming through the runtime system API

The program code directory of the runtime system API is ~/DLP-Test/style_transfer/style_transfer_offline. Edit the ./src/src/inference.cpp file and complete the program code, then compile and run the program. The input content image file is ./images/content.jpg. The network model file is ./offline_model/style_transfer.DLP.

The image generated after conversion is ./result_runtime.jpg. The commands of compilation and execution are shown in Fig. 9.8.

```
1  cd ~/DLP–Test/style_transfer/style_transfer_offline/build/
2  cmake ..
3  make
4  cd ..
5  ./run_style_transfer.sh
```

FIGURE 9.8

Runtime system API style transfer program execution.

9.1.3.2 Implementation of image style transfer based on the development board

On the development board, image style transfer can only be implemented through runtime system API programming. The implementation steps are as follows:

(1) Convert a 32-bit floating-point number model file to a low-bit-width fixed-point number model file on the cloud platform.
(2) Convert the low-bit-width model file into a model file containing DLP instructions.
(3) Compile the style transfer program through the cross-compilation tool on the cloud platform to generate the style transfer program on the development board.
(4) Download the style transfer program and the corresponding dependent libraries to the shared file directory of the local network file system (NFS) server.
(5) Connect the development board to the local NFS server so the development board can access the files on the local NFS server.
(6) Run the image style transfer program on the development board.

The concrete implementation steps are detailed below.
1. Low-bit-width conversion of the model
The directory of the model low-bit-width conversion tool is ~/DLP-Test/style_transfer/tools/pb2quantized, and the 32-bit floating-point model file before conversion is style_transfer.pb. The commands of low-bit-width conversion are shown in Fig. 9.9.

```
1  cd ~/DLP–Test/style\_transfer/tools/pb2quantized
2  python fp32pb_to_quantized_pb.py conver_quantized_style_transfer.ini
```

FIGURE 9.9

Low-bit-width model conversion operation.

The low-bit-width model file generated after conversion is ./style_transfer_quantized.pb.

2. Convert the low-bit-width model to a model containing DLP instructions

The directory of the model conversion tool is ~/DLP-Test/style_transfer/tools/pb_to_DLP, and the operation is shown in Fig. 9.10.

```
1   cd ~/DLP-Test/style_transfer/tools/pb_to_DLP
2   cp ../pb2quantized/style_transfer_quantized.pb ./
3   ./pb_to_DLP.sh
```

FIGURE 9.10

The low-bit-width-model is converted to a model containing DLP instructions.

The generated model file is style_transfer.DLP. It is then copied to the ARM program directory to be loaded by the ARM program, as shown in Fig. 9.11

```
1   cp style_transfer.DLP ../../style_transfer_arm/offline_model/
```

FIGURE 9.11

Copy model file.

3. Compile and generate the style transfer program that runs on the development board

The program directory on the development board is ~/DLP-Test/style_transfer/style_transfer_arm. The style transfer program code of the cloud platform and the development board platform are the same. The difference is that a cross-compiler is required to compile program code on the development board. The setting is specified in file CMakeLists.txt in the program directory of the development board. Copy the inference.cpp file written in Section 9.1.3.1 to the ./src directory and then compile it, as shown in Fig. 9.12.

```
1   cd ~/DLP-Test/style_transfer/style_transfer_arm
2   cp ../style_transfer_offline/src/inference.cpp ./src/
3   cd build/
4   cmake ..
5   make
```

FIGURE 9.12

Compile and generate image style transfer program on development board.

4. Download the image style transfer program and dependency libraries to the local directory

Download the image style transfer program and dependency libraries generated in the previous steps to the shared directory of the local NFS. The local Linux environment needs to install the NFS service and set the NFS service directory. Assuming that the local NFS service directory is /opt/DLP/nfs, the local operations are shown in Fig. 9.13.

```
1   cd  /opt/DLP/nfs
2   scp  −P  30300  −r  studentuser000@10.20.30.40:
3         DLP−Test/style_transfer_arm  ./
4   scp  −P  30300  −r  studentuser000@10.20.30.40:
5         DLP−Test/style_transfer/for_AT520/lib32  ./
```

FIGURE 9.13

Download the image style transfer program and dependency libraries to the local directory.

5. Physically connect two devices

Connect the development board and the local NFS server to the same switch, or directly connect the development board and the NFS server with a network cable. Set the IP addresses of the two devices to the same network.

6. Log in to the development board and run the program

Use a remote login method to log in to the development board, assuming that the IP addresses of the development board and the local NFS server are 10.100.8.234 and 10.100.8.235, respectively. The login operation is shown in Fig. 9.14.

```
1   telnet  10.100.8.234
```

FIGURE 9.14

Log in to the development board.

Next, mount the NFS shared directory to the corresponding directory of the development board, as shown in Fig. 9.15.

```
1   mkdir  /NFS
2   mount  −t  nfs  −o  tcp,nolock  10.100.8.235:/opt/DLP/nfs  /NFS
3   cd  /NFS
4   ls
```

FIGURE 9.15

Mount the NFS directory to the development board.

At this time, programmers can see style_transfer_arm and lib32 in the /NFS directory of the development board.

Set environment variables on the development board, as shown in Fig. 9.16.

```
1   export  LD_LIBRARY_PATH=/NFS/lib32
```

FIGURE 9.16

Set environment variables.

Run the image style transfer program on the development board, as shown in Fig. 9.17.

```
1  cd style_transfer_arm/
2  sh run_style_transfer.sh
```

FIGURE 9.17

Run image style transfer program.

After execution, the image file result_runtime.jpg is generated, and the image style transfer on the development board is completed.

9.2 Advanced practice: object detection

Section 8.8.3 introduces the implementation of the Faster R-CNN network. In this section, the steps of implementing this object detection algorithm on the cloud platform are introduced.

9.2.1 Operator implementation based on AI programming language

The two-stage postprocessing of the original version of Faster R-CNN is mainly executed on the CPU, which is expensive. It is necessary to develop corresponding customized operators for the two-stage postprocessing so that they can be executed on DLP.

9.2.1.1 Implementation of PostprocessRpnKernel

The postprocessing fusion operator of the first stage of Faster R-CNN (Postprocess-RpnKernel) is located after the region proposal network (RPN) network. Its main functions are:

1) Decoding the RPN output (predicted box offset and anchor box) to obtain the offset anchor boxes. Then, all the anchor boxes are cropped so that they do not exceed the original image boundary.

2) The two classification scores (whether it is foreground or background) of RPN outputs are operated through the softmax and TopK functions to obtain k highest probability scores and their corresponding anchor boxes.

3) Performing nonmaximum suppression (NMS) operations based on the sorted scores and anchor boxes, filtering out redundant anchor boxes, getting the final anchor boxes, and sending them to the next stage.

The code example of using the AI programming language to implement PostprocessRpnKernel is shown in Fig. 9.18.

```
1   __dlp_entry__  void PostprocessRpnKernel(half *bbox_pred,
2                                            half *scores_,
3                                            half *anchors_,
4                                            half *temp_memory,
5                                            half *out_proposal_box,
6                                            int batch_size,
7                                            int anchors_num,
8                                            int nms_num,
9                                            half nms_thresh,
10                                           half im_h,
11                                           half im_w,
12                                           half scale_xy,
13                                           half scale_wh,
14                                           half min_nms_score) {
15
16    __nram__ half big_nram_buf[NRAM_ELEM_CNT];
17    int AWH_ = anchors_num;
18    int AWH_PLUS_ = ((AWH_ - 1) / ALIGN_SIZE + 1) * ALIGN_SIZE;
19    half im_min_w = 0.0;
20    half im_min_h = 0.0;
21    half scale = 1.0;
22    half nms_scale = 1.0;
23    half stride = 0.0;
24    int fix8 = 0;
25    int valid_box_num = 0;
26
27    for(int i = 0; i < batch_size; i++) {
28      /* Decode the RPN output, and the two classification
29      scores output by RPN are operated on softmax and
30      TopK. */
31      CreateBox_partial(i, batch_size, anchors_, bbox_pred,
32                  scores_, anchors_num,
33                  im_w, im_h, &valid_box_num, scale_xy, scale_wh,
34                  min_nms_score, fix8, big_nram_buf, NRAM_ELEM_CNT,
35                  temp_memory);
36
37      half *box_buf = temp_memory;
38      half *box_y1 = box_buf + AWH_PLUS_ * 0 + ALIGN_UP_TO
39                      (taskId * (AWH_PLUS_ / taskDim), 16);
40      half *box_x1 = box_buf + AWH_PLUS_ * 1 + ALIGN_UP_TO
41                      (taskId * (AWH_PLUS_ / taskDim), 16);
42      half *box_y2 = box_buf + AWH_PLUS_ * 2 + ALIGN_UP_TO
43                      (taskId * (AWH_PLUS_ / taskDim), 16);
44      half *box_x2 = box_buf + AWH_PLUS_ * 3 + ALIGN_UP_TO
45                      (taskId * (AWH_PLUS_ / taskDim), 16);
46      half *box_score = box_buf + AWH_PLUS_ * 4 + ALIGN_UP_TO
47                      (taskId * (AWH_PLUS_ / taskDim), 16);
```

FIGURE 9.18

Implementation of the PostprocessRpnKernel operator.

9.2.1.2 Implementation of SecondStagePostprocessKernel

The postprocessing fusion operator of the second stage of Faster R-CNN, known as SecondStagePostprocessKernel, is at the end of the entire network, and its main functions are:

1) Performing the decode operation on the offsets of the predicted boxes (i.e., Box Encoding) of the second stage and output anchor boxes (i.e., Proposal Box) of

```
48      const int topk_num_aligned = MIN(ALIGN_UP_TO(
49                    valid_box_num, 64),24448);
50      for(int j = valid_box_num; j < topk_num_aligned; j++)
51        *(box_score + j) = NE_INF;
52      half *new_box = big_nram_buf + NRAM_ELEM_CNT -
53                    ALIGN_UP_TO(nms_num, 32) * 5;
54      /* Perform nonmaximum suppression operations based on
55      sorted scores and anchor boxes. */
56      NMS_partial(new_box, nms_thresh, nms_num, topk_num_aligned,
57                    nms_scale,im_h, im_w, AWH_PLUS_,
58                    box_x1, box_y1, box_x2, box_y2,
59                    box_score,emp_memory + AWH_PLUS_ * 5,
60                    big_nram_buf,
61                    NRAM_ELEM_CNT - ALIGN_UP_TO(nms_num, 32) * 5);
62
63      if(taskId == 0) {
64        ReshapeOutput(out_proposal_box, new_box, nms_num,
65                    fix8, i, batch_size);
66      }
67    }
68  }
```

FIGURE 9.18

(*continued*)

the first stage to obtain the offset anchor boxes, and performing cropping operations on all the anchor boxes so that they do not exceed the boundary of the original image.

2) Performing the softmax operation on the multiclassification scores of the second-stage output (COCO dataset has 90 categories) to obtain the probability scores of classification for each anchor box.

3) Performing the NMS operation according to the multiclassification results after softmax and decoding, filtering out the anchor boxes that may be duplicated in the same category, and obtaining coordinates, categories, and scores of the final output boxes.

The code example of using the AI programming language to implement the SecondStagePostprocessKernel operator is shown in Fig. 9.19. Complete and run the program based on the comments.

9.2.1.3 Fusion operator replacement

To replace the operators in the original version of Faster R-CNN code with the corresponding operators implemented with the AI programming language, our cloud platform provides an operator replacement tool, GraphTransformer, and a configuration file, FasterRCNN.config. This configuration file describes which original operators are to be replaced, the replaced operator, and the input and output nodes. The fusion replacement operation is encapsulated in the pb_generate.sh file on the cloud platform, and its implementation is shown in Fig. 9.20.

```
 1   __dlp_entry__  void  SecondStagePostprocessKernel(
 2                                half* image_shape,
 3                                half* proposal_boxes,
 4                                half* box_encoding,
 5                                half* class_predictions,
 6                                half* true_image_shape,
 7                                half* temp_buf,
 8                                half* score_buf,
 9                                half* top_detection,
10                                int batch_size,
11                                int num_classes,
12                                half score_thresh,
13                                half iou_thresh,
14                                int max_size_per_class,
15                                int max_total_size,
16                                int max_num_proposals,
17                                half scale_x,
18                                half scale_y,
19                                int int8mode)
20   {
21   /* todo: 1. Decode the prediction box offset (Box
22         Encoding ) of the second-stage and the anchor box
23         (Proposal Box) output after the first-stage
24         postprocessing.*/
25
26   /* todo: 2. Perform the softmax operation on the
27         multiclass scores output of the second-stage to
28         get the probability score of which class each
29         anchor box should belong to.*/
30   /* todo: 3. Perform NMS operation after softmax and
31         decoding, get the final anchor box coordinates,
32         class and scores.*/
33
34   }
```

FIGURE 9.19

Implementation of the SecondStagePostprocessKernel operator.

```
 1   ./pb_generate.sh
```

FIGURE 9.20

Fusion operator replacement.

9.2.1.4 Fusion operator integration

The operators implemented by the AI programming language need to be further integrated into the TensorFlow framework. The process is the same as in Sections 8.8.1.2 and 8.8.2.2.

9.2.2 Implementation of object detection

The data in this experiment are all in the FP16 format, so there is no need to perform low-bit-width conversion. Programmers can call the high-performance library API through TensorFlow to implement the object detection. Similar to the image style transfer, the implementation process is as follows:

(1) Load the model to the computational graph.
(2) Read the input image.
(3) Create a session.
(4) Get the input and output tensors in the computation graph based on the names of the input and output node.
(5) Execute the session and detect the position of various objects in the input image.
(6) Mark the detection result onto the image.

In the cloud platform experimental environment, the program code directory is ~/DLP-Test/fasterrcnn, the input image file to be tested is ./img_file/image2.jpg, the network model file is ./pb_file/output/ frozen_inference.pb, and the generated image with the detection result is ./img_file /result_image2.png. The operation of the execution program is shown in Fig. 9.21.

| python run_fasterrcnn.py

FIGURE 9.21

TensorFlow object detection program execution.

9.3 Extended practices

Readers can use the AI programming language to implement the following five operators, run them on the DLP, and then compare the accuracy with the CPU implementation.

1. Softmax

Problem description: Use a normalized exponential function (softmax) to make the sum of each matrix column (x) to 1.

The reference formula is as follows:

$$y_i = \frac{e^{x_i}}{\sum_j e^{x_j}}.$$

Generally, in order to avoid the exponential value overflow caused by a large input, all input values need to subtract the max element of x, i.e.,

$$y_i = \frac{e^{x_i - max(x)}}{\sum_j e^{x_j - max(x)}}.$$

Given an input matrix X with the size of $m \times n$ (such as 20×256), use a normalized exponential function for each column to output a normalized matrix with a size of $m \times n$.

It is recommended to use the ARE to compare the accuracy.

2. Cosine similarity

Problem description: Cosine similarity is a similarity measurement. Its output ranges from -1 to $+1$, where 0 means no correlation, a negative value means negative correlation, and a positive value means positive correlation. Implement the operator calculating the cosine similarity between two vectors.

The reference formula is as follows:

$$c(X,Y) = \frac{X \cdot Y}{|X||Y|} = \frac{\sum_{i=1}^{n} X_i Y_i}{\sqrt{\sum_{i=1}^{n} X_i^2}\sqrt{\sum_{i=1}^{n} Y_i^2}}.$$

Given input matrices X and Y with a size of $m \times n$ (such as 256×256), compute the cosine similarity of the corresponding columns and output the $1 \times n$ cosine similarity matrix.

It is recommended to use the MAE to compare the accuracy.

3. Batch normalization

Problem description: In the process of neural network training, the change of the weight parameters of the previous layer will cause the change of the input distribution of each layer afterward, making it difficult to train a very deep neural network. In order to solve this problem, a small learning rate and parameter initialization techniques are usually used, but this results in a slower training speed, especially when training models with saturated nonlinearities. This phenomenon can be solved by batch normalization (BN).

Given the input matrix B with a size of $m \times n$ (such as 128×256), calculate BN row by row and output the normalized matrix.

Reference steps:

(1) Calculate the average value: $\mu_B = \frac{1}{n}\sum_{i=1}^{n} x_i$.

(2) Calculate the variance: $\sigma_B^2 = \frac{1}{n}\sum_{i=1}^{n}(x_i - \mu_B)^2$.

(3) Normalize: $\hat{x}_i = \frac{x_i - \mu_B}{\sqrt{\sigma_B^2 + \epsilon}}$.

(4) Scale and shift: $y_i = \gamma \hat{x}_i + \beta$.

It is recommended to use the MAE to compare the accuracy.

4. Triplet loss

Problem description: The core of triplet loss is a loss function used for minimizing the distance between the anchor example and the positive example, and maximizing the distance from the anchor example to the negative example.

The reference formula is as follows:

$L = max(d(a,p) - d(a,n) + margin, 0)$.

Here, d is the Manhattan distance, that is, the sum of the absolute values of the corresponding coordinate component errors between two points:

$d(X,Y) = \sum_{i=1}^{n}|X_i - Y_i|$.

The final optimization goal is to shorten the distance between a and p and extend the distance between a and n.

It is recommended to use the ARE to compare the accuracy.

5. Pow(x,y)

Problem description: Implement the vector and matrix version of the pow(x,y) function. The reference equation is as follows:

$power(X,Y) = X^Y$,

where the input matrices X and Y with a size of $m \times n$ take the element in X as the base and the corresponding element in Y as the exponent for the exponentiation operation and provide an output matrix with the size of $m \times n$.

It is recommended to use the ARE to compare accuracy.

Fundamentals of computer architecture

In order to help readers understand the architecture of deep learning processors and artificial intelligence computing systems, this chapter introduces some basic concepts about computer architecture, including the instruction sets of general-purpose CPUs and the memory hierarchy in computing systems.

A.1 The instruction set of general-purpose CPUs

To design a deep learning instruction set, one has to learn from the instruction sets of general CPUs, obviously. Therefore, we need to review the instruction sets of general-purpose CPUs.

The instruction set of general-purpose CPUs began to evolve in the 1950s. There are four main design considerations here: versatility, compatibility, ease of use, and efficiency. Regarding versatility, for general-purpose CPUs, the importance of generality of an instruction set is beyond doubt. The instruction set of general-purpose CPUs must efficiently support a variety of past, present, and future applications. Regarding compatibility, the instruction set is the foundation of the CPU ecology and must remain upward compatible for a long time. The most successful examples are x86 and ARM, which have maintained upward compatibility after decades of development, thus supporting a huge ecology. Regarding ease of use, the instruction set should allow programmers to easily develop high-performance programs. Regarding efficiency, the instruction set must be efficient, so that the CPU can be continuously optimized in terms of frequency, energy efficiency, and performance per area.

The instruction set of general-purpose CPUs is also affected by external factors such as silicon technology, operating system, compilation, programming, and applications. From the perspective of technology, the price of early hardware was very expensive, and only circuits with a few gates could be placed in one chip. At that time, designing instruction sets focused on versatility and simplicity for hardware implementation. Today's CPU has about 1 million times more gates integrated than those of 20 years ago. Designing instruction sets requires more attention to other factors, such as how to utilize the memory hierarchy for high efficiency. From the perspective of operating system, it is necessary to consider whether to support multithreading, virtual address security, the security level, etc. From the perspective of compilation and programming, it is necessary to consider the expressiveness of the instruction and how the compiler releases the power of the instruction set. From the perspective of applications, the instruction set design needs to keep pace with the times, adding special instructions regularly for important applications. For example, x86 has added a lot of MMX and SSE instructions for multimedia applications in recent years.

From the perspective of instruction sets, two representative types of CPU architecture have emerged in the history of CPU design and are still the mainstream nowadays: i.e., Reduced Instruction Set Computer (RISC) and Complex Instruction Set Computer (CISC). RISC is the most popular general-purpose CPU architecture. Common RISC systems include MIPS, ARM, and RISC-V. A typical RISC instruction set has the following characteristics: 32-bit fixed-length instruction; one instruction that completes a very simple task (such as fetching a number from memory or completing an addition); 32 32/64-bit general-purpose registers; simple computing instructions with three register operands; memory access operations through load-store instructions; data address using base address in registers with offset; and simple conditional branching. Fig. A.1 shows RISC instruction from three different CPU designs, i.e., MIPS, ARM, and RISC-V. RISC instructions can be classified into three types: R type (register), I type (immediate), and J type (jump). The R type instructions consist of an opcode (OP), function bits (OPX), source registers (RS1, RS2), and a destination register (RD). The I type instructions consist of an opcode, a source register, a destination register, and an immediate. The J type instructions consist of an opcode and an immediate. The lengths of the opcodes and immediate numbers in different instruction sets are different, but the instruction formats are similar.

Different from RISC, CISC contains instructions for complex functions with different lengths and different execution cycles. For example, in Intel's classic CISC instruction set x86, a PUSHA (push instruction) can write many registers into the memory in a predetermined order. In order to maintain upward compatibility, the x86 instruction set has to bear a heavy legacy support. At the same time, in order to better support new applications, x86 has to continuously add new instructions. The instructions decoding module in current Intel processors is very complex, and the decoding module alone may be more complex than many industrial RISC processors. A comparison of RISC and CISC is given in Table A.1.

Table A.1 CISC vs. RISC.

Category	CISC	RISC
Time of emergence	1960s	Early 1980s
Instruction function	Complex	Simple
Instruction length	Multiple instruction lengths	Fixed instruction length
Number of instructions	More	Less
Addressing mode	Multiple addressing modes	Register with offset

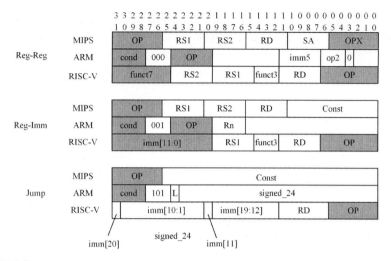

FIGURE A.1

Comparison of three RISC instruction systems.

A.2 Memory hierarchy in computing systems

The storage in a general-purpose computing system is divided into multiple levels, including I/O devices, memory, cache, and registers. Common I/O devices include traditional mechanical hard disk driver (HDD), solid state disk (SSD), compact disc (CD), and USB flash driver. These external memories have the largest storage capacity, but the slowest read and write speed. Memory refers to memory sticks, also known as off-chip memory, using dynamic RAM (DRAM). Its storage capacity is at the GB level. The read and write speed of memory has developed very slowly, compared to the computing speed of CPUs that follows Moore's law, leading to a sharp difference. To bridge the speed gap, cache is designed and adopted in CPUs. The cache is normally implemented with static RAM (SRAM). The registers have the same read and write speed as the arithmetic unit, but the storage capacity is the smallest, at the kB level.

A.2.1 Cache

Cache usually is organized with three types of placing policy for buffering a data block from memory: direct association, full association, and set association. Assuming that the memory address space is 0–31 and the cache address space is 0–7, we show how to buffer the data block in memory address 16 in cache with the three policies. The direct associativity method maps the data block in the memory to a fixed location in the cache according to the address. In this example, the direct associative method takes the memory address to perform a modulus operation on 8 to get 0 and then stores the data block to the location with modulo result, i.e., the 0th line of the cache, as shown in Fig. A.2. The full associativity method can use any location in the cache to buffer a data block from memory. The set associativity method is between direct associativity and full associativity, allowing the data block from memory to be buffered in multiple locations in the cache. Using the two-way group associative cache as an example, each data block can be stored in two locations in cache. For example, the data block at address 16 in the memory can be placed in two locations 0 and 1 in the cache, and the data block at memory address 0, 8, and 24 can also be stored in locations 0 and 1 in the cache. Therefore, which data are stored at location 0 in the cache need to be recorded with a cache tag (Tag).

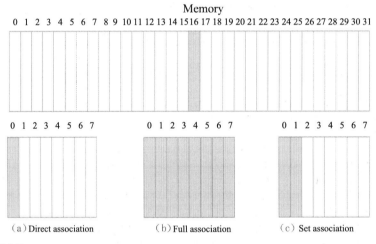

FIGURE A.2

Three types of cache associations.

In addition to the data placement, which decides where to buffer the data block in cache, data replacement, which determines which data block in cache should be replaced with new data in set associativity and full associativity, also has different policies, mainly including random replacement, least recently used (LRU), and first-in first-out (FIFO). Note that the data block location of direct associativity cache is determined and there is no replacement problem. Assuming that the fully associative cache is full or there is data in position 0 or 1 of the set associative cache, the random scheme will randomly select a location for the data in position 16 of the newly acquired memory; FIFO replaces the data that comes in first, i.e., first-in first-out; LRU will replace the least recently used data because the earliest data is not necessarily the least useful data.

When updating the cache content, the processor needs to consider the writing strategies for write hit and write miss. When a write hit occurs, that is, the address to be written is in the cache, there are write-through and write-back strategies. The write-through strategy entails writing to both cache and memory. The write-back strategy means that only the cache is written, and the dirty bit is used to record whether the cache is modified. When the modified cache block is about to be replaced, the modified cache is written back to the memory. When a write miss occurs, that is, the address to be written is not in the cache, there are two strategies: write allocate and no-write allocate. Following the write allocate policy, the block where the address is to be written is allocated from memory to the cache, and then the cache is written by the above write hit actions. Following the no-write allocate policy, the content is written directly back to memory.

A.2.2 Scratchpad memory

In addition to cache, there is another kind of on-chip memory, scratchpad memory (SPM). Unlike cache, whose data is managed by hardware, SPM leaves all the data management to the programmers. Therefore, the control logic of the SPM is relatively simple and the power consumption of the SPM is relatively low. When the data is in the SPM, the memory access latency is normally 1 clock cycle. Compared with a cache of the same storage size, the average power consumption of SPM is 40% less, the performance is 18% higher, and the area is 33% [174] smaller.

The hardware management mechanism in the cache can effectively manage data when the memory access behavior is irregular. For example, there is a lot of data in Windows, and it is difficult to analyze the memory access pattern clearly. In this case, cache is preferred. When the data access behavior in the program can be easily described, the programmer can easily manage the data access of SPM according to data access patterns in the program. In this case, SPM is preferred to improve the efficiency of data access. According to the analysis of memory access behavior in the deep learning algorithm in Section 6.2.2, it can be observed that the memory access behavior of convolution, full connection, and pooling is very regular. Therefore, the deep learning processor core DLP-S in this book uses SPM.

Cache and SPM also have significant differences in the storage capacity and the data amount of off-chip access. As shown in Fig. A.3(a), the larger the storage capacity of the cache in a general CPU, the higher the hit ratio, the lower the miss rate, and the lower the off-chip memory access data amount. When SPM is used for deep learning applications, such as the fully connected layer, the memory access of SPM has two inflection points, as shown in Fig. A.3(b). The input and output neurons of the fully connected layer are reusable, while the weights are not. Input and output neurons can be stored preferentially on SPM. When the capacity of SPM is large enough to hold all input and output neurons, the off-chip access amount will decrease. However, as the SPM capacity increases, the weight can also be placed on the SPM, but the weight is not reused. Therefore, the off-chip access will remain at a threshold. When the capacity of SPM is large enough to put down all the input neurons, output neurons, and weights, there will be an inflection point of the off-chip memory access to an extremely low value. At this time, except for the input sample that needs to be stored, there is no other off-chip memory access, so the external memory access amount will be very low. In practice, the size of SPM can be customized according to the characteristics of neural network applications to improve the utilization of on-chip memory and reduce the unnecessary on-chip memory area.

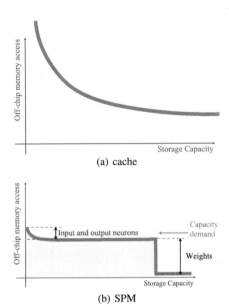

(a) cache

(b) SPM

FIGURE A.3

On-chip memory capacity vs. memory access.

Experimental environment

The homepage of this book (https://github.com/AICS-COMMUNITY) provides various resources, including the cloud platform and development boards. The cloud platform and development boards can be used by readers to program on deep learning processors (DLPs). The cloud platform contains x86 servers equipped with multicore DLPs and provides services through containers, where each user can register a unique account. Readers can log in to their own accounts to program their own code, compile, run, and get output results in their own working directory. The development, compilation, and operation of operators based on the AI programming language can be completed on the cloud platform, and the operators can be integrated into the TensorFlow framework. Readers can apply for a cloud platform account through the above website with the online login guide. The development board is an ARM32 development board integrated with a single-core DLP or an ARM-64 development board integrated with a multicore DLP. On the development board, readers can use the runtime programming interface to implement the inference of the deep learning algorithms.

B.1 Cloud platform

B.1.1 Login

Readers can log in to the cloud platform using ssh as *ssh Username@IPAddress -p PortNumber*. Username is the user name, IPAddress is the IP address, and PortNumber is the port number. Using the name studentuser000, an IP address of 10.20.30.40, and port number of 30300 as an example, the login command is shown in Fig. B.1.

```
ı    ssh  studentuser000@10.20.30.40  −p  30300
```

FIGURE B.1

Log in to the cloud platform.

B.1.2 Changing password

A unified initial password is set for each user on the cloud platform, and the password must be changed when logged in for the first time. The method is shown in Fig. B.2.

403

```
1   Input: passwd
2   Changing password for studentuser000
3   (current) UNIX password: ******
4   Enter new UNIX password: ******
5   Retype new UNIX password: ******
6   passwd: password updated successfully
```

FIGURE B.2

Changing the password.

B.1.3 Set up SSH client

In order to prevent SSH from disconnecting over times, users can modify the default configuration of the connection tool to enable the keep-alive configuration. Some commonly used ssh client keep-alive setting methods are shown in Fig. B.3.

```
1    SecureCRT: Session options - terminal - anti-idle
2        - send NO-OP every xxx seconds, set a nonzero value.
3    PuTTY: Connection - Seconds, between keepalive (0 to
4        turn off), set a nonzero value.
5    iTerm2: profiles - sessions - When idle - send ASCII
6        code.
7    Xshell: session properties - connection - Keep Alive -
8        Send keep alive message while this session
9        connected.Interval [xxx] sec.
10   MobaXterm: Settings - Configuration - SSH - SSH settings,
11       check ssh keepalive
12   Linux client configuration: edit /etc/ssh/ssh_config,
13       configure the following parameters:
14   TCPKeepAlive=yes
15   ServerAliveInterval 60
16   ServerAliveCountMax 3
17           \end{minted}
```

FIGURE B.3

SSH client settings.

B.1.4 Unzipping the file package

All experiment-related files are stored in the home directory of the user account in a form of a compressed package on the cloud platform. When logging in to the cloud platform for the first time, users need to extract the file using the tar command shown in Fig. B.4. The decompressed file is in the ./DLP-Test/ directory, and the directory structure is shown in Fig. B.5.

B.1.5 Setting environment variables

When users are logged in to the cloud platform, they need to set environment variables first. These environment variables are all defined in the env.sh file under the ./DLP-Test/ directory and are set as shown in Fig. B.6.

```
1    tar  zxvf  DLP−Test.tar.gz
```

FIGURE B.4

Extracting the file package.

```
1    |-- bcl_examples              #Example code directory
2    |  |-- data                   #Test data
3    |  |-- decov                  #Deconvolution operator
4    |  - squared_difference       #Squared difference operator
5    |-- bcl_practice              #Programming practice directory
6    |  |-- bclBN                  #Batch Normalization
7    |  |-- bclCosine              #Cosine similarity
8    |  |-- bclPowerXY             #Power(X,Y)
9    |  |-- bclSoftmax             #Softmax
10   |  |-- bclTripletloss         #Tripletloss
11   |  |-- data.cpp
12   |  |-- env.sh
13   |  - problem_set.md
14   |-- env.sh
15   - style_transfer             #style transfer directory
16   |-- for_AT520                #Cross compilation toolchain
17   |-- style_transfer_arm       #ARM platform version program
18   |-- style_transfer_offline   #Offline program
19   |-- style_transfer_online    #Online program
20   - tools
21   |-- tensorflow               #TensorFlow source code directory
22   |--tensorflow−v1.10
```

FIGURE B.5

Directory structure after decompression.

```
1    cd  ~/DLP−Test/
2    source env.sh
```

FIGURE B.6

Setting environment variables.

After completing the environment variable settings, users can follow the instructions in Chapter 9 to perform the experiments.

B.2 Development board

The experiment uses an ARM32 development board integrated with a single-core DLP or an ARM64 development board integrated with a multicore DLP. The cloud platform provides a cross toolchain for the ARM32 platform and the ARM64 platform, and the program can be compiled into the ARM32 platform version or the ARM64 platform version as executable programs. These executable programs can be downloaded to the corresponding development board to deploy deep learning algorithms on the DLP.

References

[1] Warren S. McCulloch, Walter Pitts, A logical calculus of the ideas immanent in nervous activity, The Bulletin of Mathematical Biology 5 (4) (1943) 115–133.

[2] Donald Olding Hebb, The Organization of Behavior: a Neuropsychological Theory, Wiley, New York, 1949.

[3] R. Kline, Cybernetics, automata studies, and the Dartmouth conference on artificial intelligence, IEEE Annals of the History of Computing 33 (4) (2011) 5–16.

[4] J. McCarthy, M.L. Minsky, N. Rochester, C.E. Shannon, A proposal for the Dartmouth summer research project on artificial intelligence, http://www-formal.stanford.edu/jmc/history/dartmouth/dartmouth.html, 1955.

[5] A. Newell, H. Simon, The logic theory machine–a complex information processing system, IRE Transactions on Information Theory 2 (3) (1956) 61–79.

[6] Frank Rosenblatt, The perceptron—a perceiving and recognizing automaton, Report 85-460-1, Cornell Aeronautical Laboratory, 1957.

[7] Frank Rosenblatt, The perceptron: a probabilistic model for information storage and organization in the brain, Psychological Review 65 (6) (1958) 386.

[8] Herbert A. Simon, Allen Newell, Heuristic problem solving: the next advance in operations research, Operations Research 6 (6) (1958) 1–10.

[9] Stuart Russell, Peter Norvig, Artificial Intelligence: A Modern Approach, 3rd edition, Pearson, 2010.

[10] Edward H. Shortliffe, Bruce G. Buchanan, A model of inexact reasoning in medicine, Mathematical Biosciences 23 (3–4) (1975) 351–379.

[11] Gordon Banks, Artificial intelligence in medical diagnosis: the internist/caduceus approach, Critical Reviews in Medical Informatics 1 (1) (1986) 23–54.

[12] John McDermott, R1: a rule-based configurer of computer systems, Artificial Intelligence 19 (1) (1982) 39–88.

[13] David Rumelhart, Geoffrey Hinton, Ronald Williams, Learning representations by back-propagating errors, Nature 323 (1986) 533–536.

[14] Geoffrey E. Hinton, Ruslan R. Salakhutdinov, Reducing the dimensionality of data with neural networks, Science 313 (5786) (2006) 504–507.

[15] Alex Krizhevsky, Ilya Sutskever, Geoffrey E. Hinton, ImageNet classification with deep convolutional neural networks, Communications of the ACM 60 (6) (2017) 84–90.

[16] Olga Russakovsky, Jia Deng, Hao Su, Jonathan Krause, Sanjeev Satheesh, Sean Ma, Zhiheng Huang, Andrej Karpathy, Aditya Khosla, Michael Bernstein, Alexander C. Berg, Li Fei-Fei, ImageNet large scale visual recognition challenge, International Journal of Computer Vision (IJCV) 115 (3) (2015) 211–252.

[17] David Silver, Aja Huang, Chris J. Maddison, Arthur Guez, Laurent Sifre, George Van Den Driessche, Julian Schrittwieser, Ioannis Antonoglou, Veda Panneershelvam, Marc Lanctot, et al., Mastering the game of go with deep neural networks and tree search, Nature 529 (7587) (2016) 484–489.

[18] Yoav Shoham, Raymond Perrault, Erik Brynjolfsson, Jack Clark, James Manyika, Juan Carlos Niebles, Terah Lyons, John Etchemendy, Barbara Grosz, Zoe Bauer, The AI index 2018 annual report, Index Steering Committee, Human-Centered AI Initiative, Stanford University, 2018.

[19] Arturo Rosenblueth, Norbert Wiener, Julian Bigelow, Behavior, purpose and teleology, Philosophy of Science 10 (1) (1943) 18–24.

[20] Norbert Wiener, Cybernetics, Technology Press, 1948.

[21] William Ashby, Design for a Brain, Wiley, 1952.

[22] Claude Elwood Shannon, John McCarthy, Automata Studies, Princeton University Press, 1956.

[23] Michael Huth, Mark Ryan, Logic in Computer Science: Modelling and Reasoning About Systems, 2nd edition, Cambridge University Press, 2004.

[24] Amir Pnueli, The temporal logic of programs, in: 18th Annual Symposium on Foundations of Computer Science (SFCS), 1977, pp. 46–57.

[25] E. Allen Emerson, Edmund M. Clarke, Using branching time temporal logic to synthesize synchronization skeletons, Science of Computer Programming 2 (3) (1982) 241–266.

[26] Martín Abadi, Paul Barham, Jianmin Chen, Zhifeng Chen, Andy Davis, Jeffrey Dean, Matthieu Devin, Sanjay Ghemawat, Geoffrey Irving, Michael Isard, et al., Tensorflow: a system for large-scale machine learning, in: Proceedings of the 12th USENIX Symposium on Operating Systems Design and Implementation (OSDI), 2016, pp. 265–283.

[27] Nikhil Ketkar, Deep Learning with Python, Apress, Berkeley, CA, 2017.

[28] NVIDIA CUDA, https://developer.nvidia.com/cuda-zone, 2019.

[29] Quoc V. Le, Building high-level features using large scale unsupervised learning, in: Proceedings of the IEEE International Conference on Acoustics, Speech and Signal Processing (ICASSP), IEEE, 2013, pp. 8595–8598.

[30] Here's how much computing power Google DeepMind needed to beat Lee Sedol at Go, https://www.businessinsider.com/heres-how-much-computing-power-google-deepmind-needed-to-beat-lee-sedol-2016-3?IR = T&r = UK.

[31] A LISP machine preserved in the MIT Museum, https://en.wikipedia.org/wiki/Lisp_machine, 2019.

[32] Christina Larson, China's AI imperative, Science 359 (6376) (2018) 628–630.

[33] Tianshi Chen, Zidong Du, Ninghui Sun, Jia Wang, Chengyong Wu, Yunji Chen, Olivier Temam, DianNao: a small-footprint high-throughput accelerator for ubiquitous machine-learning, in: Proceedings of the 19th International Conference on Architectural Support for Programming Languages and Operating Systems (ASPLOS), ACM, 2014, pp. 269–284.

[34] Yunji Chen, Tao Luo, Shaoli Liu, Shijin Zhang, Liqiang He, Jia Wang, Ling Li, Tianshi Chen, Zhiwei Xu, Ninghui Sun, et al., DaDianNao: a machine-learning supercomputer, in: Proceedings of the 47th Annual IEEE/ACM International Symposium on Microarchitecture (MICRO), IEEE Computer Society, 2014, pp. 609–622.

[35] Daofu Liu, Tianshi Chen, Shaoli Liu, Jinhong Zhou, Shengyuan Zhou, Olivier Teman, Xiaobing Feng, Xuehai Zhou, Yunji Chen, PuDianNao: a polyvalent machine learning accelerator, in: ACM Proceedings of the Twentieth International Conference on Architectural Support for Programming Languages and Operating Systems (ASPLOS), 2015, pp. 369–381.

[36] Zidong Du, Robert Fasthuber, Tianshi Chen, Paolo Ienne, Ling Li, Tao Luo, Xiaobing Feng, Yunji Chen, Olivier Temam, ShiDianNao: shifting vision processing closer to the sensor, in: ACM/IEEE 42nd Annual International Symposium on Computer Architecture (ISCA), 2015, pp. 92–104.

[37] Shaoli Liu, Zidong Du, Jinhua Tao, Dong Han, Tao Luo, Yuan Xie, Yunji Chen, Tianshi Chen, Cambricon: an instruction set architecture for neural networks, in:

ACM/IEEE 43rd Annual International Symposium on Computer Architecture (ISCA), 2016, pp. 393–405.

[38] Shijin Zhang, Zidong Du, Lei Zhang, Huiying Lan, Shaoli Liu, Ling Li, Qi Guo, Tianshi Chen, Yunji Chen, Cambricon-X: an accelerator for sparse neural networks, in: 49th Annual IEEE/ACM International Symposium on Microarchitecture (MICRO), 2016, pp. 1–12.

[39] Norman P. Jouppi, Cliff Young, Nishant Patil, David Patterson, Gaurav Agrawal, Raminder Bajwa, Sarah Bates, Suresh Bhatia, Nan Boden, Al Borchers, et al., In-datacenter performance analysis of a tensor processing unit, in: Proceedings of the ACM/IEEE 44th Annual International Symposium on Computer Architecture (ISCA), 2017, pp. 1–12.

[40] Wenyan Lu, Guihai Yan, Jiajun Li, Shijun Gong, Yinhe Han, Xiaowei Li, FlexFlow: a flexible dataflow accelerator architecture for convolutional neural networks, in: Proceedings of the 23rd IEEE Symposium on High Performance Computer Architecture (HPCA), 2017, pp. 553–564.

[41] Zhe Li, Caiwen Ding, Siyue Wang, Wujie Wen, Youwei Zhuo, Chang Liu, Qinru Qiu, Wenyao Xu, Xue Lin, Xuehai Qian, Yanzhi Wang, E-RNN: design optimization for efficient recurrent neural networks in FPGAs, in: IEEE International Symposium on High Performance Computer Architecture (HPCA), 2019, pp. 69–80.

[42] Yongwei Zhao, Zidong Du, Qi Guo, Shaoli Liu, Ling Li, Zhiwei Xu, Tianshi Chen, Yunji Chen, Cambricon-F: machine learning computers with fractal von Neumann architecture, in: Proceedings of the 46th International Symposium on Computer Architecture (ISCA), 2019, pp. 788–801.

[43] Mohsen Imani, Saransh Gupta, Yeseong Kim, Tajana Rosing, FloatPIM: in-memory acceleration of deep neural network training with high precision, in: Proceedings of the 46th International Symposium on Computer Architecture (ISCA), 2019.

[44] Summit (supercomputer), https://en.wikipedia.org/wiki/Summit_(supercomputer), 2018.

[45] https://699pic.com/tupian-400488635.html, 2019.

[46] Yangqing Jia, Evan Shelhamer, Jeff Donahue, Sergey Karayev, Jonathan Long, Ross Girshick, Sergio Guadarrama, Trevor Darrell, Caffe: convolutional architecture for fast feature embedding, in: Proceedings of the 22nd ACM International Conference on Multimedia, ACM, 2014, pp. 675–678.

[47] Tianqi Chen, Mu Li, Yutian Li, Min Lin, Naiyan Wang, Minjie Wang, Tianjun Xiao, Bing Xu, Chiyuan Zhang, Zheng Zhang, MXNet: a flexible and efficient machine learning library for heterogeneous distributed systems, arXiv preprint, arXiv:1512.01274, 2015.

[48] Simon Haykin, Neural Networks: a Comprehensive Foundation, Prentice Hall PTR, 1994.

[49] Tom Mitchell, Machine Learning, McGraw Hill, 1997.

[50] Ethem Alpaydin, Introduction to Machine Learning, 3rd edition, MIT Press, 2004.

[51] Zhou Zhihua, Machine Learning, first edition, Tsinghua University Press, 2016.

[52] Ian Goodfellow, Yoshua Bengio, Aaron Courville, Deep Learning, MIT Press, 2016, http://www.deeplearningbook.org.

[53] Kurt Hornik, Approximation capabilities of multilayer feedforward networks, Neural Networks 4 (2) (1991) 251–257.

[54] Adam Coates, Brody Huval, Tao Wang, David Wu, Bryan Catanzaro, Ng Andrew, Deep learning with COTS HPC systems, in: Proceedings of the International Conference on Machine Learning, 2013, pp. 1337–1345.

[55] Noam Shazeer, Azalia Mirhoseini, Krzysztof Maziarz, Andy Davis, Quoc Le, Geoffrey Hinton, Jeff Dean, Outrageously large neural networks: the sparsely-gated mixture-of-experts layer, arXiv preprint, arXiv:1701.06538v1, 2017.

[56] Matthew D. Zeiler, Rob Fergus, Visualizing and understanding convolutional networks, in: Proceedings of the European Conference on Computer Vision, Springer, 2014, pp. 818–833.

[57] Marvin Minsky, Seymour A. Papert, Perceptrons: An Introduction to Computational Geometry, MIT Press, 1969.

[58] Yann LeCun, Léon Bottou, Yoshua Bengio, Patrick Haffner, et al., Gradient-based learning applied to document recognition, Proceedings of the IEEE 86 (11) (1998) 2278–2324.

[59] Geoffrey E. Hinton, Simon Osindero, Yee-Whye Teh, A fast learning algorithm for deep belief nets, Neural Computation 18 (7) (2006) 1527–1554.

[60] Christian Szegedy, Wei Liu, Yangqing Jia, Pierre Sermanet, Scott Reed, Dragomir Anguelov, Dumitru Erhan, Vincent Vanhoucke, Andrew Rabinovich, Going deeper with convolutions, in: Proceedings of the IEEE Conference on Computer Vision and Pattern Recognition, 2015, pp. 1–9.

[61] Sepp Hochreiter, Jürgen Schmidhuber, Long short-term memory, Neural Computation 9 (8) (1997) 1735–1780.

[62] Kaiming He, Xiangyu Zhang, Shaoqing Ren, Jian Sun, Deep residual learning for image recognition, in: Proceedings of the IEEE Conference on Computer Vision and Pattern Recognition (CVPR), 2016, pp. 770–778.

[63] Chris Thornton, Frank Hutter, Holger H. Hoos, Kevin Leyton-Brown, Auto-weka: combined selection and hyperparameter optimization of classification algorithms, in: Proceedings of the 19th ACM SIGKDD International Conference on Knowledge Discovery and Data Mining, 2013, pp. 847–855.

[64] Vinod Nair, Geoffrey Hinton, Rectified linear units improve restricted Boltzmann machines, in: Proceedings of the International Conference on Machine Learning (ICML), 2010, pp. 807–814.

[65] Kaiming He, Xiangyu Zhang, Shaoqing Ren, Jian Sun, Delving deep into rectifiers: surpassing human-level performance on imagenet classification, in: Proceedings of the IEEE International Conference on Computer Vision (ICCV), December 2015, pp. 1026–1034.

[66] Andrew L. Maas, Awni Y. Hannun, Andrew Y. Ng, Rectifier nonlinearities improve neural network acoustic models, in: Proceedings of the 30th International Conference on Machine Learning (ICML), 2013, pp. 1–6.

[67] Djork-Arné Clevert, Thomas Unterthiner, Sepp Hochreiter, Fast and accurate deep network learning by exponential linear units (ELUs), arXiv preprint, arXiv:1511.07289, 2015.

[68] Bing Xu, Naiyan Wang, Tianqi Chen, Mu Li, Empirical evaluation of rectified activations in convolutional network, arXiv preprint, arXiv:1505.00853v2, 2015, pp. 1–5.

[69] Leo Breiman, Bagging predictors, Machine Learning 24 (2) (1996) 123–140.

[70] Geoffrey E. Hinton, Nitish Srivastava, Alex Krizhevsky, Ilya Sutskever, Ruslan R. Salakhutdinov, Improving neural networks by preventing co-adaptation of feature detectors, arXiv preprint, arXiv:1207.0580, 2012.

[71] Ian Goodfellow, Jean Pouget-Abadie, Mehdi Mirza, Bing Xu, David Warde-Farley, Sherjil Ozair, Aaron Courville, Yoshua Bengio, Generative adversarial nets, in: Proceedings of the Advances in Neural Information Processing Systems, 2014, pp. 2672–2680.

[72] Karen Simonyan, Andrew Zisserman, Very deep convolutional networks for large-scale image recognition, in: International Conference on Learning Representations (ICLR), 2015.

[73] Jost Tobias Springenberg, Alexey Dosovitskiy, Thomas Brox, Martin Riedmiller, Striving for simplicity: the all convolutional net, arXiv preprint, arXiv:1412.6806, 2014.

[74] Kunihiko Fukushima, Neocognitron: a self-organizing neural network model for a mechanism of pattern recognition unaffected by shift in position, Biological Cybernetics 36 (4) (1980) 193–202.

[75] Jie Hu, Li Shen, Gang Sun, Squeeze-and-excitation networks, in: Proceedings of the IEEE Conference on Computer Vision and Pattern Recognition (CVPR), June 2018.

[76] Sergey Ioffe, Christian Szegedy, Batch normalization: accelerating deep network training by reducing internal covariate shift, arXiv preprint, arXiv:1502.03167, 2015.

[77] Christian Szegedy, Vincent Vanhoucke, Sergey Ioffe, Jon Shlens, Zbigniew Wojna, Rethinking the inception architecture for computer vision, in: Proceedings of the IEEE Conference on Computer Vision and Pattern Recognition (CVPR), 2016, pp. 2818–2826.

[78] Christian Szegedy, Sergey Ioffe, Vincent Vanhoucke, Alexander A. Alemi, Inception-v4, inception-resnet and the impact of residual connections on learning, in: Proceedings of the Thirty-First AAAI Conference on Artificial Intelligence (AAAI), 2017.

[79] Ross Girshick, Jeff Donahue, Trevor Darrell, Jitendra Malik, Rich feature hierarchies for accurate object detection and semantic segmentation, in: Proceedings of the IEEE Conference on Computer Vision and Pattern Recognition (CVPR), 2014, pp. 580–587.

[80] Joseph Redmon, Santosh Divvala, Ross Girshick, Ali Farhadi, You only look once: unified, real-time object detection, in: Proceedings of the IEEE Conference on Computer Vision and Pattern Recognition (CVPR), 2016, pp. 779–788.

[81] Wei Liu, Dragomir Anguelov, Dumitru Erhan, Christian Szegedy, Scott Reed, Cheng-Yang Fu, Alexander C. Berg, SSD: single shot multibox detector, in: Proceedings of the European Conference on Computer Vision (ECCV), Springer, 2016, pp. 21–37.

[82] Mark Everingham, John Winn, The Pascal visual object classes challenge 2012 (VOC2012) development kit, http://cvlab.postech.ac.kr/~mooyeol/pascal_voc_2012/devkit_doc.pdf, 2012.

[83] Ross Girshick, Fast R-CNN, in: Proceedings of the IEEE International Conference on Computer Vision (ICCV), 2015, pp. 1440–1448.

[84] Shaoqing Ren, Kaiming He, Ross Girshick, Jian Sun, Faster R-CNN: towards real-time object detection with region proposal networks, IEEE Transactions on Pattern Analysis and Machine Intelligence 39 (6) (2017) 1137–1149.

[85] Jasper R.R. Uijlings, Koen E.A. Van De Sande, Theo Gevers, Arnold W.M. Smeulders, Selective search for object recognition, International Journal of Computer Vision 104 (2) (2013) 154–171.

[86] Navaneeth Bodla, Bharat Singh, Rama Chellappa, Larry S. Davis, Soft-NMS–improving object detection with one line of code, in: Proceedings of the IEEE International Conference on Computer Vision (ICCV), 2017, pp. 5561–5569.

[87] Joseph Redmon, Ali Farhadi, YOLO9000: better, faster, stronger, in: Proceedings of the IEEE Conference on Computer Vision and Pattern Recognition (CVPR), 2017, pp. 7263–7271.

[88] Joseph Redmon, Ali Farhadi, Yolov3: an incremental improvement, arXiv preprint, arXiv:1804.02767, 2018.

[89] Myungsub Choi, Taeksoo Kim, Jiwon Kim, Awesome recurrent neural networks, https://github.com/kjw0612/awesome-rnn, 2019.

[90] Alex Graves, Greg Wayne, Ivo Danihelka, Neural Turing machines, arXiv preprint, arXiv:1410.5401v2, 2014.

[91] Alex Graves, Greg Wayne, Malcolm Reynolds, Tim Harley, Ivo Danihelka, Agnieszka Grabska-Barwińska, Sergio Gómez Colmenarejo, Edward Grefenstette, Tiago Ramalho, John Agapiou, Adrià Puigdomènech Badia, Karl Moritz Hermann, Yori Zwols, Georg Ostrovski, Adam Cain, Helen King, Christopher Summerfield, Phil Blunsom, Koray Kavukcuoglu, Demis Hassabis, Hybrid computing using a neural network with dynamic external memory, Nature 538 (7626) (2016) 471–476.

[92] Paul J. Werbos, et al., Backpropagation through time: what it does and how to do it, Proceedings of the IEEE 78 (10) (1990) 1550–1560.

[93] Razvan Pascanu, Tomas Mikolov, Yoshua Bengio, On the difficulty of training recurrent neural networks, in: Proceedings of the International Conference on Machine Learning (ICML), 2013, pp. 1310–1318.

[94] Kyunghyun Cho, Bart Van Merriënboer, Caglar Gulcehre, Dzmitry Bahdanau, Fethi Bougares, Holger Schwenk, Yoshua Bengio, Learning phrase representations using RNN encoder-decoder for statistical machine translation, arXiv preprint, arXiv:1406.1078, 2014.

[95] Felix A. Gers, Jürgen Schmidhuber, Recurrent nets that time and count, in: Proceedings of the IEEE-INNS-ENNS International Joint Conference on Neural Networks (IJCNN), 2000, pp. 189–194.

[96] Klaus Greff, Rupesh K. Srivastava, Jan Koutník, Bas R. Steunebrink, Jürgen Schmidhuber, LSTM: a search space odyssey, IEEE Transactions on Neural Networks and Learning Systems 28 (10) (2016) 2222–2232.

[97] Martin Arjovsky, Leon Bottou, Towards principled methods for training generative adversarial networks, Machine Learning (2017) 1–17.

[98] Martin Arjovsky, Soumith Chintala, Léon Bottou, Wasserstein GAN, arXiv preprint, arXiv:1701.07875, 2017, pp. 1–32.

[99] Avinash Hindupur, The GAN zoo, 2019.

[100] Antonia Creswell, Tom White, Vincent Dumoulin, Kai Arulkumaran, Biswa Sengupta, Anil A. Bharath, Generative adversarial networks: an overview, IEEE Signal Processing Magazine 35 (1) (2018) 53–65.

[101] Alec Radford, Luke Metz, Soumith Chintala, Unsupervised representation learning with deep convolutional generative adversarial networks, arXiv preprint, arXiv:1511.06434, 2015.

[102] Emily L. Denton, Soumith Chintala, Rob Fergus, et al., Deep generative image models using a Laplacian pyramid of adversarial networks, in: Proceedings of the Advances in Neural Information Processing Systems (NIPS), 2015, pp. 1486–1494.

[103] Meng Wang, Huafeng Li, Fang Li, Generative adversarial network based on resnet for conditional image restoration, arXiv preprint, arXiv:1707.04881, 2017.

[104] Christian Ledig, Lucas Theis, Ferenc Huszár, Jose Caballero, Andrew Cunningham, Alejandro Acosta, Andrew Aitken, Alykhan Tejani, Johannes Totz, Zehan Wang, et al., Photo-realistic single image super-resolution using a generative adversarial network, in: Proceedings of the IEEE Conference on Computer Vision and Pattern Recognition (CVPR), 2017, pp. 4681–4690.

[105] Jun-Yan Zhu, Taesung Park, Phillip Isola, Alexei A. Efros, Unpaired image-to-image translation using cycle-consistent adversarial networks, in: Proceedings of the IEEE International Conference on Computer Vision (ICCV), 2017, pp. 2223–2232.

[106] Mehdi Mirza, Simon Osindero, Conditional generative adversarial nets, arXiv preprint, arXiv:1411.1784, 2014.

[107] Xi Chen, Yan Duan, Rein Houthooft, John Schulman, Ilya Sutskever, Pieter Abbeel, InfoGAN: interpretable representation learning by information maximizing generative adversarial nets, in: Proceedings of the Advances in Neural Information Processing Systems (NIPS), 2016, pp. 2172–2180.

[108] Jeff Donahue, Philipp Krähenbühl, Trevor Darrell, Adversarial feature learning, arXiv preprint, arXiv:1605.09782, 2016.

[109] Anders Boesen Lindbo Larsen, Søren Kaae Sønderby, Hugo Larochelle, Ole Winther, Autoencoding beyond pixels using a learned similarity metric, arXiv preprint, arXiv: 1512.09300, 2015.

[110] Diederik P. Kingma, Max Welling, Auto-encoding variational Bayes, arXiv preprint, arXiv:1312.6114, 2014.

[111] Leon A. Gatys, Alexander S. Ecker, Matthias Bethge, Image style transfer using convolutional neural networks, in: Proceedings of the IEEE Conference on Computer Vision and Pattern Recognition (CVPR), 2016, pp. 2414–2423.

[112] Justin Johnson, Alexandre Alahi, Li Fei-Fei, Perceptual losses for real-time style transfer and super-resolution, in: Proceedings of the European Conference on Computer Vision (ECCV), Springer, 2016, pp. 694–711.

[113] Fast-neural-style[eb/ol], https://github.com/jcjohnson/fast-neural-style, 2017.

[114] Martín Abadi, Ashish Agarwal, Paul Barham, TensorFlow: large-scale machine learning on heterogeneous distributed systems, arXiv preprint, arXiv:1603.04467v2, 2016.

[115] Paddlepaddle, https://github.com/PaddlePaddle, 2019.

[116] Caffe2, https://github.com/facebookarchive/caffe2, 2014.

[117] Jeffrey Dean, Greg Corrado, Rajat Monga, Kai Chen, Matthieu Devin, Mark Mao, Marc'aurelio Ranzato, Andrew Senior, Paul Tucker, Ke Yang, et al., Large scale distributed deep networks, in: Proceedings of the Advances in Neural Information Processing Systems (NIPS), 2012, pp. 1223–1231.

[118] TensorFlow official website, https://tensorflow.google.cn/.

[119] Chip Huyen, CS 20: TensorFlow for deep learning research, http://web.stanford.edu/class/cs20si/, 2018.

[120] Machine learning crash course, https://developers.google.cn/machine-learning/crash-course/, 2019.

[121] Bfloat16 – hardware numerics definition (white paper), https://software.intel.com/sites/default/files/managed/40/8b/bf16-hardware-numerics-definition-white-paper.pdf, 2018.

[122] config.proto, https://github.com/tensorflow/tensorflow/blob/r1.10/tensorflow/core/protobuf/config.proto, 2019.

[123] TensorBoard user guide, https://tensorboard.dev/.

[124] Keras official website, https://keras.io/.

[125] NumPy official website, https://numpy.org/.

[126] OpenCV official website, https://opencv.org/.

[127] tf.nn.sigmoid_cross_entropy_with_logits, https://tensorflow.google.cn/versions/r1.10/api_docs/python/tf/nn/sigmoid_cross_entropy_with_logits, 2019.

[128] tf.nn.weighted_cross_entropy_with_logits, https://tensorflow.google.cn/versions/r1.10/api_docs/python/tf/nn/weighted_cross_entropy_with_logits, 2019.

[129] tf.clip_by_norm, https://github.com/tensorflow/docs/blob/r1.10/site/en/api_docs/python/tf/clip_by_norm.md.

[130] Jeffrey Dean, Sanjay Ghemawat, MapReduce: simplified data processing on large cluster, in: Proceedings of the 6th Conference on Symposium on Operating Systems Design and Implementation (OSDI), 2004, pp. 1–13.

[131] Michael Isard, Mihai Budiu, Yuan Yu, Andrew Birrell, Dennis Fetterly, Dryad: distributed data-parallel programs from sequential building blocks, in: Proceedings of the 2007 Eurosys Conference, 2007, pp. 59–72.

[132] Atilim Gunes Baydin, Barak A. Pearlmutter, Alexey Andreyevich Radul, Jeffrey Mark Siskind, Automatic differentiation in machine learning: a survey, Journal of Machine Learning Research 18 (153) (2018) 1–43.

[133] Implementation of control flow in tensorflow, http://download.tensorflow.org/paper/white_paper_tf_control_flow_implementation_2017_11_1.pdf, 2017.

[134] Arvind, David E. Culler, Dataflow architectures, Annual Review of Computer Science 1 (1986) 225–253.

[135] Rasmus Munk Larsen, Tatiana Shpeisman, Tensorflow graph optimizations, http://web.stanford.edu/class/cs245/slides/TFGraphOptimizationsStanford.pdf, 2019.

[136] Gemmlowp: a small self-contained low-precision GEMM library, https://github.com/google/gemmlowp, 2019.

[137] Dense linear algebra on gpus, https://developer.nvidia.com/cublas, 2019.

[138] NVIDIA Collective Communications Library (NCCL), https://developer.nvidia.com/nccl, 2019.

[139] Mark Holler, Simon Tam, Hernan Castro, Ronald Benson, An electrically trainable artificial neural network (ETANN) with 10240 floating gate synapses, in: Proceedings of the International Joint Conference on Neural Networks (IJCNN), 1989, pp. 191–196.

[140] Dan Hammerstrom, A VLSI architecture for high-performance, low-cost, on-chip learning, in: Proceedings of the International Joint Conference on Neural Networks (IJCNN), IEEE, 1990, pp. 537–544.

[141] Marc A. Viredaz, Paolo Ienne, MANTRA I: a systolic neuro-computer, in: Proceedings of the 1993 International Conference on Neural Networks (IJCNN), vol. 3, IEEE, 1993, pp. 3054–3057.

[142] Wang Shoujue, Lu Huaxiang, Chen Xiangdong, Zeng Yujuan, Artificial neural network hardware approach and neural computer research, Journal of Shenzhen University (Science and Technology Edition) 14 (1) (1997) 8–13.

[143] Zidong Du, Shaoli Liu, Robert Fasthuber, Tianshi Chen, Paolo Ienne, Ling Li, Tao Luo, Qi Guo, Xiaobing Feng, Yunji Chen, Olivier Temam, An accelerator for high efficient vision processing, IEEE Transactions on Computer-Aided Design of Integrated Circuits and Systems 36 (2) (2017) 227–240.

[144] Yu-Hsin Chen, Joel Emer, Vivienne Sze, Eyeriss: a spatial architecture for energy-efficient dataflow for convolutional neural networks, in: ACM/IEEE 43rd Annual International Symposium on Computer Architecture (ISCA), 2016, pp. 367–379.

[145] Vivienne Sze, Yu-Hsin Chen, Tien-Ju Yang, Joel S. Emer, Efficient processing of deep neural networks: a tutorial and survey, Proceedings of the IEEE 105 (12) (2017) 2295–2329.

[146] Xuda Zhou, Zidong Du, Qi Guo, Shaoli Liu, Chengsi Liu, Chao Wang, Xuehai Zhou, Ling Li, Tianshi Chen, Yunji Chen, Cambricon-S: addressing irregularity in sparse neural networks through a cooperative software/hardware approach, in: 51st Annual IEEE/ACM International Symposium on Microarchitecture (MICRO), 2018, pp. 15–28.

[147] Patrick Judd, Jorge Albericio, Tayler Hetherington, Tor M. Aamodt, Andreas Moshovos, Stripes: bit-serial deep neural network computing, in: Proceedings of the 2016 49th Annual IEEE/ACM International Symposium on Microarchitecture (MICRO), IEEE, 2016, pp. 1–12.

[148] Mlperf, https://mlperf.org, 2018.

[149] Peter Mattson, Christine Cheng, Gregory Diamos, Cody Coleman, Paulius Micikevicius, David Patterson, Hanlin Tang, Gu-Yeon Wei, Peter Bailis, Victor Bittorf, David Brooks, Dehao Chen, Debo Dutta, Udit Gupta, Kim Hazelwood, Andy Hock, Xinyuan Huang, Daniel Kang, David Kanter, Naveen Kumar, Jeffery Liao, Deepak Narayanan, Tayo Oguntebi, Gennady Pekhimenko, Lillian Pentecost, Vijay Janapa Reddi, Taylor Robie, Tom St John, Carole-Jean Wu, Lingjie Xu, Cliff Young, Matei Zaharia, Mlperf training benchmark, in: Proceedings of Machine Learning and Systems, vol. 2, 2020, pp. 336–349.

[150] Vijay Janapa Reddi, Christine Cheng, David Kanter, Peter Mattson, Guenther Schmuelling, Carole-Jean Wu, Brian Anderson, Maximilien Breughe, Mark Charlebois, William Chou, Ramesh Chukka, Cody Coleman, Sam Davis, Pan Deng, Greg Diamos, Jared Duke, Dave Fick, J. Scott Gardner, Itay Hubara, Sachin Idgunji, Thomas B. Jablin, Jeff Jiao, Tom St. John, Pankaj Kanwar, David Lee, Jeffery Liao, Anton Lokhmotov, Francisco Massa, Peng Meng, Paulius Micikevicius, Colin Osborne, Gennady Pekhimenko, Arun Tejusve, Raghunath Rajan, Dilip Sequeira, Ashish Sirasao, Fei Sun, Hanlin Tang, Michael Thomson, Frank Wei, Ephrem Wu, Lingjie Xu, Koichi Yamada, Bing Yu, George Yuan, Aaron Zhong, Peizhao Zhang, Yuchen Zhou, Mlperf inference benchmark, in: ACM/IEEE 47th Annual International Symposium on Computer Architecture (ISCA), 2020, pp. 446–459.

[151] John L. Hennessy, David A. Patterson, A new golden age for computer architecture, Communications of the ACM 62 (2) (2019) 48–60.

[152] Kaldi ASR, https://kaldi-asr.org, 2011.

[153] Daniel J. Fremont, Tommaso Dreossi, Shromona Ghosh, Xiangyu Yue, Alberto L. Sangiovanni-Vincentelli, Sanjit A. Seshia, Scenic: a language for scenario specification and scene generation, in: Proceedings of the 40th ACM SIGPLAN Conference on Programming Language Design and Implementation (PLDI), 2019, pp. 63–78.

[154] Tao Benjamin Schardl, Performance Engineering of Multicore Software: Developing a Science of Fast Code for the Post-Moore Era, PhD thesis, Massachusetts Institute of Technology, Department of Electrical Engineering and Computer Science, 2016.

[155] Tianqi Tang, Sheng Li, Yuan Xie, Norm Jouppi, MLPAT: a power, area, timing modeling framework for machine learning accelerators, in: Proceedings of the First International Workshop on Domain Specific System Architecture (DOSSA-1), 2018.

[156] Jonathan Ragan-Kelley, Connelly Barnes, Andrew Adams, Sylvain Paris, Frédo Durand, Saman Amarasinghe, Halide: a language and compiler for optimizing parallelism, locality, and recomputation in image processing pipelines, in: Proceedings of the 34th ACM SIGPLAN Conference on Programming Language Design and Implementation (PLDI), 2013, pp. 519–530.

[157] Tianqi Chen, Thierry Moreau, Ziheng Jiang, Lianmin Zheng, Eddie Q. Yan, Haichen Shen, Meghan Cowan, Leyuan Wang, Yuwei Hu, Luis Ceze, Carlos Guestrin, Arvind Krishnamurthy, TVM: an automated end-to-end optimizing compiler for deep learning, in: 13th USENIX Symposium on Operating Systems Design and Implementation (OSDI), 2018, pp. 578–594.

[158] OpenCL overview, https://www.khronos.org/opencl/, 2019.

[159] OpenACC, https://www.openacc.org/, 2019.

[160] Liu Ying, Lu Fang, Wang Lei, Chen Li, Cui Huimin, Feng Xiaobing, Research and development of heterogeneous parallel programming model, Journal of Software 25 (7) (2014) 1459–1475.

[161] Bryan Catanzaro, Michael Garland, Kurt Keutzer, Copperhead: compiling an embedded data parallel language, in: Proceedings of the 16th ACM Symposium on Principles and Practice of Parallel Programming (PPoPP), ACM, 2011, pp. 47–56.

[162] Joshua Auerbach, David F. Bacon, Perry Cheng, Rodric Rabbah, Lime: a Java-compatible and synthesizable language for heterogeneous architectures, in: Proceedings of the ACM International Conference on Object Oriented Programming Systems Languages and Applications (OOPSLA), ACM, 2010, pp. 89–108.

[163] Michael D. Linderman, Jamison D. Collins, Hong Wang, Teresa H. Meng, Merge: a programming model for heterogeneous multi-core systems, in: Proceedings of the 13th International Conference on Architectural Support for Programming Languages and Operating Systems (ASPLOS), 2008, pp. 287–296.

[164] C++ AMP (C++ accelerated massive parallelism), https://docs.microsoft.com/en-us/cpp/parallel/amp/cpp-amp-cpp-accelerated-massive-parallelism?view=vs-2019, 2019.

[165] T.D. Han, T.S. Abdelrahman, hiCUDA: high-level GPGPU programming, IEEE Transactions on Parallel and Distributed Systems 22 (1) (Jan 2011) 78–90.

[166] Antoniu Pop, Albert Cohen, OpenStream: expressiveness and data-flow compilation of OpenMP streaming programs, ACM Transactions on Architecture and Code Optimization 9 (4) (2013) 53.

[167] The dwarf debugging standard, https://dwarfstd.org/, 2022.

[168] Introduction to the DWARF debugging format, http://dwarfstd.org/doc/Debugging%20using%20DWARF.pdf, 2007.

[169] GDB: the GNU project debugger, http://www.gnu.org/software/gdb/documentation/, 2019.

[170] OpenBLAS: an optimized BLAS library, http://www.openblas.net/, 2019.

[171] Intel math kernel library, https://software.intel.com/en-us/mkl, 2019.

[172] NVIDIA CUDA deep neural network library (cuDNN), https://developer.nvidia.com/cudnn, 2019.

[173] Common objects in context, http://cocodataset.org/, 2019.

[174] Rajeshwari Banakar, Stefan Steinke, Bo-Sik Lee, Mahesh Balakrishnan, Peter Marwedel, Scratchpad memory: a design alternative for cache on-chip memory in embedded systems, in: Proceedings of the Tenth International Symposium on Hardware/Software Codesign (CODES), IEEE, 2002, pp. 73–78.

Final words

I am a young researcher at the Institute of Computing Technology (ICT), Chinese Academy of Sciences (CAS), where my research mainly focuses on the intersection of artificial intelligence (AI) and computer architecture. Generally, the main task of a researcher in CAS is to do scientific research, and there is no mandatory obligation to do education. However, in the past two years, I have spent almost all my spare time on education and writing teaching materials. The main reason is that I have noticed an unbalanced trend in AI scientific research: we have paid more attention to the upper layers of AI (application layer, algorithm layer), while the importance of the bottom layers (system software layer, chip layer) has been seriously ignored. If such an imbalance is not addressed, the lack of hardware and software system capabilities of AI practitioners will eventually hold back the development of upper-level applications and algorithms.

The reasons for the lack of system capabilities of AI are numerous. One of the most fundamental reasons, in my opinion, is higher education (this may be because I was born into a family of teachers). For AI computing systems, both scientific research and industrial development require many different talents. These talents should be cultivated through education, since no tree can grow in the absence of fertile soil. A few years ago, no university in China offered courses about AI computing systems. It is obviously unrealistic to expect students to become masters of AI computing systems on their own if they are not given any education in this area. Therefore, we should take the initiative to change the status quo.

In recent years, hundreds of colleges and universities across the world have started to establish AI majors. I have talked with the deans of computer science or AI departments in many universities, and they all agree that it is necessary and urgent to strengthen the training of AI computing system capabilities. However, in the actual curriculum, many universities still go the way of teaching pure algorithms and applications. Such phenomenon is due to three major difficulties. First, there are few available AI computing systems courses for reference; second, not many professors teach AI computing systems courses; and third, there is no suitable textbook for the courses.

In observing these difficulties, I wondered if I could make a small contribution to filling the gaps in the availability of curricula, lecturers, and teaching material about intelligent computing systems. I asked myself, can I train some AI major students with systematic thinking by myself? In mid-2018, I made the decision to offer a course called *AI Computing Systems* to the University of Chinese Academy of Sciences (UCAS), with the hope of cultivate students' understanding of the integration of the entire software and hardware technology stack of intelligent computing (including basic AI algorithms, an intelligent computing programming framework, intelligent computing programming language, AI chip architecture, etc.). I am very pleased that this course was well received by the students, although it sprouted from nowhere with insufficient polishing and many shortcomings. Many students attended this course for the whole semester, even though they were not able to register for it. I was especially touched by the fact that some students from other institutes came from Zhongguancun to Huairou to attend the class. It took them three hours to drive back and forth for one class, and it would be late at night when they returned to Zhongguancun. This indicated that the students benefited from the AI computing systems classes.

Inspired by the students, we gradually released the PPT presentations, lecture notes, videos, codes, cloud platform, and development boards of the AI computing systems course to professors of various universities. With these teaching resources, over 80 universities, including Peking University, Tsinghua University, Beihang University, Tianjin University, the University of Science and Technology of China, Nankai University, Beijing Institute of Technology, and Huazhong University of Science and Technology are already offering courses on AI computing systems. In this way, the problem of lacking reference courses has been initially solved.

Further, we have offered a tutorial class on AI computing systems with the help of the Teaching Steering Committee of the Ministry of Education. Prof. Xingshe Zhou of Northwestern Polytechnical University was very enthusiastic to host the first tutorial class in August 2019. More than 60 professors from over 40 universities participated in this first tutorial class. In the future, we will continue to offer similar tutorial classes and strive to train hundreds of professors who can teach AI computing systems well. In this way, the problem of lack of professors will possibly be solved.

During the process of teaching and giving course workshops, students and professors suggested that they would like to have a textbook for an AI computing systems course. Therefore, a number of colleagues in our lab (Research Center for Intelligent Processors, ICT, CAS) worked together to reorganize our lecture notes into text files, which became the book *AI Computing Systems* in the reader's hands. To the best of our knowledge, this is one of the first textbooks dedicated to teaching modern machine learning computing systems comprehensively. In this way, the problem of the textbook has also been initially solved.

Looking back over the past two years, on the one hand, I feel that it is not easy to squeeze in time to teach and write textbooks in addition to the heavy research load. During the busiest time, I had to go to several schools, such as UCAS, Peking University, and Beihang University to teach classes, which was extremely stressful. Many times I went straight to the classroom from the airport or the train station (fortunately, I was not late for any class). On the other hand, it was really rewarding to work with my colleagues to start the course and write the textbook. As a human being, I think that I am similar to an AI computing system. The only differences are that I have a very low frequency and have to handle multiple tasks concurrently with frequent external interruptions. I hope that in my short remaining life, I will be able to continue working overtime to train more talents with systematic thinking for the AI industry.

Yunji Chen
11 January 2019
70th anniversary of the Chinese Academy of Sciences
Zhongguancun, Beijing

Index